C000234274

Diary of a PARISH PRIEST

To my wife, Carol

ISBN 1 84298 048 3

Design: Andrew Milne Design

Write to: John Hunt Publishing Ltd, 46A West Street, Alresford, Hampshire SO24 9AU, UK

A CIP catalogue record for this book is available from the British Library.

Printed in Singapore

Visit us on the Web at: johnhunt-publishing.com

Diary of a PARISH PRIEST

A history of England

ANDREW SANGSTER

Contents

Foreword by the Bishop of Norwich		6
Preface		9
Acknowledgements		11
Rectors of Rollesby		12
Letter to the Past		13
Chapter 1	Walter Rugg (1160)	15
Chapter 2	William de Anmere (1294-1302)	21
Chapter 3	John de Caylly (1303-1321) including Alan de Ely (1302)	27
Chapter 4	Firminus de Lavenham (1321-1324)	35
Chapter 5	Laurence Folstaff (1324-1327)	39
Chapter 6	John de Skyren (1327-1337)	45
Chapter 7	Walter Hurry (1340-1349) including Gilbert de Wellerton (1337) and John de Flete (1338)	49
Chapter 8	Simon de Rykenhale (1349-1361)	55
Chapter 9	Simon de Babingley (1361-1377)	61
Chapter 10	Nicholas de Lyons (1377-1401)	65
Chapter 11	Thomas Bradmore (1401-1424)	73
Chapter 12	James Andeley (1424-1436)	79
Chapter 13	William Thrulby (1436-1447)	85
Chapter 14	John Knolls (1449-1453) including John Selot (1447)	91
Chapter 15	John Brygge (1454-1497) including William Hoper (1453)	97
Chapter 16	Bartholomew Northern (1497-1519) including John Bulman (1497)	105
Chapter 17	Nicholas Carr (1519-1531)	111
Chapter 18	William White (1531-1554)	117
Chapter 19	John Blomevyle (1555-1586) including Hugh Twyford (1554)	125

Chapter 20 Baldwin Easdell (1586-1589) 133
Chapter 21 John Ponder (1591-1625) including William Bollinge (1589-1591) 139
Chapter 22 Hamo(n) Claxton (1625-1663) 145
Chapter 23 Henry Julyan (1663-1671) 155
Chapter 24 John Smith (1671-1684) 159
Chapter 25 John Gibson (1684-1708) 165
Chapter 26 William Adams (1708-1721) 173
Chapter 27 William Heath (1721-1742) 179
Chapter 28 William Adams (1742-1801) 185
Chapter 29 Thomas Baker (1801-1841) 199
Chapter 30 Edmund Smith Ensor (1841-1860) 213
Chapter 31 Robert John Francis (1860-1869) 225
Chapter 32 Charles H Bennington (1869-1872) 233
Chapter 33 Richard John Tacon (1872-1929) 239
Chapter 34 George Raymond Grundy (1930-1950) 259
Chapter 35 Henry Gascoigne (1950-1958) 273
Chapter 36 Roger Boys (1959-1961) 281
Chapter 37 Peter Jefford (1961-1970) 285
Chapter 38 Robin H Elphick (1971-1984) 293
Chapter 39 Kenneth Newton (1984-1989) 303
Chapter 40 Christopher Cousins (1990-1998) 307
Chapter 41 Andrew Sangster (1999-) 313

Index to Appendices 318
Appendices 319
Bibliography 335
Index 339

FOREWORD BY THE BISHOP OF NORWICH

What's special about Rollesby? At one level, nothing much. It is just one of no fewer than 577 parishes in the diocese of Norwich. Many of them have histories equally long and just as full of human incident. But Rollesby is the only one with a present-day Rector who has informed his historical research with his creative imagination to enable us to live through former centuries in the company of his predecessors. This is history, fiction, theology and an account of local traditions all rolled into one.

Andrew Sangster's book is a delight. It brings the past alive but its interest is not confined simply to those who know the parish of Rollesby well – or at all. All that's needed is human sympathy and historical curiosity, laced with a little imagination. The text is peppered with humorous asides and you are informed about all sorts of things in a peculiarly effortless way. (I hadn't really thought why **The Daily Telegraph** *was so called until I read this book and I still savour its description by a Victorian incumbent that it is "more pithy" than* The Times *though he is "not sure it will last long.")*

This is a book that reminds us that local experience is framed by national events, though the local is often paramount. None of us experience history in general but always in particular and Andrew Sangster has both a facility with language and an ability to translate the big picture into finer detail.

I hope this book will be widely read, for many will benefit from it. I hope too that those who read it will sense that what inspires it is a faith in the God of history who is not known in general, but always in the local and particular, supremely in Jesus of Nazareth, who inspired the service of all the main characters in this book.

THE RIGHT REVEREND GRAHAM NORVIC

PREFACE

I decided to write a history of a parish inspired by the list of rectors going back to the 12th century. Having looked at other parish accounts I tried to avoid an archival account for archivists. I asked myself about the nature of history and found this difficult to answer. I did arrive at the conclusion that most history is written from an objective view, when in fact history is both personal and national. So I broadened the whole project and have written the local history of a Norfolk village against the background of the broader political and social scene. I have written to all the rectors of the past, and awoken them from the dead, requesting them to write a brief account of the times in which they lived. I have asked them for local details, and about what was happening in the world at large during the time that they lived in the parish, and the way they lived. The rectors seemed the ideal vehicle because in times past they would have been central to local life; they actually existed, and they would have had a wider view of the world.

The work could be seen as falling between several stools, local and national: it includes local events and national perspectives as well as trivial aspects of history such as the introduction of snuff or famous cricket scores. I have written it from a worm's eye point of view. This is reflected in the index, where historically famous national names from the past sit side by side with local parishioners, past and present. As they are clergy writing they also make observations about clerical life. Accurate historical detail is recorded in the format of footnotes. Four of the Rollesby rectors are still alive and they have written their own accounts.

The book is historical, local and national, political and social, and each chapter hopefully reflects the ethos and mores of the era in which it is set.

Acknowledgements

If I tried to make a list of all the people who have helped me in my work it would be embarrassing because of the many I would undoubtedly omit. Nevertheless, I must mention Richard Tacon, who gave me considerable access to family papers and photographs. Also Miss Ann Bates and Frederick Youngs, who are both long serving and knowledgeable members of the parish; they gave me valuable time.

Bill Bracey, the parish treasurer, has read the text through with diligent care. Bill has taught me a great deal about my weaknesses in the English language. He supplied several thousand commas, corrected hundreds of subclauses and revealed my ignorance as to the proper placing of the word 'only'. He has accomplished this with great humour and wisdom and I owe him a great debt of gratitude. He is my own 'wise owl'.

Finally, I owe much to my wife, Carol, who never complained once about my use of our valuable free time working at this project.

Andrew Sangster

Rectors of St George's, Rollesby

1160 Walter Rugg
1294 William de Anmere
1302 Alan de Ely
1303 John de Caylly
1321 Firminus de Lavenham
1324 Laurence Folstaff
1327 John de Skyren
1337 Gilbert de Wellerton
1338 John de Flete
1340 Walter Hurry
1349 Simon de Rykenhale
1361 Simon de Babingley
1377 Nicholas de Lyons
1401 Thomas Bradmore
1424 James Andeley
1436 William Thrulby
1447 John Selot
1449 John Knolls
1453 William Hoper
1454 John Brygge
1497 John Bulman
1497 Bartholomew Northern
1519 Nicholas Carr
1531 William White
1554 Hugh Twyford
1555 John Blomevyle
1586 Baldwin Easdell
1589 William Bollinge
1591 John Ponder
1625 Hamo Claxton
1663 Henry Julyan
1671 John Smith
1684 John Gibson
1708 William Adams
1721 William Heath
1742 William Adams
1801 Thomas Baker
1841 Edmund Smith Ensor
1860 Robert John Francis
1869 Charles H Bennington
1872 Richard John Tacon
1930 George Raymond Grundy
1950 Henry Gascoigne
1959 Roger MacKenzie Boys
1961 Peter Ernest Jefford
1971 Robin Howard Elphick
1984 Kenneth Newton
1990 Christopher Cousins
1999 Andrew Sangster

Letter to the Past

Dear Parish Priests of Rollesby,

My apologies for breaking into your eternity, but I have a special request from the people of the 21st century. We were wondering whether you would be kind enough to write about your time in Rollesby parish. We are not necessarily looking for a detailed history but a short summary of the sort of matters that preoccupied you when in the parish. These matters could be local, the building of the church, the affairs of the parish and the kind of problems parishioners had during your time. It matters little whether you comment on major or trivial matters, simply those matters that caught your attention. I would be extremely grateful if you would also find the time to comment on any church matters of the Church in England, and for those of you in later times the Church *of* England. Finally, I would be most interested to know what the main topics of discussion were in your day. This could be a national or indeed international event, or anything that you and your congregation considered worthy of discussion or even prayer. If nothing significant happened in the parish the conditions of life would be of interest, and because we are typical human beings, scandals of the locality and national scene are always of interest. I suppose we are looking for a worm's eye view of history, from bottom to top rather than the usual history of looking down on events. When you have finished, please leave your correspondence at the base of the tower on the desk, or better, in the drawer that is unlocked, not that a locked drawer need worry your spiritual selves.

Yours sincerely,
THE 21ST CENTURY

CHAPTER 1

ooooo

Walter Rugg (1160)

Henry II – the beginning of Common Law & some order

Dear Future,

I was not certain whether this epistle was expected to be in French or Latin. I do not enjoy French and my Latin is only good for services, so I shall write this account in my own tongue. I was appointed parish priest of Ratholfuesby in 1160, during the reign of Henry II. Most of my fellow clerics in Norwich Priory knew the village as Rolvesbi and the locals in their crude way tend to call their settlement Rollesby. I have heard it claimed that old Godwin remembers the Viking family of Rollo who settled the area centuries before. I had only been here a few years before discovering that memories of the Vikings were mixed in emotion. Some of my parishioners regard the early Vikings as their founding and revered fathers; for others they were the sea marauders and accursed pirates. Even though it is now 1180, this wretched Saxon-Viking divide is still discussed over the cheapest ales. As I am pondering and looking at the setting sun going down over the graveyard, I can see Godwin digging his strip, and he for one makes me ever conscious that these divisions run deep in this area. When out of my hearing he still claims himself to be a son of Thor: Godwin is a heretical old fool. I wish my congregation would drop the subject; not even the incursion of the Normans just over a hundred years ago has settled the differences despite their having a new common enemy in the form of the Norman landowner and soldier.

They talk more of Vikings than of Hereward the Wake.[1] In this area of the Broads we do consider ourselves as Viking settlements and some of the Saxon villages close by still bear a degree of resentment towards us. There are those who claim the village name comes from Rolf and others Rollo; whichever you choose it was the name of a Viking Sea King: better than Ormesby which comes from 'orm' or 'worm' that means serpent, and this was only the name of one of their boats.[2] Rollesby sits by Rollesby Broad; to the north is the Broad of Ormesby and to the south, that of Filby. There are those who claim the Broads are what they are because our ancestors or previous occupants dug out too much peat. I believe this is nonsense on the grounds that this area of Anglia is so flat it's natural there should be so much water. Though, having said this, I must say that there is still some peat digging to the south.

The history of the area is somewhat remote. We are part of a fief granted to a large family variously known as Flegg and Martham or Gunton. Richard Flegg was once a tenant of Roger Bigot, and it was Richard Flegg who was one of a small band of persons to witness Herbert Losinga's charters. His son, Roger, attended on three successive bishops and the man whom we now know as Roger of Gunton holds four Knight's fees. He holds two hundred acres in Rollesby that were once owned by freemen.[3] According to the Domesday Book (1086) the main landowners in this area used to be the Bishops of Elmham and Thetford and also the Abbey of St Benets of Holm. My own patron is Richard de Rollesby and I am a good friend of his son Roger. They are both tenants of Roger Bigot.

My church dominates the local village, which is only a small cluster of houses built around the church in a very patchy way along twisting paths; drunken peasants must have laid these paths finding their way home. The church is at the highest point and the houses stretch down to the two village ponds on the Martham road.[4] It is a simple single-roomed construction with no seats on the inside. Cold and draughty it is made more so by the fact that the wooden shutters are in a state of decay. I have just finished a

---

[1] Hereward the Wake who held out against the Norman conquerors for a brief time in the Fens.

[2] *Norfolk and Norwich Archaeological Society* Vols 1-49 (1959) N&NAS, Norwich. Vol.5, p.289.

[3] *Norfolk and Norwich Archaeological Society* Vols 1-49 (1959) N&NAS, Norwich. Vol.33, Part II, p.193, for all the information in this paragraph.

[4] The two ponds were in existence until the 1740s, when one became part of White Farm property and was lost (except in bad weather) and the other pond is still a feature of this area.

Mass, all in Latin, and only one or two of the locals had sufficient Latin to join me in the creed, and that was only mimicry. The rest of the worshippers sat along the stone bench formed in the wall, and through the smoke from the candles and incense I could see and hear them discussing the day's events. The more pious ones studied the pictures of hellfire and damnation on the south wall, but few of them could follow the service and were only there to stop the wall pictures becoming a personal reality.

I wish they were a happier group: they are forever complaining about the Cistercians who are looking for yet more land on which to practise their estate management. At least my brothers in Christ know how to look after the land. If only these parishioners would cast their minds back before 1154, they would recall the civil war between Stephen and Maud. Then there was genuine fear. People spoke in whispers and hoped the soldiers would not pass through their patch of God's earth. At least Henry II has brought peace, and law, even if his justice is expensive. The Church Farm to the east of the church thrives and keeps the area in good husbandry.

It's nearly the spring but the air has a real bite. I can see smoke wafting across the church from the blacksmith's yard. I hope it has no sparks. Blackie has been in trouble before with his fires, as well as allowing his dogs to pester the cows belonging to the local abbey. I envy the monks their cloistered life. They are much better off than I will ever be.[5] Rollesby is not a rich area; even the parish priest at Little Ormesby is better off than I could ever be. We have a fair number of freemen, but the smallholdings are small and haphazard, mainly because the Prior's tenants are placed where the Prior wills.[6]

At the moment I am concerned about a popular story doing the rounds. It was told by a travelling Mass priest and has caused malicious gossip to be spread about the monks. The Mass priest claimed that King Henry had been stopped[7] by some monks from St Swithin's who had complained that the Abbot had cut down their traditional thirteen-course dinner to ten dishes. The King had been enraged claiming that one course was good enough for him and that should also satisfy the monks.

---

[5] The blacksmith's was undoubtedly where the Horse and Groom now stands: later records testify to this and the name of the Inn was probably adopted from this source.

[6] *Norfolk and Norwich Archaeological Society* Vols 1-49 (1959) N&NAS, Norwich. Vol.38, p.18.

[7] A story by Giraldus Cambrensis in *Speculum Ecclesiae*.

This wretched priest sought popularity. He had at first been a welcome visitor in Rollesby but his gossip has not helped the Christian cause in the parish. It seems to me that any outsider is always more welcome than the local priest. Occasionally it hurts me, but I know that my first duty is to be faithful and not worry about how I am considered or weighed up in the people's peculiar perspectives. It was probably the novelty of seeing an unfamiliar face that is always refreshing for anyone. I am aware that parish members have secretly whispered how much better he would be than I am. They whisper these things in secret but I hear their opinions from the so-called well-wishers. I know it to be wrong, but I was overjoyed when they discovered he was a habitual drunkard. I took even more misplaced pleasure when they chased him out of Rollesby back to Norwich once they discovered that the wicked old devil had been playing around with one daughter too many. However, it's done considerable damage to the Church, and I can take consolation only from the fact that my congregation has never seen me drunk or fooling around with parish girls. I may not be the most exciting man but at least I try to be steady: I conduct services on time, visit the sick and lonely, help in the fields at harvest, and I am pretty accomplished at catching hares. What more could they want from their parish priest?

Recently the members of the congregation have stopped talking about the Mass priest, and this is a relief. For some time they have been dwelling on the martyrdom of Thomas Becket. Godwin, Saxethorpe and Thurne made some kind of pilgrimage to Canterbury and returned two months ago almost as local heroes. I have the distinct impression that it was more of a holiday than a religious experience, and Thurne's wife is particularly suspicious about their antics. I did my best to explain the issues of the Constitutions of Clarendon to the congregation but they were not interested until the Archbishop was murdered at the King's request. I find all this ironical. The Archbishop was never popular while alive, and the locals thought that his demand that priests in holy orders should have their own courts was a travesty of justice. They were all for the King, but the Archbishop's death changed everyone's thinking. It had been the same with Blackie's old father; a huge bully of a man but when his horse threw him into the Rollesby Broad and he drowned not only did people feel sorry for him but virtually treated him as a saint. I often wonder whether people will look more kindly upon my efforts when I am dead and gone, or will I be of interest only to the worms?

I can see Morrell walking past the church ignoring me, looking his usual disgruntled self. He quarrelled all too seriously with his neighbour Freeman over the land by the Broad. When Freeman's father died, Morrell had claimed the land as his own. Freeman had little support under the old rules of the Saxon wager of law[8] because illness and the civil war had struck down most of his family. Morrell, on the other hand, is wealthy and his family has influence from Rollesby to Great Ormesby. When the Justices of Eyre[9] eventually came I persuaded them to start a case of Mort d'Ancestor[10] that had allowed Freeman to keep his land. It worked because it had been recalled that his great ancestor Geoffrey Freeman had worked the area before the Civil War. Morrell now blames me, his parish priest of all people, and refuses to acknowledge my presence. My first bishop warned me about involving myself in local disputes for fear of endangering my ministry. Twice I have tried to intervene in local issues, both times trying to reconcile warring factions, both times only out of love for my congregation and both times one or both sides has resented my efforts. All this despite the fact they had all asked for my support in the first place. It's very difficult when neighbours have disputes to walk away, parish priest or not.

I also find taking confession in a small community difficult. Mad Meg came to confession a year or so ago and told me how on a drunken evening she had allowed her next door neighbour to have his way with her, and thereafter, whenever he fancied her. I know the neighbour and Meg's husband. I said nothing but she never invites me to her hearth since the confession simply because I know. It is hardly my fault that I know what is happening, and the fact that her neighbour and husband are good friends plays upon her conscience. I heard from other confessions that she has quite an appetite for the passions of the flesh; even the most surprising people have had pleasure with her while her husband has been ploughing his strip

---

[8] Compurgation (as a word first used in 1658) was the Saxon system by which a person with a dispute could call witnesses to his claim: the witnesses could be friends and family: hardly a fair system if corruption was at work. Some mistakenly see this as a start to the jury system.

[9] Justices of Eyre or of Assize was a system of travelling justice which had its origins in the time of Henry I, but bore fruit in the time of Henry II. It was one of the foundations of common law and although expensive and sometimes feared it nevertheless ensured that justice was held in common and was fair.

[10] Mort d'Ancestor started by Henry II in 1166 that settled disputed land, demanding proof of ownership back to the time of his grandfather, Henry I thus ignoring the unhappy disputes of the Civil War between Stephen and Matilda (Maud).

or working for the manor. It's not as if she is attractive, but she no longer looks at me and there are a few others who avoid my company. The very fact I know their inner secrets excludes me from their social company. I suspect this will always be true for parish priests, whatever age or area they live and work in.

For the last few years I have served the community, kept my own fields and worked the harvest, but I have only the church for company and it can be freezing in there: I am sure the cold winters in the church will be the death of me one day. At least under Henry II there is a sense of law, even if it is still dangerous to visit other villages by night. I hope that at the last trump God Almighty forgives me my sins and those of my flock, for our sins are many.

CHAPTER 2

ooooo

William de Anmere (1294-1302)

Edward I - little order out of much chaos

When I arrived some seven years ago I found the church in Rollesby in a state of sad disrepair. It was a serious step down for me to come to this part of the northern coast. I had hoped for a position in Durham or even Canterbury. My relations had, when all was said and done, crossed with the Conqueror, and it was hardly my fault that the rules of primogeniture[1] had left me no choice but to make my way in the Church. Geoffrey, my eldest brother, now rules the roost in the Normandy estates, and I am not going to follow the military paths of my other two brothers who died fighting in Gascony. The Diocese of Norwich is the worst place for an ecclesiastical career. The last Bishop, William Middleton,[2] fell out with the King and the Diocese was known as a place of clerical intransigence,[3] and had the Bishop not offered a fine of a thousand marks, most of the clerics could have been arrested before the justices.[4] Bishops are powerful, but Edward I is not a king to be crossed even by prelates. Even before I had arrived the canons at Rochester Cathedral had teased me that I was going to a riotous place. Not that Rollesby seemed

---

[1] Primogeniture (word first used in 1602) the probate rule that the inheritance falls to the eldest son.

[2] Bishop from 1278 to 1288 was a trained Canon Lawyer.

[3] Maurice Powicke (1962) 'The Thirteenth Century' in *The Oxford History of England*, p.481.

[4] Most of this problem was to do with testamentary and matrimonial cases versus the claims of the crown. In June 1286 the writ Circumspecte Agatis was issued: it begins 'be circumpsect in your dealing with the Bishop of Norwich and his clergy. Do not punish them if they hold pleas on purely spiritual matters.'

anything but a rural backwater, and there was certainly plenty of water in the flat lands stretching away below the church.

Even in the parish there had been problems regarding who owned what land. In 1244 Simon de Peche had claimed patronage of the church against Ernald of Rollesby, and his wife Juliana de Peche had managed to claim the assize of bread and held half the fee from the Bishop of Norwich. It was all very confusing. In 1285 William de Rollesby, who owned Suckling House and land around St Andrews in Norwich, was probably the wealthiest man in the area. Although it was Simon de Lincoln and Catherine his wife, of the Gunton Manor, who secured the living for me, my real patron was William de Rollesby.[5] The other manor was that of Berking, and Richard and Joan,[6] his wife, helped towards making me financially better off than when I first arrived.[7]

My pecuniary problems arose because I had owed a considerable amount of money to a Jewish money-lender called Silas, but the King had seen fit to drive the Jews out of England and with the brutal execution of this order I am now at least without debt. I intend to make my name even in a place as remote as Rollesby. Just as I had left to take up the Rollesby cure I heard that King Edward had suppressed the Welsh revolt only to find that Scotland had allied itself to France. I know that the extra taxation is necessary in order to finance these wars, but it has impoverished yet further the rural area already badly hit by the loss of much of the wool trade. It was not a rich area since there were only eleven freemen with forty acres of land and three and half acres of meadow between them.[8]

As a cleric I found myself in some trouble in 1296 because the Pope had insisted that clergy pay no further taxes without his authority.[9] The last two years have been bad enough collecting the tithes, and in addition to this, I am now supervising the building of the new church for the Rollesby parish. It is going to take many years and many grumbles from the locals and the financial situation does little to help.

---

[5] Ann Bates' research into *Norfolk Archaeological Society*.

[6] Richard de Berking and Joan his wife were entrusted with seven messuages, one hundred acres of land, twelve of heath with four shillings per annum. *Norfolk Archaeological Society*.

[7] There may have been two manors associated with Rollesby, but the records are far from clear.

[8] Ann Bates' research into *Norfolk Archaeological Society*.

[9] Papal Bull *Clericis Laicos*, but the following summer the Pope published *Etsi de Statu* which withdrew these extreme claims.

I have demolished most of the Saxon edifice and used the stones in the foundation and the footings of the tower. It is an expensive job but I decided it would be the tallest tower in the area: if I cannot go to Durham I will have the cathedral of the Fleggs. I would prefer the new square tower, but the round tower has to do for two reasons. The first is the simple fact it is cheaper, and if it is to stretch above the skyline only a round tower will do. A square tower at that size would leave me with no resources. The second is the local input: the congregation resents any form of change. I nearly had a revolt for building a new edifice, even from people who tried to keep away from worship.

The Rawnse family, down by the broad water, were whispered still to be oak worshippers and even they had complained about the church plans. If everyone who complained actually came to church, the building would not be large enough to contain them all. People of the parish are even suspicious of me because I can speak French, even though I cope well enough with their coarse tongue.

The nave has not taken long, the chancel will have to wait, but the tower is now an impressive twenty-five feet high. My plans are working well, the main problem being the danger of wooden scaffolding. The Prior, Robert de Langele[10] from the cathedral, sent two builders from the cathedral and they have been here over a month giving advice, but the cathedral advisers have no idea what it is like in the remoter parishes. They appear to have all the money they require; it is different in the parishes. Since the burning of the cathedral in 1272[11] there have been plenty of fine artisans in Norwich, but they are expensive. They also have some fine white stone imported from Caen and Barnack in Northamptonshire, but it is too expensive for country churches.

There has already been one accident on the Rollesby tower: Granville Ellis fell and broke a leg. It did not heal properly, and now he is walking with a limp, and worse still, it causes him ongoing pain, even in his back, which seems strange. I have ensured his family does not go without food, and I have been pleasantly surprised how the peasant farmers have rallied around with various offerings. Had it been me, I am not at all certain I

---

[10] Prior from 1289 to 1309.

[11] The Norwich citizens had fired the monastery and cathedral in 1272 over a dispute over market tolls at the Fair in Tomblands: the Prior seemed to have been somewhat greedy!

would have received the same sympathy. Now the tower is growing in size, the locals are showing more interest. Stones are the problem. There were no good stones or even sound timber in Norfolk at the price I could afford; the cathedral and monastery powers had the money to ship it over from the Continent. The flint and large beach stones had to suffice in the parish, and even they are proving difficult to find in abundance. The Patron has financed some corner stones, but apart from this he is happy to collect revenues and leave me alone.

Up on the heath, to the west of the church, the villagers are having problems in the open field with their strips of land. The manor is becoming less and less important to them[12] and ownership of their particular strip is a matter of daily dispute. It has not been made easy by the necessity of a new road, now called Heath Lane, having to be cut through the centre. This has had the effect of cutting two major strips. The value of the open field with strips is that it permits individual labour to make its own way but at the same time there is a certain amount of public control.[13] Some of the villagers are giving themselves a social station they do not have; they are ascripti glebae[14] and sometimes forget this fact of life.

In my first week land disputes led me into a state of personal embarrassment. The very first confession I took in the church was from a man who had killed his neighbour up on Heath Lane over an argument over their strips. He had lived with the guilt for years and it was getting him down. I gave him absolution in return for working on the tower and the power of the Spirit worked. He was a changed man and became a leading light in the parish and rarely missed Mass or confession. He made an excellent thurifer[15] and I relied on him for his labour and support. I do not wish to name him because this document may fall into the wrong hands. Years later, in fact only a month ago, I was standing having a social chat with some villagers by the ponds on the Martham Road, and enjoying a drink when one of them asked me how I found the experience of hearing confession. I kept to the rules and said next to nothing. I told them I forgot almost everything

---

[12] G M Trevelyan. (1945) *English Social History* Longmans, London, p.4. The old feudal manorial system during this period was beginning to creak: farm leases and wages were becoming more important and taking the place of cultivating the lord's demesne by servile labour.

[13] G M Trevelyan. (1945) *English Social History* Longmans, London, p.5.

[14] 'bound to the soil'.

[15] swung the incense in church.

people confessed to me and this was good because the confessional is so strictly confidential. They pressed me a little further and asked what kind of things I heard. I told them adultery and theft were the serious problems, and then said that in the very first confession I had heard in Rollesby the man had confessed to murder. I had barely said this when up comes the thurifer, and hearing that the topic was confession, but having not heard what I had said, told the assembled group that he had come to me for the very first confession I had heard as their parish priest.

'It wasn't you, Jack,' I hurriedly said, 'it wasn't you.'

'It surely was, Father: you arrived on Shrove Tuesday and I came to thee that very night'.

'No, no,' I protested, 'there was someone earlier.'

'No,' he protested, 'I deliberately watched the church. I was determined to be the first.'

'Old Huggs was your neighbour farmer in the field, was he not?' This statement came from one of the group, Granville, who had been listening with interest and had already put two and two together. He was a relation of Huggs.

I changed the conversation as rapidly as I could, but after that the thurifer was a marked man. I learned a lesson that day, that when I have a secret to keep I have a secret to keep. The thurifer is still not aware that his secret murder is common parlance, but wonders why people are now avoiding him, and I fear for his life. Despite these problems the church is doing well and the building itself stands high above the surrounding hovels.

CHAPTER 3

ooooo

John de Caylly (1303-1321)
including Alan de Ely (1302)

Edward II - murder in the parish and of a King

Dear Reader,

In 1303 at the request of the Norwich Prior I took over the parish of Rollesby from one Alan de Ely. This unfortunate cleric lasted only one year, having taken the place of William de Anmere who left Rollesby church half built. I met William de Anmere as he travelled through to his new position at Durham. He was not popular, I gather, mainly because he wanted to change everything and had let something slip from a confession he had heard. He was the one who demolished the old church and started to build the one I am expected to finish. The Rollesby villagers believe he was obsessed with the tower. It had to be the tallest, but in fact he had only raised it to twenty-five feet when he had the opportunity for promotion and promptly left.

On the instructions of the Prior, Alan de Ely stayed for one year. There is a strange air of silence surrounding this one-year tenure: the locals hint darkly that 'not everything was right'. The Patron said he was destined for higher places. In truth, I believe that the Prior simply asked him to do a year knowing that Sir William de Ormesby[1] was demanding that I should be given the living. Obviously the gossip flourishes because the truth is not known, and if the truth is not known, people make up the facts and enjoy

[1] Rectors' list from Rollesby church.

the possibility that something is wrong. This happened with an old friend of mine: he left the parish to attend to his sick parents, but on his return he discovered that everyone thought he had run off with the miller's wife. All kinds of malicious and lewd gossip had built up about the pair of them. In fact, his departure was totally innocent and the miller's wife had simply left her beast of a husband. That is human nature but people particularly like a possible scandal amongst the clergy - even if there isn't one. I don't suppose that will ever change: thank goodness they cannot write their gossip down and spread it about in letter form.

Nor is it just the clergy that give rise to popular scandal but their betters also. The patrons of the living were Simon de Peche and his wife Juliana,[2] and their son William fell foul of the law[3] and was outlawed. It was a tragic case: young William was a fine boy and he had been riding over towards Ormesby when he found one of the village girls being molested by two strangers. He attacked them and when they fought back he killed both with his sword and dagger in fair fight. It turned out that they were servants of a rich merchant in Norwich and William fled. Had he stayed he would have had a defence. Indeed, he may have become a local hero, but he fled, was made an outlaw and the gossip started. Such is the difference between heroic status and social stigma, a mere second's careless thought. It destroyed his parents who had been good church people. The commoners loved to see their betters humbled, claiming that if murder could happen in such elevated classes why should they be regarded as better. Simon de Peche kept himself to himself but Juliana could never be seen again without a mother's tear in her eye. Then came the final effrontery to them: in 1305 William and Thomas de Reppes claimed from the Bishop of Norwich all rights to the patronage[4] of Rollesby on account of the felony of William de Peche and he was obliged to enter them as an escheat for their claim. It was an utter social degradation for the de Peche family and was the main topic of talk and excited gossip on Sundays. As parish priest I had several patrons of one sort or another: John Salmon, the Bishop of Norwich; Aymer de Valence; John de Vaus, heir of Robert de Filby; and Simon de Rollesby.[5]

---

[2] See page 22.

[3] Bates, Ann. Private research from the *Norfolk Archaeological Society.*

[4] Bates, Ann. Private research from the *Norfolk Archaeological Society.*

[5] Bates, Ann. Private research from the *Norfolk Archaeological Society*, and Rectors' list in Rollesby.

Two years after my arrival Gilbert de Heacham[6] was appointed at Ormesby and has set about building yet another church there. Quite why they need another church is beyond me but there is more wealth in that area. He is building a tall, square tower, and suggested to me that a round tower the size that William de Anmere proposed was not architecturally sound and lacked taste. He is an expert, so I have continued on the round tower's twenty-foot base with an octagonal design. The corner stones cost much money but the Prior has sent me four wagonloads from Norwich and some skilled labour. I was grateful for this since they are still rebuilding the cloisters and it is going to be years before they finish.[7] We are now at sixty foot and the church can be seen from miles away. I have to admit a certain joy as I watch it reach to the heavens.

Old Granville Ellis, who broke a leg in William's time, keeps warning me of Babel tower.

'Now look ye here, John,' he said, 'there be that story in the Bible about men trying to reach God in his heaven, and God almighty broke it all down and made everyone speak French or Latin to confuse us.'

'John, it's not as simple as that,' I tried to explain.

'It can't be more simple. French and Latin was imposed as a punishment by God because our forbears tried to reach him with a tower like yours.'

'But John, this tower is for the glory of God.'

'You're as bad as that William de Anmere. It's your glory, and that Ormesby priest has made you want to build higher, it's a sort of competition between the two of you.'

I did not prolong the argument with Granville. First it would not get me far; secondly, I need him on side because he is influential in the village, and finally there was a degree of truth in what he said. The Ormesby tower is going to be larger but there is no reason why ours should not be taller. Granville picks up most of his biblical knowledge from listening to the occasional friar preaching in Norwich. He often goes to Tomblands to the Fair, hobbles about his business for the first day then listens to any preaching friar before his long journey home.

A few winters ago our own miller, Robert of Rollesby, found his son

---

[6] Gilbert de Heacham, Vicar of Ormesby St Margaret, 1305-1308.

[7] Rebuilding of cloisters at Norwich Cathedral took from 1297 to 1430!

John murdered in the fields. Semeine, son of Henry Thedlef, was taken for the murder under the writ 'bono at malo' and flung into prison. Just before the murder Semeine had tried to drown himself in the sea, but John, the miller's son, had rescued him. With complete lack of gratitude and beyond any human reason, Semeine killed his rescuer. However, it transpired that Semeine turns mad at the crescent of the moon so he now sits in prison awaiting the King's pardon.[8] I feel sorrow for his parents. The only defence their son has is a matter of madness but at least the King's courts are civilised in this aspect.

Currently both Granville and the blacksmith are worried about their two boys, Roger and John. They were both persuaded by the Patron to support the Duke of Norfolk in these troublesome times and have disappeared as soldiers. We have not heard anything about them for years.

Although the last king made parliament important[9] his son, our current king, Edward II, is weak and his infatuation with Piers Gaveston has plunged the realm into deep tension.[10] We do not see much of the national trauma here in Rollesby, but we certainly hear a great deal from those travelling through, and now Bruce from Scotland has invaded again[11] our taxes have risen once more. It was rumoured that both Roger and John are fighting for the Despensers against the Welsh Marcher Lords.[12] I hope for their families that they have chosen the right side. The country seems dangerously close to baronial war. If the king were stronger, this need not have happened. I must also ensure that these notes are hidden! I am of the firm opinion that we would be better off with a king who is strong and a tyrant rather than some milky pleasant leader: at least there would be no anarchy

---

[8] 1316 November 19th. This story recounted in Norfolk Archaeological Records, found by Miss Ann Bates.

[9] Trevelyan, G M (1978) *English Social History* New illustrated edition with introduction by Asa Briggs, Longman, London, p.190. Edward I was sometimes known as the English Justinian because of the number of statutes he passed, especially relating to land law. He also established a form of parliament in two Houses, the Commons and Lords.

[10] Piers Gaveston, Edward II's favourite gave nicknames to the Barons and ill advice to the King. He was eventually captured at Scarborough and killed near Kenilworth by order of Thomas of Lancaster on June 19th, 1312.

[11] On the same day in 1312 as Piers Gaveston was killed Robert the Bruce invaded England as far as Durham. The North of England had to pay him off from attacking further!

[12] Churchill, Winston S (1956) *A History of the English Speaking Peoples* Cassell, London. Vol.1, p.249. Edward II tried to rebuild the royalist party with the Despensers while the Welsh Marcher Lords and Lancastrian party joined to procure the exile of the Despensers. Eventually Edward II won this round and beheaded Lancaster (March 22nd 1322).

that affects the common person so much. A tyrannical leader may not be the right thing to say, but at least he would keep law and order in the interests of his tyranny.

The local boys have caused considerable trouble over the last two years with their games on the green. They kick around a sealed pig's bladder and have become quite violent with this exercise. They played against some thugs from Ormesby and young Sam had his leg broken and lost all his front teeth. The new priest at Ormesby, John de Herling,[13] complained that one of the Ormesby men had had his ear bitten off. I have little sympathy with him because he supported the fracas and cheered his so-called side on. It was only a few years ago that Parliament tried to ban this latest fancy of game playing.[14] Old Granville reckons the game is here to stay. He believes they will be playing with balls for another thousand years. He can be such a fool with his prophecies.

The four monks on the Prior's farm, next to the church, did their best with the injuries. They have now read some medical manuscript which informs us that what we eat and the way we cook it is important for our health.[15] It does not seem very important, most people around here eat what they can, and God will call us to Him in His own time whatever we consume.

It is now 1320 and the tower is nearly complete, the nave is not finished but we have sufficient thatch to be able to worship in the dry west end of the building. The congregation members are a bit close to the altar for my liking but it will have to do for now. I am more worried about Roger's wife. He has been away at the wars for so long she has taken a fancy to young Gregory, a monk down in Ormesby. Nobody can prove a thing, but the gossip is doing the usual rounds. She is a bit flighty, and even made suggestions in my direction a few years ago. John de Herling, the new priest at Ormesby, thinks it is all talk, but I am beginning to suspect she is pregnant: that is more than talk for she is no blessed virgin. I dare not think what will happen if she is bearing a child and Roger returns. Despite the fact he has

---

[13] John de Herling, Vicar of Ormesby from 1308 to 1328.

[14] 1314 was the first law against playing violent ball games, the start of soccer: the ban was generally ignored.

[15] John of Gaddesden, the Black Prince's doctor wrote *Rosa Medicina (Anglica)*, a medical work based on observation in practice, anticipating later treatments based on diet and cookery. He is mentioned in Chaucer's *Canterbury Tales*.

been away for years she should have waited for more definite news before she looked for a new man. The fact that it is a monk makes me exceedingly unhappy, but we shall never be able to prove it even if she does have a baby. That is one thing the clever people will never be able to fathom out: what sex a child is going to be and who is the father; they will always be God's mysteries.

Young Gregory is one of those clergy who is well liked because he stops and chats with everyone, will take a drink with anyone and always has a twinkle in his eye when there is a woman about. It is common sense that the villagers are better off with the less popular priest who is at least honest, keeps to his prayers and cares for their souls. Sadly they are only taken in by the wrapping. Gregory advised Godwin to avoid the merchet[16] imposed on his daughter and Mother Huggs as well as the heriot:[17] both took his opinion and landed up paying more dearly in the long run. Popular clergy are not always the most worthy.

There are always plenty of clergy to be found but they tend to congregate in the towns of wealth and power.[18] Each one conducts the services differently. Here we tend to use the Norwich Rite, but others adhere to the confusing Hereford Rite and the more popular Sarum (Salisbury) Rites,[19] which is all very confusing for the ordinary people.

It is the ordinary people who concern me most, the people of my congregation for whom I am responsible. Their lives are tough, sometimes brutish and often short. They frequently lack proper nourishment, and all too often die from illness or from attacks by thieves and other outlaws. They indulge too much in the delights of the flesh although they have a genuine fear of hell and damnation. I have a major task before me in trying to make them more spiritually inclined in their thinking; to bring them to the way of Jesus Christ. For my own part I have similar problems with my own spirituality which can be far too shallow. I often reflect on the fact that between what Jesus said and what He actually did one could not draw a thin sword. If only my words and the better thoughts of my parishioners would come as close to our daily behaviour.

---

[16] Merchet is the fine paid to the Lord on a marriage.

[17] Heriot was the seizure of best beast on the death of a tenant.

[18] Chadwick, H (Editor) (2000) *Not Angels but Anglicans* Canterbury Press, Norwich, p.92.

[19] Chadwick, H (Editor) (2000) *Not Angels but Anglicans* Canterbury Press, Norwich, p.93.

CHAPTER 4

ooooo

Firminus de Lavenham (1321-1324)

- the English archer at home

I took over from John de Caylly as parish priest at Rollesby in the year 1321. He certainly left me with a few problems. He had become obsessed with the height of the tower. It has become a real waste of money, not least because the nave has hardly been touched. I have been asked to comment on my time here and it is nearly at a close. I promised the Prior I would do three years and I am happy because it is 1324 and I shall soon be moving on. It has not been an easy parish. There have been problems with the patronage and the Bishop has had to take a direct hand in my appointment: he had to make it clear that I was appointed with his 'full authority'.[1] The tower I rounded off at sixty-six foot; my predecessors will be happy to know it is the highest round tower in the Diocese[2] and it now has four good belfry shutters. I managed to make some progress with the nave. It now has four piers either side. The two earlier ones are rounded in the older Norman style but we can live with that archaic look. I have squeezed the Priory resources a good deal and have placed four small quatrefoil clerestory windows over the south arcade. The north side needs something but that must wait. I am especially pleased with the font, and I have mounted it on an original early English one. A chancel is needed but I

---

[1] Rectors' list in Rollesby.

[2] Still remains tallest round tower in Norfolk.

must leave that for someone else.

My main problem has been a degree of restlessness within the village. The two soldiers Roger and John returned last year. They were very quiet about the recent past, and I suspect they were somehow involved in matters unpleasant. They brought news that Mortimer has fled to France.[3] More to the point John is now worthless as a labourer because he is crippled in one leg and lost his right arm. How he survived I shall never understand. An arrow penetrated his thigh and seems to have completely shredded his muscles. The only way they could remove the arrow was by pulling it right through the flesh and, according to Roger, John nearly died from the pain. He lost his right arm in the same battle when a sword completely severed the arm above the elbow. Most men die from such injuries. Roger found his wife missing and also the news that she had given birth to a son in his absence. He went mad at first, and walked to Jermouth[4] and Caister in pursuit. He then walked to Lowestoft and still found no news except that a man with a monk's tonsure had been seen with her heading for London. After this he gave up and returned to his home, a single-roomed lodge against the Church Farm's main boundary wall. They both drink too much. Roger looks after John, but unlike other soldiers I have known they say little of what they have been up to. A soldier's silence is always a sign, in my opinion, either that there is something they are ashamed about or matters have gone badly wrong. It is quite clear that they were frightened by modern warfare. The arrow can be a ruthless weapon.

All the able men practise with their arrows at the butts either behind the church or down by the smithy next to the inn. They prefer the fields by the smithy because they can slip in for a quick ale while placing some small bets on who will win. Unlike foreigners, we do not draw the arrow but bend the bow[5] and this has the advantage of using more powerful bows and greater

---

[3] March 1323. Mortimer escaped from the Tower to exile in France where Edward II's wife was later to meet him in 1324 when they would become lovers.

[4] Ecclestone (1971) *A W Henry Manship's Great Yarmouth* Buckle, Gt Yarmouth, p.23. Late Saxon name for Yarmouth: it was once called Garianonum, then Garmud or Jhiermud.

[5] Trevelyan, G M (1945) *English Social History* Longmans, London, p.18, footnote 6. 'The secret of the greater efficacy of which English archers had the monopoly in Europe lay in the fact that "the Englishman did not keep his left hand steady, and draw his bow with his right; but keeping his right at rest upon the nerve, he pressed the whole weight of his body into the horns of his bow". Hence probably arose the phrase "bending a bow," and the French of "drawing" one.' (W Gilpin in *Remarks on Forest Scenery* 1791) This is what Hugh Latimer meant when he described how he was early taught 'not to draw with strength of arms as divers nations do, but with the strength of the body.' It was an art not easily learned.

accuracy. We sometimes refer to this art as the great English secret. Both Roger and John had been good archers in their younger days.

They both came to the church as I instructed but will not make their confessions: if Roger were not working for the Church Farm I am sure he would not even attend the Mass. I have no doubt that if he caught his wife's lover it would be a case of murder, and I suspect the village would support him.

Granville died last week; we buried him at the foot of the tower just at the very place where he fell. He had become something of a wise man to the village, but I will not miss his accusations of building a church to my own glory. Ever since he fell from the tower he distrusted the building. Already some say his ghost can be seen at the top of the tower, and that is after one week below the sod. Young Freeman dug his grave and he took it so deep I worried for the tower. I am convinced that he tried to get the body below the foundation. There is some history between the Freemans and the Ellis family I have never quite fathomed.

The Prior visited the farm and was pleased with the way the church tithes were coming into his coffers: certainly the church gains much from this parish but the poor remain as poor as ever. At least no one starves, the fish are in abundance and we do not ask too many questions about some of the game that appears on our dishes. Probably the most popular dish is the coney[6] followed by larks and thrushes caught by lime sticks and nets.[7] Bacon is one of my favourite dishes, but that depends on the amount of waste available each year.[8] Some of the cornfields are encroaching into the woodlands and that makes game less easy to catch. Although coneys are prolific other game becomes scarcer the more we extend our fields.

As well as helping with the building of the church, I have improved the priest's house. I have a proper chimney in place[9] so my eyes are not made sore: most homes just have a hole in the roof, and dry mud floors. I have a stone fireplace and have built a small outhouse for my poultry. I intend to sell my poultry before I move on, probably to Freeman, so long as he does not mention Granville Ellis's ghost again. I shall have to wait his return

---

[6] The old word for a rabbit.

[7] As they still do in parts of the continent.

[8] Trevelyan, G M (1945) *English Social History* Longmans, London, p.22.

[9] Trevelyan, G M (1945) *English Social History* Longmans, London, p.20.

from the harvest. In this area harvest is a major event, even the Norwich weavers have to leave their work to join us in the fields.[10]

That has been one feature of my life here that always irritated me. The people in Norwich make much money with their weaving, spinning and other industry; the men of Yarmouth make much with their commerce and pillage, but the rural area supplies them with the basic necessity of food and for all the hard labour receives little reward. As a country we would return to a state of anarchy without enough food to go round, and it is labour intensive, yet the rural areas are the poorest. It seems strange that townspeople are always so much better off. I have kept my own stock, laboured on my own strip, and helped at the harvest, something a cathedral priest would think beneath him. Yet whenever I meet them they always think themselves superior in all things simply because they are associated with the mother church. They strut around the cathedral with their flowing robes, hardly finding the time to look down their noses at a visiting parish priest: as far as they are concerned we are only just one step away from the peasant.

On reflection it is not a bad thing for a parish priest to be seen as one of the people. We learn to speak their language so we can communicate with greater ease, and by working alongside them we begin to understand their problems and the way they think. If a priest has no idea about the way his parishioners live their lives how can he be of service to them? Because I am amongst them they talk to me, confide in me and learn to trust in what I say. Yet I must not become part of all their fabric; I must not forget I am their intermediary with God; they expect me to be above some of the more sordid passions of life and this I have striven to do. It is not always easy but I hope history and God Himself will look kindly on my brief efforts here. If in the Last Judgement God takes a ledger out I shall hold my breath in hope that the good I have tried to do outweighs the bad I know I have done, so whoever reads this please pray for my soul.

---

[10] Trevelyan, G M (1945) *English Social History* Longmans, London, p.28.

CHAPTER 5

ooooo

Laurence Folstaff (1324-1327)

Edward III - pardoners at work

Dear Readers,

I know not what century this will be read in, but know that the times we are living through in this parish are not the best. I used to be Dean of St Chad's in Shropshire[1] and because of difficulties the Bishop asked me to come and instituted me under his full authority. It has not been an easy time. The interest in building the church has faltered. Trying to find labour has become difficult, and we are equally hard pressed with the finances. The local workers object to spending more money at a time when their tithes to the Priory are so heavy, and the wages paid for the field work is not that good. I only wish the Prior or Bishop would give some money to the area: they have spent enough on the fancy tower clock in the cathedral.[2] They are always quick enough to remove our resources on the claim that the Holy Father in Rome needs this assistance for the glory of God.

It is now nearly Christmas 1327 and the snows have stopped any work on the farm: hunger has become an issue for many in the village. I sometimes fear the temper of the mob; such angry groups have been known to

[1] Rectors' list in Rollesby.

[2] 1321. First recorded tower clock in England begun for Norwich Cathedral, with astronomical dial made in London.

kill even bishops.[3] On the whole I find it best to keep out of the way and in the warmth of the Priory Farm.

I had hoped to finish the nave before the snows, but since the masons still claim that Granville Ellis's ghost is in the belfry they have proved reluctant. I carried out an exorcism and they still claim it is there. I now believe they have used it as an excuse to avoid work.

'Now Father Laurence,' young Freeman said to me, 'we weren't scared of old Granville when he was alive, but it be another matter now he be dead.'

'My dear John,' I said to him, 'Granville is in God's hands and not in the belfry.'

'That's what I mean, Father, if he be in God's hands, and Granville be in the belfry then God's hands be too close.'

'You have no need to be worried by God's hands, my son.'

'You don't have my sinning background, Father.'

'You're young my son. You have plenty of time to repent.'

'I sometimes think I'm making matters worse by hanging on.'

I gave up; John Freeman was convinced he was wicked and that old Granville had come for him.

The village is full of superstition; they are supposed to be Christians yet they are still afraid of certain parts of the marshes. It is not the robbers that lurk there that worry them, but the spirits. For my part I am more worried about the thieves than the dark places. It only needs an owl to sit on someone's house for two nights in a row and they become convinced that a death must occur. The Prior had a procession to Priory Farm on Corpus Christi day;[4] they loved that and felt the religious demonstration gave them all safety for the next day or two.

Some pardoner[5] from Lincoln sold Reynolds two absolutions for adultery. He had committed adultery last year, it was rumoured, with the duck keeper's wife, and now with another absolution in his pocket they say he is prowling around looking for yet another opportunity, thinking it is safe. These pardoners are skilled in parchment writing and few of them have

---

[3] 1326 October 15th. London mob kills Treasurer Bishop Stapeldon: London rose in favour of the rebels against the King, Edward II. Isabella (Edward's wife) had landed with her lover Mortimer at Orwell, Suffolk on September 23rd 1326 in an effort to displace the King.

[4] 1318. Feast of Corpus Christi first celebrated in England with processions.

[5] Trevelyan, G M (1945) *English Social History* Longmans, London, p.44. '...by the travelling Pardoner with his wallet "bretful of pardons come from Rome all hot".'

genuine pardons; it is just a means of making money. They convince ordinary people that these pieces of paper are passports to heaven. Whatever crime they have committed there is always a particular pardon that will, they think, absolve them. I am determined that if I hear of Reynolds committing adultery again I shall put the fear of God in him. I also have serious doubts even about the efficacy of so-called genuine pardons: how can a pardon written in advance, and paid for with money actually absolve Reynolds? Indeed it makes him worse because he has a pardon in the bank and I fear for whoever he sets his eyes on next, or at least her husband.

Reynolds is also in trouble with me for another matter. I caught him shoeing his horse in the church just because there was a threat of a blizzard. He tried to make the excuse that it was not for his convenience but for the sake of the horse. Reynolds has taken to breeding a few sheep recently. There is real money to be made in sheep; they say we produce the best in Europe[6] and cloth-making in Norwich is becoming very important. The only problem is that the law protects skilled foreigners in the trade and this is causing all kinds of trouble in the city.[7] People resent it when people who hardly speak our own language make more money and also live in better houses than we do. I understand the nature of their vexation because so many tithes from so many parishes leave the area: they go straight into the coffers of rich monks and even foreign prelates.[8] In some parishes there is no incumbent, just a Mass priest, or visiting priest, and the tithes are collected for a priest who is living in sumptuous luxury abroad. Some priests have several parishes in Norfolk and Suffolk, choose to live in one and then employ Mass priests to do the actual work while they live off the tithes. The legal priests are the worst. The church has all the legal court franchise on marriage and probate and they make money conducting this business as well as collecting tithes as absentee landlords. It is the parishioners who suffer more than anyone else. On the other hand I have to smile at old man Ellis: he took on a corrody,[9] a sort of life annuity bought from the Prior. This meant that old Ellis gave all his money to the Prior and in return the monastery has to give him an undertaking to keep him, the creditor, for the

---

[6] Trevelyan, G M (1945) *English Social History* Longmans, London, p.36.

[7] Trevelyan, G M (1945) *English Social History* Longmans, London, p.36.

[8] Trevelyan, G M (1945) *English Social History* Longmans, London, p.41.

[9] Trevelyan, G M (1945) *English Social History* Longmans, London, p.49.

rest of his natural life. The Prior was happy to do this with Ellis because at the time he was well into his sixtieth year and always looked as sick as a dog. The Prior estimated he would be dead within a year, and that was nine years ago: old Ellis is staying alive to spite the Prior. Ellis is lucky that the Prior is an honest man: it is not the sort of transaction I would arrange with some churchmen.

Confessions of course are compulsory[10] and I am hoping that it will not be too long before I discover who Reynolds had used his second pardon for adultery on. Adultery is the main problem I deal with and it seems worse these days than ever. It all seems fun on the day, but there are always tears afterwards. Despite the promises of secrecy it eventually gets out and about. Someone will spot the couple, perhaps even a furtive glint in the eye is noted, the gossip starts and the truth emerges. Sometimes guilt sets in and they confess to their husband or wife. Sometimes they fall out but always it comes to light. Then there is hell to pay both now and undoubtedly later. It often leads to the woman being battered, or the husband seeks revenge, or the offended one leaves the village. One problem is the suffering it brings on the children: I have yet to come across a case of adultery where there is not trouble.

I shall be glad to leave this dark part of Norfolk; I am off to Suffolk where life is better. At least I hope it is, because there are ugly rumours around that the King has been murdered.[11] I am not sure whether to believe them or not.

Whenever there is trouble in high places it not only seems to permeate downwards but also leaves the world feeling unsettled. When we hear rumours of adultery among our so-called betters it gives villagers and townspeople an excuse to indulge themselves, but I have already commented on this menace of sexual deviousness. When those who lead the country lack control, a form of anarchy breaks out not only in our social lives but also on the bye-ways and highways. Thieves and robbers abound because they are convinced the official world is too concerned about its own way of life to worry itself about petty crime. I spoke to a thief only a few weeks ago. He claimed that he stole only from the wealthy and did no harm. I simply

---

[10] Trevelyan, G M (1945) *English Social History* Longmans, London, p.45.

[11] September 1327. Edward II murdered in Berkeley Castle.

failed to get it across to him that what he was doing was wrong in God's eyes and wrong in itself. He came from Caister and belonged to that unseemly group of people called wreckers. They hover on the shore waiting for shipwrecks and many people who swim ashore alive are killed for any riches they carry. The wider world is brutal and at times the message of Christ crucified seems so far away.

CHAPTER 6

ooooo

John de Skyren (1327-1337)

Edward III - monks, friars and the Scottish problem

Dear Readers,

I have been asked to give an account of my time here in the Rollesby parish. I have been here for nearly nine years now and have seen everything a parish can do to its priest.

My predecessor was not a happy man because he never coped well with the parish and was only too happy to escape to a priory in Suffolk. John Freeman teased him about an old ghost of some fellow called Granville. It was an excuse for the local people not working in the church. I called their bluff and in a service of cursing threatened to call up Granville's real ghost if they did not work. They refused to believe me but one night I dressed up large and stood at the top of the tower on a misty evening: that did the trick. Having promised to exorcise his ghost back to the grave they got on with the work and started to attend Mass a little more regularly.

I have had some help from two friars from St Francis and a Dominican.[1] They are better at preaching than I am, and friars make a change from the cloistered monk.[2] In fact the monks have become increasingly unpopular,

---

[1] Trevelyan, G M (1978) *English Social History* New illustrated edition with introduction by Asa Briggs, Longman, London, p.184. The orders of St Dominic and St Francis arrived in 1224 and helped save what was a tottering Church in England.

[2] Trevelyan, G M (1978) *English Social History* New illustrated edition with introduction by Asa Briggs, Longman, London, p.184. Monks were a product of the tumultuous past when they sought to create their own gardens of peace and soon lived off the income of green acres.

and in some places it is not safe for them to wander at large.[3] Many of my fellow incumbents, especially William Hockering[4] down at Ormesby see these friars as interlopers. I find that they are not only excellent company, but they preach Christ to all and sundry, and stir up the parishioners to attend Mass and help with the building of the church. If I did not make them welcome they would still come and preach on the green. We clergy always tend to be jealous of anyone helping with our cure of souls. We sometimes have the belief that this is our patch and others must stay out, unless it is the Bishop of course, but then bishops do not visit Rollesby. The Dominican chap is very clever: he trained at Paris and then in logic at Cambridge.[5] Despite the fact he is a learned cleric, he has not lost the common touch. I really believe that if a man knows his subject well, and is a true scholar, he is able to teach it both to the clever and to the duller spirits. Before he came to Rollesby he had been lodging in Yarmouth at The Blackfriars.[6]

I am happy with the north door and the porch that is now beautifully carved and there is no doubt in my mind that the church is doing well. The continuous repair to the thatch is the only problem, but we solve that each spring.

The King has done his best with the economy in the area. The cloth trade is thriving in Norwich and the Flemish immigrants have not only introduced new ideas into the diocese but have brought with them some considerable wealth.[7] In Rollesby new wealth has had no great immediate impact, but the patron, Roger de Gunton[8] seems better off than usual and the Priory has benefited. Some of our younger men have moved to Norwich to seek their fortunes and several have gone off to be soldiers of a mercenary cast. The last news I heard of these men came from Norwich. It was

---

[3] Fletcher, R (1980) *The East Anglians* Patrick Stephens, Cambridge, p.104. In 1327 the local people attacked the monastery at Bury St Edmunds.

[4] William Hockering, Incumbent of Ormesby St Margaret, 1328-1349.

[5] Trevelyan, G M (1978) *English Social History* New illustrated edition with introduction by Asa Briggs, Longman, London, p.183. The chief study of medieval universities was the school of logic that was needed to reconcile Aristotle with the unchallengeable doctrines of the Church. It is generally agreed that Aquinas accomplished this.

[6] Ecclestone (1971) *A W Henry Manship's Great Yarmouth* Buckle, Gt Yarmouth, p.35. The Friary was founded in 1267, domestic buildings in 1272 and the Church in 1280.

[7] Edward III attracted Flemish immigrants, granting them a Charter of protection. This ensured the cloth trade flourished and Norwich became the staple town for this trade.

[8] Rectors' list in Rollesby Church.

rumoured that they were with Edward Balliol and the King at the siege of Berwick.[9] This king is not going to let the Scots have their own way.[10] It seems to me that the wars with Scotland will never end. I am surprised that the King is so well supported because soldiers rarely return from the northern country with much bounty. What it does mean is a drain on our young men. As a parish we tend to rely too much on the middle-aged and elderly. I can never see us resolving our problem with the nation of Scotland. Unless the King's armies completely crush them the Scots will always be a thorn in our flesh since they see us as their natural enemy. This is a terrible tragedy because they worship Christ as we do.

The village around the church and farm has not grown but is still crowded. I wish the villagers would keep their houses and paths in better condition. A few have found space on the Yarmouth to Norwich path, near the blacksmith's, but not that far from the main village. Even they have built too closely together and we do look cramped. I am always concerned that one day a fire will burn the whole village down. At least the churchyard acts as a firebreak for the church.

I spoke to some men in Yarmouth about the problem of fire but they were of little use. One of them was a muringer.[11] He did suggest that there ought to be a village tax kept in a community pot to help out after any damage. But it is my belief that if Rollesby burns the whole lot will go up.

I give the congregation a brief homily or sermon each Sunday. It lasts only about a quarter of an hour but I have discovered they find it a good experience. If I make it interesting I can see that I hold their attention well. The trouble is that sometimes the things I ought to be saying cannot always be made interesting, and if I go too deeply into what I am trying to express I can see their eyelids close over. Nevertheless, I soldier on, and each Sunday try and better the standard of the week before.

'I like your talk,' Huggs said to me.

---

[9] Edward Balliol fought the Scottish after Edward III had moved the administration to York in 1332. Scottish forces tried to relieve Berwick but lost to the King's army at the battle of Halidon Hill, on July 19th 1333.

[10] By 1335 Balliol and Edward had carried the campaign as far as Perth and not until the November of 1335 did he make a truce with the Scots. David II of Scotland fled to France in May 1334 and found support from the French.

[11] Ecclestone (1971) *A W Henry Manship's Great Yarmouth* Buckle, Gt Yarmouth, p.43. In the days of Edward III the Yarmouth town appointed four expert men (Muringers) who collected money for weaponry and repairs of walls (Latin murus).

'Thank you, Huggs, I do my best.'

'If it were in Latin we wouldn't understand it, would we?'

I looked at Huggs, trying to work out what was going through his devious mind. 'That's why I use English.'

'Well, Father, why can't we have the rest of the service in English? All we hear is you mumbling away in a language we can't understand.'

'It's a sacred language, Huggs.'

'Maybe it is, but for all we know you could be talking to yourself about what you're going to be doing tomorrow, if you do anything.'

I scowled on both points, first for his attack on the language of the Church and secondly his implication that I do not work. I become more and more tired with the barb that I only work one day a week. Some people really believe it and others say it as a joke but it still hurts. The sermons they enjoy so much take me a day to prepare; I take all the confessions, the daily Mass, farm my strip, hunt game, and visit the sick and the dying. I have to listen to everyone's troubles and guard the door of my lips. At times it feels as if they are bleeding me dry. I am involved in the tragedies of their lives and all their pain I take into myself. At night I stay awake worrying about them. In return they say I work one day a week and they all think they could produce the same quality of sermon simply by telling a good yarn. I turned away from Huggs and went over to the church: perhaps a prayer would give me more strength, or just a chat with the non-existent ghost of Granville. It is not that I dislike being the priest in Rollesby, but it can be exhausting. I sometimes feel like the butts at an archery competition, everyone trying to score a hit[12] but I am the target. High and low feel that I am a good target to have a shot at merely because I am their village priest. I am their piece of personal public property, their stake in the village. This is something I have to accept because I am their servant, the servant of Christ, and while they fire their arrows I pray for their souls.

---

[12] The expression 'bull's eye' was not used until 1825.

CHAPTER 7

ooooo

Walter Hurry (1340-1349) *including* Gilbert de Wellerton (1337) *and* John de Flete (1338)

Edward III - Crecy and the rumours of plague

Dear Future Readers,

I have been asked to write some kind of time letter to the future. I must also comment on my immediate two predecessors because they stayed only a few months. Gilbert de Wellerton is supposed to have done the unforgivable I am told: he had some sort of affair with one of the parishioners. I find this difficult to believe. He was a man of considerable learning having been a Professor of Law, a Juris Civilis no less, and also Master of Tyeburn[1] Hospital in London.[2] I cannot see him as an adulterous priest; no one will ever know the truth. According to some sources he was in and out of bed with John Fletch's wife and John Fletch did not mind. According to others he was the subject of mere gossip simply because he visited Ann Fletch on a regular basis. Having met the lady in question, I have severe doubts. She is a lonely person and needs to talk a great deal because she has an unhappy marriage.

She is probably one of the ugliest women I have ever encountered, which is cause for further doubt, but there is no reason why men and women find one another attractive. It is still an active point of discussion in the village,

---

[1] Old spelling.

[2] From the Rectors' list in Rollesby church.

did he or did he not? Either way, he left and neither the Bishop nor the Prior made any comment to me, one way or the other. I have come to the conclusion that he was done to death by gossip. No one can actually say they caught him in the act; a few go so far as to say they saw him hug her, but a hug does not mean that copulation had to follow. Fletch never mentions it and no one dare talk to him about the past. Ann Fletch once told me it was all nonsense and that he was just a kind man who gave her more time than others did. I have no doubt that many clerics now and in the future will carry crosses made up of gossip and malicious hearsay. It seems to me that people just enjoy naughty talk: you can always spot them because if one happens to say that the matter is confidential you suddenly have their undivided attention and very keen interest. The patrons, Richard de Berking[3] and his wife Joan, refused to believe the nonsense of Gilbert.

The next short-term priest, John de Flete, took over in 1338 and had immediate trouble with the Freeman and Ellis families. He tried to change their minds about the height of the church tower. He believed it possible to put another six foot on the structure. They would not co-operate and he sulked. He sulked so much he was rarely seen around the parish, was late for the Sunday Mass and then did the unforgivable: he let out something John Freeman had said in a confession to a man called Beech. No one believed John had done the deeds mentioned in the confession, mainly because he was always ready to tease local clergy, but the fact that John de Flete let it slip caused outrage. Quite rightly, when a priest has a secret to keep, he also has to keep it secret that he has a secret to keep. Beech loved the potential scandal: he was a man of limited intelligence and intellect, for some reason thought himself above his normal social station, and considered he had a right to pass judgement on all his neighbours. I am so sorry he has to live in my parish.

The church is basically complete now though I do wish it had a chancel, and I have started talking to the Diocese but they, like this local area, are heavily pressed for finding taxes for the wars. It became clear after the French attacked us[4] that this is a threat the King and Parliament cannot

---

[3] Richard de Berking 'held 7 messuages, 100 acres of land and 12 of Heath' - Bates, Ann. Private research from the *Norfolk Archaeological Society.*

[4] 1338. In support of Scotland the French fleet raided Portsmouth and Southampton and attacked shipping in the channel: again in 1339 Dover and Folkestone were attacked.

ignore. The local community has never appeared so nationalistically minded. When it came to the Scottish wars there was something of an unsure attitude, but with the French all the national sensitivities[5] seem to come to the surface. Certainly soldiers find it more profitable fighting on the continent than in the Scottish mountains.[6] From the local point it is important that we hold Flanders. We have deep trade relations with that area in Ghent, Bruges and Ypres because we sell our wool to the cloth makers there. The King has made a useful alliance with Flanders.[7] At least when we put to sea we made it clear we were the masters,[8] and we are all pleased that the King has declared himself Lord of the English Sea. I was given a noble[9] the other day which makes the point well and truly because it shows our king as captain of the fleet.

The one way I can stop the village talking about the scandal of Ann Fletch is to raise the subject of the battle of Crecy.[10] The parishioners have taken great pride in this battle and have taken to practising with their longbows on a regular basis. I lend them the churchyard on rainy days because we can stand in the nave between showers. I say we, because I am quite gifted at the butts myself. The King has actually prohibited ball games under threat of imprisonment and other idle games such as cock fighting,[11] and encourages the longbow by royal proclamation. It gives the villagers the sense that they are as important as the knights when it comes to war. A good longbow can bring a knight down halfway over a field. The shaft can cut through the armour and penetrate the chain mail, and a good archer can be ready for another aim before the knight has fallen from his horse. I have

---

[5] Trevelyan, G M (1978) *English Social History* New illustrated edition with introduction by Asa Briggs, Longman, London, p.223. Froissart wrote - 'The English will never love or honour their king, unless he be victorious and a lover of arms and war against their neighbours and especially against such as are greater and richer than themselves.'

[6] Trevelyan, G M (1978) *English Social History* New illustrated edition with introduction by Asa Briggs, Longman, London, p.223. 'To pick the famous lily was an enterprise of more profit, ease and honour than to pick the recalcitrant thistle.'

[7] 1340 Jan 25th. Edward III assumes title King of France in Ghent and Flanders and is recognised as such by the Flemings.

[8] This is the beginning of what was later called the One Hundred Years War, and the first action was the battle of Sluys (1340), won by the English merchant navy.

[9] 1344. Noble, gold coin worth 6s 8d is first coined in England; it shows Edward III on a ship.

[10] 1346 August 26th. Battle of Crecy: Edward III defeats and destroys French army; Philip VI escapes.

[11] Trevelyan, G M (1978) *English Social History* New illustrated edition with introduction by Asa Briggs, Longman, London, p.227. Handball, football or hockey (pilam manualem, pedivam, vel bacularem) coursing and cockfighting, or other such idle games.

been reliably informed that the French workers are not allowed to keep any form of weapon; it is little wonder they lose against our skilled English yeomanry.

The Mass is well attended these days because there is a rumour that a deadly plague[12] is striking people down in France. Many say it is God's judgement on the French, but most of us are inclined to believe it is God's judgement on sinners in general, and it is generally feared that by the summer this angel of death may have crossed the English Seas. There are rumours, but they are only rumours, that the plague has already taken a certain hold in the old kingdom of Kent and London itself. I say it must be God's hand against sinners because it strikes the rich as well as the poor, and the rich have the greater opportunity for sin.

I spend much time collecting the tithes and however hard I try it is difficult to get it over to the villagers that I do not keep them all. Many of the tithes go straight to the Prior and many go overseas to Rome. Despite my attempts to make this known I am sure they think I am lying, and that I am extremely wealthy. They would only have to observe that I work as hard at my smallholding as they do at theirs to see I am not wealthy. Because of the wealth of the Church, both in terms of its landholdings, and because of the powerful bishops, it is assumed the parish clergy are equally as wealthy. My house is no more full of food and stores than anyone else's in the village; I have to work just as hard, my clothes are threadbare and yet there is still the assumption that I am rich. My only hope is that my riches are in heaven, because they are certainly not with me at the moment.

This is all part and parcel of a particular attitude towards clergy. The villagers place us on a social plinth and then sit back and wait for us to fall off. Most of them are very friendly on a social basis, even those from whom I have heard the most revealing confessions, but I am under no illusion. If I were to make a mistake or be caught once too often with a woman parishioner, the gossip would start. If the miller has an affair it is a nine-day wonder and there would be much laughing and joking; if I were to have a similar habit they would attack me and enjoy doing so. I suppose that they expect the priest to be an exemplar of the gospel, but allow themselves a certain leeway in their conduct. They sometimes forget that their clergy are just as

[12] The Black Death was to strike Southern England in the summer of 1348 and London by November. It is generally believed to have arrived from France.

human as they are, just as fallible, yet one slip and they simply enjoy the ramifications. I know of one friend who was driven from his living by sheer gossip: there was no substance to the hearsay and when that became apparent no one apologised. The apology would have been too late; my friend secured himself a position as a minor clerk in the cathedral.

However, Rollesby is no better or worse than any other parish, and despite the poverty of the area I have enjoyed myself here. Quite who will read this I have no idea, maybe it will be lost and never come to anyone's attention. Our main fear at the moment is the possibility that the French plague has arrived in our land, that there are signs of it in Yarmouth. If this be true my parishioners will expect me to visit them and that I must do as Christ's servant.

CHAPTER 8

ooooo

Simon de Rykenhale (1349-1361)

Edward III - the Black Death and a shortage of labour

Dear Readers,

I took over from the parish priest, Walter Hurry, just after the (Black)[1] Death, in 1349. Although we have had occasional scares it never quite returned with the ferocity of 1348. It was a dreadful time, and most especially in Rollesby and the Great Yarmouth area. By the time we reached the year of my arrival, 1349, it was claimed, with some justification, that a third of the diocese lay dead from this purge.[2]

Walter Hurry did the best he could; quite a saintly man I gather. He urged the villagers not to travel, not to mix with strangers, and to keep the village as clean as possible. Sadly, one of his flock, some self-righteous fool by the name of Beech, thought the advice was silly and continued his trade at Yarmouth quay. He brought the plague back and there was no stopping the illness after that mistake. Men and women and children fell like acorns and conkers in season, and, unlike some priests, Walter buried the dead and anointed the dying. Ironically it was because of the visit he made to the Beech family he caught the illness and died within days. Freeman and Ellis obligated a passing monk to give him the proper rites for his burial. They

[1] Ziegler, P (1997) *The Black Death* Folio Society, London, p.5. No one is certain from where or when the name Black was attached. It has been suggested it arose from the putrefying flesh or the black blisters. The earliest date for the name Black Death comes from Sweden in 1555 - swarta döder.

[2] Fletcher, R (1980) *The East Anglians* Patrick Stephens, Cambridge, p.108. In Norfolk and Suffolk 57,000 people died, 7,000 alone in Yarmouth and at least a third of Norwich City.

buried him by the tower on some strange basis that if he appeared as a ghost he would be able to handle the old ghost of Granville supposed to haunt the belfry. Future readers no doubt will have their plagues and illnesses to worry about, but I sincerely hope they never have to cope with a death like this one. The swelling of the glands and ulcerous boils that pulsate with a greeny yellow puss exude a sweet sickly smell: this is the announcement of death once it is in the nostrils. So many churches lost their clergy in 1348 and 1349 and these years will forever be remembered.[3] Down in Ormesby William Hockering died at the outbreak, then Roger Herald of Bawburgh died in 1349; he was followed by John le Smith of Worstead who died a month later. The current priest there, Warine de Runhale[4] waited until 1350 when it was reasonably safe before he arrived.

Some of the parishioners remembered a previous priest's advice about the houses being too close together; he always regarded this both as a fire risk and as a health hazard. After the Death had finished taking its toll, the remaining families burnt many of the houses surrounding the church and moved to the other side of the Yarmouth-Norwich path.[5] It has left the church and Church Farm somewhat isolated, but I have built my priest's house just to the north of the graveyard and feel reasonably safe now.

The deaths of clergy in Ormesby and Rollesby and many other parishes indicated to parishioners that the clergy at least did their job. I have been told that half the beneficed clergy in Norwich Diocese died, and altogether some 800 priests in Anglia alone.[6] Sadly, I gather that in some parts of the country the parish priests fled: I can hardly imagine them being welcomed back. There is a shortage of priests now, but then there is a shortage of peo-

---

[3] Many church boards indicate changes of Rector or Vicar in these two years: Ranworth Parish Church has three changes in the space of 24 months.

[4] Clergy of Ormesby St Margaret: William Hockering 1328-1349, Roger Herald of Bawburgh 1349-1349, John le Smith of Worstead 1349-1349 and Warine de Runhale 1350-1354.

[5] There are other views as to why St George's Rollesby stands well away from the village: see Lloyd, Virginia *Landscape Analysis: A Study of the Parish of Rollesby, Norfolk* unpublished private research. 'it would seem feasible however - and explanatory of the dearth of housing around the church that a "green-side" shift occurred, in the search for pastoral resources in the Post-Conquest period, a result of the huge population expansion in this period. East Norfolk was indeed one of the most densely settled areas of the country from the Twelfth to the early Fourteenth century. This suggestion is further substantiated by the fact that the Church stands at the highest point of the village, which forms a linear progression down towards the lowest part of the village, with its two ponds marked in the 1784 map as part of a triangular green. This would seem to be a classic example of green side settlement shift, which must have occurred before the Black Death.'

[6] Ziegler, P (1997) *The Black Death* Folio Society, London, p.122 & p.199. 48.8% of beneficed clergy died in Norwich, Exeter and Winchester: probably because of the proximity of the major seaports.

ple as well. The Bishop of Norwich, William of Norwich,[7] gained special dispensation to allow 60 clerks aged 21 years or less to hold rectories on the grounds that this action was better than nothing at all.[8] There was certainly a drop in educational standards as a result of the shortage[9] but then there were two thousand vacancies to be filled. On the 6th February 1350 the Bishop of Norwich established Trinity College at Cambridge to make sure more clergy were trained following the appalling loses. Our bishop was a good man. He had been conducting peace negotiations with the French when the plague hit his diocese. He came straight back through Yarmouth only to be told that his dear brother, Sir Bartholomew Bateman of Gillingham, was already dead and buried. The plague was raging in Norfolk and he found that his Vicar General, Thomas de Methwold, was hiding away in Essex. He ordered his return but he could not stay in his palace because of the stench of the dead.[10] Both Norwich and Yarmouth lost most of their populations. In Yarmouth there were at least 10,000 people living, and for the attack on Calais Yarmouth had gathered 220 ships and three times the number of sailors that London could muster. After the death there were few left. The tower of the town church, St Nicolas, was left unfinished for many years.[11]

In London and some other cities they say that some people went mad with wine, women and song on the grounds that tomorrow they were going to die so they might as well enjoy what was left of life. I am not sure I believe this. The people of Rollesby wailed and mourned and were terrified, but they buried their dead, moved the village away from the burial grounds of the church and life goes on. There is still considerable discussion as to what caused so much death. Some say astronomers[12] had predicted it; others that it was the judgement of God (and certainly attendance at Mass has improved); a few claim it was the French; for myself I am not sure.

The villagers are dressing more like their betters these days, more colour,

---

[7] 1344-1356. William of Norwich (Bateman).

[8] Ziegler, P (1997) *The Black Death* Folio Society, London, p.230.

[9] Ziegler, P (1997) *The Black Death* Folio Society, London, p.148.

[10] Ziegler, P (1997) *The Black Death* Folio Society, London, pp.145-6.

[11] Ziegler, P (1997) *The Black Death* Folio Society, London, p.144.

[12] In 1345 on March 20th there was a total eclipse of the moon and conjunction of 3 major planets recorded by John of Ashendon, Oxford astronomer, who claims to have predicted Black Death from such observations.

tighter fitting clothes, and Beech's son, who survived the Death, has taken to wearing a cotehardie[13] with buttons down the front. After the Death there was a different atmosphere in the village: it had left us a certain sense of careful rejoicing by those who survived. We even had a morality play[14] performed outside the church in the middle 50s. Piers Freeman, whose father John died in the Death, went off with the players to learn the skill. I remember him telling me that 'there be no work in this area, I might as well use my great skills elsewhere'.

'What skills?' I asked.

'I have considerable ability. It's only a matter of discovering it, my talents have to be discovered.'

'But you are good on the land, Piers. You till it better and faster than most.'

'There's no work.'

'With so many people dead from the Death there's plenty of scope.'

'I am not spending my energies working for that family of Beeches, and Church Farm has its own hands.'

I knew I was losing, but I persisted. 'What about your strip and your old father's strip?'

'What's a stretch of marsh bog in the new world? The Death taught me one thing and that's we've got to make our own way.'

As he walked off with the morality players I was bemused by his expression of the 'new world': because he had survived and had seen most of his family die he really believed the world was starting over again, something like the children of Noah must have felt.

I could not help but speculate that young Piers would be in trouble sooner rather than later. Since the Death, labourers have been in short supply and they tend to move around the area looking for better pay. Some of our folk have gone to Martham and Filby and even further seeking better wages. Church Farm has suffered badly from this, and although Parliament

---

[13] By the 1340s more brightly coloured materials were being worn. Men's clothes were trimmed with jagged edges (dagged) and women's with fur. Women's gowns became close fitting and the cotehardie (man's outer garment that was a short fitted tunic) was made more popular with fashionable buttons down the front and a belt on the hips.

[14] A drama that always carried a moral point: always popular as they toured the country. *The Pride of Life* is the earliest surviving fragment of a morality play and dates to c1350.

passed laws[15] against such practices, few in this area can enforce them. Where there are powerful landowners the villagers would have little choice, but around here it is mainly church land and although the Beeches see themselves as something of importance most people treat this with the contempt they deserve; and they certainly would not know how to activate the law. Managing to find good labourers has become a problem; they demand too much money and too easily move to better pastures. At least there is a truce with France after they were well and truly beaten by the King's son.[16] The French have quite a few problems; all kinds of rumours are brought back by our local boys who have served in the army. They tell us, but I do not know by what authority, that the peasants there are not like our freemen and they are in open revolt against their superiors.[17] I am sure from other evidence that our people are freer than the country folk of France. One thing I am certain of: the English labourer would never revolt against the King and his lords. Nevertheless, the labourer is now very conscious that he is needed: the Death has left too many vacancies. Even the patron, Richard de Berking, has had enough and sold up last year in 1360. He granted all Rollesby and Filby Manors to the clerk, Roger de Estreford. All he has kept is a rood of land we know as 'Old Mill Mount'. He even granted the same Roger the patronage of Filby Church that pays an annual income of twenty marks a year.[18] Times are certainly changing.

Most of my time in Rollesby has revolved around the Death's effects in the village. There has been considerable mourning and a deep sense of bereavement and loss. Some have become quite cynical about a God in heaven; for others religion has become very important. There is a shortage of labour and a certain developing arrogance amongst the workers, not just against me but against their lords and those who employ them for harvest. The ones who have spurned the church still turn to me when there is death in the family. I marry and baptise them, and they need the church for these ceremonies, but at the deathbed they need the church and a priest they can

---

[15] 1351. Statute of Labourers fixed wages at pre-Black Death rates and tried to restrict the movement of labour.

[16] The King's son was the Black Prince who defeated the French army at Poitiers (Sept 19th 1356) and captured John II of France. On March 22nd 1357 a two-year truce was made between England and France at Bordeaux.

[17] 1358 May 28th. Beginning of peasants' revolt in France (Jacquerie).

[18] Bates, Ann. Private research from the *Norfolk Archaeological Society*.

trust. I now realise how important it is for the priest to be known by all as a man who cares, because when they turn to you at the end of their lives they want someone who knows them.

CHAPTER 9

ooooo

Simon de Babingley (1361-1377)

Edward III - post Black Death

I have had the strange request to write some sort of account of my fifteen years, so far, as the priest in Rollesby. I have no idea as to whether my predecessors have been asked to do the same thing, and in what language they wrote. Since English is now allowed in the courts[1] I shall write in English though I cannot promise the style of Langland or conjure up his Robin Hood.[2] This area had suffered badly from the Death in the years 1348-9 and at the start of my tenure I was concerned it was going to be serious again.[3] Fortunately the villagers had rebuilt their houses down the road and we kept strangers out of the parish. There were no ghastly problems this time though I gather some parts of the country further south suffered badly. The main feature of our life has been securing sufficient harvest gatherers; labourers of good stature are becoming more and more expensive. Church Farm has been struggling, and it has been difficult collecting the tithes. The Beeches have become quite powerful landowners having bought or leased many of the strips left by families who have gone to the French wars or from those who were decimated by the Death. It does seem, as the last decade has passed by, that a few have become quite wealthy while the poor are becoming poorer still.

---

[1] 1362. English allowed in law-courts.

[2] 1362. William Langland begins 'Piers Plowman', poem has first mention in literature of 'Robin Hood'.

[3] 1361. Spring the plague broke out again.

During my tenure in Rollesby the church has been well attended but the village has become distant from the actual church building. The people come to the Sunday Mass if only in the hope that the Death will not revisit us, but the same disaster meant the people moved the village away from the church, instead of it being central which it should be. During the 1360s I detected a degree of anti-clerical feeling. It comes both from the national level as well as the local. Locally, it is caused by collecting tithes when there is little money around, and the labourers often escape the commitment because they have become more and more itinerant in their work habits. In the middle 60s Parliament repudiated the Holy Father's overlordship of England[4] and in 1371 a distinctly anti-clerical Parliament replaced our bishops by laymen as Chancellor and Treasurer.[5] Many of the problems regarding the papacy are because the seat of power has moved from Rome to Avignon in South France and nearly all the popes are Frenchmen. There is no doubt that with this situation the papacy nearly always favours the French side in any sort of quarrel or disagreement.[6]

Nationally we have had a few reverses against our French enemy that have caused a certain amount of disquiet, especially at sea.[7] The defeat of the navy by the Castilians has caused a special murmur because John of Gaunt married a Castilian princess! Our King Edward III resuming the title of King of France in 1369 caused much of a flurry on the international scene.

On the home front I have started to plant the idea that the church needs a chancel, and although the Bishop and Prior are encouraging me in this idea, there is little money available for such a massive enterprise. The usual complaints arise from the parishioners about every new priest wanting to change everything. I was cunning, and once I pointed out the beauty of the Ormesby St Margaret chancel it seemed to fall on more sympathetic ears. This is a strange characteristic of church life: we are all supposed to be Christians together, together in the Body of Christ, but the competitive ele-

---

[4] 1365. Parliament repudiates the Pope's overlordship of England and passes Statute of Praemunire (II) specifically forbidding appeals to Papal Court (v.1353).

[5] John Wyclif, Oxford theologian and opponent of papal domination, attends Parliament.

[6] Chadwick, H (Editor) (2000) *Not Angels but Anglicans* Canterbury Press, Norwich, p.89.

[7] 1372 June 23rd. Naval battle off La Rochelle: Castilians destroy English fleet and in August the same year Owain Lawgoch's force and French fleet defeat English reinforcements at La Rochelle; La Rochelle surrenders. On Dec 1st 1372 the French took control of Poitou.

ment can be quite dangerous. Once the villagers of Ormesby St Margaret's heard we had a new set of sanctuary bells they went out of their way and purchased a larger and overly expensive set. They spent so much on the item that they nearly impoverished themselves. Having said that, I must confess that we clergy are just as bad. Whenever I meet fellow clerics they are always supposed to be doing this or that better than I am. What I have accomplished they have already achieved. I know most of it to be nonsense because I have it on good authority that I run one of the best parishes in the Diocese. My people told me this after the drinking incident (see later).

In Yarmouth there have been the usual problems with the Cinque Ports[8] and it was rumoured that two men were killed in a brawl. Not long after this unpleasant business Piers Freeman made a re-appearance in Rollesby coming out of Yarmouth the very night of the fracas. He brought with him an expensive wagon with three hogsheads of beer[9] and gave a party to celebrate his return. He was immensely popular as you can imagine. I must confess I enjoyed the occasion myself. We held the party from Friday evening to late Saturday night. I have to confess I missed Compline and at the Sunday Mass only a few of the older ladies were in attendance. It was rumoured that old Stone drank so much he drowned in his sleep. Certainly I had to bury his bloated body the next day to comments that he would flood the graveyard and make the church damp forever. Young Piers said he had not enjoyed his time with the morality players, because they were a conceited type of people and would not give him the space to show the prowess he was convinced he had. Instead, he joined a ship sailing out of Dover plying trade with Calais. This raised my suspicions, and I could not help but wonder if the fighting in Yarmouth was the settling of some old scores.

Barely had we consumed all the beer and had a good time when Piers was up and off again. He did it just in time because two Justices arrived from Yarmouth claiming a thief had taken the wagon of beer. We had, of course, consumed all the evidence, and Piers had driven off to heaven knows where. It was rumoured he had driven towards Norwich with the two horses and wagon. I heard the Justices were coming and went to Norwich Priory

---

[8] Ecclestone (1971) *A W Henry Manship's Great Yarmouth* Buckle, Gt Yarmouth, pp.102-108. The Cinque Ports (Dover, Hastings, Hythe, Romney, Rye, Winchelsea and Sandwich) had Barons who came to Yarmouth to take control. This was deeply resented, and led to conflict even at sea during the period of the 14th century.

[9] A hogshead is a barrel containing 54 gallons.

on business to avoid any questioning. On my return I gathered that the locals had denied all knowledge; the barrels, to my annoyance, they had buried with Stone, having dug him up again to do so. I said little; it was like a village conspiracy; we just pretended it never happened.

I have found my time in Rollesby fairly rewarding but I have made my mistakes. I should not have allowed myself to become involved in the drinking incident and at times, when I look back, I was too much involved socially with my flock. I always enjoyed the festive occasions and an ale or two, but it is too easy to become slack-lipped. I always thought it was a good thing to be close to my people, and I know they enjoyed it when I joined in, and at times I felt popular, but there is the danger that familiarity breeds contempt. Like most people if I have plenty of ale I am prone to speak too much, let the occasional secret slip, express a poorly considered opinion, brag, and tell a joke I would not dare tell when sober. The villagers would revel in this but the cold light of dawn made me personally regret the night before, and the danger that they would not trust me was always prevalent in my mind. The priest's social life is always a fine line. I do not want to be a prude and stand apart; I do not want to appear above my fellow parishioners, yet at the same time I cannot just join in. I cannot be drinking with them on a Saturday night and reproach them on a Sunday morning. I cannot tell a great story about somebody I know and then expect them to trust me with their confidences. I have to learn to walk the narrow path without being superior: that is not an easy task for any priest. Being one of the people but to remain as their servant in Christ means that I have to tread with care for the sake of my soul and theirs.

CHAPTER 10

ooooo

Nicholas de Lyons (1377-1401)

Richard II, Henry IV - labour shortage and the Peasants' Revolt

Dear Whoever you are,

I was asked to write this and only hope I have time since I have left it so late; I fear I am on my deathbed. I have served in this parish of Rollesby for nearly twenty-four years, longer I believe than any of my predecessors managed in their tenures. My home was Weston and my father, Arnold de Lyons,[1] always warned me about Norfolk. My immediate predecessor, Simon de Babingley was something of a character: he was one of the boys, so to speak, always out revelling with them, but a good man who stood by the village through some difficult times. Those difficult times continued into my time here. Normally, a parish priest arrives, conducts services, hears confessions, visits the sick and dying, looks after the church and does the occasional offices. The rest of the world continues on its course, the kings, lords and their ladies ignoring the village and the village caring little for the events on a national scale. This was not the case in Rollesby; what was happening in the high courts of Parliament had serious reverberations even in a rural community as remote as Rollesby: the villagers' interest in major political figures was keen to say the least. When, for example, Piers Freeman, one of our more colourful characters, returned as a middle-aged man, he discussed the comings and going of kings and John of

[1] From Rectors' list in Rollesby church.

Gaunt to the avid interest of all in the inn by the stables. When good King Edward III died in 1377[2] the world seemed to change. John of Gaunt seemed to be more powerful than King and Parliament[3] together. The peculiar and particular finer points of the political machinations were lost on all of us working in the fields, but it did not mean that we held no opinions. I tried to do my best to explain to my flock that what happened in high places was not our business; indeed it was safer that it was not our business. The real impact was that the labourer, so essential in the fields, was a free man and sued for higher wages, while the villeins[4] struggled against the bailiff for his customary services and to be free of irksome feudal duties. It meant that much land was untended and untilled.[5] Some of the landlords in the area, especially the Beeches, have introduced more sheep to help solve the problem. The working men are no longer content to take everything with any sense of passivity. They discussed what was right and what was wrong, the level of wages and the type of work they should be expected to do. Never before in this country's history had there been such ferment amongst ordinary souls.[6] Some of the Rollesby men at Church Farm actually refused to work until the Prior paid a greater wage: such action in my youth would have been unthinkable. Personally I blamed many of the friars: they were all too keen to preach poverty, but soon the most ill educated were quoting the lines: 'When Adam delved and Eve span, Who was then the Gentleman?'

If the Prior tried to clamp down and enforce the work some of the men just left, because there was always a landowner somewhere ready to employ them and too few men to do the work. The justices[7] have tried to enforce the statutes to keep wages down but the men move. If they did not move to

---

[2] 1377 June 21st.

[3] John of Gaunt, Duke of Lancaster, younger brother of the Black Prince (who died June 8th 1376) and uncle of the new King Richard II was head of the Council of Regency and ruled the land.

[4] Villeins were not so free, under the feudal system they were tied to the land.

[5] Trevelyan, G M (1978) *English Social History* New illustrated edition with introduction by Asa Briggs, Longman, London, p.238. At least half of the rent paying farms and domain land was not functioning.

[6] Trevelyan, G M (1978) *English Social History* New illustrated edition with introduction by Asa Briggs, Longman, London, p.239. 'Professor Davis has summed up the reign of Henry III with the words: "of all the contrasts which strike us in medieval life, none is so acute as that between the intellectual ferment in the upper class and the oriental passivity of their inferiors." But in the reign of Edward III the peasants could no longer be accused of oriental passivity and the intellectual ferment in their ranks reminds us of a modern labour movement.'

[7] Trevelyan, G M (1978) *English Social History* New illustrated edition with introduction by Asa Briggs, Longman, London, p.240.

new employment, many of them hid in the wide marshes and robbed good citizens for a living. Perhaps my future reader can see why this period of time was so revolutionary. It was a huge social upheaval before our very eyes, but I did not see it at the time: it is only now on my deathbed, as I write this strange request for the future, that I have a grasp of what happened. Although it was a social change, it took political changes to spark the terrible uprising that we were to witness. The French were gaining the upper hand in the prolonged war, especially at sea.[8] We as a nation supported the wrong pope[9] and then there was the dreaded poll tax.[10] That is why I make the statement that national events impinged so much on local life, even here in remotest darkest Norfolk.

One of the key moments was when Parliament imposed a 4d a head poll tax mainly to support the war against the French. There was not a man in Rollesby who did not have an opinion, and generally against the imposition. The usual few who like to be different found it very difficult to support the measure without creating serious hostility towards themselves. The very words poll tax conjure up in my mind riots and revolutions. I am sure no government of the future would dare use the expression again even if they decide to tax more highly.

Naturally most people paid, but many moved from area to area in order to avoid the tax and this exacerbated the labourer situation. Then in November of 1380,[11] if I recall rightly, Parliament imposed a new poll tax on all aged over 15. It not only opened new wounds of contention but also drew the puss and venom from the past. A rebellious man called John Ball[12] sent agents all around Essex and East Anglia stirring up hatred against the Church, lawyers and any wealthy person. Fortunately I was left well alone because they all knew me, knew I had no wealth, and by 1381 was generally seen as 'their' type of priest. My self-rule of keeping out of politics paid for once and saved my life when an unruly mob from Caister and Yarmouth

---

[8] 1377. French burn Rye and Hastings, there was a raid on the Isle of Wight and they even sailed up the River Thames to burn Gravesend.

[9] 1378 Oct 20th. Parliament agrees to support the Roman Pope against Avignon in schism.

[10] 1377 Jan 27th. Parliament meets and grants poll tax of 4d per head.

[11] He does recall rightly.

[12] Along with Wat Tyler one of the active leaders in the Peasants' Revolt.

moved through to Norwich. They tried to lynch Henry Frost[13] down at Ormesby St Margaret but he hid in the belfry. My parishioners threatened to fight them on the spot so they moved on. It was Piers Freeman who saved the day. He spent most of his life out of Rollesby and knows more of the outside world. The night before the mob passed by he spoke to the assembled village in the Stable Inn, I can recall his words:

'You know my friends, you saw me as a youngster here, watched me dabble with the morality players, you know I fought the French out of Dover. You know I'm not all good, the beer party cannot be forgotten, nor am I all bad. I've seen London life, I've seen John of Gaunt, I've watched the high and mighty, and I can tell you the ordinary man won't win. There may well be bloodshed, but at the end of the day it will be our blood.'

'Not like you to be chicken,' young Symth cried out.

'Nor be I a chicken, and I'll take you on with sword and dagger any day. I've killed more men than you had hot meals, and it ain't something to boast of. I tell you all that it will start well, this John Ball's rebellion, but I tell you also it will end in blood and tears. Our blood and our tears but the high and mighty will always be there. They can burn down John of Gaunt's[14] property, but they'll not rid us of the John of Gaunts.'

None of us realised how prophetic Piers Freeman was at the time. Young Smyth was the only Rollesby man not to listen and he left the next day to join the band of rebels outside Norwich. We were indeed lucky, there was a serious rebellion led from Kent by Wat Tyler, and John Ball in Essex. Many men from East Anglia joined the Essex rebels or burned property locally. What was most diabolical was the killing of the Archbishop of Canterbury.[15] It all came to nought. Wat Tyler was slain by the Mayor of London[16] and the rebellion closed shut like my church door after my Mass. Many people were killed, including poor young Smyth, and there was a distinct lack of trust between the different classes thereafter. There were also some unpleasant reprisals but Rollesby was free of any serious trouble: I was able to convince the Prior and Bishop that my parish had steered clear, and

---

[13] Henry Frost, Vicar of Ormesby St Margaret, 1377-1385.

[14] 1381 June 13th. John of Gaunt's palace, the Savoy was destroyed.

[15] Simon Sudbury and the Treasurer, Sir Robert Hales both killed by the mob.

[16] 1381 June 15th. Wat Tyler killed by the Mayor at a meeting held in Smithfield: John Ball was executed with other leaders in the July.

Piers Freeman's reputation continued. Our bishop, Henry Despenser needed convincing. He is very warlike indeed, is well known as the fighting bishop,[17] and he put down the revolt in Anglia personally. There were further outbreaks up north[18] but it was a lost cause after the London killing of Wat Tyler.

Not that the crushing of the rebellion stopped the fermenting of discontent: many of the villeins wanted to be emancipated and become their own smallholders. It was a process some of our more enlightened priors allowed.[19] Personally I blamed much of the problem on Wyclif[20] and I am not at all happy that the Bible is presented in English; there are ideas in the holy book which could cause another rebellion. There is also a rumour he denies transubstantiation. Wyclif caused unsettling feelings, and a schism within the mother Church between Avignon and Rome made life very unsettled.

The politics of the mother Church led my diocese into all kinds of trouble. I was obligated to collect all the tithes with great care in the months following the Peasant's Rebellion and this was no easy matter. The Bishop of Norwich[21] took it into his head to lead a war[22] in Flanders to support the Roman Holy Father but failed to take Ypres from the French. This was a considerable embarrassment and involved our diocesan bishop being impeached. It also cost the church in Rollesby, as in many other ordinary parishes, a great deal of money. It was little wonder that the congregation resented the wider institution of the Church. Some parish priests really suffered because they were always asking for money. It was generally accepted if the priest were resident in his parish, but many had developed the habit of living out of the parish for months on end and only presenting themselves when tithes were due. I have to tell you as well that I have been privy to a

---

[17] Trevelyan, G M (1945) *English Social History* Longmans, London, p.14.

[18] Trevelyan, G M (1978) *English Social History* New illustrated edition with introduction by Asa Briggs, Longman, London, p.241.

[19] Trevelyan, G M (1978) *English Social History* New illustrated edition with introduction by Asa Briggs, Longman, London, p.242. Total emancipation was not complete until under the Tudors: mostly established in the 15th century.

[20] 1380. Wyclif and followers start to translate the Bible into English.

[21] Henry Spenser (Despenser) 1370-1406.

[22] Bishop of Norwich leads 'Norwich Crusade' to Flanders, ostensibly in support of Roman Pope against Avignon rival but failed to take Ypres from French on May 16th 1383. In October 1383 Chancellor Michael de la Pole impeaches the Bishop of Norwich.

great deal of clerical corruption in my time. Some priests marry or have women and there is no one to stop them.[23] In fact, I do believe the Church in England has serious problems because it has no means of reform.[24] All the friars and monks who permeate and influence the Church so deeply are not responsible to their bishops, but directly to the Pope. Nor can the bishops, many of whom hold secular posts, change the laws of the Church,[25] and any appeal in ecclesiastical causes lies with the papal courts. That takes time, influence and a considerable amount of money. Perhaps, dear reader, you can understand why I feel so depressed. Here I confess to having a certain sympathy with John Wyclif and his 'theory of dominion' in which he says the authority of the wicked cannot come from God since the Pope's power derives from the Caesars of Rome, not from Christ or Peter.[26] I would have more time for Wyclif if he were not so closely connected to that political schemer John of Gaunt, though I gather that there is now some contention between Gaunt and Wyclif over the subject of transubstantiation. I do believe Wyclif to be right over the Caesarean clergy,[27] although it concerns me that the Archbishop of Canterbury has expelled Wyclif's followers from Oxford. His followers are often called Lollards and the Church is beginning to persecute them.

All this passes us by in Rollesby without so much as a twinkle of an eye; they are more concerned with the harvest and finding rural labour: but they are mistaken, because all this could change the face of the Church. I have heard it said that the Church in England could break from Rome, which of course can never happen. But the first twenty years of my life in Rollesby has had these immense backdrops: rebellion by the peasants and the Church in open disarray. I doubt whether England will have such a tumultuous time again. The only real joy I have had recently is being allowed to read Julian of

---

[23] Trevelyan, G M (1978) *English Social History* New illustrated edition with introduction by Asa Briggs, Longman, London, p.243. The ecclesiastical machinery was not strong enough to enforce the full programme of Hildebrandine celibacy upon unwilling English priests.

[24] The Church in England had no autonomy: she was part of a cosmopolitan organisation centred abroad.

[25] Ecclesiastical law was Roman Canon Law, which the English Church was not competent to change.

[26] 1376-79. Wyclif writes amongst many things *De Potestate Papae* on the Pope's power, which the Pope condemned.

[27] Mainly associated with worshipping and selling holy relics, Mass priests and priests deriving their livings from Rome but not attending their parishes.

Norwich's works[28] on her visions: there is still hope that God has not abandoned our diocese.

Even as we cross the threshold of the century national events are disastrous. Good King Richard,[29] having lost his friend the Duke of Ireland,[30] was then bullied by the Lords Appellant in the Merciless Parliament.[31] It is true he later gained full power and had Gloucester murdered in Calais[32] and Arundel executed. He then quite rightly banished Gaunt's son, Henry[33] and later confiscated his lands. Henry returned, however, seizing the throne as Henry IV, and I hear persistent rumours that good King Richard has been killed.[34] While I consider all this, I am almost grateful to be on my deathbed. As a Church we are not even allowed to appeal to Rome or spread news of papal bulls:[35] England will never, I hope, know a time like this again.

I was asked to write on Rollesby, but national events have been the life blood of the village throughout the century. First the Black Death, then the Peasants' Rebellion, then the trouble in the Church and bloodshed in the royal family, and all has been so dismal. The 14th century will be the bleakest ever and I am glad to be leaving it soon. I have lived most of my life in Rollesby, a small village of no national consequence although national life has dominated us. I am not referring to the occasional villager who gets himself involved in the rebellion such as young Smyth, or whoever goes off to be a soldier, but always the fear that the events that rage across the national scene will one day move through Rollesby itself. The chaos on the national scene can also be reflected in the village. We may have managed to keep out of the actual rebellion of 1381 but there is a rebellious attitude amongst some of the workers. Wyclif has not turned up in Rollesby but his

---

[28] 1393. Julian of Norwich, mystic, writes *Sixteen Revelations of Divine Love*, reflections on her visions of 1373.

[29] Churchill, Winston S (1956) *A History of the English Speaking Peoples* Cassell, London. Vol.1, p.302. Many of the common people regarded King Richard II as an upholder of their rights.

[30] Robert de Vere, one time Earl of Oxford: much resented by the Lords Appellant, a sort of baronial oligarchy.

[31] 1388 Feb 3rd. In which all the King's friends were convicted of treason.

[32] 1397 Sept.

[33] Later Henry IV, banished for ten years: thus the seeds for the War of the Roses.

[34] 1400 Jan 6th. Richard murdered in Pontefract Castle.

[35] 1393. Statute of Praemunire (III v.1353, 1365): increased penalties for appealing to Rome; new offences of promoting papal bulls or excommunications added.

ideas have taken root in some people's minds. Fear stalks the nation and the village. The mighty lords and prelates have soldiers to guard them while their servants sleep: it is the same here. The Beeches have a guard on their door but old Blackie at the Forge sleeps well each night. There are those who say I have sought the quiet life here, but all I have tried to be is a simple servant to a small village that keeps to its own business in the hope that there is a tomorrow.

Regarding my personal tomorrow I am equally unsure. I do not know where they will find another replacement but Freeman's son, Matthew, reckons to be ordained soon: perhaps he will come here. Rollesby is not exactly the richest of livings, but the local people are good, on the whole. I have seen the rich come and go in wealth and the powerful rise and fall. What I have seen at national level I have seen reflected locally. What happens to kings and their magnates happens to farm holders and labourers in their strips. For my own part I would rather be a 'doorkeeper in the house of my God than dwell in the tents of the unrighteous'.

CHAPTER 11

ooooo

Thomas Bradmore (1401-1424)

Henry IV, V, VI - Agincourt

Dear Readers,

I came to Rollesby to the small priest's house not long after my predecessor died from old age. The congregation tells me he was a dear old soul, somewhat pessimistic about the world, and sure that if the Second Coming were not around the corner the end of the world ought to be. He was a keen observer of life but had neglected the parish to a certain extent. The church roof was leaking and there was a desperate need for a chancel to be added. Compared with other parishes in the area, and particularly with Great Ormesby, we looked like the poor relation. My patron was John Bois of Coningsby, Lincoln; he had recently become Lord of Rollesby Manor.[1]

I have found the people of Rollesby a very difficult group of rural workers, insular in their views and parochial in their attitudes. As far as they are concerned Caister and Yarmouth, a mere few miles away, might as well be in France.

One of the wealthier small farmers in this area, the Beeches, supplied the patrons of our church with money. The cynics claim they are merely trying to purchase their way into heaven, but I am of the opinion that the grace of God must be accepted in whatever form it comes, and I ordered the construction of the chancel.[2] The church now looks splendid, the chancel has a

[1] From Rectors' list within Rollesby church.

[2] The chancel of St George's, Rollesby is generally agreed to be very early 15th century.

small stone cupboard for the elements, and we are proposing to build a smaller tower where the chancel and nave meet on the south side.[3]

When the chancel was dedicated we renamed the church after our great English Saint George. It was he who brought us victory at Agincourt,[4] and for once the locals agree with me. We have to look to our own nationality and leaders for guidance because everything abroad appears to be wicked. There has even been a serious papal schism with two or sometimes three claimants to the papal throne. We tend to support the Roman based pope because those in Avignon are nearly always Francophiles.[5] Even when the Church meets in foreign council the English are not treated as a nation in its own right which is a damnable nonsense.[6]

I have been asked to comment on what preoccupied our minds during this period. I can only mention what preoccupied my mind, as for the peasants, it is only eating, drinking and wenching. While they were imbibing down at their inn, suitably named the Stable Inn because it is attached to the stables next to the blacksmith, the country faced internal rebellion. King Henry IV had to face rebellion from the wretched Welsh, under the perverse leadership of Owen Glendower, who linked himself to the Mortimers and Percys of Northumbria.[7] The King was merciful yet strong in his campaigns, and although it led to the eventual execution of the Archbishop of York,[8] the rebellions were put down. Henry's son became our new king[9] and a truly English king he was: nationalistic and always speaking and writing in

---

[3] The stairs were started but lead nowhere: it is currently used to store the elements and necessary books.

[4] Churchill, Winston S (1956) *A History of the English Speaking Peoples* Cassell, London. Vol.1, pp.318-19. Many medieval churches were re-named during this period after militaristic saints. Edward the Confessor and BVM lost favour to soldiers' saints. The Battle of Agincourt was fought on St Crispin's day, October 25th 1415 and it is reputed that Henry V's opening address prior to the battle began with 'in the name of Almighty God and St George....' - This is speculation, but it is generally agreed the chancel dates from this period and would have provided the ideal opportunity for rededicating the church's name, and St George was naturally a popular saint.

[5] Chadwick, H (Editor) (2000) *Not Angels but Anglicans* Canterbury Press, Norwich, p.89. Papal schisms 1378-1417 - 'the English government was seen as an important ally of the Popes in their struggles with a succession of Church Councils about authority in the Church.'

[6] Chadwick, H (Editor) (2000) *Not Angels but Anglicans* Canterbury Press, Norwich, p.90. 'The English delegation to the Council (Council of Constance 1414-18) which was high powered and well organised, led by the Bishop of Salisbury and included four other Bishops as well as the personal ambassadors of King Henry V, pushed hard for England to become a fifth nation, separate from Germany. The Germans proved to be England's staunchest ally, perhaps happy to shed a difficult partner.'

[7] Much of the subject material of Shakespeare's *Henry IV*.

[8] 1405 June 8th. Archbishop Scrope and other rebels executed outside York.

[9] 1413 April 9th. Henry V crowned during a heavy snow storm.

English.[10] Henry V led us to glorious victories in France, most especially Agincourt, and his early demise last year[11] was a great shock. Many of us worry that the king is so young because it places the real kingly power back into the hands of the Barons.

I rarely speak to the locals except to hear their confessions: but what I do hear is serious for the Church of God. Many of them are infected by the heresy of the Lollards. I was pleased when Sawtrey[12] was burnt at the stake for his Lollardry, and I am grateful that the bishops are pleased to kill such heretics. They even claim that when I elevate the Host at Mass it is useless, that it is no more than a 'toad or a spider'.[13] These Lollards even caused rebellion in the South and Midlands under Oldecastle;[14] they want to change our faith, share property out and hold everything in common. Such ideas are not only heretical but also dangerous for those of us with land and property. I heard that Freeman's son, who had been training to be a clerk in Holy Orders, joined the rebels. I only met him once and I was pleased to hear he had died in one of the rebellions. All this nonsense that Christ expected the riches of the world to be shared out equally shows their appalling ignorance. I rarely read the Scriptures but I do know our Lord said we would always have the poor with us; they will just have to get used to being poor, after all it was the Lord's command that they be poor and understand their place before their betters.

Freeman's visit did the locals little good. Even though we have a new chancel, fewer people want to attend Mass, and when I collect their tithes they seem to resent my justified demands. It is not as if life is tough for them: young Hudd and Freeman's grandson actually went skating on the frozen Broad last week.[15] When the papal schism ended,[16] I offered a special Mass and only twelve people turned up. I truly despair. The congregation is interested only in what strips of land still remain, avoiding payment

---

[10] Churchill, Winston S (1956) *A History of the English Speaking Peoples* Cassell, London. Vol.1, p.322.

[11] 1422 August 31st. Henry V dies and is succeeded by his child son, Henry VI with a council to rule in minority.

[12] 1401. Lollard, William Sawtrey was first man burned at Smithfield. The Statute *De Heretico Comburendo*, imposed the death penalty by burning for obdurate heretics and was passed at the request of the bishops.

[13] Churchill, Winston S (1956) *A History of the English Speaking Peoples* Cassell, London. Vol.1, p.323.

[14] 1414. Henry V put the rising down, but Oldecastle escaped but was later captured and killed.

[15] Skating was popular; they used fine bones as skates.

[16] 1417. Pope Martin V is elected.

of their feudal dues, practising at the butts and drinking themselves silly. I had to enlarge my house out of my own pocket and with paid labour: it simply is not fair. They also had the nerve to complain that I was away for a year even though I paid a travelling Mass priest to take the Mass and hear any confessions. I was going to bring the parish back a holy relic but decided they were not worth the cost.

While I was away I met John Capgrave,[17] a friar in King's Lynn: he expressed some interest in this letter I have been asked to write, but pointed out that any historical record is only valid if it shows the hand of God in history. I agree with him, and since I cannot see the hand of God anywhere amongst the Rollesby people I do not see why I need write more.

The life in a rural village is irritating, and looking back, I suspect that my letter sounds pessimistic. The fact is that I had higher hopes of my promotion within the Church than landing up in a rural backwater. In this day and age you have to belong to the nobility to achieve any chance at court, and the legal profession is extraordinarily hard work for little return. I considered the army for a time, but one looks at the injuries a sword or arrow can do so that left me with the Church. After the Death the bishops were only too happy to ordain anyone who could read and write, and I had visions of being a senior churchman within years. As it transpired, very little has come my way. Only recently I had a public row with a passing friar on this subject.

'The Church,' he said, 'is not a career; it's a vocation, a call by God and financial return and social position are not important.'

'Rubbish,' I naturally replied. 'The labourer is worthy of his hire.'

'I agree,' he replied, 'that the people whom a religious man ministers to should help keep the man in food and offer shelter, but nothing else is required. You are after all only a servant.'

'I may be many things, but I am not a servant.'

'You were a deacon before you were a priest?' I nodded agreement. He went on, 'The word deacon means servant. It does not mean you are a slave, but you serve Christ's people as Christ Himself instructed.'

'Of course I serve people, but I expect to be paid for doing so and to have a career.'

---

[17] 1417. John Capgrave wrote *Chronicle, an English history from creation to 1417.*

'The apostles were not paid, and their careers ended in martyrdom.'

'You're mad.' I was becoming angry with his silly banter. 'You will be telling me next that bishops and archdeacons should not be paid.'

'I do not deny that clergy need a roof and food, but I would pay archbishops, bishops, archdeacons just what they need to live on, no more, no less. As I said earlier we should not be in the Church for money or social status. It is not a career for bettering oneself.'

Several of the villagers heard this interchange and they all seemed to agree with the friar, so I told him off for preaching revolution and stalked away. If I have problems collecting my tithes next month I shall blame this friar for putting silly ideas in people's heads.

It has not been an easy time and the diocese has had its problems. We still have the memory of having one Bishop of Norwich flung into prison of all places. Alexander de Tottington,[18] Prior of Norwich was chosen to be bishop by the monks in 1407 but King Henry IV refused to accept his elevation and imprisoned him in Windsor for a year. The citizens of Norwich complained, as did Thomas Arundel, Archbishop of Canterbury, and so he was released. This new bishop managed to repair his palace but died[19] in 1413 and was buried in the cathedral's Lady Chapel and I managed to attend the occasion. The local people never understood the facts but it cast a shadow on the diocese.

Norwich itself was always a place of problems and generally I kept well clear of the wretched place. In the February of 1413 there was a massive fire in the city[20] that consumed all the convent of the Preaching Friars and all that belonged to them. I would not be surprised if it were the work of an angry parent over a ruined daughter. I tried to keep away from the city, but did go for a few weeks in 1415 when Henry V visited it before his trip to France. He left his coronet in pawn for a hundred marks and a further five hundred was lent by the corporation of Norwich, four hundred by that of Lynn and the remainder by William Westacre, William Walton and Nicholas Scormfet. The citizens were not repaid and sued the King in the Court of the Exchequer so the city lost the royal favour and their charter.

---

[18] Bayne, A D (circa 1880) *History of Eastern England* James MacDonald, Yarmouth. Vol.II, p.3.

[19] 1413 April 28th.

[20] Bayne, A D (circa 1880) *History of Eastern England* James MacDonald, Yarmouth. Vol.II, p.4.

This charter had been important to Norwich because the members of the religious fraternities had been able to form themselves into guilds. The members of these guilds carried themselves in great pomp and ceremony with all their possessions. The Guild of St George with the trade guilds was a particularly festive occasion.[21]

Either way, the problems of Norwich did not touch on life here in Rollesby except as gossip. As the years have passed I have become accustomed to this place and although the people are difficult and insular I have started to appreciate them as I have grown older amongst them: I have had to forgive many of their sins and I hope they will forgive mine.

[21] Bayne, A D (circa 1880) *History of Eastern England* James MacDonald, Yarmouth. Vol.II, p.4.

CHAPTER 12

ooooo

James Andeley (1424-1436)

Henry VI - French wars and the Lollards

Dear Future Reader,

I am happy about the request to write an account of my tenure here in Rollesby but because the place is of little importance I cannot but wonder why. There is trouble in Caister, and even that is a town of little importance, so why anyone in the future would like to know about Rollesby is beyond my imagination. I took over from Thomas Bradmore who was extremely unpopular. It was widely believed by some that he gave the name of Freeman's son to the Bishop of London on the grounds that he was a Lollard. I don't suppose the truth will ever be known, apart from the fact that Godwin was killed and has left a son to be brought up by his ageing family.

Godwin, one of the Duke of Bedford's archers, has engendered another source of unhappiness in the village. After the heretical Maid of Orleans[1] had turned the tide against us by the use of witchcraft and guile, as a nation we have lost all we gained in the reign of Henry V. Godwin believes that a handful of English yeoman could have defeated the French; all we needed,

[1] Churchill, Winston S (1956) *A History of the English Speaking Peoples* Cassell, London. Vol.1, p.335. Joan of Arc who entered Orleans and saved it from the English siege: she was eventually captured by the Burgundians and sold to the English who had her burned on the grounds of heresy. However, from this point on the French started to expel the English from France (with the exception of Calais). This was not helped by the King being just a baby and the Church making a fortune when it may have been better spent on the army.

he claimed, was a thousand good archers. There is no doubt that there is considerable bad feeling amongst ordinary people, saying that if they were allowed to fight we could beat the French.[2] Instead, the nobles of the land are interested only in who precisely controls the court because our King Henry VI is just a child. Apart from these intrigues, the nobles want to know who owns what land and marries whom: national interests in France are ignored.

As in the time of my predecessor the Lollards are still a danger, but given the feelings in the village against the church I do not mention my opinions on this matter too widely. The Duke of Gloucester had to crush a Lollard rebellion led by Jack Sharp[3] in the very same year that the King was crowned as King of France while he was still only ten years of age: it is a mad world in which we live.

The year after I arrived there was a general persecution of religious informers in Norfolk. Nearly a hundred and twenty Lollards suffered in this diocese alone.[4] The authorities were particularly keen to apprehend a priest called William White who had publicly renounced the errors and practices of Rome. White came from Kent and was a disciple of Wyclif himself: his main residence was Ludham where he resigned his benefice in order to marry. He claimed that men could have their sins forgiven by God alone and that we should not worship idolatrous paintings, and that the Roman Church is the fig tree Christ cursed. He was brought before Archbishop Chichele at Canterbury but managed to return to Norfolk with his wife. He continued to preach this heresy and was brought before John Wakeryng, Bishop of Norwich, and was convicted of no fewer than 30 articles. In the September of 1424[5] he was burnt in that city a week after I had been granted Rollesby Church and tenure. I disagree with the Lollard heresy, not least its attack on transubstantiation and the mother Church, but in moments of prayer I am convinced we should not be torturing, burning and killing people in the name of Christ: it does not fit with the figure of Jesus Himself.

On the whole, the question of Lollards has not affected us much in Rollesby: Yarmouth news sometimes bears testimony to news of itinerant

[2] Churchill, Winston S (1956) *A History of the English Speaking Peoples* Cassell, London. Vol.1, p.335.

[3] 1431 May.

[4] Bayne, A D (circa 1880) *History of Eastern England: Volumes I-II* James MacDonald. Yarmouth. Vol.II, p.8.

[5] Bayne, A D (circa 1880) *History of Eastern England: Volumes I-II* James MacDonald. Yarmouth. Vol.II, p.9.

Lollard preachers, but out in this part of the country it is a matter of working hard in order to survive.

Some of our winters have been particularly harsh and keeping livestock is not always easy. Most of the men break most of the game laws, and the Broads provide ample opportunities for fish, water-fowl and eels. I say nothing because I have discovered that once the locals feel you are one of them, they look after you. The village has grown a little more over recent years, and some of the labourers are spreading their houses down Martham Lane. This is quite useful for them because the larger landowners have land in other villages as well as nearby Ormesby and Hemsby. This is especially true of Thomas Bois[6] of Honing, who was the son of one of our Rollesby patrons, Roger Bois of Honing, Ingham and Rollesby. Sadly he died a year or so ago, and I attended his funeral at Grey Friars, in Norwich.[7] The other patron and local lord, John Berking, has become the first Juror of West Fleggs on the death of Judge Paston.[8] All seems changing and unsettled.

The Beeches, who provided much of the money for the chancel, have fallen on hard times. Their children seem to die young and those who survive seem intent on finding themselves in trouble. The eldest boy was caught up in a small Lollard rebellion in Norwich and it cost his father a good deal to extricate him from the bishop's prison. One of the daughters then married an off-shoot of the Godwin family so old Beech felt obligated to disavow her: this has created quite a rift in the community.

'The Beeches' background is no different from mine,' Godwin explained to me. 'My family were here at the time of the conquest, but his family crawled out from Yarmouth only three generations back.'

'He owns a lot of land and provided for the chancel,' I argued.

'His father took that land after the Black Death, and the money for the chancel was to buy himself into heaven.'

'He's had his troubles,' I tried again. It is my job to reconcile divisions within the parish.

'Where was he when we fought in France? When I was bending my bow against the King's enemies he was making money. Where was his son? He's

---

[6] In some documents Boys.

[7] 1432. *Norfolk and Norwich Archaeological Society* (1959) N&NAS, Norwich. Vol.32, Part IV, p.276.

[8] Bates, Ann. Private research from the *Norfolk Archaeological Society*.

my age and was causing trouble with the Lollards while my comrades are littered all over Flanders.'

I could not argue further. Flanders had become an English graveyard but at least it will not happen again. Once he mentioned his hostility to the Lollards I gave in and agreed. The trouble with village life in our day and age is that there are too many quarrels. One family starts to resent another, usually because of wealth. If one man has three cows and another two, it becomes a matter of unpleasant comment. If one family has a second floor and another lives on the ground, then the second storey people are regarded as better off and see themselves as superior. We all live in the same area but petty jealousy based on personal wealth is nearly always the source of village acrimony.

Geoffrey Lanham brought a piece of wood back from the French wars claiming it was a holy relic, part of the cross of Christ. He charged a penny for even his best friends to come and touch it. They would be charged extra to pray before it. I ordered him to confession on pain of excommunication and he confessed that the wood had come from a boat in Caister. He threw the wood away but I could hardly blame him, what with the trade in holy relics and the selling of absolutions by pardoners and other rogues.

Apart from the disappointment in the French wars and a degree of worry about being ruled by a king who is a mere child, life has been fairly settled in my time. Village feuds have been the most difficult aspect apart from forcing people to the Mass and collecting the tithes. I have simply tried to do my work as a priest, keep the confessions to myself, and guide the people away from the Lollards and falling out with one another.

One of the main problems I have found is being caught between different village factions. The Beech family antagonise virtually everyone: there is conflict over diminishing strips, there are those who claim rights on the Broads and rights in the woods, and I must listen to them all. The minute I express an opinion I find that I am suddenly being quoted as the authority and the last word on the subject. This alienates one group against me or against the Church. I try not to express an opinion, I just listen, but more often than not I am virtually compelled to agree that a particular action seems right, and then I have inadvertently taken sides. The priest must take so much care of local politics but at times it is impossible to be entirely neutral. The local lord has lost much of his control over the workers, but he still sits as the leader of the Manor Court,[9] and I have to be particularly careful when listening to problems relating to his interests. This has been a sensitive area for me because I have sometimes acted as his land agent. I have my own glebe farm[10] to run and it is not easy to find labourers let alone the money to pay their demands.

As a final note I might add that being a land agent for the Manor, running my own glebe farm and being a priest do not sit easily together. It is easier for the friars because they have no vested interests to conflict with their ministry. I do not know what the future holds but it would be good to think that some day clergy will receive a living wage and be able to disassociate themselves from landed interests. I know that the ordinary parishioners do not expect their local clergy to be wealthy and in a sense they are right, we must always be one of them if we are to serve them as priests.

---

[9] Trevelyan, G M (1945) *English Social History* Longmans, London, p.61. 'Feudalism proper and serfdom were dying out. But the quasi-feudal position of the landlord still survived in his powerful chairmanship of the Manor Court or Leet-Court, exercised by himself in person or by his steward'.

[10] Trevelyan, G M (1945) *English Social History* Longmans, London, p.62. Normally 50-60 acres of open field.

CHAPTER 13

ooooo

William Thrulby (1436-1447)

Henry VI - superstition and witchcraft in high and low places

Dear Future,

I have been asked to write this account of Rollesby and I find it quite intriguing why this request arrived at this precise time. Is it because it is the year 1447 and the request presupposes I am at the end of my time? I am still middle aged and neither the Prior nor the Bishop has mentioned anything to me. Even so I shall accede to the request and only the future can tell. Indeed the whole future is uncertain: Norfolk is a quiet place but there are signs even here of serious disturbance as in the country as a whole.

The baby King Henry VI was declared of age to be king not long after I took on this benefice[1] but national affairs have not gone well. We have virtually lost the wars against France and all the King seems to do is found Cambridge colleges.[2] He even founded outside Windsor a small school for twenty-five poor scholars and twenty-five paupers: he has called it Eton[3] and spends much of his time with architects. I have no doubt that it is a charitable institution and long may it serve paupers; someone needs to help them. I hope by the time this letter is read the school is still functioning for the poorest people of the kingdom. It was all very well the King spending his time in this saintly way, but in the meantime not only was there serious

---

[1] 1437 Nov 13th. Henry VI declared the right age to rule.

[2] 1441. Henry VI founded King's College, Cambridge.

[3] 1440. Eton founded under King's directions.

military misfortune in France but also tension at home. The richest man in the kingdom is Cardinal Beaufort, the Bishop of Winchester,[4] and he and others like Suffolk, and the Dukes of Somerset and Buckingham have been at odds with the powerful Duke of Gloucester. The Duke of Gloucester married his mistress, Eleanor Cobham (having put aside his first wife Jacqueline) and his enemies convicted her of trying to kill the young King by sorcery of all things. She was made to parade through London for three days and was then imprisoned for life. Later they arrested Gloucester and he died, unexpectedly, from natural causes within days of his arrest, so they say. I tell you all this to show what unpleasant and unnatural times we live in, and what has happened at the highest level of society is reflected in the lowest.

Only a few years ago, not long after the incident of Gloucester's death, it was rumoured that old Mary Hudd was sticking pins in an effigy she had made of John Godwin. She had reason to dislike the boy because it had always been intended that he should marry her daughter: instead he went off with a girl from Martham. It was not a question of love but arrangements for enlarging land holdings. Again they had the example of their betters in this idea of marriage by arrangement. Thomas Arnold of Rollesby married Agatha Fransham and so held the moiety (benefit) of the Manor of Scarning in 1441. He is also a juror for the East Flegg Hundred.[5] Also, in 1445, the Lordship of Bois in Rollesby was settled by fine on Robert Mortimer and Sibilla, daughter of John and Sibill de Bois, by John Damme the Trustee. All this was accomplished through marriage. But I deviate from my main point. Mary Hudd's expectancies were not so great but there had been an anticipation of wealth from such a union. Not long after this, Hudd's daughter died, they say from a broken heart, and old Mary Hudd was irreconcilable. It seemed to me that witchcraft had been involved and several reliable sources indicated the same. I exhorted her to change her ways, but Godwin became more and more ill. I went to her home with several members of the congregation and placed her under an excommunication. At first she did not seem to mind, but because she was excommunicated, nobody would have anything to do with her for fear of

[4] One of the legitimatised sons of John of Gaunt from his third union.

[5] *Norfolk and Norwich Archaeological Society* (1959) N&NAS, Norwich. Vol.32, Part 4, p.287.

spiritual contamination. In fact no one would trade with her and she fell on hard times: I was just beginning to feel sorry for her when I was called away to Norwich by the Prior. A week later I returned and she had died: as she was an excommunicated soul, I observed the interment of her remains in the common field outside the churchyard: no prayers were said. The interesting feature of this witchcraft was that as soon as the last sod was turned on her grave then young Godwin started to improve. After that I had no misgivings about the power of witchcraft and the validity of excommunication.

While the old witch was dying I had been to Norwich, as I mentioned earlier: while there I met William Paston who had been in his time Counsel for the City, Steward to the Duke of Norfolk and was a Justice of the Common Bench.[6] He seemed very cynical about witchcraft and more concerned about the politics of the area and problems with his family land. However, the Prior knew exactly about the nature of the problems we faced in the parishes and defended me against William Paston who thought I was a deluded fool.

The question of witchcraft persisted for some time. Certain people made accusations against neighbours that caused me to suspect it was more personal animosity surfacing. Beech came to see me and told me that Peter Payne had been collecting black cats and dogs.

'I tell you, Father, it be not natural. We all have cats and dogs, but he goes out of his way to collect black ones, and that be the colour of the devil.'

'That doesn't mean that they belong to the devil. You have a black cow.'

'But I don't go out at night and chant.'

'What do you mean?'

'He goes out at midnight and chants. I've often heard him.'

'What's he chanting?'

'I think it be the Lord's prayer backwards.'

At this my interest was aroused and I went out two nights later to observe this devilish behaviour. I heard nothing. Five nights I went and heard nothing. So I asked Peter Payne why he kept black animals and he told me that it was just for good luck. He then went on and told me that he needed good luck because Beech was trying to antagonise his neighbours

---

[6] Barber, R (Editor) (1981) *The Pastons* Folio Society, London, pp.12-13, William Paston, son of Clement Paston of Paston, born 1378, appointed to the Bench in 1429, died 1429.

because he had covetous eyes on his parcel of land near Rollesby Broad. Then I realised it was not witchcraft at all. I never trusted Beech after that: but then he was only pursuing the course of his betters. Everywhere men of high and low degree were seeking power and land. Land was the key to power and they did not care how they took it or manipulated people to achieve their aims. This was certainly the case at national level; my clerical friends in Norwich and Yarmouth were alive to the fact that the loss of France was being blamed on the House of Lancaster. Although no one appeared to blame the saintly Henry VI, it was still remembered that he was of the House of Lancaster. Rumour had it that the House of York was becoming a rival party,[7] a power in the land. This could cause a civil war, and if this happens it will bring anarchy which will assist rogues like Beech.

I dare not write on this matter much more as such thoughts are dangerous, even for a parish priest in a remote place like Rollesby. I must be about my business of ensuring the collection of tithes, attending to the Mass and keeping an eye out for genuine witchcraft and devil worship.

There are many that say that black magic and witchcraft are mere superstition. My retort to this is that there is more in heaven and earth than the human eye can perceive. The real trouble from my point of view is not the witchcraft but the problem of sorting out whether in fact it is genuine when it is reported. The alleged incident may be simply a tall story to try and entangle a hated neighbour in serious problems. The priest's job is to try and find the motive for spreading the rumour. The intention is self-evident; the intention is to rid the community of a hated neighbour. The motive is the dilemma. Is it witchcraft or merely a means of using authority to get rid of someone who has land another wants or even a creditor who is proving to be an embarrassment. For a priest it is always too easy to believe people when in fact they are scandal-mongering for their own devious purposes. I think that if I could have my time again I would simply listen and say nothing.

A good antidote to witchcraft is a holy pilgrimage. There is even a hostel in Rome for English visitors.[8] There was, I heard, a lady from King's Lynn who had fourteen children and then set out on a series of pilgrimages to

---

[7] Churchill, Winston S (1956) *A History of the English Speaking Peoples* Cassell, London. Vol.1, p.337.

[8] Survives today as the English College.

Jerusalem and Rome in 1413 and 1415, to Santiago de Compostela in 1417 to 1418 and even went as far as Norway, to Danzig in Prussia and back via Paris in 1434.[9] Her name is Margery Kempe and she claims to have direct communion with Christ because of her visits. She has become quite controversial because she is prone to large bursts of sobbing while attending services, even in the cathedral. Nevertheless, the visitation of shrines and collection of holy relics is a good safeguard against the darkness of Satan and his forces.[10]

I am personally terrified by the dark satanic forces that surround us. Even the pain of a rotten tooth did not encourage me to seek the help of dark magic. I simply took enough ale to become senseless and had it pulled by the blacksmith. I hope that one day some friar will discover a herb that takes away pain. I must put this letter aside now because I have to attend to a young mother's funeral; she died in childbirth. She lost the baby because it came feet first and then she died herself from loss of blood. In fact, over the last few years more babies have died at birth than survived. I have to baptise them as soon as possible so they do not fall prey to Satan and his disciples.

[9] Chadwick, H (Editor) (2000) *Not Angels but Anglicans* Canterbury Press, Norwich, p.110. ' "The Booke of Margery Kempe" deserves its fame not only as the first autobiography in the English language but because it offers a unique and remarkably direct insight into the female spirituality of the 15th century.'

[10] Chadwick, H (Editor) (2000) *Not Angels but Anglicans* Canterbury Press, Norwich, p.97. '...the veneration of saints and their relics and images figured prominently in the lives of the people...in 1335 nearly 8000 pilgrims visited the shrine of St Hugh in Lincoln...pilgrim badges were collected to prove shrines visited...'

CHAPTER 14

ooooo

John Knolls (1449-1453)
including John Selot (1447)

Henry VI - Cade rebellion & rumours of civil war

Dear Sirs,

My letter need only be short. I have been in Rollesby for three years and the Prior has promised me preferment to a better living very soon. I came because William Thrulby disappeared under mysterious circumstances. He had an obsession with sorcery and witchcraft and seemed suspicious of each and every person: he then vanished from sight. Some say he was taken by the devil, others that he went mad, and some say he joined some travelling friars, but I suspect foul play. He had made so many enemies with his pursuit of the devil I would not be surprised if he were murdered while on the marshes trying to spot the works and chanting of Satan himself. After William Thrulby there was what can best be described as a stand-in priest by the name of John Selot. He came simply because the Prior wanted to find someone quickly following Thrulby's strange disappearance. He only stayed for a year and a few months, a clever and ambitious man that I am told will go far.[1]

Berking Manor, of our patron, was recently possessed by Thomas Sotterby and he bequeathed it to fair Elizabeth his wife, a beautiful woman.

---

[1] Selot was to become Archdeacon of Sudbury in 1462 and later Chancellor of Norwich: from Rectors' list in Rollesby Church.

Sadly she died before Thomas, so he sold it and left the money for Masses to be said for her soul. Robert Baynard was given the first refusal but now Sir Miles Stapleton, Edward Clere of Caister and Ormesby along with Robert Baynard are the feoffees.[2] Robert was not prepared to purchase by himself. Manor ownership is like big business and is all very confusing.

The request for this letter mentions that I should put down the main topics of conversation both in terms of the locality and the national scene. News reaches Rollesby very slowly, and by the time it does reach us it has sometimes grown arms and legs. Regarding arms and legs we now have to support three of our young men who have returned from the wars with legs missing. The French wars have been disastrous. The Duke of Somerset, the least popular man in the country, has surrendered huge tracts of our rightful land to the French.[3] In fact the war with the French has lasted a hundred years and in my short time in Rollesby there has been no good news from abroad.

At home the news has also been a disaster; it is no wonder the world is so gloomy, not that one would see it touching upon the labourers in this area, they are oblivious to many of the greater events. While France was disgracing our soldiers, they were more interested in Jack Cade.[4] The country is going to the dogs; it is as close to anarchy as one can imagine. Suffolk was impeached and King Henry VI sent him into exile for five years to save his life. He sailed across the English Sea and was stopped by a warship called the *Nicholas of the Tower* and was beheaded with a rusty sword[5] for being a traitor. They say it took five strokes to execute him. A royal naval ship killing a lord of the kingdom sailing with the King's permission: perhaps the reader can see why we are close to a state of anarchy. This anarchy was also felt in Kent, a rebellious part of the country, where Jack Cade rose in rebellion.[6] One of our legless fellows knew this man Cade. He was Irish, a good soldier, but of very bad character. His rag-tag army caused the royal army to

---

[2] Bates, Ann. Private research from the *Norfolk Archaeological Society*.

[3] 1449 Oct 29th. Duke of Somerset surrenders Rouen to French; on July 1st 1450 he surrenders Caen and leaves Normandy. By 1451 Bayonne surrenders to the French and it is the end of English rule in Gascony. On July 17th 1453 the battle of Castillon, in which Talbot was killed: it was a decisive battle and was the last battle of the Hundred Years' War.

[4] See note 6.

[5] Churchill, Winston S (1956) *A History of the English Speaking Peoples* Cassell, London. Vol.1, p.338. 1450 May 2nd.

[6] 1450 May 24th. Jack Cade begins revolt in Kent with men of Surrey, Sussex and Middlesex.

flee and the King sought safety in the north. The rebels then occupied Southwark, pillaged London, and killed the Treasurer, Lord Say as well as William Crowmer, Sheriff of Kent.[7] The Lancastrians blamed the Yorkists, but I think it was just a revolt like that of the peasants in 1381, which my father told me about. Cade was eventually killed[8] and I was disappointed when the king pardoned the rebels: he really is quite weak.

This anarchy does not help locally: the labourers here are always gossiping that the kings and queens will one day go, the lawyers and clergy will follow and we will have a country ruled by farm workers in which everything is held in common. I know that will never be the case; maybe in some distant country in some distant time, but not in England. However hard I try to explain this to the congregation on a Sunday morning I know it falls on deaf ears. Fortunately we are a very small village of some two hundred souls and the work is hard here; there is little time for a real revolt so they content themselves with gossip of a new future instead. There is some talk that my patron is going to move into the area and build himself a manor house: that should be interesting if it happens. Apart from this chatter, the main concern locally has been the poor harvest. Had it not been for the fish we might have been close to starvation, and keeping warm in the winter has been a problem. The trees have been felled so much that there is little good wood around which is not owned. The Beech family sells wood but they put the prices up in the autumn and had I not the tithes I would be as cold as the farm worker. It is a good job they have their drinking inn by the stables.

Three of our younger and more able men have left the work of the fields and joined the royal army: the country is in severe danger of civil war between the York and Lancaster Houses.[9] Quite why the young men are so keen I do not understand; these are dynastic struggles that have little to do with us. There have been serious problems with the great families of the nation.[10] The land and power disputes are destructive to the good order of the country and the King has been obliged to travel on judicial business. He

---

[7] 1450 July 2-5th.

[8] 1450 July 7th.

[9] 1452 March 1st-3rd. Yorkist and Royal armies confront at Dartford: York yields and is pardoned.

[10] 1453 August 24th. Fighting breaks out between the Neville and Percy families. On July 21st of the same year the Council had been forced to meet to settle a dispute over the possession of Glamorgan between Duke of Somerset and Richard Neville, Earl of Warwick, later known as the 'Kingmaker'.

came to East Anglia[11] last year and I caught a glimpse of him at Norwich. I have heard in the cloisters that all this pressure is causing him to have a weakness of the mind, almost a mental breakdown:[12] it seems strange that a man who can have everything at his command should suffer like this.

The country is definitely unsettled: only in 1350 there was a special commission of oyer and terminer[13] for Norfolk and Suffolk: there have been plenty of them in the land since Cade's rebellion. This one seemed to be investigating powerful men of Norfolk, such as Sir Thomas Tuddenham and John Heydon. John Paston had a case against Lord Moleyns but it was dismissed. Paston complained that the judges were biased against him.[14] It is also clear that troops of soldiers are being gathered and several times we have witnessed small armies being assembled.[15]

It is an age of litigation and conflict. Even in the parish we have our problems: Beech continues to contest everyone's right to land if it touches the Broad, and even the village pond is in dispute. A newcomer in the village has claimed the right to the pond, and thereby the ducks. The villagers, especially the Freeman family and the Godwins are almost up to the point of taking up arms - over ducks! Several times I have intervened to stop bloodshed, but what can one say when the great families of the nations are also at one another's throats. If the King is weak, barons create disorder and anarchy, and this permeates even down to the village pond. No leadership gives way to a primitive form of survival.

This has been the main thrust of my time in Rollesby, a small village of rural souls whose main talking points have been the lost war with France, the disputes of the great families of the land and the duck pond. I find it truly aggravating that some of the most serious quarrels in a small community are engendered by the most trivial of circumstances. A lost chicken, a small encroachment on an old strip, urinating in someone's paddock, matters of little or no moment cause bad blood, and I am expected to step in and heal the problems. I can understand it in cases of adultery, fornication,

---

[11] 1452 September 6th. Henry VI starts judicial tour of East Anglia.

[12] 1453 August. Henry VI suffers first mental breakdown.

[13] A special court designed to deal with grievances or problems of a region, or a difficult case.

[14] Barber, R (Editor) (1981) *The Pastons* Folio Society, London, p.55.

[15] Following Henry VI's breakdown the Duke of York emerged as the protector of the realm, and rival factions emerged, even in Norfolk.

murder and theft, but a duck pond! All my education and experience having to be brought into focus to solve who owns what duck and what part of the pond. On the other hand if I resisted such work then heaven knows what the consequences would be. Being a servant here means being prepared to do the most menial of tasks alongside trying to save souls for eternity. One minute I am giving reason on ducks and chickens and the next trying to save a man's soul from eternal damnation. It is very hard work and at times tedious. I take strength and comfort from the fact that priests before have done the same thing and those who follow me will also tread the same ground. I only hope that this effort of mine will one day be read by a future priest of the parish, and that he may pause a moment between tasks to pray for my soul.

CHAPTER 15

ooooo

John Brygge (1454-1497)

including William Hoper (1453)

Henry VI, Edward IV, Edward V, Richard III, Henry VII - the War of the Roses

Dear Readers,

I have been the rector of Rollesby for over forty years and have with my parishioners lived through the most dangerous period of our country's life. My patron was Brian Bois, and in 1483 requested in his will that he be buried in the chancel before the altar of St George.[1] That has been duly done and now John Smith LL.D, Chancellor of Norwich has given the Rollesby Manor by his will to St Gyles's hospital in Norwich for eighty years, and on licence for mortmain for ever.[2]

The parish has managed to keep itself to itself: being a small village of simple souls we have avoided the tumult of civil wars, the change of kings and the machinations of barons, in what has now been dubbed the War of the Roses.[3] I am not a historian, nor a person who can make a social comment on the times in which I lived. I am a simple country priest who spends most of his time dissuading our young hot-blooded men from taking sides and joining baronial armies unless they are obliged.

I should account for my immediate predecessor, William Hoper: he came as a caretaker priest for a few years but stayed just one. He had strong affiliations with the Yorkist cause and disappeared as a chaplain to one of

[1] Bates, Ann. Private Research from the *Norfolk Archaeological Society*.

[2] Bates, Ann. Private Research from the *Norfolk Archaeological Society*.

[3] The term War of Roses not actually used until 1829 by Sir Walter Scott.

their armies. He was here a matter of months and the parishioners hardly knew him. For my part I arrived in 1454 when the Lancastrians were in power. Perhaps I ought to explain the nature of the division between York and Lancaster. It was not a war between the two northern counties as some of my more ignorant folk think. Both the Lancastrians and the Yorkists are of the same family line: both belonging to the greater family of the Plantagenets. Because Henry VI had been but a baby at the start of the reign the great lords brought him up and ruled for him: this gave them a lust for power and they were factious about their individual power. Henry VI was, of course, Lancastrian but his wife, Margaret of Anjou, was French. She was a powerful person, and some say she was the one who conspired in the death of Gloucester. They held the royal lands including the Duchy of Cornwall and the Lancaster earldoms. In this area East Anglia was seen as Lancastrian, but civil war bites deep and part of York's strength was to be found in Norfolk. His main strength was with the Mortimer family on the Welsh borders and, of course, that turbulent county, Kent. The personal ambitions of these great nobles drove us close to national suicide. Even parishioners, who had never met a noble lord, and who at the very best had only seen them at a distance, argued the case for and against whom should be king. Most of the Rollesby folk believed Henry VI to be saintly, but that a stronger person like the Duke of York should hold power.

This was basically the cause of much trouble in the parish and the kingdom. An MP called Young[4] had made this suggestion in parliament and although he gained good backing he soon found himself in the Tower. Then the next thing we hear is that the saintly King had gone mad and it made sense for York to be Protector of the Realm.[5] The King's wife, Margaret, gave birth to a son, causing some mischievous people both in the parish and in high places to suggest it was a sham to confirm the Lancastrian line. When the King regained his sanity Margaret screamed for revenge and I personally think that that was the time the civil war started, and it lasted for most of my time here in Rollesby. It's one of the reasons I stayed and did not seek preferment: it was much safer to stay in one place, keep quiet and do the job for which I was ordained and inducted. It was a war made up of

---

[4] 1450. Henry sent him to the Tower as soon as parliament was dispersed.

[5] March 27th 1454. Council appoints York as Protector.

battles and skirmishes, and intelligent folk kept out of the way - wherever possible.

I had been in the parish for only six years when the war heated up to an unpleasant temperature. The King was captured at Northampton even though he had new cannon guarding his line[6] and it was agreed that he should be king for life but York was to rule and succeed him. We all thought at the time that this would solve the problem, but we had not counted on his wife Margaret, who, with her son the Prince of Wales, was hiding in Harlech Castle. At a battle in Wakefield[7] she routed the Lancastrians and the Duke of York, with other nobles, was put to the sword. But it did not end there: hundreds of ordinary soldiers were massacred: this had never happened before; most of the ordinary soldiers hardly knew what they were fighting for and to kill them as prisoners was the undoubted work of Margaret. The whole war turned unpleasant, and Rollesby villagers who had opinions now spoke in whispers.

The Duke of York's son, Edward, returned the compliment of brutality at the battle of Mortimer's Cross,[8] and again no quarter was spared. It seems to me the more modern war becomes, the more horrific and less gentlemanly. Edward IV was crowned[9] and I am told that a third of English estates changed hands in a day. We all hoped that that was the end of the matter but Queen Margaret continued the Lancastrian fight, seeking help from the French and Scots. The newly designed artillery meant that sieges were no longer sustainable and Margaret fled to France leaving Henry aside to be captured later.[10] They led him into London with his feet bound by leather thongs to his stirrups and wearing a straw hat, made him circle the pillory three times and then placed him in the Tower. The locals in Rollesby were outraged by this behaviour. They do not expect cruelty from their betters.

It was about this time that I found one of the Beech family dead in the churchyard. They are not a popular family because they have capitalised on other people's misfortunes. I had to call the justices because when the women were cleaning his body for burial they discovered burn marks around

---

[6] July 1460. Battle of Northampton.

[7] 1460 Dec 30th.

[8] 1461 Feb 2nd. Edward, amongst others executed Owen Tudor.

[9] 1461 June 28th.

[10] 1465 June 24th. Henry VI captured at Ribblesdale.

his rectum. He had died from a red hot poker we believe: a dreadful way to die but it leaves few marks and no doubt the perpetrators hope not to get caught. The cruelty at the national level seems to permeate all levels of society. Young Hugg was suspected of the murder and was hanged in Yarmouth a month later. This was a great shame because years later I was to hear a deathbed confession about the murder and it was not Hugg. The Beech family is full of wily intrigue, always manipulating themselves into positions of power in order to gain property and wealth.

The top and bottom of society reflect one another. The Beech family and their local enemies were just the same as the Neville family, the Earl of Warwick who was nicknamed the 'King maker' and fell out with Edward IV because of his secret marriage.[11] Because the King gave his wife's family eight new peerages, shifting the balance of power, there was a revolt in Yorkshire.[12] Soon Warwick had two kings in prison,[13] Henry VI and Edward IV: perhaps the reader can see why these were such complicated and dangerous times.

Eventually, after the promise of pardons, Edward IV was back on the throne, and not far from here, too close as far as I was concerned, was the battle of Empingham in Lincolnshire.[14] The loss of this battle caused Warwick to flee to France: there he betrothed his daughter Anne to Queen Margaret's son, the Prince of Wales, and promised to restore Henry VI to the throne. Such machinations may seem unbelievable to future readers, but they did happen. He kept to his word and poor old Henry VI, who had been rotting in the Tower for five years, was put back on the throne.[15] It did not last long, Edward IV returned to the open arms of London[16] and following the battle of Barnet[17] Edward won and Warwick was killed: poor old Henry VI was finally put out of his misery by having his head chopped off in the Tower.[18]

---

[11] 1464 May 1st. Edward secretly marries Elizabeth Woodville: he did not reveal this to the Council until September of that year when the Earl of Warwick had hoped to marry him into a French alliance.

[12] 1469 Spring. Robin of Redesdale raises revolt in Yorkshire denouncing the Queen and her family.

[13] Follows battle of Edgecote July 1469.

[14] 1470 March 12th.

[15] 1470 October 13th.

[16] 1471 April 11th.

[17] 1471 April 14th.

[18] 1471 May 21st.

Nor were things peaceful in the parish while all this was going on. There was a rising in East Anglia because of Clarence[19] and two of the young Beech brothers were caught up in this mischief. No doubt they joined to improve their lot but they paid the price. A sword struck down one brother, and the other died on a new torture instrument imported from abroad:[20] during this torture he virtually implicated the whole village of Rollesby, especially the Freemans and Godwins of whom he had a special dislike. Fortunately I stood in high enough favour to deny the validity of his death claims. It was easily done in all conscience; all the Freemans and Godwins were interested in was closh and kayles.[21]

I was annoyed at this because I had received an opportunity to travel to London with a fellow cleric to see the new printed books[22] but had to delay the enjoyment of this respite to save the villagers being examined one by one. This episode did not endear the Beech family to the people.

While the village was fuming at the intrigues of the Beech family Edward IV suddenly died[23] in his prime after a few day's illness: they say it was because of his promiscuous behaviour.[24] His brother, Gloucester, was made Protector for the young Edward V but almost before this piece of news reached Rollesby it was followed by the news that Edward V was declared illegitimate and, with his nine-year old brother Richard, was cast into the Tower. We had no sooner gleaned this news than we were told that Gloucester was the new King Richard III[25] and that his son was to be invested as the new Prince of Wales at York. No one in the village or elsewhere liked this usurpation especially since the two princes were never heard of again. I had learned to keep out of politics because one never knows who will be in power next, but I heard because I listen. Everywhere I went, from Rollesby to Yarmouth, from Yarmouth to Norwich everyone was

---

[19] 1477. Clarence, implicated in East Anglia Rising is imprisoned in tower and murdered there the following year on February 14th. Clarence was the King's brother and a possible heir to the throne! According to Shakespeare he died in a barrel of malmsey wine: a legend which held good in the 16th century.

[20] 1468. The Duke of Exeter imported the rack, first used in the Tower of London.

[21] Closh and Kayles, a form of skittles forbidden about this time by statute.

[22] 1476-7. Caxton sets up printing press in precincts of Westminster Abbey.

[23] 1483 April 9th.

[24] Probably from appendicitis, unknown in those days.

[25] 1483 July 6th. Gloucester crowned King Richard III.

suspicious of Richard III. He was regarded as a dangerous usurper and a man who could not be trusted. They say we should have taken warning of this because of his physical deformity,[26] but one of the holiest men I have ever known was terribly deformed in his body.

Nor was this the end of the civil war: the King could not be trusted. Even his great supporter, Buckingham, rose against him and was duly executed in Salisbury.[27] However, Buckingham was part of the Beaufort family and therefore Lancastrian. His son, the Earl of Richmond, Henry Tudor crushed Richard III at the famous battle of Bosworth.[28] The soldiers in the King's army had no heart to fight for such a monstrous king and Richard III was slain on the field and carried naked to his burial place without ceremony. That ended the civil war and Henry VII is now our king, supported by both Yorkists and Lancastrians because of their mutual detestation of Richard III. There is a sense of peace in the land at long last: even the villagers have taken to football on the green[29] and stopped talking about the ups and downs of the great families they have never seen. I thought it could be a time for me to seek preferment now the country is less restless. The civil war had taken thirty years and I am too old to venture out of the parish unlike the rumours of one, Christopher Columbus, who has discovered a new world across the great seas[30] and Henry VII has commissioned a John Cabot[31] for similar discoveries. Such travels are beyond my comprehension: I have travelled to London twice in my life, but to cross the seas so far and discover new lands is something I find difficult to contemplate: the world is changing. I have seen kings and queens come and go in my time here in Rollesby. Much of it I have had on good authority, because a local man, John Paston, passes on the information. He was MP for Norfolk,[32] but of latter days has been more concerned about his property and the will of a Sir John Fastolf regarding property in Caister.[33] The case of John Paston illus-

---

[26] Hunchbacked.

[27] 1483 November 2nd.

[28] 1485 August 22nd.

[29] 1486. The word 'football' is first applied to a game where the ball is kicked.

[30] 1492. Christopher Columbus discovers Bahamas, Cuba and Haiti.

[31] 1496. Henry VII gives patronage to John Cabot.

[32] Barber, R (Editor) (1981) *The Pastons* Folio Society, London, p.80.

[33] Barber, R (Editor) (1981) *The Pastons* Folio Society, London, p.74. Sir John Fastolf died November 5th 1459: the probate on his will was a concern for many years in the Paston Letters.

trates the problems of this day and age: it is a period with no real law and order. If a man had a claim against another he will not stop short of murder and assault to gain his way. Even jurors go in fear of their lives. If a man is powerful enough or noble enough he can take over that to which he has no legal right. The sheriff of Norfolk told John Paston that it was useless to think of suing Robert Hungerford, Lord Moleyns, because the Sheriff had received 'writing from the King that he make such a panel as to acquit the Lord Moleyns'.[34] There is no recourse to law in a day and age when the greed of important men has led us to the brink of anarchy.

We nearly had similar problems with the Huggs: after the execution of his son the old man died and his land was claimed by the Beech family. In times gone by the Huggs had been villeins but they had been granted the land by the Prior. I claimed the land on behalf of the Church as a case of natural reversion. The Beech family tried to stop me but both the Freeman and Godwin families stood testimony that it was Church land. Normally the Freemans and Godwins are antagonistic towards the Church; they attend Mass only on festive occasions, but they would support the devil if he stood in opposition to the Beeches.

'I tell thee, priest,' old Godwin said to me, 'the Church has treated us badly with these tithes, but the Beeches are worse.'

'The church, Godwin, has a natural right to tithes.'

'And what exactly is a natural right?'

'The Church marries you, baptises and buries you, gives you absolution, blessing and the holy sacraments, and for this the Church must be paid.'

'And grow rich.'

I didn't follow the conversation through, it was enough they stood with me against the Beech family. The Godwins, Freemans, Smyths, and Huggs, and other well known names in the parish have been here since the earliest of times. They move house, leave, return, grow in wealth in one generation and lose it in the next. There was a time when the Beech family was poor and the Freemans rich: no doubt these fortunes will change again with their children. It is the same at national level, one moment the Yorks, next the Lancasters, all ambition and power, true amongst the great families and true

[34] Trevelyan, G M (1945) *English Social History* Longmans, London, p.60.

in the parish. If, dear reader, I have told you more about national events than local it is mainly because at local level the civil war did not touch us, but we talked of nothing else. Indeed it seemed to me that the more fractious the national scene became the more fractious it was in the parish. It was as if if the nobles of the land could behave the way they did then so could ordinary people. When it was rumoured that a well-known landed character had a mistress as well as a series of whores it almost caused an outbreak of fornication in the village. 'If they can and get away with it why can't we' was unsaid but felt. So when the lords of the land went to war over land so did villagers. There was a continuous stream of contentious claims against one another's landholdings. Who can blame the villagers when we had a panoramic view of the misbehaviour of our betters?

I did achieve one heart's desire and built the porch to the church last year.[35] I found the money from a well-endowed gentleman, one Edmund Churche. He gave ten marks and with this we were able to make the north porch a fine construction. It is a fine addition, so long as my successors and I can stop Smithy changing horseshoes in there every times it rains. I hope that whoever walks through that porch on a rainy day will remember me, John Brygge, and pray for my soul.

---

[35] *Norfolk and Norwich Archaeological Society* (1959) N&NAS, Norwich. Vol.38, p.262. 10 marks left by Edmund Churche for a new North Porch.

CHAPTER 16

ooooo

Bartholomew Northern (1497-1519) *including* John Bulman (1497)

Henry VII, Henry VIII - Tudor despotism

Dear Readers,

I have been the rector of St George's, Rollesby for over twenty years but I fear I will not make the same target of service as my predecessor, the Reverend John Brygge. He came as a young man and died in post: he never moved because of the civil war. He was, I gather from the parishioners, a man obsessed with the politics of his betters, and would frequently hold forth on the subject of Lancastrians and Yorkists. However, he is remembered kindly because he had the good sense to stop most of our young men joining the itinerant armies and there was little loss of life in the village despite the blood letting elsewhere in the country. He had his critics of course; what clergyman does not? Some say he was a coward and when soldiers were passing through the village he could not be found; it was rumoured he used to hide in his priest's house or the church tower. On the other hand he argued forcibly with those proposing to take sides and thereby probably saved their lives. On the whole he is remembered well, most especially for standing up against the Beech family and doing his job as a parish priest. He did visit the sick and dying, and there was a daily Mass without fail, even if few people attended except on Sundays. I, on the other hand, came for a few years and stayed twenty, but I am old now and am sure

I will be buried alongside John Brygge. Just before I came there had been another Rector by the name of John Bulman but no sooner had he arrived than he fell ill and died. He took only one Sunday service, spent two days in bed and was buried the next Saturday. It certainly reminded the villagers of our mortality.

I did build into the south-east corner of the sanctuary a stone cubicle. I had intended to use it as a place to deposit altar material but it proved too small. Sometimes I have used it as a confessional because it is open to public view and I can see from this vantage point if anyone is eavesdropping. Generally it has proved most unsatisfactory and of latter years I have disregarded it.[1] My patron, James Bois, thought I had gone mad. Sadly he died in 1509 and his son Richard shows little interest in the church.[2]

The village of Rollesby is poor and undermanned on the farms[3] and there is a certain degree of sluggishness amongst the work-folk. They plant only sufficient grain for their own needs and leave much to pasture. If it were not for the occasional swan, rabbit and bird I would sometimes go hungry.[4] When I first came, I was unpopular because I had been asked to collect Peter's Pence[5] along with the tithes: fortunately William Palmer[6] from Greater Ormesby took it over; he is a man of some avarice. When I first took the parish on, Henry VII was well and truly on the throne. He was Welsh, but Lancastrian by birth and he had the good sense to marry Elizabeth of York, Edward IV's daughter, and this kept both sides happy and a civil war at bay. Henry VII cherished justice, and there were many hangings at the start of the reign, but certainly it is now safer to travel than the time before he was king. I gathered he had his problems with pretenders to the throne, usually stirred up in France, especially Burgundy. One was too

---

[1] Pevsner, N (1976) *The Buildings of England: North-East Norfolk and Norwich* Penguin Books, Middlesex, p.305. 'most interesting still the unexplained cubicle in the south east corner with an entry (with four centred head) from the altar as well as from the west. It is only 4'6" by 3'6" and 6'8" high: it is very small for a vestry and not well guarded for a treasure chamber.'

[2] Bates, Ann. Private research from the *Norfolk Archaeological Society*. The patronage stayed with the Bois family until 1541 when it passed to the Cappes family.

[3] Even as late as this period the rural areas felt the effect of the 1348-9 Black Death. Before the Black Death the population was between 4 and 5 million. At the end of the 15th century it was only 2.25 million, though during the next 100 years it was to rise by 90%.

[4] Seabirds were a popular part of the diet.

[5] 'Peter's Pence' was levied on land of a certain value: it was 1p a year and sent to Rome. The Archdeacon of Wells was the chief taxman.

[6] William Palmer, Vicar of Greater Ormesby, 1494-1534.

funny for words; he was Lambert Simnel who was crowned in Dublin as King Edward VI[7] and arrived to claim the crown. He lost and the King made him work in the kitchens![8] This was seen as quite a funny punishment except by Godwin's wife who looks after my kitchen: she claimed she could be the queen pretender. More serious than this was the pretender Perkin Warbeck who claimed to be one of the lost princes in the Tower: this was not so amusing and he was soon executed.[9] The Irish of course did their best to cause trouble, but the king's army had artillery that knocked the Irish castles down. The Irish are quite capable of using artillery but they can't make them; they lack the means, thank God.

We had an Irish priest pass through the village and he stayed a month. As soon as the locals heard he was Irish at first they all wanted to throw him back on the road. Instead they liked him: he drank with them in the Stable Inn and they enjoyed his stories. They were tall stories but the locals did not mind. He was only in his thirties but had the locals any historical sense they would have realised he would have had to have been at least eighty years old to have seen all the things he claimed.

'I tell thee, Father,' Godwin said to me, 'if all priests were like that Irishman the church would be full. If all Irishmen are like that priest I like the Irish.'

'Just because he drinks you under the table doesn't make him a good priest.'

'He's one of the people,' Godwin retorted.

'A priest cannot be one of the people; he must be apart to a certain extent so they can come to him, he's not just one of the boys.'

'We can go to him; he's always where we are, in the inn.'

There was no point in arguing. Old Godwin thought I was stand-offish so I shrugged my shoulders and left him to meditate upon the drinking priest from the Irish land. The travelling priest had only been gone three months when Godwin discovered his youngest daughter was pregnant by the Irishman. That changed his mind and he has always been more respect-

---

[7] 1487 May 24th.

[8] 1487 June 16th. The battle of Stoke near Newark. Simnel is defeated, captured and sent to royal kitchens; Lincoln is killed: Lovell escapes but died in hiding.

[9] 1499 Nov 21st. Perkin Warbeck executed in the Tower of London after an alleged conspiracy with Edward, Earl of Warwick.

ful of my position since. After that the locals were never too happy with people who were not local and certainly not foreigners. It was not that long ago that Londoners rose and attacked foreign workers and their property.[10] Fortunately Rollesby is not a prosperous place and attracts few outsiders.

Henry VII was good at keeping the French at bay. He aligned himself with Spain and in his reign matters looked quite prosperous. I was one of the first men in the area to receive the new shilling:[11] I kept it for years but necessity made me part with it for housekeeping. It was a more peaceful time than we had been accustomed to, although one or two of our young bloods talked of joining a private army of the Earl of Suffolk,[12] but his early imprisonment by the King brought that to nothing. I was personally concerned when the King died[13] because his son, Prince Arthur,[14] had predeceased him. However, we need not have worried because his next son, our current king, Henry VIII, married Catherine of Aragon, his brother's widow. They had a son but he lasted only fifty-two days.[15] He now has a daughter Mary,[16] so all seemed stable again.

The locals liked Henry VIII because he thrashed the French again; they called it the Battle of the Spurs[17] because the French fled the field so fast. While the King was achieving victory in France the Scots invaded but they were crushed by the Earl of Surrey even though the enemy outnumbered us two to one.[18] As a nation we are regaining our respect and it shows even in village attitudes.

The King is something of a theologian and his theological works have pleased the Pope. I am concerned, as are other clerics, with his choice of Thomas Wolsey: because it was rumoured that the King has a dislike of hereditary peers he chooses people of a mean estate. Wolsey, and I hope he

---

[10] 1517 May 1st. Evil May Day riots in London: artisans attack foreign workers and their property.

[11] 1489 November 29th. Henry VII reforms coinage; first gold pound coin (sovereign) is minted. Then in 1504 the shilling coin worth 12 pence; the first English coin to carry recognisable portrait of a king.

[12] 1506 April 24th. Edmund de La Pole, Earl of Suffolk, imprisoned in Tower as the chief Yorkist claimant: he was executed in 1513 June 4th.

[13] 1509 April 21st. Henry VII dies at Richmond Palace.

[14] 1502 April 2nd. Arthur died in Ludlow.

[15] 1511 January 1st.

[16] 1516 February 8th. The future Queen Mary.

[17] 1513 August 16th. The Emperor Maximilian and Henry VIII defeat the French at Guinegate.

[18] 1513 September 9th. Battle of Flodden: Thomas Howard crushes Scots and James IV killed.

never reads this, was the son of a mean butcher from Ipswich of all places. His father was pilloried for selling bad meat. First the King made him a Papal Legate (which meant that the English Church was under a man of the royal household), then the Bishop of Lincoln,[19] next Archbishop of York,[20] then a Cardinal and finally in 1515 made him Chancellor. Wolsey is corrupt, we all know that: he has an illegitimate son, and while he was still a mere boy Wolsey gave him eleven Church appointments. I must say no more, I have no wish to find myself in the Star Chamber.

In the village we are concerned about enclosures: we are a poor area and it is not too serious, though I gather more so in Ormesby. The Beech family has enclosed much of the common land and it is causing strife and poverty. Wolsey has promised to send commissioners to the rural areas to investigate the problem[21] but we are concerned that the corrupt Beech family will bribe their way through the issues. There is more money to be found in Yarmouth and Norwich, but in the villages it is still a matter of scraping a living, and losing land to the powerful landowners is dangerous for the common purpose of survival. Rollesby has always been a backwater, but stealing the land could lead them and other villagers into revolt.

My main problem in the village has been lack of attendance at the Mass and few come forth for confession unless I put pressure on them. Even the dullest wits in the local inn have discussed the viability of the Mass. They claim that it is no mystery, that the bread and wine do not become the actual body and blood of Christ. This attack on transubstantiation is dangerous. Indeed I have noticed that they are more inclined to attend Matins, Evening Prayer or Compline than the Mass. They gathered much of this silliness from the Irish priest I mentioned earlier. He had picked this nonsense up while travelling in northern Europe. They protest that they cannot follow the sacred language of Latin even though I explain it to them piece by piece. One of the young Freeman family came to see me about this, asking why the Mass had to be in a dead language.

'It's not dead,' I explained. 'It's used throughout Christian lands.'

'But it's no good if we can't follow it.'

---

[19] 1514.

[20] 1514-1531.

[21] 1517 May 27th. Wolsey sends out 17 Commissioners to 35 counties to investigate enclosures.

'It was the language of our Lord,'[22] I exploded.

'I suppose that's the end of the debate,' Freeman said. 'We are not allowed to argue against that.'

I felt I had put him in his place; the idea that the sacred Mass could be read in English was absurd and will never happen. The problem is that most lay people could not care less, and those who show an interest start to be precocious and want to change things. The time will never come when lay people have 'a say' in the affairs of the Church. Having said that, I would prefer some lay people to Thomas Wolsey.

Rollesby's people tend to be insular because they spend most of their time in the fields. The only time I recall them leaving in their droves was a few years ago in 1515 when the French queen and Charles Brandon, Duke of Suffolk, visited Yarmouth.[23] We all flocked there to see the spectacle. The entertainment lasted for three whole days and the Duke was so pleased with Yarmouth's efforts that he promised to try to arrange for the King of France to visit.[24] We all knew this to be unlikely because the kings of France and England are rarely on friendly terms. We had, after all, only gone to see the Queen because it was rumoured she was beautiful.

In this type of rural parish, which is not well endowed, the parish priest has to do all the work. I am expected to take services, prepare the altar, open and shut everything, and even keep the place clean. Nor am I helped when everyone tells me how much better it used to be in the old days, when people came to church on a regular basis. Their having told me this, I am then told again and again what a saint my predecessor was. When I catch them off guard I gather that there were ups and downs with my predecessors and many people stayed away from the Mass as they try to do now. I expect the Rector who takes over from me will get the same treatment: I will be beatified in their memories and it will be claimed that the church used to be packed to overflowing. I shall soldier on and do what I do to the best of my ability in the hope that God will recognise my small service to this community.

---

[22] Jesus spoke a form of Aramaic: the first MSS of the NT were written in common Greek.

[23] Bayne, A D (circa 1880) *History of Eastern England* James MacDonald, Yarmouth. Vol II, p.83.

[24] Bayne, A D (circa 1880) *History of Eastern England* James MacDonald, Yarmouth. Vol II, p.84.

CHAPTER 17

ooooo

Nicholas Carr (1519-1531)

Henry VIII - stirrings of religious unrest

Dear Readers,

Ten years I have worked in this village and during that time have watched a little more wealth slowly creep into the community. My predecessor Bartholomew died in post, as he anticipated. The parishioners spoke highly of him, though he always laboured under the impression that he was not appreciated. I am never sure whether people speak well of the last person to make the new incumbent feel on the wrong foot, or whether it takes a man's death for them to appreciate him. I know that I am a source of some of their jokes, that I am frequently criticised in public and I wonder whether they will change their tune about me after I have gone: I can only hope.

The affairs of the Church are felt especially dangerous during my time here. Although Pope Leo X pronounced the King 'Defender of the Faith',[1] Henry is now causing problems with a suggestion of a divorce. Wolsey, now the Papal Legate, has supreme authority over the Church in England (I could not help but wonder, in the letter requesting me to write this, why there was an obscure reference to the Church *of* England) and twice Wolsey

[1] 1521 October 11th. Pope Leo X confers title 'Defender of the Faith' on Henry VIII for his 'Assertion of the Seven Sacraments', a Latin study refuting Lutheranism.

had tried to get himself elected as Pope.[2] It has been suggested that this was an effort to secure the divorce for the King. Wolsey sent his secretary, Stephen Gardiner, and the King's almoner, Edward Fox, to Rome to seek consent.[3] It can of course never happen: there is no pope who will ever allow the King of England to divorce a queen. Now, I am picking up news from fellow clerics at the cathedral that Wolsey has either been arrested or died, or perhaps both:[4] Wolsey will not be missed but it does not augur well for the Church.

In addition to all this the King has appointed a mere layman as Lord Chancellor for the first time.[5] I gather he is a very clever man and also a man of integrity, but the Lord Chancellor's post has always been a Church appointment, and many highly placed clerics are concerned about what the future holds for the Church. His name is Sir Thomas More[6] and I have to confess that I once was able to read in the cathedral, his book on Utopia:[7] I could not understand it all because my Latin is not very good once I leave the type of vocabulary one finds in the Mass. He had been Speaker[8] and I would have thought that good enough for him. We are all concerned about his friendship with Erasmus and Colet in Cambridge: they want to challenge all that is sacred.

Furthermore there have been serious doctrinal attacks on the Church overseas; some madman called Martin Luther has committed the heresy of attacking the Pope.[9] It will never develop in this country and I am sure he will be burnt as a heretic to save his eternal soul. I know there is some corruption within the Church but the Church itself will eventually solve these

---

[2] 1522 January. Wolsey fails to be elected Pope: instead a Spaniard, Adrian VI. This Pope died in November 1523 and Wolsey tried again only to fail against Cardinal de Medici as Clement VII.

[3] 1528 Feb. And on July 13th 1529 the Pope ordered that the divorce question be settled in Rome.

[4] 1530 November 4th. Wolsey arrested at York and dies at Leicester while under escort to London on November 29th. In December of this year clergy were accused of breaking the Statute Praemunire (v.1353) in recognising Wolsey as legate.

[5] 1529 October 26th. Sir Thomas More is first layman to be appointed as Lord Chancellor.

[6] Elton, G R (1997) *England Under the Tudors* Folio Society, London, p.111-112. 'When Thomas More succeeded Wolsey as Chancellor, and such Bishops as Nix of Norwich and Longland of Lincoln (in whose dioceses the dangers of heresy was greatest) could at last act on their own, a minor wave of persecutions followed: More's record in the matter is rather that of the convinced and high-minded sixteenth-century believer that he was, than that of the nineteenth-century moderate liberal he is so often made out to be.'

[7] 1516. First edition in Latin of Thomas More's *Utopia*, printed and published in Louvrain.

[8] 1523 April. More elected Speaker.

[9] 1516 October 23rd. Wittenberg - Martin Luther's 95 Theses concerning Papal indulgences which are often seen as marking the start of the Reformation.

minor problems. Amongst the problems is the news that in Germany they have had the nerve to print an English translation[10] of the Bible: I really do wonder what will happen next. I have no doubt that if the peasants and workers read the Bible in English, it will be open to abuse, misunderstanding and, apart from putting clerics out of work, it could lead to a revolution in the Church, if not out in society as a whole.[11]

While all this has been going on there has been much fun as far as the court is concerned. Jousting and tilting has become popular with this king: Richard Clere[12] from Ormesby attended the King at one great event called the Field of the Cloth of Gold,[13] so dubbed because of all the splendour and wealth. The Ormesby folk have been boasting about their connection with this event ever since. Some of the less genteel folk have started their own version but by racing horses,[14] and I suspect they are gambling on the event, but I have no doubt this will soon lose its fascination.

More importantly than this has been a studied interest in farm work, and although the workers cannot read, our patron and several serious landowners have turned working the fields into a study. Fitzherbert's[15] book has become quite popular and there are two copies at the cathedral. On a more serious note we are concerned about plagues; in London two or so years ago there was a dreadful outbreak[16] and we have been very cautious about welcoming visitors from the cities.

The Godwin family brought this news back with them and we kept them at a distance until we were convinced they were safe. Young Godwin has trained to be a lawyer: how they afforded the fees I will never understand. Master Beech has implied it was illegally acquired but then he is

---

[10] 1526. German printed English translation of the Bible by William Tyndale reaches London: in Scotland by 1530.

[11] Chadwick, H (Editor) (2000) *Not Angels but Anglicans* Canterbury Press, Norwich, p.127. 'in England there was hostility towards it. In 1523 William Tyndale asked Cuthbert Tunstall, Bishop of London, for help with the necessary expense of translating and printing the New Testament. He was refused, and sought help abroad. By 1526 copies were available, and, by 1527, Robert Necton of Norwich was importing them by the dozen and then by the hundred. Ann Boleyn had a French Testament and probably a Tyndale, too. Thomas More wrote against Tyndale's translation in vitriolic terms, and a royal proclamation of 1530 forbade translations in English, French or Dutch, "printed beyond the sea" to be imported.'

[12] Sir Richard Clere (died 1529) and Lady Alice Clere (died 1538) aunt of Queen Anne Boleyn. His memorial is under the Sanctuary carpet in Ormesby St Margaret's, three miles away.

[13] 1520 June.

[14] 1530. First organised horse racing at York.

[15] 1523. Anthony Fitzherbert's *Book of Husbandry* is first practical manual of agricultural technique.

[16] 1528 July. Sweating sickness (plague) severe in London.

always casting aspersions. As a family, the Beeches seem on the social ascendancy. The Freeman family has had trouble with the youngest son; he went off to be a soldier and was employed by the Duke of Buckingham[17] and this led him into all kinds of problems. After his master was sent from this earthly coil young Freeman, it was rumoured, travelled abroad with a group of mercenaries to fight in Germany. I am not so much worried about his fighting for money, but Germany is full of dissident rebellious people against the Holy Father. I have been asked, because of my learning in theology,[18] to consider how we react, and I have had many interesting and instructive hours with young Godwin on this. I have to confess that although he is trained to be a lawyer, he has a sound mind for theology. It is unusual in a small rural village to find anyone of sound education apart from the patron and one or two local lords. Some of the parishioners are showing more care in the fabric of the church, and we have a set of very valuable vestments at our disposal. I would like to see the bell tower equipped with decent bells and a new silver chalice for the altar, but we are getting there only slowly.

I have not commented widely on local issues simply because they are of little importance considering the breathtaking challenges against the Holy Church: my only fear is that the locals start taking some of these foreign ideas seriously. They worry me too, because I am like other clergy: we tend to be very conservative by nature. I have an intense dislike if not fear of any kind of change. This is especially true if it impinges upon my faith: it is like a challenge I fear to stand against. I fear being tainted by ideas that could lead me down to the recesses of hell itself. I also fear that some of these new ideas, as ridiculous as they are, will appeal to ordinary people like the folk here in Rollesby. If that were to happen, it could have unhappy consequences: either a form of persecution by the authorities or, worse still, people may lose their faith. That has always been my main concern, the faith of my parishioners. If they go wrong I may well be held to account in the day of the final judgement. There are so many winds of change and more often than not it is those who lack learning who are blown into the way of heresy. I know there are heresies and heresies, but some of these foreign ideas are

---

[17] 1521 May 17th. Execution of Edward Stafford, Duke of Buckingham for treason.

[18] This Incumbent, Nicholas Carr, held the degree of Doctor of Divinity.

base and their very nature could cause a weak man to lose his eternal soul. As that weak man's servant in Christ I feel heavily responsible for protecting him from these dangers. Trying to affect what people think, what goes on in their minds, is a difficult and nebulous task, yet my neighbour's soul and therefore mine is at stake.

CHAPTER 18

ooooo

William White (Whight)[1] (1531-1554)

Henry VIII, Edward VI, Mary - when religion became dangerous

Dear Future,

I was the incumbent of two livings, Trowse[2] and Rollesby but I lived most of my time in Rollesby and employed a curate in Trowse simply to collect the tithes. I say 'was' because I am obliged to leave these parishes next week for being honest. I challenge any other rector of this parish to any claim that he has lived through stranger or more devastating times than I experienced in my twenty plus years here. The request has come through to me in the year of our Lord, 1554. Quite how it has arrived is a mystery to me. I used to be a lawyer[3] and I tend to be suspicious of strange requests, especially in this day and age. So much has happened in my time here that there is no sensible or systematic approach I can think of in laying out such a brief note on such a vastly important time. I have seen kings and queens come and go, especially queens! First we were astonished when Henry married Anne Boleyn,[4] Cranmer having pronounced Catherine's marriage void.[5] Then a few years later the King had Anne Boleyn decapitated.[6] The very

---

[1] In some documents White is spelt Whight.

[2] *Norfolk and Norwich Archaeological Society* (1959) N&NAS, Norwich. Vol 32, Part 2, p.89.

[3] This Rector, William White, held a law degree, the LLB.

[4] 1533 January 25th. Henry VIII marries Anne Boleyn, she was crowned on June 1st same year.

[5] 1533 May 23rd.

[6] 1536 May 19th.

same month he married Jane Seymour[7] but she died the following year.[8] Next Thomas Cromwell arranged for him to marry Anne of Cleves[9] but the marriage was annulled in the same year![10] In the month this marriage collapsed he married Catherine Howard,[11] niece of the Duke of Norfolk and with a touch of irony he had Cromwell executed on the very same day as this particular marriage. We had only just grasped the enormity of what was happening when he had the Queen executed[12] and married his sixth wife, Catherine Parr[13] in the same year. I have lived through six queens, something that has never happened before nor is likely to happen again. No one dare make a comment because it is very easy for the axe to fall, and even though this letter is for some far-away period of time I would not have dared write this account if Henry VIII were still alive.[14] Since then I have seen young King Edward VI[15] ascend the throne and die, and now Queen Mary, a monarch who worries those of us who are of the reforming faith.

My patron, Richard Bois, died and the patronage was granted to the Cappes family in 1541: William Cappes had little interest in the area but his wife Ethelreda came to Mass on several occasions. Then in 1550 when there was a redistribution of monastic lands, Anne Shelton, who had been a servant to King Edward and Queen Mary in turn was given a life grant of Rollesby Manor, worth at least £6.13s. The old Berking Manor had been conveyed to the King in 1535 on an exchange of land between Bishop Rugge and Henry.[16] None of this helped with the fabric of the church. The tower bells are in a bad state of repair and the vestments are worn; my wardens, Robert Fferyer and John Yeates[17] do their best, and eventually they raised enough money for two new bells in 1552.[18]

---

[7] 1536 May 30th.

[8] 1537 October 24th.

[9] 1540 January 6th.

[10] 1540 July 9th.

[11] 1540 July 28th.

[12] 1542 February 13th.

[13] 1542 July 12th.

[14] Henry VIII died 1547 January 28th.

[15] Edward VI was 9 yrs and died on July 6th 1553 at Greenwich. Mary proclaimed Queen on July 19th.

[16] Bates, Ann. Private research from the *Norfolk Archaeological Society*.

[17] Bates, Ann. Private research from the *Norfolk Archaeological Society*.

[18] These two bells are inscribed with: '+ hec fit scorum. Campa laude Bonarum' and '+in multis annis. Resonet campa Johis'.

Although nationally these are momentous times, they signify little compared with what has happened to the Church. The year I arrived in the parish, King Henry was recognised as 'Supreme Head' of the English Church as far as the Law of Christ allows, and the clergy were fined.[19] It was not a time to argue, especially since I witnessed in Norwich[20] the death at the stake of Thomas Bilney, a gentle ascetic reformer and a so-called heretic: at night I can still hear his screams. The following year the clergy had to formally submit and we had to accept that there could be no ecclesiastical laws without royal approval.[21] Not only this, but Thomas Cromwell forbade the study of canon law at English universities. No one that I knew was prepared to protest: I shall never forget the flames licking around the skin of Bilney the heretic. Then we had to swear an oath to the succession of Anne Boleyn,[22] which brought to a sudden halt those of my brother clergy who had pronounced on the King's sin. I am grateful for being in Rollesby; it is a place where if you keep yourself to yourself it is possible to avoid the prying eyes of Cromwell and his spies. Cromwell had a grotesque sense of humour: he put Friar Forrest to death by the fire which was started with a large wooden image from a Welsh Shrine which was supposed to have the legend that one day it would start a 'forest' fire. No one but idiots found it amusing.[23]

As the Church reformed itself life could be quite dangerous. When the crown seized all the chantries[24] it did so on the grounds that praying for the souls of the dead was a waste of time because purgatory was a vain fantasy. This worried me as well as my parishioners on two counts. First, few of us want to go to hell, and most of us do not feel good enough for heaven, and so purgatory seems fair and reasonable. Secondly, when we pray for the dead it is not simply to arrange their arrival in heaven, but to indicate our love for them. This denial of prayers for the dead was much more serious than the replacement of the Latin services by a single set of rites in the 1549 Prayer

---

[19] 1531 February. Clergy pay £100,000 to purge breach of Praemunire.

[20] 1531 August 19th. Bilney burnt at the stake in Norwich for heresy.

[21] 1532 April 15th. Formal submission of clergy.

[22] 1534 March 30th. Succession Act: oath required from peers, MPs and clergy; slandering of Boleyn marriage is treason.

[23] 1538. Morrill, J (Editor) (1996) *The Oxford Illustrated History of Tudor and Stuart Britain* Oxford University Press, p.276.

[24] 1547 Chantries Act.

Book. I did not mind even when altars were demolished in 1550 and replaced by wooden tables; not even when Cranmer took out 'sacrifice' from the Mass, and when the forty-two articles of doctrine were published in 1553; all was acceptable, all except the removal of purgatory, which for many of us is our only hope!

After the Act of Supremacy[25] when the King was confirmed as Head of the Church he had Bishop John Fisher and Thomas More beheaded: after that I decided to keep myself hidden away in the Broads and utter nothing of any consequence. That at least was my intention, but twice I became embroiled in national politics. Early in 1536 the smaller monasteries were dissolved and by the end of the decade so were the greater monasteries. The money went straight into the royal coffers, but it caused a social upheaval. At least the monasteries had kept people in employment and looked after beggars and vagrants. Now these people are a positive nuisance despite the Statute against Vagabonds:[26] even the children sing about the problem, 'Hark! Hark! The dogs do bark; the beggars are coming to town. Some gave them white bread, and some gave them brown, and some gave them a good horsewhip, and sent them out of the town.' The local Franciscans who have moved into Church Farm tend to look after such beggars but that is only if they can pass through the village to the farm. Once the alarm is up the Freemans, Godwins, Blacks and Beeches are out chasing them as if they are French infantry.

The new Bible was given to the parish translated into English[27] and the Six Articles published, which were against the Pope: I am no hero so I accepted all that was done by my superiors. I have seen what happens to those who protest. The village has enjoyed the Bible now they can understand it, but they are beginning to ask a good number of questions. It was only a few years ago that they imposed a Prayer Book on us as well.[28]

I rather took to the new Prayer Book, although many clergy did not like the imposition of the same liturgical routine. I had hardly used it when,

---

[25] 1534 November. Act of Supremacy.

[26] 1531 March. Statute against Vagabonds: impotent beggars licensed by JPs; sturdy beggars pilloried or whipped.

[27] 1539. English 'Great Bible', based on translations by Tyndale and Miles Coverdale, circulated to parishes: in the same year the Six Articles which were anti-papal, but reaffirm Catholic doctrines.

[28] 1549 January 15th. Act of Uniformity: imposes Book of Common Prayer: first used in English churches in June 9th the same year.

with Thomas Brooke[29] I was caught up in a serious rebellion lead by Robert Kett from Wymondham. I have no idea what the experts in the future will say about this rebellion but I knew it had to happen. Life had become extremely unfair for ordinary people and, while I do not mind what prayer books we have to read from, I could not stand by and watch parishioners starve and lose their livings.

However far in the future you may be, dear Reader, you will have heard of Robert Kett's rebellion. I saw it first hand because I became involved, and gained much of the original gossip from Alexander Neville.[30] Despite what people may say it was not a political uprising but we went to war because of the economic and social problems in our area.[31] The old system of the village being a viable economic entity under the manor started to disappear at the turn of the century, but by the 1540s most of the strips had been enclosed and even the best freeholders and copyholders were losing their rights to land. Rollesby had more landless labourers than ever before. Because the cloth trade had become profitable more sheep[32] were needed in the newly enclosed land, and the landless were all too tempted to pull the fences down. This consolidation of land, along with inflation, caused they say by the King's continual debasing of the realm's coinage, meant that many villagers in Rollesby, as in many other parts of the kingdom were without work, without their own land, and in danger of starvation. The seasonal weather had not helped and several times we thought we would die from lack of victuals and good water.[33]

The Lord Protector, Lord Somerset,[34] seemed at one stage to be on our side, and good commonwealth men such as the MP, John Hales, and Hugh

[29] 1549. Thomas Brooke of Rollesby was one of the ringleaders in Kett's rebellion along with a William Whight, Rector of Rollesby; a university graduate of King's, a dispossessed clergy. According to a note of 1567 Brooke was a Gent. Of Rollesby who wrote verses. Excerpt from *Norfolk Archaeological Society.*

[30] Champion, M & Sotherton, N (1999) *Kett's Rebellion 1549* Timescape Publishing, Norfolk, p.3. Alexander Neville, secretary to Archbishop Matthew Parker who at the time of Kett's rebellion was serving as Vice Chancellor of Cambridge.

[31] Land, S K (1977) *Kett's Rebellion: The Norfolk Rising of 1549* Boydell Press, Ipswich, p.7.

[32] Land, S K (1977) *Kett's Rebellion: The Norfolk Rising of 1549* Boydell Press, Ipswich, p.9. The Fermors of East Barsham had 17,000 sheep in 1521.

[33] Champion, M & Sotherton, N (1999) *Kett's Rebellion 1549* Timescape Publishing, Norfolk, p.25. In 1542 there was an unprecedented drought: the Thames dried to a trickle and salt water reached only as far as London Bridge. In Reepham the church and High Street burned down because there was no water to fight it.

[34] Lord Somerset fell between two stools, neither pleasing the working classes because he would not go far enough and the landed classes because he went too far: he fell from power in October 1549.

Latimer were equally opposed to the enclosures. We called them commonwealth men because, like me, they were dedicated to a country where the common good for all was seen to be the only Christian way forward. The whole rebellion was made easier because we were some way from London and the potential lordly power in Anglia was rotting in the Tower of London,[35] and Norwich had been weakened by a bad bishop with a corrupt brother.[36] In our part of the world, East Anglia, most of us were of the reforming party[37] and Robert Kett knew that he would gain rapid support. My only concern was his twenty-nine articles of protest. Most of them were fine since they dealt with necessary land reform, but at least six attacked the clergy for enriching themselves, which I considered to be unfair. Nevertheless, in our area, the Fleggs, our two signatories, attached their names, first Symond and then William.[38]

The Rollesby men, especially the Freemans and Blacks were involved with me in joining the rebellion. Ormesby was very quiet in the whole matter. First they did not have the same issues regarding enclosures and, more to the point, their lands belonged to the Sir John Clere family and they were cruelly active against their people.[39]

As you undoubtedly know, the rebellion collapsed, mainly because we failed to take Great Yarmouth,[40] and Robert Kett failed to spread the rebellion. Although we beat Northampton, and despite the fact that we had captured the best artillery, we could not win against Warwick: most of our men were armed only with agricultural tools.[41] The failure to take Yarmouth was serious. The people of that port drove us rebels away and even captured some of the guns that we had taken from Leistofte.[42] The Yarmouth men

[35] Thomas Howard, Third Duke of Norfolk was attainted and sent to the Tower in 1546 for complicity in treason. He stayed there during the reign of Edward VI.

[36] Land, S K (1977) *Kett's Rebellion: The Norfolk Rising of 1549* Boydell Press, Ipswich, p.40. William Rugge, Bishop of Norwich was so cruel in his polices a petition had been sent to the King to have him removed. His brother, Robert, was Sheriff of Norwich in 1537 and Mayor in 1545 and 1550.

[37] Land, S K (1977) *Kett's Rebellion: The Norfolk Rising of 1549* Boydell Press, Ipswich, p.73. Eastern counties ahead of the government in adopting protestant reforms.

[38] Land, S K (1977) *Kett's Rebellion: The Norfolk Rising of 1549* Boydell Press, Ipswich, p.55. Symond English and William Pecke members of the old Hundreds of East and West Flegg.

[39] Sir John Clere, whose family memorials are to be found in Ormesby St Margaret's parish church, had heard the Surrey treason trial and was pro-active in Northampton's army sent to quell the rebellion.

[40] August 17th 1549 was the first attempt to capture Yarmouth.

[41] Champion, M & Sotherton, N (1999) *Kett's Rebellion 1549* Timescape Publishing, Norfolk, p.79.

[42] Lowestoft.

engaged us at Gorleston and many were killed before the day was done.[43]

The main issues were soon forgotten, and Kett's enemies claimed that Robert Kett was a mischief maker who had simply fallen out with the lawyer, Flowerdew.[44] This was untrue: it was a rebellion to draw attention to the fact that villages like Rollesby were being starved to death by greedy landowners; we were no longer prepared to live a servile life. I hope history does not condemn us.[45]

Freeman, Black and I fled by mingling with the crowds. We witnessed the death of Miles the Gunner,[46] they partly hanged him, disembowelled him while he was still alive and then beheaded and quartered him. That was enough for us. We hid ourselves and kept out of the way for some time. Later we heard that Robert Kett was captured at Swannington and his death was inevitable.

I have returned to Rollesby only recently and although the Beech family, who have been enclosing strips as fast as possible, tried to indict me, they failed. Freeman also returned but Black died from an accident in Norwich when a cart, with a drunken lout in charge of the horses, crushed him. Some say I should not have involved myself with politics but my religion tells me that I must fight that which is unjust. How far clergy should be involved with the politics of the world is a problem that will occur again and again. The Church has its own politics: the authorities are doing their best to ensure we all sing the same chant, so to speak, and they have published the forty-two articles of the Church of England. Cranmer wanted the King to grant the power to insist all clergy be obliged to subscribe to them.[47]

My main problem in life has been my wife. I have lived with her most of my life but she has to all appearances been only my housekeeper. A few suspected but dared say nothing, but celibacy was the expected and unreason-

---

[43] Palmer, C H (Editor) (1847) *Foundation of Great Yarmouth (Henry Manship's MS)* Charles Sloman, Yarmouth, p.25.

[44] When the Abbey at Wymondam had been dissolved the townspeople had pleaded for the retention of the church of St Thomas as their parish church. This had been granted but the lawyer and sergeant at arms, Flowerdew had been over zealous in demolition: this contention with the locals, led by Robert Kett had been the spark of the rebellion.

[45] In 1949 a large stone was fixed to the wall of Norwich Castle by the citizens of Norwich in 'reparation and honour to a notable and courageous leader in the long struggle of the common people to escape from a servile life into the freedom of just conditions.'

[46] 1549 August 28th. In Norwich.

[47] 1549. They are the originals of the current Thirty-Nine Articles.

able law of the Church.[48] Under the young but wise Edward VI clergy were allowed to marry, and I promptly did so in order that my parishioners might see I had nothing to hide. In my other parish of Trowse there had been as much gossip as that in Rollesby so it was a relief to marry my so-called housekeeper. No sooner had I married than Edward died and Queen Mary started to reverse all the gains we had made. In November 1553 she published a series of eleven articles that authorised the bishops to deprive of their livings all who had been married. It was a complete change of direction and touched three hundred and thirty two university graduates in this diocese alone. This was serious for the Church and us. The Church could hardly lose so many graduates: as graduates we are distinguished from the rest by having the prefix 'Mr'.[49] I was examined by the Bishop at the cathedral and was given the opportunity to deny marriage. I could not do so because I had married not only in public but more importantly in the eyes of God. I was therefore dispossessed of my living[50] and I cared little. I have saved sufficient to buy some land and I leave Rollesby soon to start a new life. I wish the next man well: he will be safe enough in Rollesby, so long as he keeps himself to himself.

---

[48] During the time of Pope Gregory VII at the end of the 11th century celibacy became the firmly established rule.

[49] *Norfolk and Norwich Archaeological Society* (1959) N&NAS, Norwich. Vol.32, Part 2, p.89.

[50] Thus on the church wall this rector has 'Dispossessed' after his name.

CHAPTER 19

ooooo

John Blomevyle (1555-1586) *including* Hugh Twyford (1554)

Queen Mary, Elizabeth - the first Elizabethan period

Dear Readers,

I have been in the Rollesby parish for thirty years now and so far I have avoided the stake and charges of heresy or treason and have just about managed to control the parish with its many problems. My immediate predecessor was one Hugh Twyford: he was a down and out papist and the locals chased him out after two Sundays. He simply fled and a few months later, in the year 1555, I was appointed.

Before Hugh Twyford was a William White, some kind of fancy lawyer type priest who became involved in Kett's attempted rebellion. He married under the Edwardian legislation and dejectedly watched the rules reversed in the Marian period, leading to his dispossession. This struck me as a serious misfortune; many clergy were secretly married, even Archbishop Cranmer. It is no worse than the arranged marriages that are so prevalent these days. Bishop Chaderton, in 1582, married off his only daughter Joan, aged nine, to a boy of eleven with unhealthy consequences. There was even a rumour a clergyman carried a three-year-old boy, one John Rigmarden in his arms and coaxed him into the words of matrimony to a five-year-old girl and then told him to go and play with her.[1] However, my predecessor, William White, was more interested in the politics of land ownership than

---

[1] Trevelyan, G M (1945) *English Social History* Longmans, London, p.69.

true religion: today, the way events are running, it is a question of religion that occupies all men's minds. I have been asked to give an account of my time here, but I cannot do this without explaining the religious turmoil we have been through and still, I suspect, have to come.

The very word 'religion' means 'binding': it is meant to bind men together and yet I am living through a period of time when it has the opposite effect. It is not that the church is not central: the building binds us, it is the only place large enough for the whole village to meet. They try and cram into the Horse Inn but if it is a serious meeting it has to be the church. The Christian Church is also central in our lives; our bishops and archbishops are national figures, the Church deals with all cases of birth and death, cases of divorce and adultery, of defamation and probate and wills. But the actual religion divides us; it no longer binds us. There are those who call themselves truly Catholic, then there are Protesters, now called Protestants, and there are reformers like Protestants who want the one church. The old Lollard heresy has taken a certain grip and although it will not prevail there are some ideas of the new reforming Protestants that link to the old Lollard movement. The Lollards and most Protestants do not believe in transubstantiation,[2] and now Mary is no longer on the throne I am happy to join myself to that number. I still see the priest as a sort of pipeline between God and His people, and the Holy Communion, as we now call it, connects people with Christ's sacrifice and God's grace. My predecessor was an old fashioned papist and spent all his time selling rosaries and candles, for profit. He also prayed incessantly to the saints: he treated each saint like a specialised lawyer, so the parishioners had to pray to St Margaret of Antioch every time there was a difficult birth. Nor would he attend what he called Mass on a regular basis, or go more than a mile to hear a deathbed confession.[3] As a Protestant minister I do not believe God needs a middleman, an intermediary, but each man can depend on his own faith: I am only there to assist. When the papists elevate the host, they act as a superstitious witch-doctor, worshipping a god made from bread: as a Protestant minister I am

---

[2] The belief that the bread and wine become the actual body and blood of Christ.

[3] Morrill, J (Editor) (1996) *The Oxford Illustrated History of Tudor and Stuart Britain* Oxford University Press, p.265. Two of the most common complaints about clergy.

more of a teacher.[4] Everything is predestined and although I am not for 'leaping out of Peter's boat'[5] I believe we will have to unless Rome opens itself for reform. In my father's day, during the reign of King Henry VIII, you had to believe in the Mass and deny the Pope, it was very difficult because all too easily you could be either a traitor or a heretic. I do not deny the central importance of the Mass or Communion. In fact, out of my own funds I purchased from Norwich in 1567 a new silver chalice.[6]

The parish has taken very easily to the new reforms; my papist predecessor made it so much easier as well. It strikes me that the people of East Anglia, especially the rural ones, are more blessed with insight and want to rid themselves of superstitions. They have taken to the new prayer books with considerable ease.[7] I have no doubt this prayer book will bind the Church together. Wherever a person travels in this part of Christendom the same service will be used. It is like a series of bricks placed in the right order and will give order to the Church.

We have had several changes back and forth. At one stage we were expected to throw the altars out of the church and put in simple wooden tables more appropriate to the commemorative act of Holy Communion than to the sacrifice of the Mass.[8] Old Godwin was all for this change, but Freeman and Black insisted that the altar be kept at the back of the church. I was never sure whether it was because they thought the old papist ways would return or whether they were being cautious. We had Edward VI reforming, Queen Mary going back to Rome,[9] our current Queen Elizabeth a Protestant but she has no heir: heaven knows what will happen next. The sweating sickness in London is seen by many as a punishment by God for all the changes: it is a dreadful illness, the victim breaks out in a sweat and a few hours later he or she is dead. I think Freeman and Black by not losing the altar are hoping Rollesby will avoid the sweating sickness by having a

---

[4] Morrill, J (Editor) (1996) *The Oxford Illustrated History of Tudor and Stuart Britain* Oxford University Press, p.269.

[5] An expression for leaving Rome.

[6] Still in use today - Pevsner, N (1976) *The Buildings of England: North-East Norfolk and Norwich* Penguin Books, Middlesex, p.305.

[7] 1552. Act of Uniformity imposes Second Book of Common Prayer: Eucharist a purely commemorative act. 1559 May, revised edition of Prayer Book. By June 24th used in all parish churches.

[8] Morrill, J (Editor) (1996) *The Oxford Illustrated History of Tudor and Stuart Britain* Oxford UP, p.278.

[9] 1554 November. Formal reconciliation with Rome and the mass reinstated.

foot in both camps. I cannot blame them: I recanted once to avoid the fire, we are after all only men. I have it on good authority that the Queen's Secretary of State, William Cecil, who is clearly a Protestant, keeps a certificate in his desk that he regularly attended the Mass during Mary's reign: it is signed by the Vicar of Wimbledon.[10] If a man like him is cautious why should not parish priests and their flock take care?

We tread a fine line; we still wear vestments and make the sign of the cross at baptisms[11] and until the Pope excommunicated and deposed the Queen[12] it felt best to choose the middle way. The bishops have produced the Thirty-Nine Articles and at least this has cleared some of the confusion with the doctrinal muddle into which we are all sinking. I can still clearly recall John Hopton, Bishop of Norwich, who was a zealous adherent of Princess Mary. He was a bigoted papist[13] and Mary on her accession promoted him to the see. He persecuted the Protestants in great fury, and survival during his time was not easy. He died in 1559 and we happily buried him in the cathedral.

In a way, survival means turning a blind eye and keeping one's own counsel. The last Bishop of Norwich, Bishop Parkhurst, was an expert at this, but his successor, Bishop Freke is dangerous.[14] He has sternly demanded conformity and the type of conformity he demands has put him in conflict with the leading Protestant gentry in Norfolk, including I might add, the son of the Lord Keeper and even his own Diocesan Chancellor. In 1583 he was embarrassed when it was discovered that his butler and lawyer were regularly attending Mass.[15]

So my dear reader, I hope you can understand the difficult times through which the Church is travelling. I am, like my people in Rollesby, Protestant in terms of belief, a little Catholic in style of worship given the demands of

---

[10] Morrill, J (Editor) (1996) *The Oxford Illustrated History of Tudor and Stuart Britain* Oxford University Press, p.280.

[11] Morrill, J (Editor) (1996) *The Oxford Illustrated History of Tudor and Stuart Britain* Oxford University Press, p.282.

[12] 1570.

[13] Bayne, A D (circa 1880) *History of Eastern England: Volumes I-II* James MacDonald, Yarmouth. Vol.II, p.110.

[14] Morrill, J (Editor) (1996) *The Oxford Illustrated History of Tudor and Stuart Britain* Oxford University Press, p.284.

[15] Morrill, J (Editor) (1996) *The Oxford Illustrated History of Tudor and Stuart Britain* Oxford University Press, p.284.

the Prayer Book, but having to be prepared to change attitudes in case we are faced with the stake. In our time we have seen Thomas Cranmer, author of the prayer book and Archbishop, burnt at the stake[16] and Cardinal Pole ordained priest on one day and consecrated Archbishop of Canterbury two days later.[17]

It was no surprise that the Cardinal died only twelve hours after his beloved Queen Mary.[18] Within a year we saw the anti-papal laws of Henry VIII restored, and an Act against papal bulls which declared all instructions from the Pope treasonable.[19] God above must wonder what we are doing; it was no wonder St Paul's Cathedral in London nearly toppled when it was struck by lightning.[20] One of the greatest sorrows of my time was the loss of our own beautiful rood screen during my predecessor's time. Along with all the other changes demanded was its removal. It had the crucified Christ, with His mother Mary and John standing at the foot of the cross. It was supposed to have been replaced by one carrying the regal arms to enshrine who was the head of the Church, but we never had the means to replace it and now it is a void.[21]

In the meantime good old Rollesby kept its head; at least we were not struck by lightning.

'What next?' Freeman was always asking me.

'Keep our heads down and follow conscience,' I replied.

'And what if my conscience leads me to the stake?'

'You will be a martyr if your views eventually predominate.'

'And if they don't?'

'You will have been the enemy.' He did not like this.

'What will you do?' he persisted.

'I am no martyr. I shall recant and then recant again. I have no intention of becoming a public spectacle on some Norwich bonfire. I shall keep my views in my head and say what is necessary to avoid following Cranmer and others into the fire.'

---

[16] 1556 March 21st.

[17] 1556 March 22nd. Cardinal Pole ordained priest on Mar 20th and consecrated Archbishop on this date.

[18] 1558 November 17th.

[19] 1571 May. Act against papal bulls.

[20] 1561 May. Lightning destroys spire and sets roof ablaze of St Paul's Cathedral.

[21] Evans, George Ewart (1977) *Ask the Fellows who Cut the Hay* Faber & Faber, Boston, p.132. 'the rood was taken down and destroyed in most churches during this time.'

'Well,' he replied, 'I hope you consider it your duty to guide your parishioners either to say nothing or the right thing at the right time.'

And that, dear reader, is what I did. We were Catholic, then Protestant, then Catholic, then Protestant: we had feet in two camps, but our hearts were in one. We were Protestants, we were the English Church, but we were prepared to compromise and that way we survived. No martyrs in Rollesby, but we lived and we enjoyed the Horse Inn.

When I say we had no martyrs we came close to having one on the political front. Thomas Brooke[22] of Rollesby with friend George Redman of Cringleford found himself caught up in the Norfolk Rising of 1569. The main cause had been that our traditional market of English cloth was in danger because of too many Huguenot settlers in Norwich. This sense of unease and suspicion was increased in the locality when the Duke of Norfolk was sent to the Tower.[23] The JPs were instructed to keep public order and on December 1st the new Sheriff of Norwich, Sir Christopher Heydon, assured the Privy Council that all was well in the Shire, whereas we the local people knew that serious resentment was simmering.[24] It was no surprise when just before Christmas the men of Kenninghall, the trusty tenants of the Duke, showed their hand: they had been encouraged by the successful rebellion in the North by the Earls of Northumberland and Westmoreland. It was soon put down and we have not seen anything of Thomas Brooke to this day. Rollesby is a quiet village but there is always one ready to join rebellion.

The Manor of Rollesby changed hands in my time: Lord North bought the reversion of the Manor of Rollesby from the Bishop of Norwich. There is talk that he will build an estate up by the Martham Road.[25,26] Then in 1561 Thomas Gawdays, of Rockland, sold the reversion of Rollesby Manor to William Cappes of Acle with all the rights, liberties and members of the

---

[22] *Norfolk and Norwich Archaeological Society* (1959) N&NAS, Norwich. Vol.32, Part 2, p.76.

[23] 11th October.

[24] *Norfolk and Norwich Archaeological Society* (1959) N&NAS, Norwich. Vol.32, Part 2, p.73.

[25] *Norfolk and Norwich Archaeological Society* (1959) N&NAS, Norwich. Vol.34, Part 1, p.20.

[26] Lloyd, Virginia *Landscape Analysis: A Study of the Parish of Rollesby, Norfolk* unpublished private research. 'presumably, when Edward Lord North became Lord in 1558, he and his descendants and successors subsequently inhabited the Hall, as their rightful home. By extension, it is logical that the new Hall was built after this date, in a bid to improve and personalise their acquired manor house, and firmly stake their claim.'

advowson of the Church of St George's.[27] Even at the local level all is change and concern for us.

In the meantime Yarmouth has grown to be of some importance: in 1559 the Port obtained the important privilege of holding an Admiralty Court[28] on every Monday throughout the year. This gave them the power to try all the maritime causes within their jurisdiction except that of piracy. Yarmouth has sufficient piracy within its own market!

The Guildhall of Yarmouth is used as a place of feasting. I recall an occasion on March 18th 1563[29] when all were ordered to hear Divine Service and were then charged 2/8d towards a feast. All brothers and sisters had to pay 12d. The feast was good though: more spice cakes, breads and ale than I could consume.

A few years after this the Queen gave licence for a body of seafaring refugees to live in Yarmouth.[30] Some of the local people did not like the idea of overseas refugees, but they are very parochial and small-minded in their outlook. They are when all is said and done, refugees. When we appear before our Lord at the last judgement how will we look if it transpires He was there: I never forget those lines from the New Testament, 'Where were you when I was hungry and thirsty, where were you when I was in prison?' These refugees are Flemings and they established our fishing industry better than did the Dutch who have always held the upper hand in this way of making money and providing food. In fact these Fleming refugees have brought wealth to the area.

The Queen herself was due in Yarmouth[31] and the town made for her a silver cup in the form of a ship. She never left Suffolk for there was a plague in Yarmouth. Some lords of her retinue came and they were royally entertained.

Despite these high occasions, everyday life is really a matter of keeping oneself to oneself to avoid having to go to the block. With the religious changes and all the rebellions and especially having landed gentry in the

---

[27] Bates, Ann. Private research from the *Norfolk Archaeological Society*.

[28] Bayne, A D (circa 1880) *History of Eastern England* James MacDonald, Yarmouth. Vol.II, p.114.

[29] Bayne, A D (circa 1880) *History of Eastern England* James MacDonald, Yarmouth. Vol.II, p.114.

[30] Bayne, A D (circa 1880) *History of Eastern England* James MacDonald, Yarmouth. Vol.II, p.117. They established the Yarmouth fishing industry.

[31] 1578. Bayne, A D (circa 1880) *History of Eastern England* James MacDonald, Yarmouth. Vol.II, p.127.

area, clergy even in remote rural areas have to walk with caution. It is probably safer to be a soldier than a cleric in this day and age. Looking back I feel as if I have been finding my way through a maze while at the same time leading my sheep in such a way they too do not lose their heads or their souls.

CHAPTER 20

ooooo

Baldwin Easdell (1586-1589)

Elizabeth I - anti-Catholicism

Dear Future Readers,

I have no idea who will be reading this in the future. I will not know whether you are Catholic or Protestant, whether the papist plots eventually succeeded or whether Protestants survived. Perhaps, as is my ardent hope, Protestants reformed the Catholic Church and there is but one Church again. My predecessor, John Blomevyle, was much loved in Rollesby: he taught them how to survive during these turbulent times. He died in harness and is much missed. Thomas Brooke, a gentleman of the parish and well known for his verse writing[1] speaks most highly of John Blomevyle. It is rumoured that Thomas Brooke was mixed up in Kett's Rebellion, but he never says anything to me. He keeps Robert Shancke company: Robert was admitted[2] to Gonville and Caius College, Cambridge in 1561 and is probably the best-educated man in the village. The two of them generally attend church but they seem suspicious of me. I feel insecure because the parishioners have grown to distrust churchmen. I keep telling them I am a safe Protestant, but they are always looking in their huts and cupboards for seminary priests, or worse still concealed Jesuits.[3] I am, I keep

---

[1] Bates, Ann. Private research from the *Norfolk Archaeological Society.*

[2] Bates, Ann. Private research from the *Norfolk Archaeological Society.*

[3] 1574. First seminary priests arrive in England and in 1580 the first Jesuits. In 1577 the execution of priests began.

telling them, their minister, not a Catholic priest. They are concerned that if a Jesuit or priest is found locally then all hell will break loose. There is no question that Catholics are not going to leave our shores easily. Catholicism is not going to die; it is going to have to be actively controlled.

Nor can the Catholics be trusted; we are under threat from Spain and other Catholic countries and the papists are trying to murder our queen. I was actually in London when Sir Anthony Babington and two others were executed at Tyburn;[4] no one in my circle is other than grateful to Walsingham for seeking out these conspirators. We positively cheered when the Court of Star Chamber[5] sentenced Queen Mary to death, and drank Queen Bess's health when the Catholic queen was executed at Fotheringhay.[6]

However, we do not live in easy times because suspicion is deep and corrupts everything. Whenever I am in company I am careful what I say, because you never know who is going to repeat what one has said or to whom: even a humorous aside can be dangerous. If there is someone in the company whom I do not recognise I almost pretend I am mute. I cannot believe that recently a Member of Parliament urged the Commons for greater freedom of speech[7] in this day and age: the man was either a fool or had too much courage. I was not surprised that he was imprisoned for his stupidity. In this day and age one must be circumspect, keep to the Prayer Book, keep one's own counsel, and above all keep out of the way of mysterious strangers. In this sense, Rollesby is an ideal place to live, as everyone knows everyone and the moment a strange face appears he is greeted with open hostility. I can recall when a new man called Jack Snape appeared in the village; although he regularly attended Divine Office the village remained suspicious of his presence for many years. The parish chest[8] was tampered with one day and the new man had to flee. It was years later we discovered the would-be thief was someone else.

One of Blackie's sons has gone to sea, and it was rumoured that he

---

[4] 1586 September 20th.

[5] 1586 October 25th.

[6] 1587 February 8th.

[7] 1587 March 1st. Peter Wentworth MP again imprisoned for urging greater freedom of speech.

[8] Evans, George Ewart (1977) *Ask the Fellows who Cut the Hay* Faber & Faber, Boston, p.148. 'each parish had a chest usually kept in the vestry, it contained any valuables and special fabrics.'

served with Drake when we sank the Spanish ships sent to invade us.[9] This very threat of foreign invasion should warn all and sundry of the dangers of supporting the papists. I know for a fact that the proposed threat stopped many wavering. The Huggins and Heap families have, we believe, erred on the side of the Catholic, but once they learned the Spanish were about to invade they became staunch Protestants overnight!

Just as I arrived there was trouble with a travelling Jesuit: he was making his way to the Midlands having landed at Great Yarmouth and the Beech family gave him shelter. The parishioners were delighted with the news and leaked the information rapidly. The Beeches have never been popular, and when the authorities examined their house they discovered a crucifix, holy water stoups and more candles than a cathedral would need. Freeman and his local cohorts were thrilled at the discovery but badly disappointed that the Beech family escaped. They simply disappeared. They have lost their house and holding but it was rumoured the family were excessively rich and that they have established themselves in another town. For their sakes I hope the local people never find out. I am not entirely sure what has happened in the past but it goes back a long way and there is considerable bad feeling.

In the church we use morning and evening prayer and celebrate the Communion service once every three months. The church is reasonably well attended but I am not convinced that this is because of spiritual needs. Neighbour wants neighbour to know that they are devout in the Protestant cause. Another reason I am suspicious is that when I am reading the office and the exhortations, snoring often interrupts me. My sermons are instructive teaching sermons, I am careful to keep to the Thirty-Nine Articles and I never preach for more than an hour. The old crucifixes and thuribles have all disappeared, as have the candlesticks. There are those who gossip that they were hidden in the graveyard, and that the Beech family had retrieved them. They were certainly not in the house when it was searched.

I am living in a tiny rector's house north of the church, and it appears so much smaller now Thomas and Margaret Godwin have built their palace across the lane to Filby. It was duly completed in 1583[10] and now they have

---

[9] 1588. The Spanish Armada defeated.

[10] This cottage, known as 'Old World Cottage' still stands to this day. It was the birthplace of the famous Thomas Godwin DD, Cromwell's chaplain. See later.

had a stone laid in the side with the date, 1583 and 'God Bless us, TG & MG'. Many of the locals are quite jealous of the living space, but old Godwin, whose roots in the village stretch back centuries, is a keen supporter of the Church: and I enjoy the occasional meal there. Godwin has risen in the world and seems particularly pleased that the Beech family had to flee. He has purchased most of their land from the Crown.

Unlike some parishes, Rollesby still has a large number of smallholders, particularly on the heath and to the south of the church in the small valley - if one can describe it as a valley in flat Norfolk. It does make the collecting of tithes tedious, and I am forever sending my man and his wagon out to collect every tenth sheaf of corn.[11] I also pay for the occasional woman and her children to stone pick my land on the grounds that the fewer stones the more the soil will grow good crops. They also work at the weeds with their grubbers and dock-chisels.[12] Mrs Godwin is particularly effective. They work hard but I often wonder what the future holds for them.

As regards my own future I am uncertain. While Rollesby is a quiet and safe place the financial rewards are appalling. I am hoping to move to a more financially rewarding benefice in the future. The main problem has been the whispering. There is always, as I have mentioned, the possibility of being misreported with the direct consequence that a harmless word lands one up in front of a tribunal where not only one's living is in danger of being suspended, but also one's life may be at stake, literally. Then there is the usual gossip. No one cares if Blackie is up to something, or whether Huggs drinks too much. If you have money like the Beech family used to have, people sit back and wait for you to die so they can gloat. The Godwin family, once they had built their splendid home, became the subject of gossip, mainly as to how they could afford such a fine place. The implication was, of course, that Godwin had involved himself in some nefarious dealings in Yarmouth smuggling. In point of fact Godwin is a very religious man, very clean living and simply gained his wealth by prudent saving and good husbandry. As the Rector, I have found myself the main focus for idle tongues.

---

[11] Evans, George Ewart (1977) *Ask the Fellows who Cut the Hay* Faber & Faber, Boston, p.98. 'the tithe is a church tax ... the church based its right to do so in reference to the Old Testament; but it is probable that the tithe is a vestige of the old Roman tribute of the one tenth. Up to the beginning of the 19th century most tithes were paid in kind; but under the Tithe Act of 1836 a rent charge was established.'

[12] Old weeding tools.

My main church officer is always polite and pleasant to my face, impeccably polite and supportive and yet I have it on good authority that when my back is turned he spends most of his leisure time criticising me and waiting for me to make some small error. I cannot react to this scandalous behaviour because it is never done within my presence. The people who tell me this I trust, but if I let the cat out of the bag there would be trouble because as the senior lay officer in the church others are afraid of his caustic tongue. The only consolation is that whenever I meet other parish clergy they tell similar stories. I suppose that one of the main reasons is that the villagers put the rector on some sort of plinth and they would like to see him fall off; it would create a sense of excitement in some dreary lives. It is of course impossible to please all the people all the time, so I do my best the way I see it. I pray and meditate and hope that the gossip remains a nine-day wonder, whatever its latest cause. If some future rector reads this I would like to think that he is not suffering the same problem. It is impossible to avoid village gossip, but if Christian values mean anything it should not happen amongst God-fearing people who attend church.

CHAPTER 21

ooooo

Dr John Ponder (1591-1625) *including* William Bollinge (1589-1591)

Elizabeth I and James I - surviving the plague years

Dear Mysterious Future,

I found the request for this letter but cannot quite understand how and from whom it arrived. I take it that in this new age of science someone wants to save it for the future. I am not at all interested in writing any sort of account of Rollesby because I am far too busy, but somehow I feel compelled to do so. It is not that Rollesby keeps me busy, as a Doctor of Law I have often felt that my real calling is in London or at the very least in Norwich.[1] Nor do I understand why just Rollesby parish is of interest and not my other parish in Suffolk, Thelnetham. It is twenty-seven miles away and much more important. I hold both parishes by special dispensation from the Archbishop of Canterbury.[2] My patron in Rollesby is Lady Catherine Drewry, and she is a very fine lady. Her husband is my lord Sir Drue Drury,[3] but he shows little interest in the area; he resides here in order to stay out of the city. Having noted this, I must confess I fled London to come to Rollesby for fear of the plague; there had been several outbreaks and I knew that the rural areas were safer on the whole. It was a good deci-

[1] Dr Barbara MacAllan. Private research: in the comperta records at Norfolk Records Office there is a complaint from parishioners that Dr Ponder was never in the parish.

[2] *Norfolk and Norwich Archaeological Society* (1959) N&NAS, Norwich. Vol.10, p.49. An examination by the Bishop as to what clergy held dual livings.

[3] Sometimes spelt Drewry and sometimes Drury.

sion because a year later the outbreak nearly wiped out half of the London population.[4] I hope that you understand that the plague is a very serious matter, because when it strikes there is no remedy and there is no way of avoiding it once it is in the area. Spiritually the effect is like a double-edged sword. There are those who feel closer to their Maker and take a very religious view of life, some become almost pious at the close proximity of death. Others see the devastation and reject any notion of a good God and seek a good time, as they perceive it, while they have the time to use. Such people drink themselves silly in the taverns and wench away the night hours. I have seen a similar reaction amongst soldiers before they go to war. When life is so precarious the human predicament changes because as humans we are never sure how to deal with the possibility that we will die.

Not that these ponderous thoughts had much effect on the new Lord of the Manor, Leonard Mapes. He had built himself a magnificent Jacobean Hall on the Martham Road with a splendid if somewhat pretentious driveway for carriages. Apart from the church itself, it is Rollesby's only claim to a building of any architectural significance. Leonard died in 1619[5] and we have placed a magnificent memorial tablet to him in the chancel on the south wall. Leonard Mapes had been the Town Clerk of Norwich between 1596 and 1609, and his son, Francis, JP[6] succeeded him. My wardens, William Rainham and William Quinns[7] said that it was one of the finest memorial services they had ever attended. I had various wardens during my time in Rollesby and generally they were always complaining about the state of the church, especially John Smyth and Christopher Clarke[8]. Some of the parishioners can be just as difficult. The Lady Harris claimed she would not come to church to hear Divine Office because I am told she is popish.[9] I had problems with one, William Cubitt, who insisted that his servants worked on Sundays, as well as the wife of William Bullyvaunt whom I had

---

[4] 1592 December. The plague in London killed 17,000 within 12 months.

[5] The Mapes family became entwined with the Ensors and it remained with that family until 1906: the last owner was Sir Ion Benn.

[6] Francis Mapes JP was High Sheriff in 1632.

[7] Dr Barbara MacAllan. Private research.

[8] Dr Barbara MacAllan. Private research.

[9] Dr Barbara MacAllan. Private research.

to take to task for slanderous speeches against her neighbours.[10] These wretched people use and abuse the church, even keeping their horses nearby so the nave becomes covered in horse dung and then I am blamed.[11]

Politically, London is the centre of all activity. At the beginning of my incumbency Queen Elizabeth was on the throne. They were dangerous times; one only had to suggest problems about who should be the next monarch and prison waited.[12] If the question of the Queen's supremacy over the Church was raised there was an excellent chance one's head would be separated from one's body as happened with that fool, John Penry.[13] To make such a statement was just as dangerous as being a Portuguese Jew trying to poison the Queen.[14] Executions in that period of time came thick and fast: I actually witnessed at Tyburn the death of Robert Southwell, a Jesuit priest after he had been tortured on thirteen separate occasions.[15] Southwell was a local Norfolk man: he was born at Horsham St Faith, near Norwich, and his family was related to the Cecils and Bacons. Fortunately I am a thorough Protestant and I keep my opinions to myself and speak only of those matters of which I am certain. Unlike my predecessor, William Bollinge: he was only here for a couple of years and he was a strange fellow. On the one hand there were rumours that he had Catholic leanings by taking the Holy Communion service three times a month, and then on the other hand he took not only a wife but a mistress as well. The parishioners were furious, especially old Godwin who is very strict in his views. Either way, all I know is that William Bollinge simply disappeared: some say he went to Rome, others that he died from the pox. For my part I have been here well over thirty years: I keep my sanity by working outside the parish as far as possible.[16] Some scurrilous parishioners suggest I am enjoying myself, and while I confess I like watching Shakespeare's plays, especially the come-

---

[10] Dr Barbara MacAllan. Private research.

[11] Dr Barbara MacAllan. Private research.

[12] 1593 February 23rd. Peter Wentworth (again!) imprisoned for raising the succession question in Parliament.

[13] 1593 May 29th. John Penry, probable author of Martin Marprelate Tracts, executed for denying Queen Elizabeth's Church Supremacy.

[14] 1594 June 7th. The Queen's doctor, Roderigo Lopez, a Portuguese Jew, executed at Tyburn for allegedly trying to poison her.

[15] 1595 February 2nd.

[16] See note 1.

dies,[17] I also work, and being a man of private means I do not see what business it is of rural labourers and such like. When I went to see William Kempe[18] dance into Norwich, nearly every clerk in Holy Orders was there, and I don't expect their congregations complained. They are, I feel, envious of my wealth. Rollesby is a poor area and although there is no poor house here,[19] the farm workers have some difficulty in surviving. They seem to expect me to work as they do in the fields. They forget that in the old days the clergy were not so well educated and had to work for a living. I do paper work and to a labourer this is not seen as work. Because I sit at my desk working farm workers see it as one long holiday.

Despite their poverty and ignorance, they discuss national events as if they were on the Council themselves. They spoke for the Earl of Essex one moment, the next they are baying for his blood.[20] One minute Essex is the hero and even a possible successor to the Queen, the next he is a rogue worthy only of death. I suppose it will always be true of politicians and people in power: the people's darling one moment and the devil incarnate the next. The labourers are very coarse and blunt in their outlook: they lack all sensitivity. After the gunpowder plot[21] and Guy Fawkes' trial[22] they started a celebratory bonfire. It really is quite gruesome, the burning of the effigy: I am sure such a profanity will not last because it is so distasteful. There is a cruel streak in people: not content with fighting their dogs or cock fighting they gain some kind of vicarious pleasure out of watching an effigy burn. They would not be so keen if they were the cause of the attraction.

I was actually in London when good Queen Elizabeth died[23] and was pleased that James VI of Scotland became James I of England.

There was some concern when the heir, the Prince of Wales, died from

---

[17] 1593/94. First production of Shakespeare's *The Comedy of Errors, Two Gentlemen of Verona, Love's Labour's Lost* and *The Taming of the Shrew.*

[18] 1600 Feb 11th. Comic actor, William Kempe, leaves London on his Morris dance to Norwich (reached March 11th) - nine days dancing between nineteen days of rest.

[19] 1598 March. Poor Relief Act: local poor rate, workhouses set up.

[20] 1599 September. Essex signs unauthorised truce with Tyrone, returns to England and Elizabeth orders his arrest. 1600 June, Essex sentenced to lose his titles for his misdemeanours. 1601 January 7th-8th, leads revolt against Queen and on February 25th duly executed.

[21] 1605 November 4th.

[22] 1606 January 27th. Executed January 31st.

[23] 1603 March 24th. At Richmond Palace.

swimming in the dirty water of Windsor[24] but not as much as when Charles, the next heir contracted a marriage with the Catholic Princess Henrietta Maria, daughter of the French Henri IV. Now that Charles I is officially King,[25] it is of some concern that he may be deeply influenced by this Catholic relation. Under James I we all felt safe, his main problems were parliament and money, which is no problem compared with the dangers of religion. His wife is due in the country next month[26] and I intend to travel to London to witness the occasion for myself. I only hope the place is plague free. When one lives in the rural backwater, as I do, it is exciting to see for oneself what is happening at the national level. Anyone who has been fortunate enough to witness an important event is frequently sought out by others to describe what happened. It is a strange phenomenon that when a person lives a humdrum life or, like me, lives in a remote area, one's life is more fulfilled by seeing what happens in the higher echelons of society.

I intend to travel without giving the parish notice; I am fed up with their complaints about my rightful time out. The young Godwin, who is only twenty-five years of age, is particularly outspoken about my holidays. To think I baptised him in 1600; I should have dropped him in the font whilst I had the chance. It is so much better in the parish with the wealthier residents: they are more educated, more understanding and certainly more sensitive. The Claxton family[27] now has influence over the advowson[28] of the parish and I am sure they are priming their son for such an advancement in life. Sadly, Rose their lovely daughter died in 1601.[29] She was only twenty-three but she always attended service and did a good deal of charitable work among the undeserving poor. Her knowledge of the prayer book was profound. The other major family are the Mapes, whom I have already mentioned, though my old hunting friend Leonard, as I said died a few years

---

[24] 1612 November 6th. Henry, Prince of Wales, dies at St James's Palace from typhoid contracted when swimming at Windsor.

[25] 1624 March 27th. James I dies at Theolbalds and Charles accedes as King Charles I.

[26] 1625 June 12th. Henrietta Maria lands in Dover.

[27] The next incumbent was a Hamo Claxton.

[28] Right of living to church.

[29] Rose Claxton died 1608. The tomb chest and effigy are preserved to the north of the altar. She is wearing a ruff and elaborate Elizabethan costume and lies on her side propped up by her elbow. Her other hand clutched a prayer book until it was chopped off.

ago in 1619.[30] He was a gentleman, brought his family up to respect the Church and enjoyed hunting. In so far that these were civilised families, Rollesby was the better for it: at least, unlike Greater and Little Ormesby, the village is not fleeing to the New World. I speak to the local workers, on occasions, but I cannot bear the familiarity some of them assume. I feel this attitude goes back to the days of the Catholics when the priests saw themselves as part of the people in the community.

I have no idea as to who will read these notes of mine, nor why I have been asked to write them. On reflection, I am like so many others, a product of my age. No doubt future rectors of this parish may hold different views, but like my predecessors, I have been confronted by the peculiar circumstances of my age. I have lived through a politically turbulent time, the fear of the plague has cast a very serious shadow upon our lives, and boredom in a small parish has done my soul little good. I have done my best to prepare useful sermons, buried, married, and baptised members of my parishes, but have kept myself sane by travelling. For this I have been criticised, but had my life been caught up only in the lives of the ninety inhabitants[31] of this village I would have gone mad. I am fairly old now and cannot help but wonder if I would have been of better service to my Lord and to the Church if I had been given greater responsibility. Naturally most parish clergy must think this from time to time, but I have had the distinct impression that because I came here and just did my job I have been forgotten. Had I made some noise about this or that issue, or caused some minor disturbance, I may have been made a canon at the least, if only to keep me quiet.

---

[30] Leonard Mapes died 1619. Alabaster wall monument: kneeling figures of children behind the parents in the predilla or lower part of monument. There are seven sons and two daughters. Surviving members of this family live in Arizona, USA.

[31] *Norfolk and Norwich Archaeological Society* (1959) N&NAS, Norwich. Vol.10, p.49.

CHAPTER 22

ooooo

Hamo(n)[1] Claxton (1625-1663)

The English Civil War, Puritans and religious dissension

Dear Reader,

My predecessor, Dr Ponder, known by the parishioners as 'Dr Absent', had an inordinate fear of the plague. He fled London to escape it but returned only this year to die from a new outbreak![2] I think he went to London as much out of curiosity to see the new wife of King Charles I as to flee from the Goodwin family. Their young son, Thomas, graduated from Christ's College in 1616[3] and was training for Holy Orders. He is a very zealous young man and highly critical of anything that smacks of the old days. My family, which is probably one of the most influential families in the area, preferred candles on the altar for the celebration of the Holy Communion. When old Goodwin mentioned this to his son at Cambridge I had a letter of remonstration, of all things. Naturally I ignored the matter; he was but a boy.[4] But on the other hand, I have to admit he is both clever and scholarly. His main problem is that he is an extremist and I used to dread what would happen if ever his type managed to rise to power. I have since learned, but I shall save that for later in my

---

[1] Hamo in Church Register, elsewhere it is spelt Hamon, see *Norfolk and Norwich Archaeological Society* (1959) N&NAS, Norwich. Vol.3, Part I, p.388.

[2] 1625 August. Plague in London sends court and Parliament to Oxford.

[3] Thomas Goodwin entry in *Encyclopaedia Britannica*.

[4] Thomas Goodwin born in the cottage opposite church was to become a zealous Puritan, a well known divine and chaplain to Cromwell.

account.

My rectory is now a little more prominent in the village because my family has invested some money in making me more comfortable, and I was also fortunate to have my own income from some family trusts. My family was also connected with Roger Drury who died in 1599. He was the man who through his will devised the site of Blackfriars as well as the Manor of Eccles. He asked to be buried in Rollesby Church.[5] Because of the Drury connection my father, Henry Claxton, was able to present me with the living of Rollesby. My family is quite well known. In 1559 Hammond Claxton of Chediston in Suffolk was in favour with Thomas, Duke of Norfolk, and his namesake the century before was Mayor and Sheriff of Norwich.[6]

I was never sure that Rollesby was the right place for me, but once national events turned dangerous I was glad to be here. Even Norwich can be dangerous just for a cathedral visit. Not long after I arrived, I recall that Irish soldiers had been quartered in the city and they were creating havoc. The soldiers were abusive, more often than not drunk and capable of assaulting anyone who objected. Their officers were either oblivious to their behaviour or ignored it by treating even clergy with the utmost contempt.[7] In Great Yarmouth people would not go to church because the Dean and Chapter appointed Matthew Brookes in a town where Puritan feeling was against this type of ecclesiastical appointment.[8] They stayed away at Easter in their droves just to avoid giving to the Easter Offering.[9] Times are not easy for clergy.

Even one's name can be dangerous: I was interrogated as to whether I had any connection with Laurance Claxton[10] or, maybe, was even the same man. This was all nonsense; the man was a fanatic of the worse type, Baptist

---

[5] *Norfolk and Norwich Archaeological Society* (1959) N&NAS, Norwich. Vol.3, Part I, p.387.

[6] *Norfolk and Norwich Archaeological Society* (1959) N&NAS, Norwich. Vol.3, Part I, p.388.

[7] Bayne, A D (circa 1880) *History of Eastern England* James MacDonald, Yarmouth. Vol II, p.166. 'There is a very curious letter from the Mayor of Norwich dated 19th March 1627, protesting against the quartering of Irish soldiers in Norwich, on the poverty and distress of which city ... he bitterly complains of the outrages and disorders of these Irish soldiers and their officers who ... utterly terrify the country people.'

[8] Dr Barbara MacAllan. Private research.

[9] Until quite recently the Easter offering went to the incumbent.

[10] Laurence Claxton (sometimes spelt Clarkson) preacher and pamphleteer, leader of radical English religious sect known as the Ranters. Originally a tailor by trade he wrote several tracts. Later he was converted to another extremist Puritan sect, the Muggletonians. He died in debtors' prison.

by profession. Once the visiting chaplain had met me he dismissed the ideas as absurd.

As a rector, I became quite used to being examined about my religious practices. I have always been only a country parson, second to the squire, but the authorities have been inquisitive about how we conduct our affairs, mainly, of course, because we have such influence over the way people think. The main problem was that during my time here we all lived through the dreadful Civil War. Staying alive was a matter of treading a very thin line: it has at times almost been a circus act, a theological circus act. I cannot recall the number of times I have stood in the parlour of Rollesby Hall warming myself against the fire hearth and discussed survival with my family. Whenever I see that parlour fireplace,[11] I reflect on those intellectual and spiritual gymnastics, which I had to perform in order to survive.

The main causes of the war started when Charles I had financial problems with Parliament and Oliver Cromwell, MP[12] for Huntingdon (and can anything good ever come out of Huntingdon?), took a leading hand. A few years ago I would not have dared put this in writing, and am only doing so now because I am told it will be read after my death. The following year Charles dissolved Parliament, in 1629: it seems a lifetime away. In those days I was leaning towards William Laud's traditions and I was most hopeful when he was made Bishop of London,[13] and more especially when he was made Archbishop of Canterbury.[14] Once Thomas Goodwin left Rollesby, I put candles and a silver crucifix back on the altar: and I was calling it an altar again and not simply a table, and we bowed. But life was appalling in the parish, the religious differences paling into insignificance compared with the problems with the harvest. The weather was against us and many came close to starvation.[15] I spent some of my private income on alleviating the more local problems. It was not much and it was not until later that I realised how grateful the locals were for this effort. I had always

[11] Pevsner, N (1976) *The Buildings of England: North-East Norfolk and Norwich* Penguin Books, Middlesex, p. 305. 'Rollesby Hall ... the parlour's fireplace was dated 1620...'

[12] 1628 March 17th. Charles opens third Parliament: MPs include Oliver Cromwell elected for Huntingdon.

[13] 1628. William Laud becomes Bishop of London: like Richard Montagu Bishop of Chichester he was an 'Arminian' High Churchman, and opposed by Puritan Parliamentarians for their ritualistic traditionalism.

[14] 1633 August 6th.

[15] 1631. Social distress caused by poor harvest for second year running.

thought them an insensitive, uncaring bunch, and I know they looked at me with suspicious eyes, but this little charity was to save my life later. Because labourers are not overly effusive with their gratitude does not mean they are not grateful, and their memories, fortunately for me, were long.

Had I been politically more sensitive, I might have read the signs more carefully. I thought the old Church rituals were returning, especially when William Prynne[16] had his ears cut off, but the Puritans were growing in strength. Some of our local gentry, especially my family, were taking to wearing silk and jerkins fitted to the waistline.[17] Others were wearing the dowdy colours of the Puritans. By the division of people's clothes alone I should have seen the country dividing down the centre: with the benefit of hindsight it now appears obvious. Many people simply moved out of the country; it must have appeared to them the safest thing to do. I remember hearing in 1637 how nearly sixty people from Ormesby St Margaret and Scratby had left from Yarmouth to settle in New England. It felt as if half their parish had disappeared overnight. Amongst them went the Moulton and Carver families, as well as the Marstons, Eastows, Dowes and Pages. Even my old friends, the Palmers, packed their bags, gathered up their three children and left at the same time.[18] Francis Mapes,[19] High Sheriff and a family member of Rollesby Hall, warned me of the storms. Although we were preoccupied with local matters such as the harvest I heard the first serious warning bell when news crept through that Archbishop Laud had been impeached.[20] He had done so much to give some traditional form to the Church of England. We had only just heard this when it was rumoured that the King had tried to arrest some MPs while in the House, including Mr Pym.[21]

After this it all became inevitable: civil war raged, first one side then the other; tragedy followed tragedy. At first we thought the King must win,

---

[16] 1634 May 7th. Puritan pamphleteer, William Prynne had his ears amputated after a trial in the Court of Star Chamber for libelling Henrietta Maria in *Histrio-Mastix, the Players Scourge* (1633).

[17] 1630s. The cavalier style in vogue.

[18] University of East Anglia computer site: http://www.uea.ac.uk/his/virtualnorfolk/migration/ormesby.htm

[19] Francis Mapes JP High Sheriff 1632 - Bates, Ann. Private research from the *Norfolk Archaeological Society*.

[20] 1640 December 18th.

[21] 1642 January 4th. Charles I enters House of Commons to arrest five MPs including Pym and Hampden.

especially after Prince Rupert's arrival,[22] but Cromwell and the Parliamentary cause were popular in this part of England. He built up an army called the 'Eastern Association' and this was formidable. Future readers will know this history, as it was like a scar across England: brother fought brother. Most Rollesby men were of the Parliamentary hue and those who were inclined to the royal house, myself included, kept a discreet silence. I was especially concerned about Thomas Goodwin, the man born opposite Rollesby church. He had become Vicar of Holy Trinity, Cambridge, but because of Archbishop Laud's persecution of Puritans he had fled England for a little known place called Arnhem, in Holland. With the execution of Archbishop Laud[23] and the Puritans and Parliamentarians rising in favour I dreaded the return of this man. The civil war continued to rage: I heard news that an old Rollesby family called the Beeches had taken to the royal side and that some of our men, including the Freemans and Blacks, had met them in battle. After the Battle of Oxford[24] most of us considered the royalist side defeated, and I discreetly removed the candlesticks and crucifix from the altar and hid them up in the belfry. I also made sure I had in very prominent and public view the Directory of Public Worship, which was full of rubrics and biddings, but no prayers.[25] I was horrified when the episcopacy[26] was abolished, but what could I, a mere country parson, do?

Even to a country parson in remote Rollesby events were always uncomfortably close: I even kept clear of Yarmouth. The town had declared for Parliament and the town received orders from Parliament not to billet soldiers. All the buildings by the town walls were taken down and the gates that were ramped were locked up and the east leaf of the bridge was drawn up every night.[27] Not everyone in Yarmouth was happy about this. It was a real civil war and families and towns were divided. The Puritans sent the Royalist mayor to prison in Cambridge and when Colonel Cromwell came

---

[22] Charles' nephew, Prince Rupert of the Rhine defeated Parliamentarians at the Battle of Powick Bridge on September 23rd 1642 and again at the Battle of Edgehill, October 23rd.

[23] 1645 January 10th. At Tower Hill.

[24] 1646 June 24th.

[25] 1664 February. This Directory replaced the old Prayer Book.

[26] 1646 October. Episcopacy formally abolished.

[27] Bayne, A D (circa 1880) *History of Eastern England* James MacDonald, Yarmouth. Vol.II, p.173.

on March 17th 1643[28] to deal with Lowestoft, I had real fears that the war would spread as far as Rollesby. Cromwell was a frequent visitor to Yarmouth and used to stay at the house of his Presbyterian friend and counsellor, John Carter, on South Quay.[29] There is something in the Norfolk character that always causes rebellion. On October 7th 1649, there was an intended insurrection near Norwich in favour of Charles II and three judges were sent to hang six men at New Hall (St Andrew's Hall).[30] Many others were hanged. On May 29th 1660, the restoration was celebrated in Yarmouth with great rejoicing.[31] First Parliamentarian, next Royalist: whole towns and families swung with the tide like petulant schoolchildren taking sides in the streets. It would have been almost amusing had it not been so distressing and dangerous.

In the midst of this we had the local excitement of Matthew Hopkins, the 'Witch Finder General' of East Anglia. He was more terrifying for unlearned labourers than the Civil War. If he believed a woman was a witch, he had her bound and cast into the water: if she sank she was innocent, if she floated she was dragged out and hanged as a witch. We were safe in Rollesby, but there were several villages nearby which suffered from his cruelty. I gathered that several men had their wives done away with in this fashion by accusing them of witchcraft, and one woman accused her lover's wife in order to remove her from the marriage bed. He supervised over two hundred executions, and eventually he was tested by his very own method, bound and flung in water and he floated: they dragged him out and hanged him.[32] Personally I have no belief in witches. From swimming in the summer I know that by expelling air I can sink, but by holding my breath, which is the natural thing to do, I float. The trouble is that many rural folk in these parts tend to be superstitious.

We talked about Matthew Hopkins nearly as much as about the civil war, but after they executed the King[33] there was no room for any other discussion. It cast a gloom on everything. Even those staunch supporters of

---

[28] Bayne, A D (circa 1880) *History of Eastern England* James MacDonald, Yarmouth. Vol.II, p.174.

[29] Bayne, A D (circa 1880) *History of Eastern England* James MacDonald, Yarmouth. Vol.II, p.178.

[30] Bayne, A D (circa 1880) *History of Eastern England* James MacDonald, Yarmouth. Vol.II, p.196.

[31] Bayne, A D (circa 1880) *History of Eastern England* James MacDonald, Yarmouth. Vol.II, p.225.

[32] 1647 August. In Bury St Edmunds.

[33] 1649 January 30th. In Whitehall.

Parliament were uncertain about such an extreme act of barbarity. It seemed to me in those days that the world was turning upside down. In this county of Norfolk a mad group called the Fifth Monarch arrived and stirred up trouble. They did not recognise Cromwell as Protector nor Charles II as king: they looked to a prophesy in Daniel and Revelation[34] and thought they were to succeed the Romans! I always thought the book of Revelation to be a happy hunting ground for cranks. They were fairly active between February and March of 1649 but they were soon tracked down and executed. There were a number of silly sects around at this time.

It was not long after this that I heard that Thomas Goodwin, now chaplain to Cromwell himself, was sending a representative to see how the reformation was going in his old parish of Rollesby. I was terrified. I knew that he sat as an official at the trial of heretical ministers[35] and he had undoubtedly not forgotten the admonition he gave me for the use of candlesticks and which I had so obviously ignored. I re-entered the belfry and threw the treasures into Rollesby Broad and hoped for the best. When the Commissioner arrived it was Goodwin himself. He called a public meeting to ask me questions. I pretended I was truly Puritan in thought and all the parishioners, to my incredulous surprise, backed me. Technically I was thrown out of Rollesby and my oversight of Holt, but in reality I just kept going without collecting the tithes and glebes so as not to draw attention to myself. I had to wait until 1660, a few years ago from this time of writing, to be restored to my rights by Sir Drury.[36] At least the parishioners backed me, even the Goodwin family.

'Why?' I later asked old Goodwin himself, father of the dreaded Thomas.

'Because when the harvest was down in 1630 and 1631 you fed us, and that be better than the bread of heaven.'

'Bread of heaven?' I thought, this was truly manna from below; they could so easily have told the truth and had me condemned. Sadly the commissioners damaged my sister's monument in the sanctuary, because they

---

[34] Daniel 2 v44 & Revelation 20 v4.

[35] Under Thomas Goodwin entry in *Encyclopaedia Britannica*.

[36] Bates, Ann. Private research from the *Norfolk Archaeological Society*. 'Order dated 10th December 1660 by Commissioners, after reciting that Hamo Claxton an ejected minister out of the benefices of Holt and Rollesby had made his election ... to be restored ...'

saw she was holding a prayer book. They actually chopped her hand off. It was such a beautiful monument, put up in 1608.

Fortunately my parents were not alive to see this remarkable piece of barbaric stupidity. I am not a papist, but just like the King and Archbishop Laud I tend to belong to the High Church, Anglican through and through. Because it was High Church with due reverence to ceremonies and ritual the ignorant perceived it to be Catholic. I had to pretend to be Puritan to survive, but it went against every muscle in my body. The Civil War had opened a Pandora's box in religious matters. The main problem was that people were unable to combine a firm faith in their religion with an acceptance that others might also be right.

Religious toleration was the cry, and to find it, people from Great and Little Ormesby[37] fled to the New World, but one's livelihood and indeed one's life depended on an ability to switch allegiance with a mental agility which did not offend one's personal spiritual integrity - difficult. Had my parishioners not convinced Thomas Goodwin that I was a Puritan there would have been a very good chance that the Commission[38] would have placed a genuine Puritan here in my place. I would not have appreciated this and certainly the ordinary parishioners were, by this time, becoming tired of the puritanical strictness. It was as if a religious hurricane had swept through the land. Almost as a warning, we suffered a real hurricane;[39] half the trees were uprooted in Church Farm, a barn was laid low and old Goodwin claimed he saw our tower sway in the wind.

The Church of God seemed to suffer its own hurricane. The Prayer Book authorised one moment was banned the next: it was all very confusing. I shall never forget hearing about the layman, John Evelyn, being attacked on Christmas Day 1657 by Parliamentary troops simply because Evelyn and his followers were devotees of the Prayer Book.[40] There was also the case of John Hackett (who later became Bishop of Coventry and Lichfield)[41] who continued to read the Prayer Book service even though a Parliamentary soldier of the Earl of Essex held a pistol at his head.

---

[37] Research shows that up to a quarter of the people in the Ormesby area left for the Americas.

[38] 1654. Commission of Triers: fills vacant Anglican benefices with Puritan ministers.

[39] 1658 August 30th. Hurricane winds sweep southern England, the worst storm for centuries.

[40] Chadwick, H (Editor) (2000) *Not Angels but Anglicans* Canterbury Press, Norwich, p.162.

[41] In 1661.

When the time came, at least Oliver Cromwell refused to accept the crown, his son Richard was weak, and I cannot tell you how relieved I was when Parliament[42] voted for the restoration of the King Charles II. I thought it rather tasteless the way they treated Cromwell's body[43] because although I never liked the man or what he stood for, he was still one of God's children. However, I was mightily relieved when the revised Prayer Book was introduced in 1662.[44] This time the boot was on the other foot in so far that over two thousand non-conforming ministers were ejected from their livings. No one questioned me this time: although I had been queried on several occasions about the truth of my puritanical standing it was now understood that I was High Anglican and was at long last left to my own devices. As for Thomas Goodwin, I was reliably informed that he attended Cromwell on his deathbed, assuring him of his salvation. After that he disappeared somewhere in London. He never returned to Rollesby as far as I know, certainly not at the time of writing, which is 1663.

The people of Rollesby were by nature Parliamentary and fought with Cromwell, but they did not like the puritanical restrictions on their lifestyle and they too welcomed the relief of the return to monarchy. They knew I was a true Anglican parson and defended me against the Puritan inquisition by Thomas Goodwin. For that I shall always be grateful to them. In the meantime I continue to marry, bury and baptise them, laugh with them on festive occasions and mourn with them at their gravesides. The Civil War was a lesson we all learned from, and whatever other wars our country may enter in the future, none of us would want a civil war again. Out of respect for the way the parishioners defended me, I conduct the services between my old style of Anglicanism and what some call low churchmanship. We follow the new prayer book with care; we have two candles on the altar, a wooden cross but no crucifix, and celebrate the Holy Communion once a month. This causes the least offence as the wounds heal.

This has been my main task as a rector, reconciling the different factions and shades of opinion that grew out of the quagmire of civil unrest. War with a neighbour over the sea is one thing, but war between neighbours and

---

[42] 1660 May 1st. And on May 25th Charles welcomed in Dover.

[43] 1661 January 30th. Corpses of Cromwell and Ireton hanged at Tyburn.

[44] 1662 August 24th. Revised Prayer Book imposed on England and Wales: it is still authorised and still used in many churches including some services at Rollesby in 2001.

families in the same land is another. It taught me to understand my own frailty and personal weaknesses. I had been obliged to eat humble pie and pretend I was a Puritan. I knew that my parishioners lied for me, and they knew that I knew they lied. It was to save me that they did so, so I could hardly admonish them when they disagreed with my churchmanship. They had saved my life, how could I criticise them for preferring simple Morning Prayer to sacramental worship? They saved me not because of my religious convictions but because I had fed them when the harvest failed. I resolved thereafter to speak only if my words passed three tests: is what I am going to say truthful, is it necessary to say it, is it kind? The latter years here in Rollesby have been a commitment to healing and reconciliation.

CHAPTER 23

ooooo

Henry Julyan (1663-1671)

Charles II, the Great Fire and the Dutch Wars

Dear Reader,

I used to be the Vicar of Clippesby, a nearby and smaller parish, but the Patron of Rollesby, Leonard Mapes,[1] persuaded me to take on this living because he needed someone to stabilise the church after the ups and downs of my predecessor. Leonard Mapes[2] lived in the manor and was deeply concerned that the last Rector, Hamo Claxton, had vacillated between strong Puritanism on the one hand to High Anglican on the other. The parishioners had to sit back and watch their minister twist and turn, changing colour according to the season of the day. The congregation was more sympathetic to poor old Hamo than the Church authorities were: he had been a kind parson who had helped them through the bad harvests and they simply smiled at his vacillations, putting it down to survival instinct. He was not the only parson who had to change the colour of his liturgy and style of worship, but no one doubted Hamo's deep felt Christianity. For my part I was happily Prayer Book, what people have started calling Low Church. I did place candles on the altar for Communion service but held it

---

[1] Church Records.

[2] An impressive monument to the Mapes family can be found on the south wall of the chancel in Rollesby Church. He occurs in the list of gentry for 1673. His son, also Leonard Mapes, 1710-1775, was High Sheriff of Norfolk. He married Priscilla. Their son, Edmund, was a noted member of the Norwich Militia in 1767. Edmund's daughter, Amphilles, married John Ensor and thus the interweaving of these two well known Norfolk families.

only once a month. The strength of Rollesby worship is in the Matins and Evensong, and the Litany.

The 1662 Prayer Book has resolved many but not all the religious problems. At least it has rejected most of the puritanical demands, made a healthy distinction between the orders of priesthood and established the important sacramental nature of baptism. In fact the 1662 (May) Act of Uniformity made the assent to this new prayer book mandatory for Clerks in Holy Orders, a position I was most agreeable towards. It also meant there was a structure between the state and the Church and only a Roman Catholic monarch, which is unthinkable, could ever undermine this stability.

The religious contentions did not die away immediately. The Civil War had set free all kinds of religious pretensions: anyone who had an opinion and could articulate it formed a sect. It became so absurd that the government decided, quite rightly in my opinion, to ban all religious meetings if there were more than five people present.[3] There can be only one true religion and one expression of it, and to allow mad groups to start up of their own volition will lead people astray. I have opinions on how to run the Navy, but this does not make me an authority on the subject, and certainly gives me no right to try and take over his majesty's fleet. One of the major issues was that during the Cromwellian period a number of nonconformist ministers were given benefices: they have been obliged to give them up but they still pester parishioners in their old localities. It is the very sort of divisiveness that both the Mapes and I wish to avoid. As the local gentry, the Mapes feel very strongly that the Church of England should be uniform and the only Church. We were all very pleased when Parliament insisted that ex-ministers of nonconformist nature should stay away from towns where they had formally held a benefice.[4] I have no doubt that by the time this letter is read, the modern reader will not know what we mean by nonconformists, because they will disappear within a few years. Having said this, I am particularly concerned about the group called the Quakers. They are a very simple minded group but seem very determined.[5] There is some

---

[3] 1664 May. Conventicle Act: bans unauthorised religious meetings of more than five people.

[4] 1665 October 18th. Five Mile Act; keeps nonconformist ex-ministers from vicinity of towns where they had once held benefices.

[5] 1668. William Penn is imprisoned for *The Sandy Foundation Shaken*, a pamphlet attacking Trinitarian beliefs.

talk that many of these sects have travelled to the New World and are establishing themselves there, which is beyond the practical control of Parliament. I find it very difficult to imagine that they will ever catch on against the interests of the established church.

When I said earlier that I had opinions about the Navy most of us even in rural Norfolk held such opinions while the war with the Dutch raged at sea. I travelled down the coast to Lowestoft[6] and watched and heard the great naval battle in which we were so victorious. Even ashore the sound of the guns was deafening, and I heard that in Rollesby itself the sound of gunfire was heard. This may have been a victory but a seriously black day followed when we heard that the Dutchman, Ruyter,[7] had sailed up the Thames and sunk three warships in Chatham and had the audacity to tow our flagship back to Holland. Goodwin and Freeman thought it the blackest day in our history; I thought that the blackest day was when we murdered Charles I but said nothing. These wounds are still open and the subject is best kept at a distance.

Some of the winters we have had in Rollesby have been terrible: we have had to pray for warm weather. Crops and animals have suffered and down in the village old Ma Huggins died from the cold. Even in the Rectory with five open fires it is difficult to stay warm. The two Broads of Ormesby and Rollesby froze over and some went ice-skating: tragically two boys broke the ice and although they were pulled out they died from the cold.[8] If the weather had continued in this way, life would have been very difficult to sustain in the rural areas. New thatches and better fire systems are essential. Having noted that, I ought to point out that it is first necessary to control fire. In London the fires got out of control and most of London, including St Paul's Cathedral, was burned to the ground.[9] Thousands of homes were destroyed and it was a lesson to us all not to build too closely together. There was the usual chatter about Divine retribution but I asked the pundits why the people of London were more at fault with their sins than we were in Rollesby.

I travelled down to London quite recently, and managed to purchase

---

[6] 1665 February. Second Dutch war begins on July 3rd. Naval victory over Dutch just off Lowestoft.

[7] 1667 June 12th. And he attacked Sheerness on the same day.

[8] 1664 November. Severe frosts. The River Thames froze over until March 1665.

[9] 1666 September 2nd-6th. Great Fire of London; 13,300 buildings destroyed.

John Milton's Paradise Lost;[10] it cost me a lot of money but I am very proud of the edition and pleased to have it in my study. Rollesby people do not read much, though there is a growing attention to the subject, especially since the Bible and Prayer Book are so available.

Goodwin is now very old and he hears little of his son, but his nephews keep him company and his smallholding still is one of the best in the area. The Freemans and Blacks have also survived the winters but there has been a good deal of movement away from the area because of the lack of work. Some have taken to fishing out of Yarmouth and Lowestoft, and some have moved further afield. The population is as low as two hundred and many of these are women and children.

I have made a point of visiting people in their homes. I think this has been important because over the last few years a considerable amount of distrust has built up over the Church. There is still the feeling that one has to be careful about heresy and whom one speaks to, but on the whole they treat me as they do the squire and keep a respectful distance. I certainly never frequent the Horse and Groom Inn as it is now called. It is a kind of informal staging post between Yarmouth and Norwich or Cromer, and all kinds of unpleasant people gather there at odd times of the year.

Looking back, my main concern has been the people's attitude towards the Church. It has changed from one of utter servility to one of total cynicism. The lowest social order feels that it has a right to question every service and every prayer. The validity of the service and the minister himself are all too frequently major topics of conversation. I can see in the faces of the villagers the suspicion that I, as their minister, and the Church, tend to be held in in this day and age. I am equated in their minds with the gentry, the landowner, and thereby the ruling class: it amounts to a simmering resentment. They come to me caps in hands for baptisms, weddings and funerals, but uppermost in their minds is the fact that I collect the tithes from them. I put the blame on the religious difficulties of the Civil War and the continuing dissension between different denominations. Every man is now an expert on all matters religious, and I worry for the future.

---

[10] Written in 1658-63 and published 1667.

CHAPTER 24

ooooo

John Smith (1671-1684)

Charles II and more religious conflict

Dear Future Readers,

I have always been suspicious about being asked to write down anything unless it pertains to the gospel of Christ. In these days there are people around who will take anything a parson writes and they deliberately misconstrue his intentions. Only a few years ago a friend of mine in holy orders expressed an opinion on the saints and he was condemned as a papist and was therefore a traitor. He was called before the authorities and cleared but the parishioners hounded him from the parish. I never discovered what happened to him apart from the rumour that he had gone to Ireland. There is a frightening lack of toleration in our society, most especially in religious matters. Even stating this makes me nervous and I am doing so only on the grounds that I have been assured that this document will not re-emerge until some time after my death. I would not dare express my true feelings in public. As far as the parishioners know, I am anti-Catholic and anti-Dissenter: I am certainly not for the Dissenters' way of thinking and practice but I would not persecute them in the way that is happening. I am sure Christ did not intend any of this to happen to His children. They may be mistaken, but they are still the sons of God.

In the first days of my tenure here I thought that the problem would be a nine-day wonder and I was grateful to King Charles II for the Declaration of Indulgence.[1] This lifted the dreadful penal laws against Catholics and Dissenters in general. It was a truly humane and civilised thing for the King to do. Sadly Parliament reared its head again and refused to vote the King funds[2] until he had withdrawn the Declaration, which he duly did, and did so very quickly out of sheer necessity.[3] The Declaration lasted for barely a year. Then Parliament behaved like a mediaeval monarch and passed the Test Act[4] demanding that all office holders had to declare their rejection of Catholic doctrines of the Mass and to prove by certificate that they had recently received the Anglican Communion. Several times I had strange gentry from Yarmouth and Caister make their communion at St George's and then ask me to sign a letter to the effect they had attended. This became quite a nuisance until it dawned on me that I could make a small charge. It certainly helped my income and made lesser mortals think twice before they asked. I used to feel guilty about this charge, because the Communion service should not be a validation for citizenship, nor should a man participate in the Lord's Supper for that reason. It must have been embarrassing for the King because his brother, the Duke of York, had to retire as High Admiral because he was Catholic.[5] I actually saw the Duke of York twice within a few days. I just happened to be in Yarmouth on March 10th 1681 when the Duke was returning from Scotland and landed in Yarmouth. A few days later I saw him enter New Hall[6] in Norwich when he dined with the important people of the city.[7] At that time few of us knew much about his character. There is some concern about the Duke of York because he could be the next heir to the throne, and he compounded that concern by marrying Mary of Modena, an Italian Catholic, despite Parliament's protest.[8] Parliament is now more powerful than the monarch in many ways, even obligating the King to accept peace with the Dutch.[9]

---

[1] 1672 March 15th.

[2] 1673 February.

[3] 1673 March 8th.

[4] 1673 March 29th. Test Act.

[5] Duke of York was in fact the future James II and was forced to retire on June 12th 1673.

[6] Later called St Andrew's Hall.

[7] Bayne, A D (circa 1880) *History of Eastern England* James MacDonald, Yarmouth. Vol.II, p.229.

[8] 1673 November 23rd.

[9] 1674 February 9th. The Treaty of Westminster: enforced by Parliament.

Rollesby people discuss such matters little, but if they do, it is always on the side of Parliament. It may well be that Parliament is the true future of this country, but it has to learn to be less cruel and less open to paranoid bigotry. They imprisoned a brilliant preacher[10] simply because he did not have a licence to preach: Jesus never had a parliamentary licence.

It was not long after this that there was a frightful frenzy of anti-Catholic feeling and plots instigated by one Titus Oates. This madman, and unlike others I always perceived him to be a madman, even said that there was a popish plot to kill the King. The King himself wisely ignored this threat,[11] but this Oates fellow stirred up further feeling by swearing to a magistrate that there was such a plot to place the Duke of York upon the throne as King James II. There followed a number of arrests of priests and any Catholics bold enough to claim themselves as such were barred from nearly every walk of life.[12] This fear of Catholics stretched across the country, city and town and even villages like Rollesby. Our own gentry were a mixture of Whigs and Tories[13] and the fear of treason based on the papacy was common to them all. I am convinced that Titus Oates will one day be exposed as a complete fraud.[14] The divisions he has created may well last a lifetime if not beyond. With others, he has turned the term Catholic into something that is alien and foreign and not to be trusted.

When Black's forge caught fire it was rumoured that the instigators of a Catholic plot had caused the conflagration. I found it inconceivable that there could be any reason behind such an incident apart from the fact that Black was in his drink and neglected his forge fire. As it was, the rumour spread that this was a plot against the Church and monarch. Quite how the destruction of Black's forge would bring the King and Church down was beyond me, and beyond others once I had managed to draw their attention to the nature of such ridiculous claims. Even here I had to be careful in case I was seen as defending Papists. We had two fires in the village and the safety of the inhabitants is of some concern. We have had a tendency to

---

[10] 1672. John Bunyan released from Bedford gaol after serving 12 years for preaching without a licence.

[11] 1678 August 13th. King Charles II learns of the plot from an intermediary but discounts it.

[12] Reached a climax in November-December 1678.

[13] 1679 was the year the terms 'Whig' (generally a Country party, opposition group led by Shaftesbury) and 'Tories' (Court party led by Danby) came into use.

[14] This happened in May 1685 when Oates was whipped through the streets of London.

build some buildings too close to one another. The reason is that as families grow they simply extend the house until the thatch of one is practically growing into that of the one next door. This was probably the reason for the fires in London's Wapping and Southwark.[15] The only good side of such disasters is the lessons we learn, and the better buildings that are designed after the conflagration. I travelled to London and saw Wren's masterpiece of St Stephen's and witnessed the laying of the foundation stone for the new St Paul's Cathedral.[16] I also attended Westminster Abbey and heard their beautiful organ. I can never imagine a country parish like Rollesby having its own organ; it would fill the whole nave even if we could afford it. A few years after my initial visit I also heard Henry Purcell[17] play the organ: it helps lift one's soul heavenwards.

Lifting the souls of some of my Rollesby parishioners in the same direction is not always easy. Many years ago there was a family called the Beeches in the area. They had left some time during the Civil War and never returned. Last year one of the family returned and purchased some land, lying between Ormesby and Rollesby. They were unpopular and amongst other things Black and Greggs blamed them for the burned down forge. I had to intervene. I saw Mark Goodwin about the matter. Mark was the cousin of the infamous Thomas Goodwin, but the Goodwins are an old and respected family in the area.

'Well, Parson Smith,' said Mark leaning casually on his gate as he spoke to me, and having little regard for clergy or gentry, 'the Beech family not only backed the wrong side but they were Catholics to boot.'

'This Mr Beech tells me he is prayer book Church of England, and has a certificate of Holy Communion from St Nicholas's Parish Church in Great Yarmouth.'

'That may be true, Parson, but it goes deeper than religion. The Beech family drove families out of the area by forcing the purchase of land in the hard times. They are greedy and the locals have never liked them.'

'Surely this is a new generation and we must give them a chance?' I asked, but I had the feeling that it was too much to hope for.

---

[15] 1676 May 26th. Fire of Southwark in which 625 houses burned to the ground and on November 19th 1682, 1,500 families were made homeless after a fire in Wapping.

[16] 1672-79. Sir Christopher Wren's St Stephen's, Walbrook: the foundation stone for St Paul's was laid in the June of 1675.

[17] 1679. Henry Purcell becomes organist for Westminster Abbey.

'Fine by me, but memories run long and deep in a small village like Rollesby. There's not much that happens so what does happen is remembered.'

Mark Goodwin was wise in these comments. In a rural village like Rollesby little actually happens, and when it does it is discussed at great length by everyone, and never forgotten. I reflected on an old clerical friend of my father's who had found too much comfort in drink: thirty years later the village mentioned his name every time drink was discussed, and every time his name was mentioned the drink problem would be raised. It would never happen in a city or a town. Being a cleric in the rural life has its drawbacks; one's life is public property, and there's no room for deviation or even a hint of deviation.

I am regarded as public property as much as the church itself. If I visit old Simon twice in a month there is the immediate rumour that the poor old boy must be dying. In fact, because I called in to see him only a few days after my last visit, Simon convinced himself that he was dying: he was concerned that I knew something he did not. A few years ago Mother Howard asked me to call on spiritual matters and I obliged. I could not answer her question at once but followed it up the same week. Her neighbour saw me enter her house twice in a few days and I need not tell you how far a certain flavour of gossip travelled after that incident. It was all perfectly innocent and legitimate, but after picking up the suggestive nuances from a so-called concerned friend I dared not visit her again. Then there was the occasion when some family members visited me and the villagers convinced themselves that there was something dreadfully wrong. When an old Cambridge friend stayed a few days, the rumour gathered force that we were the centre of some plot. It could be that it is all because of the nature of our current society where lack of religious toleration is prevalent. As I stated earlier, neighbour suspects neighbour of being either a Dissenter or a Roman, and I hate the way that many people attend church with a great flourish but only to indicate to their neighbours that they are socially acceptable because they are Church of England. In the meantime, I tread a fine line of careful conduct, measure my words and bear the burden of being the centre of everyone's interest. It may be that even in an age of toleration, any minister of religion will always attract attention. It gives me a sense that they are waiting for me to commit some sin, to fall into my grave or to be in trouble with the authorities.

When I was a young ordinand, I had always hoped to be a parish priest whom the parish would love and cherish; life is not like that in any way. The year a new minister arrives he is treated as God Himself, the second year as an apostle, the third year as a mere mortal, and after that for some he becomes the devil incarnate. They clap when you first arrive in the parish and you do not hear that sound again until you announce you are leaving. It has made some of my colleagues quite sceptical but I have decided to keep it all in perspective and see it as part of a cross I must carry.

CHAPTER 25

ooooo

John Gibson (1684-1708)

James II, the Glorious Revolution, William and Mary and Queen Anne

Dear Readers,

I took over the parish church of Rollesby from the Reverend John Smith: he was a kind man and all too forgiving. It seemed to worry him that we took a stand against Catholics and Dissenters. He completely failed to understand the dangers we were in as a nation; he could not see that the Papists were undermining the country. The people of Rollesby forgave him this weakness because he was essentially a kind man, but under my guidance, they came to see that he was also soft. As a parish and diocese as well as a country, we had to take a firm hand against the insidious influence of popery.

When I took over, Charles II was dying. He had been Church of England[1] and apart from his love of women and spaniels we had been contented with his monarchy. As a nation, we had once again accepted the Divine Right of Kings, and that is why his brother, James II, was accepted, although he was Catholic. When he was crowned on St George's Day,[2] we in Rollesby had high hopes that this was a good sign. But on the second Sunday after his accession it was noted that he attended Mass in his private chapel with much pomp and ceremony. This was a bad sign and made some

[1] Converted to Roman Catholicism on his deathbed.

[2] 1685 April 23rd.

of us think that his zeal for the Roman cause could be trouble. Nevertheless, we were still with him when the stupid young Duke of Monmouth landed at Lyme Regis[3] to deny him the crown: even though Monmouth was Protestant, all Rollesby supported the King and rejoiced when Monmouth was defeated at Sedgemoor[4] and then executed on Tower Hill.[5] He had stood no chance, a bunch of peasants against the Household Cavalry and the Dragoons. The two infantry regiments were led by a Colonel Kirk, and some of us had doubts about how he behaved with the losers. They saw that this man and his officers hanged the captured rabble one by one while they imbibed strong drink. This was immediately followed by Judge Jeffreys, who, when he was not drunk, was always in a blind rage. He told those brought before him they would be dealt with leniently if they confessed and when they trusted him and confessed he then promptly hanged them. We were told the King delighted in Jeffreys' letters and this started to leave a bad taste in people's mouths, especially in Rollesby once the hearsay started to leak out several months later.[6] I heard the information in Norwich when I had gone to have a tooth drawn. The pain was agonising and all the drink I took beforehand did not alleviate the agony, and then I had to pay the man eighteen shillings for his efforts. Since I pay only two pounds a month for my daughter's singing master, I thought I was ill-used. I would like to have put that man before Judge Jeffreys! This singing master was little better with the church, and although we had a good flautist and two good fiddlers the singing was appalling.[7]

My fellow ministers in Norwich informed me that the new king had released the imprisoned Roman Catholics and even paid their fines, and had then made four Catholic peers privy Councillors.[8] When I look back on the sequence of events from my current position, I wonder why we as a nation were so patient with King James II. I can remember that in 1687 he made

---

[3] 1685 June 11th.

[4] 1685 July 6th.

[5] 1685 July 15th.

[6] 1685 September 2-24th. Judge Jeffreys conducts the Bloody Assize in the West Country against those who were supposed to have assisted Monmouth.

[7] Bates, Ann. Private research from the *Norfolk Archaeological Society*. '...where the chancel and nave join there used to be a rood screen with a loft for two fiddlers & flautist ... the steps leading to the loft are still in good condition and various records are now kept there.' (Or it may have been another projected tower.)

[8] 1686 July 17th.

the Declaration of Indulgence,[9] which suspended all the sensible penal laws against Catholics and Dissenters. He even tried to expel the Fellows of Magdalen College for refusing to Catholicize their college, and then passed an Order in Council that the Declaration should be read in all Anglican churches.[10] Any future reader must know the history of all this: we discussed nothing else. I never saw what had to be read out because before the distribution was complete, the Archbishop of Canterbury, and six other bishops were sent to the Tower.[11] They were of course found not guilty and this impressed upon Whig and Tory alike the fact that this king had to be opposed. The King's character was all very confusing. He was unquestionably Roman Catholic and dangerous to our Protestant way of thinking. Yet years later I heard that just before the Revolution, James II sent an order to the Norwich Mayor, Aldermen and Common Council of Norwich to admit thirty Quaker freemen without taking the oaths:[12] this was however rejected at the next assembly.

I truly wondered whether we were on the brink of another civil war. As a parish priest I knew little of what happened in high places but it soon transpired that the discontented aristocrats and landed gentry had contacted the Protestant Prince William of Orange, King James II's son-in-law. The King was giving commissions to Catholic officers, and even the birth of a son did not stop the rebellion against him, indeed it inflamed it. There were those who saw the papist monarchy going on forever, and most who believed it was not his son, but a brat smuggled in, concealed in a bed-warming pan. We, as parish priests, were actively encouraged to preach against popery and to produce pamphlets for the literate to illustrate the dangers of Catholics. The Anglican Church had openly attacked the monarchy. It had to be done because James II was openly subverting the faith of the Church of England and undermining our constitution. He made this clear when he prorogued Parliament in the November of 1685, and Parliament never sat again while he was king.

It had all happened by the time news reached Rollesby. I can recall sit-

---

[9] 1687 April 2nd.

[10] 1688 May 4th.

[11] 1688 May 18th. Archbishop Sancroft.

[12] Bayne, A D (circa 1880) *History of Eastern England* James MacDonald, Yarmouth. Vol.II, p.239. July 25th 1688.

ting in my rectory to this very day when young Goodwin arrived hot foot from London.

'I tell thee, Rector, it be true. Lieutenant General John Churchill, the King's own man defected to the Dutchman and it was all over. The King fled. Magistrates at a place called Faversham detained him for a time. Then he fled the country.'[13]

I heard this news in the February of 1689; it is amazing how fast news travels in the modern world. Mary and William were made King and Queen[14] and we then had our famous Declaration of Rights,[15] which no doubt is celebrated as a national holiday even in your days, dear reader. We were saved from another war and from a Catholic take-over. The monarchs prepared the Toleration Act, which granted freedom of worship to most Protestants but fortunately excluded Catholics and Unitarians. The only aspect I never understood was how the Archbishop and many of my High Church clerical friends refused to take the oath of allegiance, still holding that they had given it to the bigot, James II. Not only the bishops and Archbishop but some of my parson friends were suspended for refusing.[16] Personally, I had no problems and, like most, I was glad to see the end of a Catholic monarch, and so Rollesby continued peacefully through this potentially dangerous time. I was at last able to get back to looking after my glebe land. Apart from the fact it costs me one shilling and sixpence to have an acre cut I still make a fair guinea out of the land belonging to the church and me personally.

When I look back on those days, and with the benefit of hindsight, we should be grateful that Louis XIV of France did not threaten to invade Holland, or James II had not called for Louis's help, otherwise William and Mary would not have come. I talk of kings and queens, but the ordinary people never saw them although we saw the effects of their government in our lives. Many of us did see King William III when he landed at Yarmouth in 1691 on his way back from the continent.[17] Many of the Rollesby people

---

[13] 1688 December 12th.

[14] 1689 April 11th. The joint coronation of William and Mary.

[15] 1689 February 12th.

[16] 1689 August 1st. Archbishop Sancroft, eight bishops and 400 clergy suspended: they formed the nonjuror schism which lasted several decades: a form of High Church separatism.

[17] Bayne, A D (circa 1880) *History of Eastern England* James MacDonald, Yarmouth. Vol.II, p.243, Oct 16th.

went to the town to catch a glimpse of the royal personage. The corporation entertained him royally at a cost of £106.[18]

The politics of the world is becoming more and more like a game of chess. I read a pamphlet only the other day, although it had been published for some time, in which a William Penn proposed a federation in Europe.[19] I thought it made sound sense but it will never happen. There will always be war in Europe and the idea that countries of different languages and religious views will ever co-operate is ridiculous. I might add, and only the future reader may have a better idea of the reality, that even if all the countries in Europe tried to work together, England would never join. We shall always see ourselves as different, and as a nation we can be awkward.

In my parish, as in other parts of England, the harvest failed badly in 1692 and the highwaymen grew in number,[20] but generally Rollesby prospered during the reign of William and Mary, and even now during the time of Anne.[21] Again we were pleased when she was crowned on St George's day and this time we had higher hopes because it felt as if the papacy threat was no longer serious. There is now a lightness in the air as there are lights in London's streets.[22] The Catholic problem is now an outside problem, especially with the Scots and Irish. Here in Rollesby I know of no Catholics, and there are no Jacobites hiding in the Broads.

In the mid-1690s I spent a brief time in London. I saw the destruction caused by the fire at Whitehall Palace[23] and the new money foundation of the Bank of England:[24] I do not lack personal wealth and I was interested in this enterprise. Above all I was thrilled to see St Paul's Cathedral[25] consecrated, and joined the ranks of clergy for the occasion. This cathedral will always stand as a triumph of our age, as a mark of our worship of God and as a sign of the strength of the Church of England. I am fortunate in my

---

[18] Bayne, A D (circa 1880) *History of Eastern England* James MacDonald, Yarmouth. Vol.II, p.243.

[19] 1693. William Penn's *Essay on the Present and Future Peace of Europe*.

[20] Bayne, A D (circa 1880) *History of Eastern England* James MacDonald, Yarmouth. Vol.II, p.243.

[21] 1695 January 13th. Princess Anne returns to court and acts as royal hostess on state occasions for seven years; 1702 April 23rd, Queen Anne crowned at Westminster.

[22] 1685 September. First organised street lighting: Edward Hemming authorised to light main London Streets with oil lamps outside every tenth house on moonless winter nights.

[23] 1698 January 4th. Whitehall Palace destroyed by fire.

[24] 1694 July 27th. Bank of England established with William Patterson as the founder director.

[25] 1697 December 2nd.

wealth, but some of my fellow parsons have a very bad time and could not travel to London. It was good tidings indeed when Queen Anne used money from the Tudor monarchs to supplement the income of impoverished clergy in Anglican orders.[26] I was disappointed to find my colleague in Martham had spent his pot on this wretched new idea of snuff:[27] it seems a dirty habit and makes his nose run all the time, and makes his congregation sneeze when he persists in taking it while in the pulpit.

The villagers seemed to forget the religious problems; there is nothing like an overseas war to take away domestic problems. Instead we talked about Marlborough's victories abroad, especially Blenheim, and again I made a point of going to the victory parade[28] in London, I would not have missed that for the world. We also united with Scotland about this time[29] though it was not until 1707 that the Scottish Parliament accepted the Act of Union. I have a depressing feeling that although the Scottish intellectuals and leaders have worked together for this, it will not create great friendship between the two countries.

In the village there is a small degree of prosperity, and we have started to sing some modern hymns with the help of Hudd's fiddle. My favourite is 'When I survey the wondrous cross' and the congregation also like 'O God, our help in ages past'.[30] My snuff-snorting colleague in Martham resents these hymns because they were written by a Dissenter, but their use has certainly brought some life to our services and increased the congregation. The Patron was not too happy so I tend to announce them when he is off hunting.

'I tell you, Parson,' the Patron said to me from his horse one day, 'these new fangled songs are heathen. They degenerate the atmosphere; you'll have us dancing in the pews next.'

Since he pays some of my stipend I said little, but his theology and religion stop at his stables; he is more interested in fishing, shooting and hunting. In some ways I quite enjoyed the patron's company, but he is a greedy

---

[26] 1704. Queen Anne's Bounty - the Queen set up a fund from money confiscated by Henry VIII to assist impoverished clergy.

[27] 1703-4. The taking of snuff becomes popular after capturing huge amounts from Spanish ships at Vigo.

[28] 1705 January 3rd.

[29] 1706 July 23rd. Treaty of Union ceremonially presented to Queen Anne by English and Scottish Commissioners.

[30] Issac Watts was a dissenting pastor in London and published his *Hymns and Spiritual Songs* in 1707.

man, forever taking land and resenting any smallholder, even freeholders of less than a £100 a year.[31] He certainly resented even comfortable freeholders shooting their own ducks or partridge; he was under the impression of most gentry that all game, fur, feather or scales was his by right.

I had two bay windows placed in the front of the rectory, which not only extended my room, but also gave it more light, and now the building has a certain grandeur which reflects my standing in the community.

Life has been peaceful in the village; I did have trouble with some of the locals over my policy in the occasional offices. I refused to bury John Gregg when he threw himself off the church tower because his wife had run off with a soldier. I cannot bury suicides in consecrated ground.

'That don't be fair,' opined Freeman who was quite angry about my position. 'John was a good man.'

'He may have been a good man but at the end he took his own life, and that, my good man, is a sin.'

'He was depressed, not in his right mind.'

'Still a sin,' I replied.

'Did you sack that parlour maid of yours when she dropped the tray of bone china?'

I was surprised he knew of this incident. 'No, I didn't,' I replied. 'She was so upset over the loss of her mother that she was beside herself with grief. I should not have told her while she was holding the tray.'

'You forgave her because she was not in her right mind?'

'True, I do have some compassion.'

'Parson, we all noted the compassion, especially letting her work the day her mother died, but John Gregg was not in his right mind. Can't you forgive him?'

'I must leave that to God, so in the meantime enough of your argument. Go and dig the grave the other side of the graveyard wall, and just cover him up.'

I was pleased that Freeman and others thought me compassionate, but it did not hold for long when Mary Black had a baby out of wedlock. I refused to baptise the bastard and then it died. The parishioners objected to this but

---

[31] Trevelyan, G M (1978) *English Social History* New illustrated edition with introduction by Asa Briggs, Longman, London, p.525. 'In Anne's reign the acquisitive tendency of the large landowners was becoming more than ever marked...'

if we are going to have a national Church we must follow Canon Law in all matters.

I sometimes feel that we do not do enough for the poor, but it is a matter of their laziness and if we make too many gifts they will never want to prosper by their own efforts. I have three servants and two gardeners so at least I keep some of them in employment that way.

I know that some of the village feel I am somewhat haughty, but they must realise I hold an important position as a minister of the Established Church. It is almost like being a government official, and because of my position it is right that I mix with the better off and the educated classes. I take their services and do the occasional offices for them, but it is not my place to mix with them socially. The labourers doff their hats and call me 'Sir' and that is the way I expect it will always be. Jesus Himself said we shall always have the poor with us, and so long as clergy of the Established Church show necessary compassion to the lower classes then our social strata should be safe. My fellow clerical colleague in Martham disagrees with me; he has some dissenting notion that we are servants to the people, but at least I do not sneeze snuff all over them from the pulpit.

CHAPTER 26

ooooo

William Adams (1708-1721)

Queen Anne, the South Sea Bubble and the start of the Hanoverians with George I

Dear Future,

I have received this strange request to write about my tenure of office at St George's, Rollesby, and with my loss of wealth, which I shall come to later, I have no other better use of my time than to expend some ink on this request. When I first arrived I was dismayed at the weather in the area of the Broads; it was so bitterly cold that I felt as if I had fallen off the edge of the world. The Broads froze and for months it was difficult to find any water that was not frozen. The farm animals died in their droves and the cereal crops found the land too hard.[1] The heavy taxes of the war and the bitter winters caused the price of grain to rise and there was much suffering in Rollesby. I gathered later that it was worse in the cities but at least the country people of Rollesby knew how to poach game. It was a much better life in the cities from the point of view of wealth and ease of living. In Norwich even horse racing[2] was popular and many artists were able to maintain even their lifestyles thanks to rich city patrons.[3] In the countryside it was more a matter of survival.

One of my parishioners, young Briggs, had returned from fighting in

---

[1] 1709 January to March. Extraordinary cold weather in Western Europe: there were even icebergs in the North Sea.

[2] Porter, R (1998) *England in the Eighteenth Century* Folio Society, London, p.220.

[3] Porter, R (1998) *England in the Eighteenth Century* Folio Society, London, p.228.

France. He had been at the battle of Malplaquet won by Marlborough, but at what a cost. Our army was over a hundred thousand strong and we lost over twenty thousand men at this small French town called Mons. The name, Mons, will forever stay in the English memory as a place of unprecedented slaughter. The Whigs claimed it as a victory, the Tories as carnage. When the Tories took over the war, they negotiated the Utrecht Treaty, which meant that the English army left their allies in the field and returned via the town of Dunkirk. Young Briggs said Dunkirk will go down as a name of infamy, a time when the army fled because of politicians: we hope that never happens again. At least it concluded the war of the Spanish Succession, not that England gained much. As a country we were granted a toenail of Spain called Gibraltar and the small island of Minorca. One of my friends wondered what use Minorca was to anyone apart from sending Dissenters and other unruly people there. My opening years in the parish were a time of turmoil, and when Queen Anne died[4] many of us feared there would be another civil war over the succession. Marlborough exiled himself in disgrace having been accused of keeping money meant for the war: he claimed that he had spent it on bribing spies.

The next thing we knew was that we had a German king for our king, based on the grounds he was a Protestant. The fact that it is rumoured (and I have been assured this letter will not see the light of day for many years) the King is dull, indeed almost a blockhead, and can speak not a word of English, is irrelevant compared to the fact he is not a Catholic. He was called the Elector of Hanover because of some right to vote for the Emperor. He was already fifty-two years of age when he arrived in 1714, and just because he was the son of Sophia of Hanover, who was the granddaughter of James I, he had the right to spend English money in Hanover, wherever that place is. At least it showed that as a nation we were staunchly Protestant, and somewhat superior to those on the continent.

Politics has not always been easy either locally or nationally. The Whigs and Tories are always battling. Indeed, it seemed that the Tories might go to war over the Hanoverian succession. Their leader, the Earl of Oxford, Harley, was nearly always drunk, and they were divided over the rightness of the Treaty of Utrecht. Bolingbroke fled the country in aid of the Stuart

---

[4] 1714 August 1st. At Kensington.

Restoration, the Jacobites as we call them (adherents of James II). They tried in 1715 to win a war but were defeated at the battles of Sheriffmuir and Preston.[5] The Tories were now a broken force in politics because most people associated them with the Jacobite cause.

Norfolk is a place of sound common sense and mainly peopled by Whigs and people who can think rationally and clearly. Politically Norfolk people are fairly active, especially in the City of Norwich and port of Yarmouth. Norwich is especially active in the production of its own newspapers. I remember the first ever published was a small quarto sheet costing a penny and called the *Norwich Postman*. Also a Mr Collins near the Red Wall in St Andrew's published the *Weekly Courant* and *Weekly Packet* though neither of these contained much actual news.[6] In 1721 he had the *Norwich Weekly Mercury* and *Protestant Packet* that were much more substantial.

Yarmouth saw itself in competition with Norwich. As soon as Queen Anne had come to the throne the Corporation of Yarmouth appeared to be as anxious to change their old bailiffs for a mayor and aldermen. A committee of nine persons drew up the petition that was duly presented to the Queen who granted the charter. It cost the town £412 9s 10d. but secured the rights and privileges of the corporation as in the last charter of Charles II.[7] As a county we were politically active and it was no surprise that the leader of the Whigs is a Norfolk squire, Walpole, and his Secretary of State, and brother-in-law, Townshend, is a Norfolk farmer. They say that Walpole is the first minister,[8] or Prime Minister, a strange title that I do not think will last long.

Walpole has started to put the country back on a financial footing. We all, me included, went through a period of considerable greed when we thought we could use money to make more money. I put much of my fortune into the South Sea Company[9] only to find it was false, that it was corrupt and full of bribery and I have lost all. They have used a word called 'sleaze'; it comes from a thin textile but means in short, corrupt. Only

---

[5] 1715 November 13th and 14th.

[6] Bayne, A D (circa 1880) *History of Eastern England* James MacDonald, Yarmouth. Vol.II, p.272.

[7] Bayne, A D (circa 1880) *History of Eastern England* James MacDonald, Yarmouth. Vol.II, p.273.

[8] 1721 April 3rd. Walpole created Prime Minister, a title he did not use himself.

[9] 1720 January. South Sea Company offer to take over national debt, the 'bubble' burst by the end of the year.

Walpole had had the good sense to oppose this venture and is now trying to clear up the mess, but too late for individuals like me. I was even approached at one time by a company that was developing a system of firing square cannonballs and another company trying to sell areas of Irish bog. I refused these incredible offers, but because many bishops had invested in the South Sea Company I thought it was safe: I might as well have invested in the square cannonballs. Even the high and mighty fell, including hundreds of peers and most of the House of Commons: the Postmaster General killed himself with poison and hundreds of others also committed suicide. At least I was in good company: who would have thought that an economic market or private enterprise could bring such ruin. It brought the country to its knees and ruined the lives of thousands of people. I am sure we shall learn from this lesson and it will never happen again. Although I have lost most of my money, I have sufficient funds to put my son, who bears my Christian name as well, through Cambridge and I hope he will take over this benefice from me in the fullness of time.[10] At the moment he is just a baby, but I have put the money in trust for him. I could barely afford a copy of Daniel Defoe's exciting story of *Robinson Crusoe.*[11] I felt sorry for the Goodwins, who had also invested in the South Sea Company on my advice: they had to sell their house that had been in the family since it was built in 1583. The Patron bought it and at my request, gave them a reasonable price. They now have a humbler dwelling next door to the Inn, The Horse and Groom.

Walpole has been careful over the Catholic problem. Roman Catholics are still rightly regarded as dangerous, especially because of the Jacobite threat. They are not allowed to be MPs, or vote for that matter, and are not allowed to carry weapons. Other non-conforming Dissenters, so long as they are Protestant, can obtain an annual act of indemnity, but although they are fools, because they are Protestants they are not dangerous. The Church of England is the Church of common sense, non-persecuting and holding the balance. We hold the balance between the extreme positions of

[10] William Adams Junior was Rector of Rollesby from 1742-1801.

[11] Published in 1719. Regarded as one of the first novels but didactic in nature.

the fanatics.[12]

My four servants had no idea of the problems the country faced. They have only an interest in who is marrying who and what scandal dwells in the village. I insist they attend Morning and Evening Prayer, as I do with all the tenants, so the church is nearly always full. I try to educate them in the finer points of theology, but all too often gain the feeling that they sleep in the pews. It is not as if my sermons go much over the hour, and I am careful not to give them too much Latin or Greek. I sometimes worry about their lack of education, but it means little to them: they seem interested only in feeding themselves and staying warm in the winter. I always rise by nine in the morning, and like to go hunting with the squire: when we chase across the fields I always give the workers a cheery wave. They respond in a respectful way with little enthusiasm but I expect that is because they have been up since first light. In the summer many of them work from five in the morning to nine in the evening, but that does them good both financially and morally.

Sometimes I feel a little uneasy with myself because I do have a life of considerable ease. Although I lost much of my fortune, I am better off than most, for I can still maintain a reasonable household, and can afford my gun and horses. To put it bluntly there is little for me to do in such a small village. There are barely two hundred souls here and most of them are at work from daybreak to night. In the evenings they eat, drink and then collapse into sleep. Last year I had seven funerals, four marriages and eight baptisms. On Sunday there are two services and little else. I read a great deal but even the most basic theology is difficult to communicate to many in the congregation. If the squire and family are there I can raise the level of my intellectual input, but then I lose the rest. If I aim my sermon at the mass of the villagers the squire accuses me of being patronising. I rarely write my sermon out for this reason, and if the Mapes or Ensors are there I raise the level, and if not I can be more homely in my approach. I call in and visit

---

[12] Chadwick, H (Editor) (2000) *Not Angels but Anglicans* Canterbury Press, Norwich, p.180. 'This idea of the middle way had a long pedigree, but in this period it was invoked endlessly in a variety of formulations. In the Spectator article, the moderation of the Church offered a path between "Bigotry and Atheism". It was also claimed that the national Church occupied a median position between the competing ideals of religious unity and religious freedom. It maintained a middle way between the infallibilist authoritarianism of the Church of Rome and the excessive individualism of radical Protestantism. By distinguishing itself sharply from both deism and Methodism, it was charting a path between what Bishop Gibson described as the contrary evils of "lukewarmness" and "enthusiasm".'

anyone who is sick or injured, but that takes only a half-day at the most. I know that some of my rural clerical friends from nearby parishes relieve their boredom by travelling to London and leaving the parish in the care of clerks and curates. I cannot afford this so I content myself with country pursuits, especially hunting and fishing. I no doubt will have my critics who will say that I was not ordained for this life of ease, and all I can reply is that I am at least in the area of my parish if I am needed. If I were not here someone would have to be doing the Christian work because without a rector the villagers would be seriously let down. I only wish they appreciated this more even if my own conscience pricks me somewhat.

I made considerable efforts with the new thatch on the church roof. As soon as the winter harvest of reed cutters finished I personally supervised the grasping of the right canes and had severed them with my own sickles. The scythes are also fitted with a looped wand of hazel (called a bile) to clear the swathes.[13] I also purchased for St George's a new paten made by John Eastt in 1716.[14] By my own evaluation as I look back over my life here, I know I have committed the sin of negligence by not always paying due heed to the needs of my parishioners, but I have tried to do my best.

[13] Ellis, Ted (1982) *Countryside Reflections* Wilson-Polle, Norwich, p.115.

[14] Paten still in use on special occasions: the Sunday paten was presented by Dorothy Beare in memory of her husband.

CHAPTER 27

ooooo

William Heath (1721-1742)

George I, George II - gin drinking and the growth of trade

Dear Readers of the future,

This request landed up on my desk and I have no idea how it arrived here. I have asked the servants and at first suspected the cook, but I have given up and since the request has a peculiar novelty about it I shall pen a few words about my time here. Rollesby has been a comfortable tenure for me, although it was fortunate I had my family fortune. The patron is not particularly well off and my predecessor was foolish enough to lose his own income in the South Sea Bubble disaster. He died last year and his son is now under the patronage of my own patron. It is the intention that he will train at Cambridge and one day follow me in this benefice. I am, in a sense, a holding curate for the family. Even so, I am the rector and purchased an expensive flagon to go towards the church treasures.[1]

I have purchased several fields in the area by the trinity of Broads east of Rollesby. I tried to purchase some land by the smaller common along Back Lane, but a local man, White, has purchased most of the area. White is building a farm and already it is known as White's House Farm.[2] I have

[1] Still in use, dated 1728 it has the leopard's head crowned, lion passant: the marks are on the lid as well.

[2] Lloyd, Virginia *Landscape Analysis: A Study of the Parish of Rollesby, Norfolk* Unpublished private research, dates White Farm from early 18th century. This White Farm was to become a rectory in the 20th century during the time of the Reverend Raymond Grundy (see chapter 34) and is currently lived in by a churchwarden, Mrs L Lloyd, and her husband Dr A Lloyd.

joined a few other gentlemen and purchased a wheeled seed drill[3] and a hoe drawn by a horse to weed between the straight rows. This not only gives a neater appearance to the field but it is also much more efficient and there is not so much waste as with sowing by hand. We grow mainly corn at the moment because the normal buyers not only purchase it but also gin is in fashion and corn is its main constituent[4] and anyone with a distillery is open to good purchase. It is cheaper than ale and women in particular are fond of it as a tipple.[5] I have a concern that some people drink too much and I gather it has a detrimental effect on young mothers and their children, but I believe in freedom of choice and the corn sells well to those who distil this particular drink. I gather the Whig government are especially concerned about gin drinking in London, and there is gossip that they intend to tax gin out of the reach of the poor. This would not only be a shame for me economically, but I feel it unfair on the labouring classes. The poorer classes tend to die young anyway, because of the way they abuse themselves, and possibly because of their long hours of labour, not that honest labour should kill anyone. I said this only the other day to my stable lad when he was asking for two days off after Christmas; I could not grant this because I had guests staying in the rectory.

The labouring classes are not aware of the needs of hygiene as they should be: some of the homes here in Rollesby are nothing short of squalid. I had reason to call into the blacksmith's hovel next to the Horse and Groom Inn the other day and I saw inside his dwelling place: it was disgusting. It is no wonder I spend a good deal of my time burying children and babies: I spend more time in the graveyard for children under six than I do for their elders.[6] We had a measles outbreak in 1723 and it killed nine adults: there was little the doctors could do apart from bleeding the patients, and I am not sure that this is the best cure. When people have painful illnesses the doctors are lost and it is little wonder they look to gin for relief. Certainly when they have the occasional tooth drawn, a bottle of gin helps the moment pass and another bottle helps the mouth settle down.

---

[3] Invented by Jethro Tull in 1701.

[4] Gin was almost an epidemic at this time and in the cities it is claimed that one in ten died from this drink. See Hogarth's paintings.

[5] At this period distilleries could be set up by anyone and the tax was low.

[6] 20% of babies died in their first year, and in London fewer than a third of children reached the age of six years.

Several of the local people have taken to trade in a large way. The Youngs down Heath Lane have opened a stall in Great Yarmouth Market, and from what I gather they are flourishing. I purchased my favourite author's book, Daniel Defoe's recent publication of *Moll Flanders.*[7] I gather his father was a tradesman, a butcher, and Defoe himself a hosiery merchant of sorts. The world is changing in so far as some tradespeople are making plenty of money. It is a grubby way of life but it enables them to send their children to university: I hope that they are not allowed to lower the tone of these great institutions. Although Defoe is a Dissenter I find his literature quite entertaining. I keep the volumes out of sight whenever the patron calls in for a glass of wine.

My patron, although like most Norfolk men a Whig, has become highly critical of the Prime Minister, Walpole. The Tories have used this peculiar title of Prime Minister in a sneering way, but we Whigs feel it most appropriate. He tells me that whenever Walpole wants anything out of King George I he bribes one of the King's many mistresses. These German mistresses have been given English titles and they are very greedy. The King himself speaks no English and he and Walpole are obliged to converse in Latin. Many of the great men in court have mistresses; I gather it is quite the done thing. I suspect my patron of indulging in affairs of the heart in Norwich, and I have entertained the idea myself. The labouring classes do not have such ideas but they have little regard for the wedding vows when they are in their cups. So long as it does not entail the break-up of the family home I see little wrong in such indulgences. At least under Walpole the taxation is lower, the land tax most especially has been reduced and I suspect that the entente with France has been of some help in the financial security of the country. As a country we are important because we are Protestant, and even Spain's demand for the return of Gibraltar worries us little.

One of my main concerns has been the growth of local taxes such as turnpikes and tolls,[8] imposed on the grounds that the roads need upkeep. It costs me a penny every time I take the Yarmouth road by horse, but when I

---

[7] Published 1722.

[8] Bayne, A D (circa 1880) *History of Eastern England* James MacDonald, Yarmouth. Vol.II, p.312-313. 'Turnpikes continued to be a popular form of income during this century. In 1770 turnpike roads were made and opened from St Stephen's Gates, Norwich to Trowse; from the same gates to Walton; from St Benedict's Gates to Swaffam; from Bishop's Bridge to Caister; and from Norwich to Dereham, Swaffham, and Mattishall.'

go to Norwich in the coach it is as much as four pence, and a score of my cattle can cost as much as for a wagon which is six pence. There were some localised riots in 1726 regarding these charges but they came to nothing. None of us would mind paying such fees if they could use the soldiers to clear away the latest pestilence of highway robbery. I spent a Christmas holiday in London in 1724 and while at Tyburn I saw the infamous highwayman, Jack Sheppard, hanged.[9] Many regarded him as a hero, and most of London turned out to watch the event.[10] He made a heroic speech and I enjoyed my picnic and a bottle of good port while he spoke and then swung. It took me hours to get back to my lodgings because of the carnival atmosphere. I made another journey the following year to see Jonathan Wild executed at the same spot: they say he was the master of all criminals.[11] I have to confess to enjoying such occasions because they are always very festive. While in London I took quite a fancy to the tea and coffee shops; both drinks are inexpensive and one meets such interesting company in the better areas.[12] Tea drinking by the gentry and their ladies is quite the round in Rollesby: tea afternoons often dominate my diary. Soon it will be coffee mornings as well! That could make my social life in Norwich and Yarmouth very busy.

The religious upheaval of my youth has virtually disappeared; Roman Catholics are not to be seen in the proper walks of life, and the Bishop of Rochester, Francis Atterbury, was even sent to the Tower because he was suspected of conniving with the Jacobites.[13] On the more amusing side I gathered that a Charles Wesley, John Wesley and someone called George Whitefield had set up a Holy Club at Oxford. They are very strict in their religious observances and because of their systematic approach to religion they have been dubbed 'Methodists':[14] it will not last because it is too serious and takes the levity out of life. They sneer at hunting and all the good and pleasurable pursuits in life.

---

[9] 1724 November 16th.

[10] An estimated 200,000 onlookers.

[11] 1725 May 24th. 'Thief-Taker General' Jonathan Wild executed at Tyburn as master of the criminal underworld. Some histories discount this account.

[12] 1723. Reduction of duty on imported tea and coffee made the drinking more widespread.

[13] 1722 September 24th. In May 1723 the House of Commons passed the Bill of Pains and Penalties depriving the Bishop of his See and sent him into exile.

[14] Derisively named Methodists about 1733.

The gentry, with whom I naturally mix, generally have a poor opinion of the monarchy, though they are not Jacobites. When George I died[15] there was some hope for George II but it was misplaced. He abhors England and anything English, and Walpole has to rely on his friendship with the King's wife, Caroline of Ansbach. The Hanoverian King fails to understand the power of the English Parliament and resents the wealth of us English. I am told he is a short-tempered man who dabbles in all the political appointments. I did have the good fortune to see George II in 1736. He had sailed from Helveotslugs (a small port in Holland) and was exposed to extremely dangerous weather and landed in Lowestoft at a time I was fortunately staying with friends in that port. He arrived on January 14th and some local sailors met his barge as it beached and actually hoisted the King and the Countess of Yarmouth on their shoulders to bring them ashore! John Jex of that town greeted them and acted as their coachman for their two-hour respite in Lowestoft before heading for London via Ipswich.[16]

Sadly Walpole quarrelled with Townshend but to our betterment in the fields. Townshend, whom we have christened Turnip Townshend, came back to Norfolk[17] and had worked out a rotation of crops that I must confess seems to work. On the farms we have also found Tull's work on horse-hoeing very useful.[18] Townshend's departure has benefited our crops but Walpole is now floundering. He lives in a very grubby house at 10 Downing Street but virtually has a monopoly of power. Even some Whigs now oppose him, mainly because Walpole angers many and inspires no one. His main opposition comes from a young politician called William Pitt and I am sure that we will hear more of this man as times passes. Many of us feel the country needs an issue to unite us, and it may be we have found it with the war currently in progress. Our slave ships, which were very productive, were being searched by Spanish coastguards, and a Captain Robert Jenkins had his ear cut off by a Spaniard. The nerve of this action, a Spaniard assaulting an English officer, was almost too much to bear. Captain Jenkins brought his shrivelled ear in a pickle jar to the House of Commons and the MPs all

---

[15] 1727 June 11th. George I dies at Osnabruck.

[16] Bayne, A D (circa 1880) *History of Eastern England* James MacDonald, Yarmouth. Vol.II, p.280.

[17] To Raynham Hall, Norfolk.

[18] 1733. J Tull publishes *The Horse-Hoeing Husbandry*, a scientific treatise to serve as a guide for the agricultural revolution.

rose in rebellion at what the Spaniards had dared to do.[19] Walpole had to declare war[20] and all over the country we rang bells in celebration. A few weak-minded people wondered why we should ring bells at the beginning of war, but they have no patriotic feeling. We all sang 'Rule Britannia' during Evensong.[21] Sadly Walpole is no leader for a nation at war; he was a manager of money and patronage, and after twenty-one years in office had to resign.[22] There are those who want to investigate his time in office because they say he made much money out of it. Such people are small-minded. There are those of a similar type in Rollesby, always sticking their obnoxious noses into my affairs. They seem to think that because I am the rector of the parish they have the right to know my business. I have heard rumours that they say I charge too much for funerals and weddings, pay my servants too little, race my horses too far, and have a mistress in Martham. I actually like the occasional gambling flutter in Yarmouth; they never mention that little weakness. I have a social station in life and it is my duty as a rector to uphold it and not bow to the servile demands of labouring parishioners. They should be grateful that I do bury and marry them, I even give up the occasional afternoon to baptise their brats. A few years ago in the great frost[23] I allowed the downstairs servants a fire in the scullery, they forget these little pleasantries which I have done for them: instead they watch my every movement and gossip about my private life. As a member of the gentry I am above their silly hearsay, but I cannot help but be conscious of their coarse observations. It is not easy being a country parson and most people would lose their minds with the boredom. I do my duty when called upon but have to have an active life between Sundays in an effort to keep my sanity.

---

[19] 1738 March 28th.

[20] 1739 October 19th. Walpole reluctantly declares war on the Spanish, now known as the war of Jenkin's Ear.

[21] 1740 August 1st. Composed by Thomas Arne.

[22] 1742 January 11th. Succeeded by the Earl of Wilmington, with Carteret as Secretary of State.

[23] 1739 December 25th. 'Great Frost' in South and East England until February 8th.

CHAPTER 28

ooooo

William Adams (1742-1801)

George II, George III - winning an Empire to the Napoleonic War

Dear Reader of some time future,

I have been the rector of Rollesby for some fifty-nine years and my father held the tenure before me, although he was not my immediate predecessor. Had he been asked to write a similar letter, dear reader, you would have heard how the malicious bankers ruined him in the days of the notorious South Sea Bubble. He saved sufficient funds for my education. At the time of the financial disaster I was only five years of age and he had to dismiss my tutor and educate me himself. I was eventually ordained at the age of twenty-three and did a small curacy before I took over from William Heath in 1742. My father allowed Heath to be rector on the understanding that on my father's death I was to take over the incumbency. My father was sixty-two years of age when he died and I paid for him to be placed in a vault below the sanctuary. I placed my mother there when she died in 1755. She survived until she was seventy-five years old. Sadly I also buried my wife, Elizabeth, there in 1784.[1] Also interred in the same vault is my daughter Mary and her husband William Hurnard. I seem to be outliving everyone.

I have now passed through the eighteenth century and am now in my eighty-fifth year, considered by some of my parishioners as past good serv-

[1] The tombstone with the family details is beneath the carpet in the chancel just at the edge of the sanctuary.

ice, but I think held in high affection, if only for my age. Whether I shall see the year 1801 out is another matter, and I take each day as it comes, and only hope I have sufficient energy to complete this task. I own several prosperous farmlands in the area, relying heavily upon the good work of Thomas Palgrave to maintain the work. I married him to Mary Carmen of Rollesby in 1773 and they have both proved very supportive of me in my older age.[2] The farms are reliable and bring in a steady income.[3]

There has never been a century like the one I have lived through and I suspect the mysterious request has arrived on my desk because of this fact. I have seen so many changes in the parish and in the world. Throughout my life there has been perpetual world war with the rise and fall of empires. In the parish I have seen the rise and fall of families as I have seen the rise and fall of eminent politicians and countries. I have been blessed to have lived so long and seen so much. I know other centuries have had their lows and highs. I was sharply reminded of this in 1753 when I heard that a Lambeth Palace gardener had killed William Laud's tortoise. I reflected on Laud's execution in 1645 and worked out that his tortoise had survived another hundred and eight years[4] but died a death similar to that of his master. I have always been an admirer of William Laud and the death of his strange beast caused me to read about the past. Nevertheless, the period through which I have lived has to be unequal to other moments of history in many ways.

When I took over Rollesby in 1742 we were, as we still are, caught up in European wars with alliances coming and going. In the Austrian War of Succession we were allied to that country against France, then allied with Prussia against France and today in 1801 we are still at war against our traditional enemy across the channel. I can recall the days when Pitt was a rising star and disliked by the then king, George II. Pitt, whatever views history may place upon him, was a gifted leader. In Pitt's early days as a

---

[2] Palgrave, Derek A *The Palgraves of Rollesby, 1773-1973* Private publication undated.

[3] Palgrave, Derek A *The Palgraves of Rollesby, 1773-1973* Private publication undated. 'Marshall, whose *Rural Economy of Norfolk* was written at the very end of the 18th century visited the area on May 12th 1782 to see the country and the celebrated husbandry, of the Flegg Hundreds. He noted the rich soil and standards of husbandry which in Rollesby he considered passable. Apparently the farmers in the area were noted for their quick dispatch of business, and for the great quantity of work they got done by a given number of servants and labourers. Marshall was clearly impressed by the state of the hedges in Flegg. "in this necessary piece of husbandry the Flegg husbandmen excel."'

[4] Chadwick, H (Editor) (2000) *Not Angels but Anglicans* Canterbury Press, Norwich, p.158.

member for Old Sarum[5] the King had bitterly opposed Pitt's entry into government. The King himself was not much liked; he preferred Hanover to England and we preferred him to stay in Hanover. Apart from his personal bravery in 1743, at the battle of Dettingen,[6] he was not much liked.

However, he was Protestant, and our enemies, France and Spain, had encouraged the Roman Catholics in Scotland to rise in yet another Jacobite rebellion. As we were English, we always had a distrust of Roman Catholics, and whoever reads this in the future probably still feels the same. If anyone in the parish was suspected of being Catholic they were and are virtually unemployable and in danger of being chased from the parish. I have since heard the Jacobite leader described as 'Bonnie Prince Charlie'[7] but he was a mere pretender and an insidious enemy of the state. It is true there was a slight panic when the Jacobites first rose and invaded England. I was in London at the time the news started to percolate through. There was a run on the banks and one could withdraw only sixpences at a time. In Rollesby a passing Scotsman was badly beaten and had to flee for his life. This part of Norfolk has always been staunchly Protestant and Parliamentarian and does not take to strangers easily. It is not so much a matter of principle as a matter of rural isolationism. The King's son, the Duke of Cumberland, put paid to Scottish hopes at Culloden. It was a pitiless battle I am told and many of the captured were put to death whether they were of high or low estate.[8] After that, kilts were outlawed and the bagpipes banned: I always thought it silly men wearing skirts and the bagpipes deserved to be banned; they are as musical as a dying cow. Strangely enough the Jacobite scare soon subsided and Scottish people could travel through Rollesby fairly safely once again.

In the parish we were soon concerned about the Gin Act[9] which was put in place to tax the drink and thereby restrict the sale. As with my predeces-

---

[5] Old Sarum was a bump in the ground and the owner could nominate whom he liked for Parliament, thus the expression 'pocket borough' because it 'was in his pocket' - a 'rotten borough'.

[6] Battle of Dettingen June 27th 1743. George II was the last English monarch to lead troops in battle. The allies won but 2,000 men were lost against 4,000 of the enemy and little gained.

[7] 1745 July 23rd. Prince Charles Edward, 'the Young Pretender', lands on Eriskay Island.

[8] 1746 April 16th. Battle of Culloden was the last chance of the Stuart Succession. A thousand Scots were killed within half an hour, many prisoners were hanged and leaders beheaded. Others were deported. Cumberland himself became known as 'the Butcher'. Charles led a life of drink and debauchery, had no heir and died in 1788.

[9] 1751.

sor and my father before him this caused me some concern. The grain was part of my income and I have always been cynical about politicians using tax as a moral force when in fact it is just another form of governmental income. I am sure future governments will never do this. Having said this I have to confess that gin drinking is a serious vice: when I was in London I was told that in the capital alone there are over seven thousand gin shops! On that occasion I was fortunate enough to hear Handel's *Messiah* performed at Covent Garden in the presence of George II.[10] I could not help comparing the gin-sodden women on the pavement selling their bodies to the beauty and sophistication of Handel's music. It is the same in Rollesby; life in the agricultural cottages can be brutish compared to the patron's Hall and the Rectory. One friend told me that gin was a pleasant escape for the working classes: personally I care little for their standards, it is a free world and so long as they pay their dues the choice must be theirs.

Some of the better landholders in Rollesby are respectable, and there is even discussion of forming a parish cricket team, especially after the Kent match.[11] I doubt whether it will come to much as a game, and it was certainly not helped by some parish women wanting to join.[12] I personally objected because it lowers the proper esteem in which women should be held. To see women chasing after a bat and ball, from whatever class they come, is most unseemly. It can also be a dangerous game and I can recall the Prince of Wales dying from being struck with a cricket ball.[13] Personally I prefer the more genteel sport of golf and I sometime practise this game on my lawns, even at the age of eighty-five.[14] I always preferred quieter games because I have an intense dislike of losing my wig in public. I did so while out shooting by Rollesby Broad. I lost the wretched thing in the mud and it cost me a full guinea to buy a new one.[15]

Although I lost money after the Gin Act my wealth soon recovered. The American colonies had a demand for sheep and wool and I invested in the

---

[10] 1743 March 23rd. *Messiah* at Covent Garden when George II originated the custom of standing for the Hallelujah Chorus.

[11] 1744 June 18th. First fully documented cricket match between Kent and All England at Finsbury, along with printed codes of cricket law.

[12] 1745 June 26th. Earliest women's cricket match: Bramley v. Hambleton, Gosden Common, Surrey.

[13] 1751 March 20th. Prince of Wales dies from pneumonia following a cricket accident.

[14] 1754. First written rules for golf agreed at St Andrews, at the foundation of the Royal and Ancient Club.

[15] Woodforde, James (Editor) Beresford, John (1978) *The Diary of a Country Parson 1758-1802* OUP, p.1.

East India Company. At first I thought the investment a disaster, especially after the disastrous and callous brutality of the Black Hole of Calcutta.[16] Eventually, of course, under Clive we were successful[17] and my investment is giving due and proper return, enabling me to start rebuilding the Rectory in a style proportionate to my station in life. There is little talk amongst the parishioners about the great events in the colonies; they are concerned only about their income and livelihoods. They are not far-sighted, even the best informed amongst them has little idea where India or America is apart from 'across' the sea. I have sometimes tried to explain to them the immense distances involved, but few of them have left Norfolk or even the Flegg area. When Admiral Byng[18] was shot for the loss of Minorca they had no idea where Minorca was, and as for poor old Byng they could not care less.

They did however come close to a riot along with the working classes elsewhere in the country when we changed the calendar in 1752. Up to that period in time we English used Julius Caesar's calendar, the Julian calendar, and our New Year's day was always March 25th. The continent used the Gregorian calendar named after Pope Gregory XIII and we came in line with them by having September 2nd immediately followed by September 14th. There were two types of protest. From the thinking classes there were those who strongly objected to us following Europe, a sort of fear that we would become part of Europe, that they would dictate to us: that will never happen of course, the concept of England being part of Europe. We are a world Empire. The working classes who could articulate their thoughts believed they had lost a period of their lives! Old John Greives, whose birthday fell on September 8th, thereafter claimed that for two years he was forty-two and when he died twenty years ago his gravestone had his age a year younger than he was in reality. For many years after this there only had to be the slightest local trouble and superstitious people blamed it on the calendar changes. As late as 1756 we had a slight earthquake, which was felt in Norwich through to Rollesby and Yarmouth.[19] Down at the Horse and

---

[16] 1756 June 20th. Siraj-ud-Daula, allied to French in Bengal, seizes Calcutta; over 120 victims die in the Black Hole.

[17] 1757 June 23rd. Clive defeats Siraj-ud-Daula at the Battle of Plassey.

[18] 1756 May 20th. Admiral John Byng breaks off naval action against French off Minorca and in 1757, on March 14th, was shot at Portsmouth for cowardice. Pitt opposed this since Byng was an obvious scapegoat.

[19] Bayne, A D (circa 1880) *History of Eastern England* James MacDonald, Yarmouth. Vol.II, p.282. Jan 10th.

Groom Inn pundits were blaming the calendar change, quite why I could never fathom. There had also been a disastrous fire in Norwich which nearly destroyed the old city, Bridewell[20] and many adjoining houses.[21] As with Holt in 1708 (May 1st), which had had a similar fire that nearly destroyed the town, it was undoubtedly caused by a careless accident. However, the same pundits later blamed it on the calendar despite the fact that the Norwich fire occurred on October 22nd 1751, a year before the calendar change. Such foolery is beyond belief.

When I say we are an Empire we certainly felt that we were in the mid-eighteenth century, especially after the defeat of the French in the Americas and Canada. The only sadness was the death of Wolfe at Quebec.[22] Perhaps the reader can understand why I refer to a world war. Pitt's policy of giving British money to Frederick of Prussia has worked. He occupies the French in Europe while we beat them around the globe; it is a policy that stretches their resources.

On the other hand our parish resources are also stretched. The patrons, the Mapes-Ensors, have paid for a few box pews in the church for the family and visiting guests, and other chairs have been provided, but I have had to finance them myself which is most annoying. It all came at a time when I had paid out for two good hunting horses. I no longer ride at my age, but in those days it was important that as the parson of the parish, I had the best and was seen in the right company.

Money is always a problem both for the church and myself. It always amazes me how some people seem lucky in life while others lose their fortunes. I had a good friend in Norwich, Mr Renden Deave, who in 1768 found his foreman wishing to sell one of two lottery tickets he had purchased. Deave bought one, No 42,903, and he won £20,000. He was already rich being a manufacturer. He felt sorry for his foreman so he wrote him a cheque for £500 but the chap still hanged himself. Deave gave the ticket to his London lawyer to draw the proceeds and the lawyer disappeared never to be seen again.[23] I think lotteries are immoral and should be banned; they

---

[20] Bridewell - an old building first erected in 1370 by Bartholomew Appleyard: his son William was the first Mayor of Norwich in 1403.

[21] Bayne, A D (circa 1880) *History of Eastern England* James MacDonald, Yarmouth. Vol.II, p.282.

[22] 1759 September 18th. British capture Quebec; both Wolfe and Montcalm killed.

[23] This true story is related on p.312, Vol.II of Bayne, A D (circa 1880) *History of Eastern England* James MacDonald, Yarmouth.

never seem to bring happiness.

I can clearly remember hearing the news of George II's death[24] and the succession of his grandson, George III. It was supposed to be a time of a greater constitutional monarchy with no more talk of divine rights of kings but a matter of political expediency. Our only concern was the new king's age, at only twenty-two, and it was no relief when the Earl of Bute,[25] his old tutor took political sway, but it did not last long. The locals who knew little of such matters, except what I told them, did hear that unlike the previous Georges the new king was English, spoke English and appreciated being English. That certainly helped the popular cause.

Not that kings and their governments are popular for long: whoever you are, mysterious reader of the future, I am sure you still criticise your monarch and Prime Minister. When the Treaty of Paris ended the Seven Year War[26] there was much bitterness in the parlours of the well-to-do and thinking people and it was generally agreed that we had given too much away simply to end a war. It certainly made Bute unpopular and he soon resigned. The King was not held to blame but he made himself unpopular when Wilkes published his newspaper, the *North Briton*.[27] Indeed it was a scurrilous paper, satirical and cynical and rude, but we have reached a stage where free speech is important. Later of course Wilkes was found guilty of seditious libel and obscenity[28] and fled the country. I never read the *North Briton* or his *Essay on Woman*, but I have been told it was not the kind of writing a parson should read. I have seen some drawings of naked women and although I find them quite entertaining I dread to think what would happen if the working class had access to them for it would inflame their base passions out of control.

We are a heavily populated country, over seven million live in these islands but many are just poor and working class. Many of the population are virtually outcasts, and no better than the slaves that can be purchased at the ports. The pregnant women and elderly are a serious problem because

---

[24] 1760 October 25th. George II dies at Kensington Palace.

[25] Bute, who had next to no political experience, was Prime Minister for a very brief time.

[26] 1763 February 10th. Peace Treaty ends war: Canada, Nova Scotia, Dominica, Grenada and Tobago ceded to Britain.

[27] 1763 April 23rd. *North Briton* No 45 and Wilkes being hostile to George III landed him up in the Tower.

[28] 1764 February 21st.

the issue always falls on the parish. It was about this time that we started thinking of a poor house down New Road in some fields I own. I shall touch upon this enterprise later, but its origin was our concern with the parish being littered with labourers who could no longer work or care for themselves, and pregnant spinsters in the hedgerows. I spoke with Francis Miles[29] about the problem and he set to with plans to erect a Poor House. There is, if I am being honest (and at my age there is no point in being otherwise), a mixture of motives. As a parish we did not like the litter and debris of humanity scattered over our landscape and we also felt a Christian obligation to do something. Many deserved all that came their way, such as loose women who had allowed themselves to be seduced by sons of landowners and old labourers who had made no provision for their old age. A sense of compassion provoked us into action, but also a sense of righteous anger at their being in our parish.

Money of course was always the issue, as we were heavily taxed;[30] I even filled in two windows of the Rectory to avoid the window tax.[31] Many of the problems arose because of poor and corrupt administration from London and the fact that we were conquering the world. We are a worldwide power without embarrassment: it is a good thing because we take Church of England Christianity wherever we go, with justice and good order, but it costs very much. Captain Cook even opened up the great sea routes to the other side of the world in my time here.[32] But all the time we had to fight the dastardly French who tried to thwart our natural rights as the superior nation. In America we had to garrison the place in order to protect the colonists against not only the French but also the savages, sometimes called Red Indians. When we tried to tax them to help pay for this they objected and then the colonists declared a war of independence during which they took control of our land. The elderly Pitt seemed to side with the American colonists, claiming they should not pay taxes if they were not represented in Parliament: that of course was a nonsense because everyone in this country has to pay taxes and only a few, quite rightly, are allowed to vote.

---

[29] Whose gravestone can be found in the north part of the graveyard by the 20th-century war memorial: Francis Miles, husband of Mary, who died August 6th 1791.

[30] In the mid-18th century the government collected over four million pounds a year in tax, by the end of the century it had risen to thirty-two million pounds.

[31] Window Tax since 1696 and much used and abused in this century.

[32] 1769 October 7th. Cook reaches New Zealand and on April 28th 1770 discovers and names Botany Bay.

There was plenty of money in Yarmouth because of smuggling, which was very popular and still is. I have to confess that I have purchased smuggled goods myself, especially silk handkerchiefs, tea at only three shillings and sixpence a pound and rum at a few shillings a bottle. We all know that the government is against such enterprise but then they tax us to poverty so it is justified in some ways. It is not real crime, of which there is plenty. The back streets of the cities are just as dangerous as the countryside at night. At least in London they have thief takers and Bow Street Runners started by Henry[33] and John Fielding. We have been obliged to hang many a young thief from this small area alone. Poverty and starvation can never be the excuse for theft from the better off. I was robbed by a pickpocket in Drury Lane, London when I went to see Garrick act on the stage.[34] I heard later the scoundrel, who had stolen one of my prized smuggled handkerchiefs, was only nine, but he was duly caught and properly hanged.

We had a boy in Rollesby caught breaking into the Manor house, what we call the Hall. He was apprehended by the senior servant but escaped on the way to the assizes. No doubt he will eventually be caught. I know the family well. They tried to get some sort of so-called Methodist preacher to marry them, but since the Marriage Act they were obliged to come to St George's and pay the proper fees.[35] The new system of banns being called helped stop many irregularities, not least establishing that the two people could legally be married. I recall it was about 1754 that I was about to marry a young couple when the banns were interrupted because the girl was accused of being Jewish: we soon put a stop to that nonsense.[36]

I travelled to Oxford and London in 1770 and I was proud to be English. Whilst I was away on this journey Norfolk suffered the most terrible storm.[37] The Happisburgh and Strumpshaw Mills were blown down, many ships were lost off the coast and Freeman claimed that St George's bell tower swayed with the wind. I was glad I missed this. The storms

---

[33] 1749 May. Henry Fielding becomes Bow Street Magistrate, enlists help of 6 mobile 'thief-takers'; succeeded in 1754 by half-brother John, who further developed system of runners.

[34] 1747 September 15th. Garrick begins twenty-nine years as actor-manager at Drury Lane.

[35] 1753 July. Marriage Act: ends marriage by unlicensed ministers and regularises calling of banns.

[36] 1753 July 7th. Jewish Naturalisation Act tried to remove disabilities but was repealed a year later because of widespread hostility against Jewish people.

[37] Bayne, A D (circa 1880) *History of Eastern England* James MacDonald, Yarmouth. Vol.II, p.312. 1771 Dec 19th.

brought out the worst in people along the coast. The wreckers all along from Hunstanton to Caister were busy murdering survivors for any wealth the poor creatures had managed to bring ashore.[38] However, despite this setback the country was flourishing, full of ornamental gardens and large stately homes. I also travelled for a brief way on the canal they were constructing between Birmingham and the River Severn:[39] now I am an old man I realise the importance of these canals for the cheap transport of heavy materials, especially coal. The canal system is very effective and cheap, and although we are now building better roads with more durable surfaces the canal system seems to be the answer for the future. Since James Watt patented his 'fire engine'[40] it has proved to have many uses at collieries and tin mines. I have no doubt that although we are and will always remain an agricultural country the century I have just entered, the 19th, will be a century of industrial progress. I hope that the new urban working classes can fulfil their working obligations. Having noted this, I must express a concern regarding some of the ruling classes where gambling has become something of an obsession. Only the other day I heard of a young lord putting twenty thousand pounds on a game of cricket. I know that thousands change hands on a game of cards and horses but I was surprised to hear of betting on cricket. Some MPs have also indulged in these pursuits and this is not something I find satisfactory.

I had a mind to support the elderly Pitt's speech for Parliamentary reform in which he argued for the end of pocket boroughs and more seats for the counties: it was of course, lost.[41] Politics is still the main discussion in the thinking homes and the Hall. In Norfolk we are all country Whigs and were disappointed when Lord North was made Prime Minister in 1770. He is a Tory and we must not forget the origin of the word Tory, an Irish outlaw! Tories are still associated with Roman Catholics, and even the smell of a Catholic can cause a riot.[42] The King still controls the government by patronage, especially by posts and pensions. I was always glad that

[38] Bayne, A D (circa 1880) *History of Eastern England* James MacDonald, Yarmouth. Vol.II, p.333.

[39] 1772 September 14th. Completion of the link canal.

[40] 1769. James Watt patents steam engine.

[41] Parliamentary Reform had to await 1832 but Pitt the Elder spoke on the subject many times fifty years earlier.

[42] 1780 June 2nd-8th. Anti-Catholic hysteria leads to Gordon Riots in London: mob caused widespread damage and about 850 people were killed.

North was able to keep Wilkes out of Parliament, even though he was re-elected three times while inside prison,[43] and surprised at his bothering to insist on Spain recognising our rights on some rocky islands in the South Atlantic, called the Falklands.[44] Such a waste of time, whoever will care about tiny islands called Falklands? It is typical of politicians to be stirred up on the silliest of issues. When Wilkes was made Lord Mayor of London[45] I despaired: I hope never again that there will be another Lord Mayor of London so popular among the people.

London is a long way from Norfolk but transport and new roads make it closer, and I gather that there is a mail service from London to Bristol, which takes only seventeen hours.[46] The Prince of Wales travels from London to Brighton and back, some 180 miles simply by saddle! There is talk that one day it will be possible to travel from Norwich to London in a single day, but I doubt that will ever happen to those reading my account in the future. There is only so much that horse power can achieve. My newspaper, the *Daily Universal Register*, now very stupidly calling itself *The Times*,[47] is always full of such futuristic predictions. The paper has gone downhill and spends too much time on scandal, not least when King George III went mad, and also gives too much time for those who would set slaves free; they are, after all is said and done, private property.

As I look back over the last few years there have been two things in particular that have caused me concern. If I remember rightly, the first dates back to 1784 when the nondescript John Wesley provided for the continuance of the 'Yearly Conference' for the so-called Methodists and named a hundred ministers. This is a heresy I am surprised to see grow and I am equally surprised that the bishops do little about it. It will not last long because they are a challenge to the Established Church. The main issue is that they make themselves popular with the masses by entertaining hymns and songs: it will soon lose its momentum. I was told recently that the Reverend John Wesley and his brother Charles had visited Norwich as early

---

[43] 1770 April 18th.

[44] 1771 January.

[45] 1774 October 13th.

[46] 1784 August 2nd. John Palmer established first mail-coach service.

[47] 1788 January 1st. *The Times*, from the *Daily Universal Register* founded by John Walter on January 1st 1785.

as 1754 but at that stage they were generally unknown except by some old soldier at Lakenham, a small hamlet of the city. It was there Charles Wesley preached his first so-called Methodist sermon to the locals, I am told.[48] I was further informed by the Dean that John Wesley visited again the following year and on July 1st 1755 preached his first sermon at a place called Foundry, near Orford Hill.[49]

Yarmouth Methodism was started about the same time (1754) by an itinerant preacher called Thomas Olivers, and he had several public meetings in the market place. In Rollesby they meet in an old cottage now named Chapel Cottages part way down Back Lane.[50]

The second was the fall of the Bastille in Paris in 1789,[51] which led to the bloodshed in France and now the current war against Napoleon. The war worries me little: I am personally convinced that despite his victories, Napoleon will burn out. Our Royal Navy and the King's Army will eventually triumph. Only last year (Oct 6th 1800) the illustrious hero, Nelson, a fine Norfolk sailor, arrived in Yarmouth having been absent from England for two years seven months. He was received with due honours and given the freedom of the borough. Nelson will put the French in their place. But I do fear revolution. I recall in 1795 (Jan 19th) being in Yarmouth when the Princess of Holland, her son and several Dutch nobility sought refuge in the port. The lower classes can be frightening and a Statute in 1795 put an end to public meetings where the topics were political or religious.[52] This was none too soon because a year later Thelwell, a political lecturer, was declaring on the rights of man at Yarmouth when a party of sailors broke into the room to seize the orator. After the general fighting it was discovered that over forty people were seriously bruised in the scuffle, though the orator escaped. The real danger was the popularity of the revolt amongst the labourers in this country: the talk of revolution was not healthy. Several times I spotted Freeman and Goodwin, two smallholders down Heath Road, looking greedily at the Rectory and the Hall as if anticipating the day

---

[48] Bayne, A D (circa 1880) *History of Eastern England* James MacDonald, Yarmouth. Vol.II, p.287.

[49] Bayne, A D (circa 1880) *History of Eastern England* James MacDonald, Yarmouth. Vol.II, p.287.

[50] Lloyd, Virginia *Landscape Analysis: A Study of the Parish of Rollesby, Norfolk* unpublished private research - 1784 map ... Chapel Cottages.

[51] July 14th.

[52] Bayne, A D (circa 1880) *History of Eastern England* James MacDonald, Yarmouth. Vol.II, p.321.

they would take them over. I spoke sharply to them both and was astounded with the confidence with which they replied.

'Well, Parson Adams, you have the lands around here and you charge us much, but the aristocrats in France have paid the price in France for their abuse of power.'

'My dear man, you're not accepting regicide are you?'

'Regi what?' Freeman asked.

'The killing of kings.'

'We've done it before.'

The thought chilled me, and I dug my spurs into my horse and left them with a sharp rebuke that I expected to see them at Evensong.

I wondered why I had ever bothered with these labourers, these so-called parishioners; to think that in 1775[53] Miles and I and many other landowners spent hours and money on erecting down New Road the House of Industry for the poor and destitute. I spent hours working out the inscription for the founding stone: it reads 'The Old Court House for the Instruction of Youth, the encouragement of industry, the relief of want, the support of old age and the comfort of infirmity and pain.'[54] We have nearly a hundred in there now, with ages ranging from nine months to eighty-nine years. I am chairman of the Board of Guardians, not that I manage many meetings these days; we always meet on a Tuesday morning and hold the Petty Sessions for the local crime in the afternoon. Some people now call New Road, Court Road[55] because of this development. Many of the petty criminals are or have been workers in the House, and we manage their lives in such a way they have little time for their nefarious activities. This has been a massive load of work in my latter years but I see it as Christianity at work, and a House of Industry, or as some insist on calling it, a Workhouse, would meet the approval of God Himself. I am not a complicated man and I hope that when my last day comes I shall be judged as a simple Christian soul who did his best to love his neighbours, with the obvious exception of the French.

---

[53] The House of Industry opened in 1777: it took in eighty-nine inmates and was what we call a Workhouse. It cost £2,300 and was built on twenty-two acres for up to 400 people.

[54] Original stone tablet dated 1776.

[55] There is no reliable evidence as to when Court Road took on its new name.

CHAPTER 29

ooooo

Thomas Baker (1801-1841)

From the Napoleonic Wars to Queen Victoria

Dear Reader,

I have been Rector of St George's, Rollesby for forty years, but I fear that because of my ailing health I shall not reach the age of my predecessor, William Adams, who died in April 1801. He was well respected by the parish because of his age and wisdom: he lived to eighty-five years of age and when the Bishop asked him to consider the possibility of retirement he replied that he did not view his appointment as temporary. Through the patron's gift of advowson and my own family fortune, I purchased considerable land as well as the necessary glebe property. This glebe land was important because it provided a most satisfactory income. The main problem was the sudden growth of rabbit warrens. The locals had made little effort to clear out these pests because they provided meat for their tables: they call rabbit meat 'hollow meat'[1] but I employed Goodwin as a gamekeeper to solve the problem. Rollesby is not a wealthy parish but I have managed to do well here in my time. Being responsible for the sanctuary, I had it fully restored as soon as I arrived with the addition of some scriptural texts painted upon the walls. The wardens are responsible for the nave and they did their best.

My main problem has been averting scandalous talk: I have led a clean

---

[1] Bayne, A D (circa 1880) *History of Eastern England* James MacDonald, Yarmouth. Vol.II, p.332.

living life that one would expect from a clerk in Holy Orders. Because I had trouble finding a decent housekeeper when I was a bachelor, and having had six housekeepers in three years, my early time in my first parish was riddled with hearsay and local gossip. One of these housekeepers was made pregnant by a stable lad and together they fled to King's Lynn. A passing sailor from Yarmouth made the third one pregnant and because I felt sorry for her I paid her ten guineas. Many of the parishioners believed this to be a statement of personal guilt rather than Christian charity. It all came to a head when the country's papers and magazines were alive with the scandal of Dr Edward Drax Free, Rector of Sutton Church, Bedfordshire. He had fornicated and had had criminal intercourse with several housekeepers; he had been forced to pay for their children. He had sold the lead from the chancel roof, used the graveyard as a farmyard, kept pigeons in the church, failed to take services, refused to bury the dead unless exorbitant fees were first paid and committed many other misdemeanours.[2] This excited the public at large because everyone enjoys seeing a public figure pilloried in the press, especially the clergy. The inhabitants at the Horse and Groom Inn, who cannot read, had the son of the parish clerk read them all the facts of the case. They were all of the opinion that the Church of England was rotten through and through and that I must be as bad as Dr Drax Free. I reprimanded the clerk's son, but it was to no avail since his reading lessons earned him a few pints of ale each evening for his entertainment. Many of them started to leave the Church and attend Methodist meetings and I blame Dr Drax Free and other similar corrupt clergy for the growth of Methodism. Even the gentry started to gossip and speculate, which was ironic indeed, because the housekeepers at the Hall and other servants often leave unexpectedly and return a few years later dependent on the good offices of the Workhouse. I married my wife, Ann, before I came to Rollesby. This action stopped the local gossip here, but sadly the Methodists and Baptists[3] in Ormesby grew in strength because of my perceived weaknesses. It was only silly gossip based on the illogical thought that because I was Church of England I was therefore corrupt. I protest my innocence at this stage of the letter but do believe that the weaknesses of other clergy have brought the church into ill-

---

[2] Outhwaite, R B (1997) *Scandal in the Church: Dr Edward Drax Free 1764-1843* CUP, pp.145-6.

[3] 1813. Baptist General Union established for Britain and Ireland.

repute.

The House of Industry established by my predecessor, which I mentioned earlier, has run well. I have imposed new rules about drinking and smoking: both are now prohibited and the inmates must learn to live together in perfect Christian harmony without recourse to bad language. If it occurs, the master of the workhouse is to punish those responsible most severely. I insisted that a door that led from the male to the female quarters be blocked.[4] Money was a problem and we had to reduce the remuneration of all officers including the Governor.[5] I was concerned about the morals of the inmates, and all single men employed by the herring fishery industry and admitted to the house were confined and could leave only by permission of the committee.[6] We employed John Chapman as a Relieving Officer[7] for outside relief in 1837 but he resigned within three months and we never found a suitable replacement. Norman Britten[8] has been the main officer there during my tenure and agrees with me about moral conduct. Punishment of vice I believe to be an excellent virtue, which was why I was dismayed to hear the outcry in Norwich when German mercenaries flogged English militiamen.[9] Why should not wrongdoers be flogged? The poor especially need some form of discipline to keep them in place. We do enough for them anyway: there are soup kitchens in London,[10] and even industrialists show much zeal with their so-called philanthropy.[11] Not only this, but the Royal Lancastrian Institution was founded to promote the education of the poor on Joseph Lancaster's so-called monitorial principles.[12] If we are not careful, the poorer working classes will dominate this country; it is not always wise to teach the labouring classes to read and write, they may well get ideas above their station. We held the first ever census in this country in 1801 and I was shocked to hear that our population in England alone

---

[4] *Norfolk Fair - County Magazine,* May 1971, article by D A Palgrave, p.17. 1819.

[5] *Norfolk Fair - County Magazine,* May 1971, article by D A Palgrave, p.17. 1822.

[6] *Norfolk Fair - County Magazine,* May 1971, article by D A Palgrave, p.17. 1829.

[7] *Norfolk Fair - County Magazine,* May 1971, article by D A Palgrave, p.18.

[8] Bates, Ann. Private research from the *Norfolk Archaeological Society.*

[9] 1810 July 9th. Cobbett fined £1,000 and jailed for two years for denouncing flogging of militiamen at Norwich by German mercenaries.

[10] 1800 January 8th. First soup kitchens to relieve hungry poor in London.

[11] 1800 Autumn. Robert Owen begins philanthropic reforms for workers employed in his mills at New Lanark.

[12] 1808.

is 8.3 million:[13] in Rollesby there are only three hundred souls. Most of the population lives in the cities and industrial areas and I hope the landowners can keep them there. In the same year as the census, the Act of Union became effective and it is hoped that this will stop all the traditional problems we have had with that part of Great Britain. We have had problems in Rollesby as well; the General Enclosure Act,[14] which enabled many of us to enclose most cheaply large amounts of the common land for tillage was resented. The smallholders objected but they failed to regard the country's overall need for more food: they accused me and a few others of making money, which was most unfair. I was always grateful to my patrons for never levelling such silly accusations. When I first arrived it was the Mapes family but in 1824 the Hall formally passed to the Ensors,[15] really another branch of the Mapes through past marital arrangements.

Life can be very unfair for those of us in the educated classes: I recall the resentment I felt when clergy were excluded[16] from the House of Commons: along with the gentry we are among the few educated people in the land. I was even put under some pressure by the Bishop to consider an Interdenominational Sunday School.[17] I have never heard of such nonsense, and did not appreciate the Bishop trying to dictate such matters to an incumbent of a major parish. I have a good choir and there are four boys I oblige to attend, but this new fangled idea of Sunday Schools is a passing silliness, as is the idea of the Church promoting its own schools.[18] The Bishop even wrote to the clergy about not attending horse-racing, just after I had enjoyed a brief holiday at Ascot.[19]

I should mention that during my early tenure in Rollesby, we, as a nation, defeated the French dictator, Napoleon. Just before I arrived in Rollesby there had been a mutiny in the fleet in Yarmouth[20] but there was a

---

[13] 1800. First ever British census supervised by John Rickman: 8.3 million in England; 1.6 million in Scotland; 0.5 million in Wales; 5.2 million in Ireland.

[14] 1801 June.

[15] Women's Institute Federation (1990) *The Norfolk Village Book* Countryside Books, Norwich, p.173.

[16] 1801 June 23rd. Clergy Disqualification Act: clergy excluded from the Commons, but the Reverend John Horne Tooke, radical MP for Old Sarum, allowed to stay until the end of that session.

[17] 1803. Interdenominational Sunday School established in London.

[18] 1811 June. National Society set up to spread Anglican Church Schools.

[19] 1807 June. Ascot Gold Cup first run.

[20] Spread from Nore and Spithead, May 12th 1797.

general peace with France until 1803 when a dispute over Malta ruined it. It was a Norfolk sailor, Horatio Nelson, who defeated the Franco-Spanish fleet at the now famous battle of Trafalgar:[21] as a country we were proud of the achievement, especially in Norfolk. I actually travelled to Yarmouth to see this great man. It was summer, June 29th 1801, that the Vice-Admiral Lord Nelson arrived in our port in the kite sloop, Captain Donnett, from Copenhagen. He proceeded immediately on foot from the jetty to the hospital to enquire respecting his brave comrades. After staying for about three hours the great hero left the town for London attended by the volunteer cavalry.[22] The French then exhibited their true nature and established what we called the Continental System, an effort to stop us trading anywhere in Europe.[23] I predict that the French will always do their best either to keep us out of Europe or to try to marginalise us. They cannot of course succeed. We were somewhat concerned when Napoleon beat the Russians and Austrians at Austerlitz[24] but then the French were not dealing with us directly. I remember the concern when Wellington landed in the Spanish Peninsular, and reading Henry Crabb's[25] report in *The Times* all about Corunna. We had barely got over the continuous excitement of the Peninsular war when the Americans had the nerve to declare war against us;[26] this was of little consequence compared to the European war. It was a great relief when Napoleon took the war to Moscow[27] but was beaten by one of the harshest winters ever recorded in those parts. This was a sure sign God was on our side. After that it was downhill for the French: Wellington beat them at the battle of Vitoria[28] and so destroyed their hold on Spain. Then Napoleon was finally defeated at Leipzig,[29] exiled to Elba, escaped,

---

[21] 1805 October 21st.

[22] Bayne, A D (circa 1880) *History of Eastern England* James MacDonald, Yarmouth. Vol.II, p.361.

[23] 1806 November 21st. Napoleon's 'Berlin Decree' bans trade with British possessions through any port under French control.

[24] 1805 December 2nd.

[25] 1808 June 20th. First despatch from a specialist war correspondent.

[26] 1812 June 18th. US Congress declares war on Britain over naval interference with American shipping in blockading France.

[27] 1812 June 24th. Napoleon invades Russia; enters Moscow 14th September; last retreating troops leave Russia 14th December.

[28] 1813 June 21st.

[29] 1813 October 16th-19th.

and finally lost to Wellington at Waterloo[30] with a little help from Blucher.[31] I recall going to London to join in some of the celebrations, and in time to hear of the British Museum purchasing the elegant Parthenon Marbles from Lord Elgin:[32] it seemed that as we are the masters of Europe this was an appropriate acquisition.

However, while in London, I was conscious of the kind of trouble I had experienced in Rollesby. Ellis and Freeman had returned from the French wars first as heroes then as troublemakers. The main problem was the shortage of work and idle hands lead to the devil's work. They had been reported to me as claiming that the English should have the sort of revolution the French had had thirty years ago. They had gone so far as to suggest that the Enclosure Act was illegal, that there should be no bishops, and that gentry-type 'aristocrats' should have their heads lopped off and their land given to the villagers. Whilst I was not overly concerned about their drunken dribble in the Horse and Groom, my newspaper brought it to light that this kind of radical talk was more nation-wide than I anticipated. As I look back to those days of my middle age I realise that the main problem was the sudden reappearance of thousands of servicemen[33] with no work to do.[34] It was an awkward time: George III was mad and the Prince Regent, whilst stylish, was content to play in Brighton. It is true that I was personally more interested in Jane Austen's latest novels[35] and fascinated by the new gas lighting, especially for Evensong, but the politicians and monarch who should be in charge were in danger of losing control of crime and order. They passed a variety of Seditious Meetings Acts,[36] which gave magistrates the right to bring in the militia and treat crowds as the enemy. It is true that hunger was a problem[37] and some fellow clerics at a meeting expressed a degree of sympathy for the labourers, but I begged to differ. When the labourers next con-

---

[30] 1815 June 18th.

[31] A great deal of help!

[32] 1816.

[33] Over 300,000 unemployed servicemen cast adrift after 1815.

[34] During the war iron sold at £20 per ton, after the war only £8: ergo unemployment as well.

[35] 1816 *Emma* published; *Persuasion* and *Northanger Abbey* published posthumously in 1818.

[36] 1817 March.

[37] 1817 March 10th. 'Blanketeers' begin protest hunger march from Manchester to London, but 160 arrested at Stockport the next day. June 9th some 200 labourers from Pentridge, Derbyshire march on Nottingham but checked by cavalry. Similar uprisings in Huddersfield.

gregated in St Peter's Fields without informing the authorities in Manchester, it led to the so-called Peterloo massacre[38] when the yeomanry killed eleven people. At the next clerics' meeting I felt justified in my original assertions that the labourers were out of control, but a few still felt the government was too heavy handed. For my part I am convinced that a few more Peterloo massacres would solve the problem, and when I heard the local Methodist minister at Martham had criticised the government I wrote to him expressing my views. In Rollesby I could detect a high degree of resentment, but the labourers depended on our fields for their food so it stayed only at the resentment level. I did make a point of ensuring that Ellis and Freeman found no work. These people had to be taught a lesson. I rubbed further salt into the wounds of my clerical friends when it was revealed that some dangerous dissidents in Marylebone had plotted to assassinate the cabinet and take control of the government. They called it the Cato Street[39] conspiracy: they were all caught and, properly, five were hanged. The government banned meetings of more than fifty people and put a stamp duty on newspapers to stop radicals printing their own editions. I was sorry that the government had placed it as high as fifty people and excluded Quakers and Freemasons:[40] had it been around ten I could have had all the grumblers and disturbers of the peace in the Horse and Groom arrested and deported.

Life in the parish can be very frustrating: I become extremely annoyed when I read of other churchmen who see our task as mere social workers amongst the poorer classes. I blame it on affluent evangelicals like the 'Clapham Sect'.[41] We need more of the Oxford Movement where we must stress the importance of the sacraments and a sense of holiness and disciplined devotion.

It was during this period of my time in Rollesby that a great embarrass-

---

[38] 1819 August 16th.

[39] 1820 February 28th. Conspirators led by Arthur Thistlewood.

[40] 1819 December. The Six Acts passed.

[41] Chadwick, H (Editor) (2000) *Not Angels but Anglicans* Canterbury Press, Norwich, p.195. 'The leadership of early Evangelicalism was concentrated in the hands of a small group of affluent Anglicans, including the Wilberforces, the Venns, the Thorntons and the Macaulays - the Clapham Sect. William Wilberforce's *Practical View of the Prevailing Religious System of Professed Christians* (1797) was a passionate and extremely popular appeal for the recovery of a due sense of the seriousness of sin, repentance, and Christian responsibility ... he was prominent in the development of missionary work overseas, including the foundation of the Church Missionary Society and the Bible Society.'

ment occurred in the royal family, which I hope will never occur again. It was, and still is, a well-known feature that monarchs have problems with their children, especially the Princes of Wales. When George III died,[42] his son, the Prince Regent became George IV. He was a man given over to gambling, drinking and whoring. He had married a Mrs Maria Fitzherbert many years before. She was a Roman Catholic, a commoner and twice a widow. It was against the Royal Marriages Act, but on the other hand they had been married by an Anglican clergyman, Robert Burt, in Mrs Fitzherbert's drawing room in Mayfair. The Prince of Wales was then obligated to marry Princess Caroline of Brunswick: he was so devastated by her appearance it is said he was drunk at the altar and remained so for the first twenty-four hours of their married life. At the time of his father's death he tried to rid himself of her but the investigation by the government into her alleged adultery failed. She also had the support of the mob and ill-educated populace. I started to suspect her when she allowed a letter she had written to the King to be published in the press: this type of manipulation of the press is morally reprehensible. They barred her from the coronation[43] but a few months later she died unexpectedly at the age of fifty-three.[44] Her death solved several major embarrassments for the country. I hope nothing like this ever occurs again in the royal family. The labourers of Rollesby discussed this issue with amazing impertinence and fervour, as if they were all part of the royal family problem.

I have to confess that the masses terrify me. They are always demanding better conditions and there has even been talk of forming unions. Yarmouth can be a place of ugly social fermentation. On February 3rd 1825 there was a particularly unfortunate high tide in that port which did much damage to that area by the quay. Southtown was completely overflowed and made impassable and many lower rooms on the west side were flooded. Consequently much grain and other merchandise was spoiled. The masses not only indulged in looting but seemed to blame the high tide on those who were better off![45] Even in Norwich there has been serious unrest. The

[42] 1820 January 29th.

[43] 1821 July 19th.

[44] 1821 August 8th.

[45] Bayne, A D (circa 1880) *History of Eastern England* James MacDonald, Yarmouth. Vol.II, p.389.

camlet weavers resisted a proposed reduction in wages.[46] The main problem was that those camlet weavers in the north were paid more though their work was inferior. In Norwich some worked for a Mr Robberds and others protested and there were serious disturbances.[47] I was pleased when some rural labourers in Tolpuddle[48] who tried to join ranks were transported to Australia and only sorry when they were allowed to return. In the industrial areas Luddites destroy machinery, and there is unrest even in hitherto quiet agrarian areas.[49] There are a few in the Horse and Groom I would like to transport. The government has proved weak in control and I was sadly disappointed when they allowed the 1832 Reform Bills[50] to pass into law. I did not object to the new constituencies, but getting rid of the pocket boroughs was a mistake, some of our better political leaders started with such boroughs without having to convince the ignorant populace that they were the right men.

It is not that I lack Christian charity, though the Vicar of Ormesby implied that not long ago. I fully supported the Factory Act[51] forbidding children under nine years old to labour and restricting the working day to nine hours for children under thirteen. Mind you, I was impressed by the argument that the earlier children work in the mines the better, because they become used to working with a deformed back earlier and this makes them more productive as adults. It must be difficult for a thirteen-year-old working in the mines stooping because he has been allowed to develop a straight back. I also supported the argument that all slaves in the British Empire should be legally free.[52] They should be paid as servants although at a lower rate but they should not be slaves. I also supported the Poor Law Amendment Act which curbed outdoor poor relief and set up the Workhouse. In Rollesby we were ahead of the government in this: our House of Industry in Court Road had already been named a Workhouse,

---

[46] Bayne, A D (circa 1880) *History of Eastern England* James MacDonald, Yarmouth. Vol.II, pp.418-9.

[47] 1838 August 27th.

[48] 1834 March 18th. Tolpuddle Martyrs sentenced to 7 years' transportation and returned in September 1838.

[49] 1830 August-October. 'Captain Swing' agrarian riots in South England against enclosures and threshing machines.

[50] 1832 June 4th. Reform Bill approved: constituencies created in new towns; rotten and pocket boroughs abolished; franchise extended to include all upper middle class.

[51] 1833 April.

[52] 1834 August 1st.

and it is a very fine institution. When God calls me to account one day I shall point to the work I have done in Court Road. I hope, dear reader, that you will see in this modern age that I have been charitable towards my fellow creatures.

I have to confess I feel less charitable towards other denominations being allowed to flourish within the kingdom. The Methodists in particular are roaming through the area like poachers on my estate. There is even talk that they are considering building a chapel down Main Road and this does not impress me. In Yarmouth there is another breed called Congregationalists[53] but I do not think they will come as far as Rollesby. The Baptists are certainly active in Ormesby, but the Vicar there does very little to try and stop them. These Dissenters are certainly growing and take too much upon themselves. They are beginning to manifest open hostility to the Church of England in Norwich and other places, passing resolutions for the separation of Church and state.[54] These dissenters differ from one another in many different ways but somehow find a common bond in their opposition to the Established Church. The counter petitions have been effective and indeed helped to unify the Church of England. Indeed, there is a revival in the Church of England. John Henry Newman, Vicar of St Mary's, Oxford has published some fine tracts along with Keble,[55] and they are generating what has been described as the Oxford Movement. This return to proper sacramental worship should put the Baptists, Methodists and the Vicar of Ormesby in their place. I was bitterly disappointed when the government allowed licences to be issued for weddings in nonconformist chapels, and further irritated when we had to start keeping registers: the paper work is ridiculous.[56] The state feels all too free to meddle in Church affairs. Now we have ecclesiastical commissioners authorised to administer the estates and revenues of the Church of England:[57] the only amusing feature about this interference was the fact they equalised the stipends of the bishops. I thought that an excellent idea, so long as they steer clear of meddling with the structure of the parishes. The Church must stand up for

---

[53] 1831. Congregational Union of England and Wales established.

[54] Bayne, A D (circa 1880) *History of Eastern England* James MacDonald, Yarmouth. Vol.II, pp.395-6.

[55] 1833.

[56] 1836 August 17th. Marriage Act: the Registrar General appointed and registration became compulsory.

[57] 1836. Established Church Act.

itself, as when University College was set up in Gower Street, London for non-sectarian education[58] we established King's College in the Strand as an Anglican rival. I have no doubt that King's will prove to be the better college.[59]

In my time here I have seen the world become modern overnight. In Rollesby Hall they have added a new white brick wing which is more fitting with this modern age.[60] We have stagecoaches and mail coaches covering every part of the country[61] but I do not think the new steam railways will be effective, they are too slow and dangerous.[62] My only fear is that this instant type of communication can spread some diseases too easily: we do not want cholera and other city illnesses spreading to the rural areas such as Rollesby.[63] I am sure crowds and fast travel spread disease: when I went to Henley to watch my old university beat Cambridge at rowing[64] I came back with influenza, undoubtedly caught from someone in the immense crowds gathered for the occasion. My last trip to London was to watch the wedding of our Queen Victoria to her first cousin,[65] and again I caught an illness from the crowds from which I am still suffering. I did send myself a letter by means of the new penny post[66] and when this small correspondence arrived at the Rollesby Rectory before I did, I knew then the world was changing.

I wondered whether this letter was a hoax, and that it will simply gather dust in some diocesan archive, but if it is read in the future, even say in 1940, know, dear reader, that the modern world started in my day. In fact, I will be surprised if the world will change much more in the next hundred years than it has in the last forty.

I have worked hard for the Workhouse in Court Road, and spent many

---

[58] 1826.

[59] 1828 and this editor thinks his assertion right!

[60] Pevsner, N (1976) *The Buildings of England: North-East Norfolk and Norwich* Penguin Books, Middlesex, p.305.

[61] 1836. 3,300 stagecoaches and 700 mail coaches in service and over the next two years forty-four railway companies were established.

[62] 1830 September 15th. William Huskisson killed by Stephenson's Rocket at opening of Liverpool-Manchester railway.

[63] 1832 February 13th. Cholera comes to London (Rotherhithe, Limehouse).

[64] 1829 June 10th. First University Boat Race: Oxford beat Cambridge at Henley.

[65] 1840 February 10th. Queen Victoria marries her first cousin Prince Albert of Saxe-Coburg, at Chapel Royal, St James's.

[66] 1840 January 10th. Penny Post introduced by Rowland Hill.

hours on the bench as a JP: I feel that as a responsible Anglican cleric these are necessary tasks. Looking back over my time in Rollesby, I have felt a degree of anger and sorrow that the labourers view the church as a place to avoid and when they are obliged to attend I can see it is of little interest to them. In addition to this, I have always had the feeling they have viewed me with a degree of suspicion. I think it comes from the fact that they perceive me as a member of the landed class: this is of course true; nevertheless, I had hoped that they would treat me more as the shepherd of their souls. In my quieter moments I wonder whether I have always got it right. I have had to be tough with those labourers who have fallen foul of the law and landed up in the Workhouse, but sometimes it is necessary to be strong to be kind. This has always been my dilemma, the clash between my social duties as Chairman of the Workhouse and senior JP and my role as Rector and as shepherd to their souls. Despite my feelings towards some of my parishioners I nevertheless acceded to demands and gave the necessary land for the building of the first National School.[67] This edifice was designed for up to ninety children[68] and I was happy for them to have this basic education so long as it did not give them ideas beyond their station and encourage them to leave their natural labours in our fields.

I was thirty-two years of age when my wife Ann and I arrived in Rollesby. We came to escape the sadness of losing our five-year-old daughter Anna Maria in 1799.

The sadness did not stop in Rollesby. In 1822 we lost William Henry aged sixteen, two years later we lost another Anna Maria aged only thirteen. It broke our hearts. I wondered whether my wife Ann would cope with the losses. We had high hopes for our other children, but in 1828 Frances Jane died aged twenty-nine, and a year later my favourite son, Edward George died only twenty-one years of age. He had just passed into manhood. In 1834 my last son, Charles James died aged twenty; he did not make even manhood. All our hopes were founded on our last daughter, Georgiana Mary who married Major General Cock of the Bengal Lancers: together they bore us four grandchildren, but then, in 1840, last year no less, she died at sea whilst returning from India: she was only twenty-eight years old.[69]

[67] Stood where the village hall now stands.

[68] Women's Institute Federation (1990) *The Norfolk Village Book* Countryside Books, Norwich, p.174.

[69] All these tragic family details are to be found on two monuments attached to the south wall of the nave.

Ann and I have felt the loss of our family deeply. When Amphilles,[70] the wife of my good friend John Ensor, died at the age of fifty-six we felt that was tragic, but to lose seven children! I found considerable comfort from my friends, especially John Ensor and his young son the Reverend Edmund Ensor. Even some of the village people were kind, especially Annison the wheelwright, Appleton the blacksmith, Spanton his worker and Boyce our veterinarian. My gardeners, Crane and Gorble also expressed genuine sympathy.[71]

Although there were parishioners who cared little for us, nor I for them, some were fine upstanding people. I shall never forget the work of Thomas Palgrave who married Judith London at Runham in 1807.[72] He worked at the gardens of Rollesby Hall all my time and was a wise and wonderful craftsman. His eldest daughter, Susanna married Edward Annison (whom I have just mentioned) in 1836 and they became excellent yeoman farmers as a family. His other daughter, Mary Ann married Robert Frosdick in 1829 and they are becoming well known farmers in the area.

However, I do not think this letter requires me to list parishioners, so I shall close on the note that I have changed as the years have passed. The death of my seven children has affected me badly, and although many describe me as old fashioned, I have tried to do my best given the circumstance of the age in which I have lived. I now await my Maker to call me to Him in the hope I shall be reunited with my dear children.

---

[70] Memorial on north wall.

[71] Names extracted from Whites 1836-45.

[72] Palgrave, Derek A *The Palgraves of Rollesby, 1773-1973* Private publication undated.

CHAPTER 30

ooooo

Edmund Smith Ensor (1841-1860)

Early Victorian Period, poverty and wealth and war with Russia

Dear Reader,

I have at long last decided to reply to the mysterious letter. It has a semi-official request about it and for some reason I feel compelled to comply though my initial feeling was that it was a waste of time. My family is a longstanding component of the Rollesby parish and indeed have been patrons holding the advowson for some time. The family has two strains, the Mapes and Ensors and we have lived in the Hall since the 17th century.

I trained for Holy Orders without any intention of serving a title in my home parish, as it were. Our Lord said a prophet was never welcome in his home town but I came at the request of my family and not for any betterment or self-service. It was argued that a different style of pastoral leadership was needed after my predecessor, Thomas Baker. I always found Thomas a pleasant and easy man to live alongside, but that was because I am a member of the gentry. Thomas rightly considered himself a member of the upper middle classes and spent most of his time in our drawing rooms or those of our social equals. He had little or no time for the rest of the parishioners who are all agricultural labourers. Thomas was more at home hunting or fishing, and he gave short shrift to the members of the congregation. Thomas had a number of family tragedies that preoccupied him. He drove many away from the Church, some attending the Methodist meetings and others attending to nothing but their own frugal needs. From what I saw of the way he talked to the average parishioner I could hardly blame them, and indeed welcomed the attention they received from the Methodist minister. The Church both in Rollesby and elsewhere had stopped being the only Church for the people of England.[1]

The parishioners were, of course, sceptical when I was announced to the living, and who can blame them. They said nothing to me but I could feel them saying that we were keeping it in the family. That is not the truth, but as my father said to me, the Patron has a vested interest in the local community and that includes the care of their souls. They were equally suspicious of me because I had adopted the new style of clerical collar, what has been the dubbed the 'dog collar'.[2] I am of an evangelical inclination, but do not abhor the Oxford Movement's High Churchmen as many of my brother clerics do. I made a point of wearing the new collar to indicate that as a Christian I belong to no camp except Christ's. Furthermore, the dog collar has the advantage of letting any stranger know exactly who you are, and that there is a Christian presence at hand. I accepted the benefice on the day the Queen had her first son, and if he succeeds as the new monarch he will be King Edward VII.[3] I only hope that he does not give the Queen the same problem as all the Princes of Wales seem to have done in the past. On the day of my induction and installation the church was packed and the Bishop of Norwich spent the night with the family. The next Sunday, St George's was also fairly full, and I rightly judged that the congregation was out in force to hear how I preached. After the initial flourish of curiosity the numbers fell back to the usual fifty or sixty for Morning Prayer and thirty odd for Evensong.

I have mentioned that my predecessor had some unfortunate family

---

[1] Chadwick, H (Editor) (2000) *Not Angels but Anglicans* Canterbury Press, Norwich, p.214. 'a religious census of 1851 (the only one carried out by a government in England) revealed that practising churchmen and dissenters were about equal.' p.219. 'less than half the population went to any church. No longer the traditional claim to be England's Church.' p.220. 'inevitably, the statistics were not totally accurate. Out of some 14,000, almost 1000 places of Anglican worship never filled in the form, and their support had to be guessed ... villages varied. In some there was no church, or the population was scattered; but in others the parson really cared about the welfare of the whole community, - or less nicely, a squire who went to church could be thought capable of making employees who did not go jobless and homeless ... in East Anglia, Anglicans and Nonconformists were neck-and-neck: in Liverpool, Roman Catholics led.'

[2] 1835. Dr Gentili, an Italian priest placed in charge of a seminary at Prior Park, Bath, introduces the clerical dog collar to England.

[3] 1841 November 9th. Future King Edward VII born: made Prince of Wales, 7th December.

bereavements in his time; my own family suffered as well. My uncle, John Mapes Ensor, with whom I was very close when I was younger, was Her Majesty's Vice-Consul at Lorient. He was there for only three years when he died at Concarneau. For some extraordinary reason his dear wife had him interred there and did not return him to Norfolk. As a family we never understood her reasons. I have placed a memorial to him on the south chancel wall. I was with my Uncle John and his eldest son, John Mapes Webb Ensor, when we shot a great sea-eagle with a wing span of 2.20 metres.[4] Uncle John died on the 23rd February 1852, and barely three years later we heard that his son, who was a lieutenant with the 10th Foot Infantry in Bombay, died on April 22nd 1855, aged only thirty. I had another memorial erected in his memory on the same wall as that of Uncle John. It was at this stage that Rollesby Hall passed into my hands.

Enough of my family problems; my parishioners had more difficult times than I could ever experience. Although even the better off complained about the first ever peacetime income tax[5] being as high as 7d in the pound, one still had to earn more than £150 a year before having to pay this tax. I suspect that there are only five or six families in my parish who have this type of income; the rest make do on much less. In fact survival is still difficult, and when I first arrived there had been a succession of poor harvests[6] and even the hardiest of families were beginning to worry. Poverty was widespread and in 1842 we had 270 inmates in the Workhouse.[7] As the Chairman of the Board of Guardians I did my best but there were a number of attitudes I had to change following the tenure of Thomas Baker. He had instructed the Workhouse overseers to be tough and disciplined to the point of cruelty and it took me several years to change their attitudes to more compassionate ways of thinking. The numbers drop in the summer but in winter the Workhouse bulges at the seams. There are forty-eight Guardians but for many it is just a social title and they are of little practical help.

One of the great steps forward was the building of the National School. It was completed in 1840 and although Thomas Baker made it known that the children of labourers needed no education I gave it my full support once

---

[4] For details of this person see Appendix 1.

[5] 1842 May 11th. Introduced by Peel.

[6] 1842. Fourth successive year of bad harvests.

[7] Ann Bates notes.

I arrived. It is built behind the Horse and Groom, down the road from the church, and takes ninety children from an area wider than Rollesby itself. I really believe that in this day and age the poorest must learn to read and write, or how else will they elevate themselves from their poverty, for hard work alone does not achieve this. I think it is appalling the way we expect children to work for their living from the earliest years. Even Ashley's Mines Act did not go far enough in my opinion since no child should be in a mine and no child should be expected to work before the age of fourteen.[8] I am not surprised that the Chartists cause so many problems: if my family were affected by the social injustices of the day I am not so sure I could simply sit back and wax lyrical, but would rather be out doing something about it.

The general health of the poor is appalling and a Royal Commission set up in 1844[9] achieved very little, and only looked at cities. Health in rural areas is equally bad, the sanitary needs of the village are the same as in any town, and the disease and stench in the summer is appalling. In the Rectory and the Hall we are well equipped, but the average labourer's cottage has, at the very best, shared provision at the edge of the fields. During the 1830s cholera from Russia entered via Sunderland and spread rapidly: it is a frightening and deadly illness. It causes more deaths than the authorities care to notice[10] and when they did eventually inspect water systems in fifty towns, they discovered thirty-one of them to be impure. Despite all the warnings the governments of each day do little: it was not that long ago that 10,000 died in London alone, and at long last it was identified that the cholera was water-borne.[11] Many of us had suspected this for a long time, and I had a furious row with the Vicar of Martham who suggested that the illness was God's punishment upon the wicked. Considering his lifestyle I asked how he and I survived God's wrath. I suspect that as country clergy, we are sometimes too remote from the realities of life. Many of the clergy in this area hold several livings and enjoy travelling to and from their various

---

[8] 1842. Ashley's Mines Act: children under 10 and women not to work underground.

[9] 1844. Royal Commission on Health of Towns set up.

[10] More people died from cholera than war and during this period there were few years without a war being fought somewhere on the globe, from India to Africa and Europe.

[11] 1854 April-May.

residences.[12] For others, the rural isolation drives them slowly mad.

If the failing harvests in Norfolk and the poverty in general made the life of the average person miserable, life was far worse for the Irish. Not only had their harvests been bad but there was also a potato blight. I gathered from an informed friend that in that wretched part of Great Britain's neighbour island four million people lived off potatoes, and that problems with that crop were as bad as being struck by cholera and a medieval plague at the same time. Although in the 1840s trade revived, the price of bread was high because the import duties stayed on corn to protect our own farmers. The landowners, like my family, were more than happy with this situation, but I disagreed with them many times on this issue because I could see the suffering caused by high prices, and in Ireland it was insufferable. It was not until 1846 that the Corn Laws were repealed, but the famine in Ireland was massive and to my dying day I shall not forgive those in power for ignoring the plight of that island race. I was not surprised to hear of the mass emigration to America by all those Irish who could muster the fare. I also believe that the Irish will never forgive the English for this and it will cause trouble in the future. When I heard that there had been an attempt on Peel's life I was sure it would be Irish in origin.[13] The main problem within Ireland, and to a lesser extent in this land, is that the rich are very rich and the poor very poor. I would make Charles Dickens'[14] *A Christmas Carol* compulsory reading for those who lack charity.

The Church does its best but is still hampered by internal bickering. There was more interest in Newman's interpreting the Thirty-Nine Articles[15] in a so-called Roman Catholic light than any interest in poverty and Irish famines. Then when it was proposed that children too young to work should be educated in Church maintained schools it was dropped

---

[12] Chadwick, H (Editor) (2000) *Not Angels but Anglicans* Canterbury Press, Norwich, p.199. 'the crucially important 1838 Pluralities Act resulted in a shake-up for the parochial ministry by putting a gradual brake on the holding of more than one living (unless one was within ten miles of the other, and the populations and revenues were fairly small) ... for the beneficed clergy it meant isolation by taking up residence in remote parishes where perhaps no clergyman had lived for years ... the Act spelled the disappearance of the curate in sole charge, and the arrival of the resident incumbent.'

[13] 1843 January 20th. Peel's Secretary, Edward Drummond, shot dead in Whitehall by Daniel McNaghten in mistake for Peel. He was acquitted of murder on grounds of insanity. The legal rules regarding insanity as a defence for murder are still known as the 'McNaghten Rules' to this day.

[14] 1843. Charles Dickens writes *A Christmas Carol.*

[15] 1841 February 27th. Newman's *Tract XC* caused the above controversy.

through sectarian hostility.[16] I was deeply annoyed by this, for as Anglicans or Catholics or Methodists, we should put the poor first. The Vicar of Ormesby disagrees with me but that troubles me little. After all was said and done George Williams managed to found the interdenominational Young Men's Christian Association in London,[17] so why could the churches not co-operate on the issue of the poor who need us most? Instead, in 1846 I was asked to join the Evangelical Alliance to combat Tractarianism: it seems to me that our leaders are never happy unless there is some internal conflict they can fight over. I was going to Yarmouth to attend a meeting on the disunity of the churches when a dreadful accident occurred. Some clown calling himself Nelson was being pulled by four geese down the River Bure in a tub. It was a fine afternoon[18] and large crowds had gathered on the old suspension bridge to watch this fool, and all being on one side the bridge collapsed and above eighty persons were drowned.[19] I hope that when suspension bridges are built in the future they use a more common sense and safer design.

On the lighter side of events, the parish next door, Great Ormesby, stretches to the coast north of Caister and encloses a small hamlet called Scratby. Undoubtedly a Danish settlement but the name suggests some itching illness. Some boy to the south of the hamlet found a sea chest full of gold on the beach. Since this coincided with the gold rush in California[20] they have now called that part of my neighbour's parish, California. It annoys the Vicar greatly, but I have the distinct impression the name will last.[21] Whenever we meet I mischievously mention the name only to watch him mutter that it will all pass: I wish I could look into the future. I walked on the beach only a few years ago with my father, and we laughed and talked about the new name: I also laughed at his new style of hat. They call it a bowler hat, and it is very much the latest fashion.[22] He bought them for

---

[16] 1844 June 15th. Factory Act: 12 hour day for women; 6 hour day for children 8-13; proposal they should attend Church maintained schools dropped through sectarian hostility.

[17] 1844.

[18] !845 May.

[19] Bayne, A D (circa 1880) *History of Eastern England* James MacDonald, Yarmouth. Vol.II, p.427.

[20] 1848 January 24th. Gold discovered at Sutter's Creek, California.

[21] California south of Scratby has a few residences and a holiday area still known as California but is not yet included in the official Church of England benefice title.

[22] 1849 December 17th. First bowler hat made by T and W Bowler of Southwark for Norfolk gamekeepers.

his gamekeepers but has taken a fancy to one for himself.

One of the most fascinating trips I made out of the parish in my time was to London to visit the Great Exhibition.[23] It was built as a Crystal Palace in Hyde Park, and was truly fantastic. Many countries exhibited there but it was clear that Great Britain leads the world in industrial matters, though I must confess I was impressed by some of the growing industrial ingenuity of the Americans. It was opened only for six months but in that time it had a million visitors a month. I expect at the end of the millennium there will be a similar occasion that will attract even more visitors.

Perhaps the saddest moment of my time in Rollesby was watching our country go to war against Russia.[24] As a country we have always been at war, many times in Africa, Afghanistan, India and even New Zealand, but the war against Russia brought untold misery to many soldiers and to families in my parish. The Gregg boy never returned, and young Goodwin came back a bitter and broken man: he had left us as a cheerful young lad full of life. Basically the Russians had moved in on the old Turkish Empire, the Ottoman Empire, on the pretence of looking after Christian Serbs, and the Sultan made the mistake of attacking the Russians, so with the French we joined the Turks and took the Russians on in a bitter and unnecessary war. I might say that I hold the unpopular view as usual. We were told of great successes at the battle of Inkerman[25] and then the Siege of Sebastopol[26] as well as the bravery of Cardigan's charge of the Light Brigade into the Russian guns. I heard from some officers, old friends of the family, that it was all a disaster. There were mistaken orders, wrong orders, orders deliberately misconstrued all for personal glory, but resulting in the death of thousands of ordinary soldiers. We heard about the glorious efforts of Florence Nightingale, but not before thousands of soldiers died from the cold because army administration had given them no appropriate clothing, and hospitals where my father would not have kept his foxhounds. It was no wonder young Goodwin was bitter. He had miraculously recovered from a bout of cholera, but a bullet wound in his leg had been so badly treated that it festered and had to be amputated after he was dismissed and came home. I

---

[23] 1851 May 1st. Opened by Queen Victoria.

[24] Crimean War. 1854 May 31st Britain declares war on Russia.

[25] 1854 November 5th.

[26] Begins October 17th 1854.

paid for the surgeon myself, and then found Goodwin a job as a junior administrator in the Workhouse. He is personally very grateful to me as his parish parson, but I have heard he has very strong views on the so-called 'upper classes', and who can blame him.

When I went to London to find a top surgeon I saw the first postal pillar-boxes,[27] and purchased one of the first newspapers called the *Daily Telegraph.*[28] It is written in much more pithy style than *The Times* but I am not sure that it will last long. It is called the Telegraph because of the latest invention: it was only a couple of years ago that Queen Victoria communicated with President Buchanan in America by this scientific marvel.[29] But I deviate; I went to London to secure the surgeon for young Goodwin and heard about the institution of a new award for bravery, the Victoria Cross.[30] I felt quite cynical that a few gain bravery awards while thousands of young men like Goodwin lose their limbs and their livelihoods without any talk of compensation or even compassion. I nearly wrote to the government but my father implored me not to and I do not like clashing with him unless it is unavoidable. There is a great deal of unnecessary cruelty in this world. This was more than apparent when the Indian Mutiny occurred,[31] on both sides of the divisions. I was amazed that the sparking point was the rumour that the Lee Enfield bullets were greased with animal fat, and that the Hindus objected in case it were cow and the Muslims in case it were pig. But we are no better; there were actually riots in London against the ritualistic movement in the Church![32] For relaxation I have been reading one of Anthony Trollope's Church novels, *Barchester Towers,*[33] and although it ridicules the behaviour of churchmen it does it with mild humour and a gentility we do not deserve.

I last went to London in July 1858 but the smell from the River

---

[27] 1855 April 11th. The first six experimental pillar boxes installed by the Post Office in London.

[28] 1855 June 29th. *Daily Telegraph* is first published.

[29] 1858 August 17th. Completion of Atlantic telegraph cable linking Ireland and New Foundland.

[30] 1856 January 17th. Victoria Cross instituted, and in 1857 (January 26th) Queen Victoria distributes the first sixty-two VCs in Hyde Park.

[31] 1857.

[32] 1859 June. Violent anti-ritualistic demonstrations at St George's-in-the-East, Wapping: they continued on and off until May 1860.

[33] Published 1857.

Thames[34] was so overpowering that I cut my journey short and returned to Rollesby for the rest of my break. It will probably be the last time I travel to London because it is unbearably overcrowded. Time has passed quickly, and I read that the Queen is now a grandmother of a member of the German royal household.[35] Sport has become the Englishman's pastime: Fred Lillywhite organised a tour of twelve cricketers to Canada and the United States.[36] Cricket is such an English game that I doubt if anyone will ever beat us at it. I have organised a cricket XI in the village, and Black the iron-monger is so brilliant as wicket keeper I doubt whether we will ever lose.

As I write this a great controversy has blown up over the publication of Charles Darwin's *Origin of the Species by Natural Selection:*[37] it is causing debate in the highest and lowest places. Monkey or man, God-made or the survival of the fittest; these are the debates in Parliament and in the Horse and Groom. I will not preach on this because I am ambivalent. The Bishop is furious with Darwin's theory, and I am quite sure that if it were two hundred years ago he would have had the man burnt at the stake. I keep silence because I have always had my doubts about the creation account in Genesis. Even if there were some evolutionary origin to explain our development nothing will shake my invincible belief that God was behind the design. The parish clerk raised it in a meeting as if intimating that the Church were about to fall and we could close St George's and use it as a barn. I told him that 'if we had all descended from apes, some of us,' I said, glaring at him, 'had not descended far enough'. The committee laughed but I felt bad about my reply and I apologised afterwards. Fortunately he took it in good humour and later I heard him using my quip on someone else.

Most of my time in Rollesby has been taken up with visiting. I use a horse for this, rain or shine, and going into my parishioners' homes I have learned a great deal about the way they live. It has made me feel uncomfortable in the Rectory, and when I mentioned having fewer servants not only did my wife raise her voice for the first time in our married life, but the servants took it unkindly too.

---

[34] 1858 July 2nd. The smell of the Thames was so bad because of the hot summer that both Disraeli and Gladstone were taken ill.

[35] 1859 January 27th. Future Kaiser Wilhelm II born.

[36] 1859 September 6th.

[37] 1859.

'But Parson,' Mrs Youngs said to me, 'you may appease your conscience by having fewer servants, but then we have less income.'

'But I don't need so many to look after one man and his wife, Mrs Youngs, it does not feel right. You don't have servants.'

'If you paid me more I would.' She laughed and I laughed.

I kept the servants, paid them a little more than I could afford and wondered how long the clergy could go on living in this style. It does not sit easy with my conscience and the way I perceive the Christian gospel. I know my predecessor, Thomas Baker, thought servants necessary and no mere luxury, but he never saw inside their homes. I am sure he imagined they lived like him on a slightly smaller scale. Perhaps an evolutionary process may work this problem through. Perhaps there will be a time when one person does not have to survive by being a servant to a richer man. If this letter is ever read in the future I hope it is a keyhole as to how we lived, but I would give anything to look at Rollesby in a hundred years' time. In 1960 will the Rector still have a serving staff of eight as well as two stable lads?

Life in Rollesby has been comfortable for me but I have often felt distinctly uncomfortable living alongside the squalor and poverty of my parishioners. There seems to be an inequality in society that I find difficult to accept and impossible to change. Cottages are too few and they are always overcrowded and I blame the current criminality on these appalling social circumstances, and the lack of education. Too few children attend day schools, though I am pleased that Sunday School numbers are increasing.[38] Several times I have considered throwing myself into the mission field overseas to do the work of the gospel, but then I look at the villagers and recall that in my absence they may find themselves with a rector who cares little for them. I content myself with the fact that this is my parish and that God called me to work here. In many ways it is a privilege to work so closely with people in their lives, and as I have lived longer and visited my parishioners I have some warmth from the knowledge that they trust me more and more. Despite this I shall never rid myself of the feeling that I have always had food on my table and warmth by my hearth whilst those who join me in worship are more often than not on the threshold of serious poverty. I have

[38] Bayne, A D (circa 1880) *History of Eastern England* James MacDonald, Yarmouth. Vol.II, p.437. 'in 1858 the estimated population of Norfolk was 464,613 including 41,215 children who attended day schools and 50,684 who attended Sunday Schools.'

helped out where I can but it has not been enough. The smallholders up on Heath Lane might as well still be living in medieval times despite the considerable wealth in the upper reaches of society.

CHAPTER 31

ooooo

Robert John Francis (1860-1869)

Railways, industry and still poverty in mid-Victorian times

Dear Reader,

I found the request for this letter only this morning and since I am about to move on to another parish I had better write down my thoughts today. I took over from Edmund Ensor who quite literally worked himself to death in this parish. He was only fifty-one years of age when he died (January 28th 1860) and his poor wife predeceased him at an even younger age of forty-one years in 1850. After her death he suppressed his grief by working twice as hard for the parish. His predecessor had been a dreadful man, I gather, and Edmund had a great deal of work to do in the parish to make sure the population knew the Christian Church existed for them and not just the gentry. I have done my best to emulate Edmund's high standard of constant visiting and it is a thankless task. People are pleased the Rector has called, they make a fuss of one when there, but that does not mean they will attend church except for Easter and Christmas and the occasional offices of baptism, matrimony and funerals. Some do not even attend at Christmas and Easter, so they come only twice in their life and once afterwards. The Methodists have grown in number and have built themselves a new chapel in Main Road: it is a Primitive Methodist Chapel[1] called 'Ebenezer': no one can tell me what it means. The Methodists have very

[1] Built 1866.

strict moral standards and they impose many restrictions on their members. I heard recently that the Scratby Society had informed its members to desist from collecting flotsam from the beaches since it has a connection with their sinful past of plundering shipwrecks.[2] It seems sad that in a small Norfolk village of barely three hundred souls there should be two churches in rivalry. However, only a hundred come to either chapel or church and that means two hundred go nowhere. I put it down to the fact that the Methodists have more modern and racy hymns to sing. I have to confess that some of their hymns make me want to tap my foot, which I am rarely inclined to do in Matins or Evensong. Our own hymnal[3] is a vast improvement on the past but it will take time for the typical congregation to take it to heart: the average congregation resents any form of change. The Horse and Groom has a better attendance on a Saturday night.

There was something of a stir in the Horse and Groom when I first came because Ned Gregg, a local farm labourer won several bare-fist boxing matches[4] in Yarmouth. When his young wife asked him to stop, he did so to the annoyance of those who placed money on his dubious pugilistic abilities. I admired Ned for following his wife's common sense guidance and was later delighted to find that he had joined her in the choir. Ned was also handy in helping to put out a fire in one of the great barns. Had it not been for his speedy reactions in summoning help and organising the water, we could have had another Southwark.[5]

I took a brief holiday that year; I travelled to France for two months without the aid of some travelling company that is now becoming the fashionable thing to do.[6] When I returned I deviated a little to observe *HMS Warrior*, the first all-iron warship.[7] I find it impossible to comprehend how

---

[2] Patterson, Arthur (circa 1900) *From Hayloft to Temple (1865)* '...that the Society at Scratby be informed that we decidedly disapprove of their conduct in concealing derelict goods, as we consider it to be sinful...' (this refers to flotsam from wrecks).

[3] Chadwick, H (Editor) (2000) *Not Angels but Anglicans* Canterbury Press, Norwich, p.206. '*Hymns Ancient and Modern* had its rivals and its detractors, but it was the supreme hymn book from 1861 to the beginning of the 20th century. Then came *The English Hymnal* of 1906, stamped with the genius of Ralph Vaughan Williams and the flair of Percy Dearmer ... even more lively and modern was Percy Dearmer's *Songs of Praise* (1925) ...'

[4] 1860 April. Last major bare-fist boxing contest in England: Tom Sayers and American John Heenan over forty-two rounds for £200 each at Farnborough, Hants. A drawn match.

[5] 1861 June 21st-26th. Much of Southwark destroyed in great riverside fire.

[6] 1861 May 17th-24th. Thomas Cook's first continental holiday tour: six days in Paris.

[7] 1861 October. Completion: in 1866 *HMS Albert* was the first warship to have guns mounted in an iron turret, and the engineer, Robert Whitehead constructed the first self-propelling torpedo.

so much iron and steel can actually float. Nowadays steam ships carry more than sailing clippers and can go further whatever the weather does. It is particularly good for steamships now the Suez Canal has been opened.[8] I am amazed at the technology at sea and feel certain that the shipping revolution must have peaked: I cannot believe that ships can be built any bigger or faster.

After I returned from my adventures abroad I heard the news that the Prince Consort, Prince Albert, had died.[9] This may seem a strange thing to comment upon but the fact is that during my tenure at St George's no member of the public has seen the Queen since. Although everyone was at first deeply sympathetic at her loss, it soon became rumoured that she was cherishing her own grief too much. Indeed some questioned her sanity[10] and it was not kindly received that the Belgian king had taken up residence in Buckingham Palace to cover royal duties.[11] Public sympathy was short-coming after a few year's absence by the Queen. Mr Goodwin, who works in the Workhouse, and fought in the Crimea, made the pertinent comment that the Queen and Government send thousands of soldiers overseas to fight and die in gruelling circumstances, but the Queen cannot face the death of a husband in his bed attended by the best doctors and with all the comforts the modern world can provide.

The 1860s have been a time of prosperity yet the squalor in the working class home remains. The population is almost growing out of control[12] and there is much poverty in the cities, towns and the rural areas. According to the official census the vast majority of workers are still agricultural or domestic servants. Life for neither of these classes is easy, not least because during this decade we have had some of the worst winter weather ever recorded. The River Thames froze solid and so those who unload in the docks were immediately laid off and became paupers overnight. The pawnshops filled up with the most mundane and sad articles and death stalked the streets. I find it a strange contradiction that we have such advances in

---

[8] 1869 November 17th. Prince of Wales attends opening of Suez Canal by Empress Eugenie.

[9] 1861 December 14th. Prince Consort dies from typhoid fever at Windsor.

[10] It seems more than likely that the Queen suffered a nervous breakdown.

[11] 1862 January 14th. Royal duties are exercised by her uncle, King Leopold I of the Belgians.

[12] 1861 census indicates 21 million in England and Wales: 2.25 million are agricultural workers or domestic servants.

this modern age; railways stretch across the country and grow under the country,[13] suburbs with new houses are created on the outskirts of great cities and yet paupers still die in the streets. It is no wonder that people migrate to America and to the colonies, and that a quasi-religious leader called William Booth can stir up so much feeling.[14] Some people have so much wealth that they have purchased mechanical road transport, and have to employ three attendants, one of whom has to walk in front with a red flag, keeping the dangerous vehicle at a maximum speed of four miles an hour.[15] I have seen some of these monsters both in Yarmouth and Norwich. Wealth and poverty are an enigma: I have little understanding as to how some people accumulate so much wealth, and how easily it can be lost. There was a so-called 'Black Friday'[16] a few years ago when things went wrong in the City and people lost their money. I can understand this with poor harvests or loss of merchandise at sea, but not over a desk. I am sure it will never be allowed to happen again.

Although I am concerned about the poverty in this country at least we are not in the turmoil of civil war as in America. We were all sad to hear about the assassination of Abraham Lincoln; he had liberated the slaves in an effort to civilise that great land.

I tried to tell the children in the school about him, but they have no idea of current affairs in our own country let alone overseas. They can concentrate only on the three 'R's because in order to gain the governmental grant they have to be tested by official inspectors to assess their progress.[17] This is not what education should be about, it will soon be the case that they will introduce some kind of national curriculum and kill off all decent education by insistence on more and more paperwork.

In 1864 I went back to my old university, Oxford, to hear the public debate in the Shedonian Theatre on the vexed problem of evolution. I voted for Disraeli who declared himself on the side of the angels. No one in the

---

[13] 1863 January 10th. World's first underground railway opened to public: Paddington to Farringdon Street.

[14] 1865 July 2nd. William Booth leads his first evangelical Christian Mission meeting in Whitechapel, London; not yet called the 'Salvation Army'.

[15] 1865. Road Locomotion Act.

[16] 1866 May 11th. First 'Black Friday'. City panics as bankers Overend, Gurney and Co. fail; financial instability leads to many bankruptcies over the next few months.

[17] 1862. 'Revised Code' of education introduces government grants to individual schools on a 'payment by results' basis, dependent on tests by official inspectors to assess progress in the three 'R's.

pews at St George's doubts that we were made by God in His image, and although a few in the Horse and Groom have other opinions they are ill educated. I do attend the Horse and Groom from time to time, but only to organise the village cricket. We do rather well at Rollesby, and I took a couple of my better players to the first county cricket championship ever played. I also watched the MCC play against New South Wales at Lords; a young sixteen-year-old called W G Grace scored fifty in his first match; he is a very good player. It is such a fine gentlemanly sport, unlike Ned's boxing, even though they are trying to make that game more civilised.[18] As a Christian country we must try and be civilised, which was why I was so pleased the government has now finished with public hangings.[19] I have no doubt that it is necessary to execute habitual criminals but to do it in public is tasteless. For the same reason I was thrilled to read about a Dr Thomas Barnardo who is to open a children's shelter for destitute boys in Stepney,[20] and the end of transportation to Australia.[21]

In some ways life has improved during the 1860s: the First Trades Union Congress was able to meet in Manchester[22] and in 1867 there was the Second Parliamentary Reform Act.[23] This Act virtually enfranchised all men in the towns and extended it in the countryside, but sadly excluded all poorer agricultural workers. This meant that only a few in Rollesby have the right to vote. Mr Goodwin said this was unfair and I could not disagree with him. He also believed women should have the vote! John Stuart Mill had introduced this notion in Parliament[24] but it was given short shrift and is never likely to happen. Having said that I once claimed it would be impossible for all Anglican bishops from around the world to get together, but that happened.[25] I do think women have an unfair share of the activities in today's world, and I hope that whoever reads this in the future may be able to smile and tell me that women do have the right to vote and have

---

[18] 1867. Marquis of Queensbury, in collaboration with J G Chamber draws up rules to govern boxing.

[19] 1868 May 26th. Last public hangings: Frances Kidder at Maidstone; Michael Barrett at Newgate.

[20] His first home for Destitute Boys built in 1870.

[21] 1868 November 12th. Last sailing of a convict ship.

[22] 1868 May 25th-29th.

[23] 1867 August 15th.

[24] 1867 May 18th. Defeated by 196 votes to 73 with 290 abstentions.

[25] 1867 September. First 'Lambeth Conference' of Anglican bishops world-wide is held under presidency of Archbishop Archibald Tait.

equal education. We have made a start: in 1868 the Cambridge Higher Local Examination was opened to girls as well as boys, and Emily Davis founded a women's college at Hitchin.[26]

For the women in Rollesby it is all hard work. If they do not work in the fields they are domestic servants. Then when they get home they are expected to cook, clean and care for the rest of the family. On the other hand my wife has so many servants she has nothing to do, except read and ride. The world is making progress but it lacks real equality. I felt the Church was making progress and was thrilled, when in October 1865, the Church Congress was held in St Andrew's Hall, Norwich, and was filled every day for a week with bishops and high-ranking clergy. I attended the debates along with many High Churchmen for the Eastern Counties and I was most interested that they felt Bible history was ably vindicated against the objections of the Freethinkers.[27] Some of these people question the very authority of the Bible.

I sometimes have despaired at the numbers in the congregation; they are all too few. I do understand that when a family has been in the fields all day they are exhausted, and Sunday is all too often their only day off. Tenants come but then I know that in some cases they come only because they are my tenants or the tenant of the patrons. I should not make this kind of judgement, but I am trying to be quite frank as I look back over my time here. I do my best to visit as many homes as possible, and they respond with attendance, but the man of the house is often out working, as may be the rest of the family, and the last person they want to see in the evening is myself. My wife would also object if I spent every evening out and about. In terms of congregational numbers it feels like pushing a large snowball up an icy slope. The tragedy is that when some of the non-attenders fall seriously ill and death knocks at their door they regret their lack of attention to their faith. A few that I know of have been convinced atheists, and like convinced believers are content to leave this life. The vast majority have not given it much thought and die in a state of turmoil, wanting to believe they will be gathered up into God's loving care, yet wondering whether the faith I offer is true, and then, if true, the mediaeval concept of hell is valid. They live in

[26] 1869. She moved it to Girton, Cambridge in 1872.

[27] Bayne, A D (circa 1880) *History of Eastern England* James MacDonald, Yarmouth. Vol.II, p.459.

such a spiritual wilderness that I sometimes cross myself in moments of doubt.

CHAPTER 32

ooooo

Charles H Bennington (1869-1872)

Sporting times

Dear Whoever you are,

I cannot understand why I need to write this letter on several counts. The first is I have been in Rollesby for barely two and half years and intend to leave as soon as possible. The second reason is connected to the first: nothing ever happens here for me to report on. My predecessors were obsessed with the parish, and visited all the residents, even in the agricultural cottages: I could not bring myself to do this type of common charity work. I was ordained into Holy Orders and that is not the same as being a mere charity worker. I laboured hard to produce erudite sermons for the benefit of all classes and they complained about their length and, because of their appalling education, claimed they found them difficult to follow. I also tried to bring a better churchmanship to the rural scene, a crucifix and a few minor vestments, and they treated me as if I were trying to lead them to Rome. I knew within months I was not welcome nor did I feel at home. If these people wanted only a visitor and a brief popular sermon for the very few who attend they would have been better off with a minor curate or a retired schoolmaster.

It was also a difficult time for me personally. I had just married and I was anticipating considerable property from the arrangement. My wife decided that she would retain title to the property and the lands and refused to sell any of it. After the Married Women's Property Act[1] this was her legal entitlement. I almost considered moving to Scotland where the Act was not effective.[2] I did not fight the issue because she comes from an influential and difficult family, but in my next post I intend to help her change her mind.

I did enjoy doing some teaching in the local school, not of the pupils who are the dullest creatures on earth, but of the small teaching staff there. The school is growing and of course has more money to spend now the government has accepted that basic schooling is a government responsibility.[3] I have never been sure of the wisdom of the Government in this Act. They do, when all is said and done, pay for this luxury out of my taxes. Independent schools have to pay their own way and at least they educate those who are going to be the natural leaders in society. I was amazed when young Goodwin claimed his son should be educated at the country's expense. He is not a dull boy but I cannot see what good it will do him. I employed him as a 'back'us boy'[4] for my housekeeper, and although he spoke well at family prayers after breakfast I could see it was by memory, for he could read little. I paid him £1 a quarter and gave him the right to half the eggs if he found a hen's nest in the hedgerows and marked it with a sticker.[5] The Palgraves had similar attitudes to Goodwin but after Benjamin John Palgrave, who used to live in Workhouse Road, left for Newcastle[6] to become an iron worker I heard little more of this family. I did hear more recently that James Palgrave, George and Lucy's son, has become something of a scholar.[7]

At times the Government seems quite soft and almost motherly towards

---

[1] 1870 August 9th. Married Women's Property Act acknowledges the principle that wives may have property of their own.

[2] Extended to Scotland in 1877.

[3] 1870. William Edward Forster responsible for Education Act - existing church schools to receive government backing.

[4] Evans, George Ewart (1977) *Ask the Fellows who Cut the Hay* Faber & Faber, Boston, p.23. A back'us boy or back-house boy was at that time the lowest rank in the rural hierarchy. He was under the command of the farmer's wife.

[5] Evans, George Ewart (1977) *Ask the Fellows who Cut the Hay* Faber & Faber, Boston, p.25.

[6] Palgrave, Derek A *The Palgraves of Rollesby, 1773-1973* Private publication undated.

[7] Palgrave, Derek A *The Palgraves of Rollesby, 1773-1973* Private publication undated; this young man was described as a scholar in the 1871 census.

the working classes. They started giving public holidays, Bank Holidays[8] as they are sometimes called. Again it is the employer who has to pay the wages, not the Government. Now they have allowed people to vote secretly[9] and employers could well find themselves employing people who have voted against them or their man. I find it all very frightful.

Both my predecessors played cricket with the locals from the Inn, which I found below my status. Not that I do not enjoy sport, but certainly not cricket. Last year I travelled to watch Scotland beat England at Rugby Football,[10] and only a few months ago attended the first Football Association final at Kennington Oval, and watched Wanderers beat the Royal Engineers 1-0.[11] I will be travelling to see the first international football match to be played in November.[12] It is not as if the locals can say I am out of touch, but just because I do not choose to play in their teams they think I am above myself: that I am not but I am above them socially and educationally.

Some of the labourers are far too quick with their impertinent thoughts. Down in the Workhouse a retired soldier with only one leg, his name is Goodwin, works as the clerk because of the good offices of one of my predecessors. Because he has held the position for some time and because a previous rector appointed him, he considered it within his right to suggest I visited some of the sick at the back of the Workhouse.

'Mr Goodwin,' I said, 'and if I fall ill because of such a visit will you conduct Matins tomorrow morning?'

'No, Sir, begging your pardon, but the last two rectors always called in before Tuesday lunch, I just thought you may continue the custom.'

'And who exactly are you to instruct me in my duties?'

'I am a nobody, sir, an absolute nobody, but apart from serving the Queen in the Crimea I have spent all my working life in Rollesby and thought you may be interested to know something of the past.'

---

[8] 1871 August 7th. First Bank Holiday, resulting from recent enactment of John Lubbock's Bank Holiday Bill, giving three leisure breaks between spring and autumn each year.

[9] 1872 July 18th. Ballot Act: ensures secrecy at elections; first secret ballot is at Pontefract by-election, 15th August.

[10] 1871 January 26th. Rugby Football Union founded, London; Scotland defeat England in first international, Raeburn Park, Edinburgh, 7th March.

[11] 1872 March 16th.

[12] 1872 November 1st. First international football match in the world: it was a goalless draw between England and Scotland at Partick.

'In future please keep your thoughts and opinions to yourself.'

He did not reply but he did not take his eyes away from mine: it was as if he were treating me as an equal, and was quietly passing judgement on me. I spoke to the other Guardians about his contemptuous attitude and was astounded to find that they thought highly of the man. Personally I would have sacked him despite the fact he had a leg missing. Someone told me he was a distant relative of a Thomas Goodwin, who had something to do with Oliver Cromwell and although it did not impress me, it helped explain to me as from whence his attitude came. He actually saw himself as an equal to other men of better social standing. The local people are fairly basic in their outlook on life, looking only to the fundamental necessities of existence. Their staple articles of diet are the three 'Bs' - bread, bacon and beer.[13] Many of them brew their own beer. They make their own utensils from wood. A brewing-tub called a keeler, an underdeck called an underback, a beer stool and a horse-hair sieve for straining. I have never tried this brew and have no wish to do so. There is a man down Court Road[14] who makes so much he sells it from his own front room to the annoyance of the Horse and Groom. Because we grow so much barley, beer is easy for the locals to produce. The whole business is grubby by my standards.

I found Norfolk, and most especially Rollesby and Norwich, a dark brooding place. Only last week I was reading of a man called William Sheward who presented himself to the Chief Inspector at Lambeth Police Station and confessed he had murdered his wife in Norwich way back in 1851![15] He claimed to have cut her throat, hacked her body to bits and distributed them around the city. At the time of the murder he was an assistant to a pawnbroker and had lived at St Martin at Oak. Aged witnesses were recalled and could in fact recollect finding bits of bodies but thought they had been discarded by medical students from dissected corpses. They executed him in Norwich. The whole business makes me shudder, especially with all the body snatching that is supposed to take place in Norwich and Yarmouth. They have even named one of the lanes in Yarmouth off the Market Square as Body Snatcher's Row.

---

[13] Evans, George Ewart (1977) *Ask the Fellows who Cut the Hay* Faber & Faber, Boston, p.55.

[14] This common ale-house survived into the early 20th century.

[15] Bayne, A D (circa 1880) *History of Eastern England* James MacDonald, Yarmouth. Vol.II, p.485 for more details of this incident.

I told the Bishop about my unhappiness and he seemed to understand. It almost seemed as if he had been told before I arrived there, and he appeared more than happy that I should seek preferment elsewhere. In a month I shall leave Rollesby where nothing happens and quite why anyone in the future wants to know about the place I shall never understand. The future of churches in places like this parish must be in doubt. In this day and age clergy are educated people and it is difficult for them to adjust to the appalling ignorance of farm labourers. Any small rural parish will always be insufficient to occupy a man of my education and talent, especially when the Methodists are always appealing to the lowest common denominator in the parish. They do not worship like we do, they simply have 'sing-a-longs' rather like simple Sunday Schools. Rollesby is more in need of fervent missionaries who have had some experience in darkest Africa. The Bishop disagreed with me on this point, and he led me to believe that I would not find employment as a canon in the cathedral where my talents would be better tested. He mumbled on about Christian humility and charity, and that is why I shall seek preferment in another diocese. The Church is changing. Too much attention is given to people like Bishop Colenso[16] and Charles Darwin. There was nothing new about Darwin's idea: theologians had long had to consider the ramifications of geological discoveries.[17] Now we are being told that the Old Testament is untrue and we are all descended from apes and the weak Church leadership does nothing. If one disturbs the water one becomes a public nuisance or if one quietly does the work one is ignored. I shall seek better pastures.

---

[16] Chadwick, H (Editor) (2000) *Not Angels but Anglicans* Canterbury Press, Norwich, p.224. 'The radical biblical criticism of German scholars such as F.C.Baur had little direct impact in Britain. But it was quite otherwise with J.W.Colenso, the Anglican Bishop of Natal, whose exposure of the mathematical absurdities in the Pentateuch was devastating. It horrified orthodox churchpeople in Britain, engineered a schism in the Church in South Africa, and prompted the calling of the first Lambeth Conference in 1867.'

[17] Chadwick, H (Editor) (2000) *Not Angels but Anglicans* Canterbury Press, Norwich, p.225.

CHAPTER 33

ooooo

Richard John Tacon (1872-1929)

Victoria, Edward VII, George V - the Boer War and the Great War

Dear Readers,

It is now January 1929 and I have been Rector of this parish for some fifty-seven years, I am eighty-two years of age and confess of failing health. This request came to me a few months ago. I thought that if I do nothing about it now, I am not likely to have time in the future. I was ordained in Rochester as a deacon in 1870 and priested in the same diocese in 1871. I did my basic training as a curate in Kelvedon for two years and came to Rollesby under the patronage of N Bennington, Esquire. I did my initial training at Corpus Christi, Cambridge, where I was stroke for the college boat. Strangely I have a Spanish background but that was generations ago. In Spain the family was of some importance, one member being the Governor of Madrid in the fifteenth century and another Captain-General of Cuba in the eighteenth century.[1] When my father, Charles Tacon of Hinton Hall and Mansion House at Eye, died the executors purchased the land and patronage of Rollesby, and so I became patron not long after being inducted as Rector of Rollesby. I am also Lord of the Manor of Walcott but would rather be known as a man who did my duty as the Rector of Rollesby.

When I arrived in the parish, top hats, striped trousers and silver canes

[1] *Burke's Landed Gentry* centenary edition 1937.

were the fashion[2] but had I worn this in Rollesby I would have been seen as something of a dandy so I wore more robust rural clothes. About this time the American evangelists, Dwight Moody and Ira David Sankey, were undertaking a two-year revival mission[3] throughout the country using their own Sankey and Moody Hymn Book. It was not something that reached as far as Rollesby. Nor did the Public Worship Regulation Act that sought to curb ritualism within the Church of England.[4] Fortunately, being a Norfolk rural area, we were hardly High Church; this was more a city phenomena. It certainly caused some divisions amongst my clerical friends in Norwich, but out in the Broads it was merely a point of casual interest.

More serious was the agricultural strike.[5] It started south of us in Suffolk but soon spread around the country. I had a degree of sympathy for the labourers because they suffered compared to city and town workers. For those in industry there had been a series of legislative acts to make their lives better, and even in the year of the strike there was another Factory Act.[6] The agricultural labourer, along with the domestic servant, had been forgotten, especially in terms of electoral franchise and wages. There was a new author on the scene that year, and I read his novel *Far from the Madding Crowd:*[7] his name is Thomas Hardy and whether he becomes a great author we will have to wait and see. He based his book on the agricultural scene and although many politicians saw rural life as idyllic, this was far from the facts, as Hardy's book illustrated. Life was tough for the labourer, and it was almost unsustainable during the strike that lasted half a year. There were few luxuries for the ordinary people of the village. It was the same in surrounding villages. Indeed Rollesby at least had its own fire appliance, and when the mill burnt down in nearby Martham it was our fire appliance that was the first there.[8] Families found themselves out on the streets, and the

---

[2] 1873. These items became popular during the early 1870s, women's fashion favoured long sleeves and draperies, a bustle, small hats with a veil, gloves, high necks.

[3] 1873 onwards.

[4] 1874 August 7th.

[5] 1874 February 20th. First organised strike of agricultural labourers begins (to August 10th); spreads from Suffolk to much of East England.

[6] 1874 August 30th. Factory Act: 56-hour working week; further safeguards to protect children from employment as chimney sweeps.

[7] Published 1874.

[8] *Norfolk and Norwich Archaeological Society* (1959) N&NAS, Norwich. Vol.36, p.189. On April 2nd 1898 the Rollesby fire engine was in attendance at the Martham Mill fire.

Workhouse, of which I was a Guardian and later Chairman, filled to the brim. I had to admire the workers' tenacity. I often paid for entertainment in the Workhouse, and along with my clerical colleague, the Reverend J Dredge (chaplain) we would provide both food and fun.[9] Some saw this as patronising, but year after year I personally, along with Mrs Butt, gave twenty-two stone of prime beef to the Rollesby poor on Christmas Eve, and we received only grateful thanks. I remember my warden, Mr Thomas Webster, used to help distribute this gift and in 1908 fell ill from the effort, eventually dying in March of 1909. Mr Silcock my other warden was never entirely himself after this. My daughter, Ethel, played for the funeral: it was 'Saul's March' and one of the best renditions she ever gave. It can be strenuous walking around Rollesby on a cold day. My parish clerk used to catch a cold every Easter when he went from house to house claiming his right of two rashers of bacon and six eggs per household.[10] It was a strange custom but most welcomed him at the door.

From just after I arrived there were serious problems with English agriculture. Not only did we have a series of bad seasons but also American wheat was pouring into the country at a rate with which we could not cope.[11] The men had to move to find work; some of them moved as far away as America and the colonies and others moved to the cities. When I took over Rollesby parish we had a population of 557 souls[12] and I have steadily watched the decline ever since. While the rural labourers suffer, few in the towns and cities seemed to notice. Never has there been such a gulf between town and country. I recall reading about Matthew Webb swimming the English Channel[13] and the press becoming more excited about this sporting

---

[9] Flegg Parish Magazines 1907-10. Feb 1907.

[10] *Eastern Daily Press*, 26 April 1922. 'The ubiquitous Easter egg crops up in a rather curious fashion in connection with an ancient custom in vogue at Rollesby. On Easter Monday the Parish Clerk makes a round and visits every house claiming at each the perquisite of his office in the shape of two rashers of bacon and six eggs. Inquiries show that such a custom has long existed in Rollesby.'

[11] Trevelyan, G M. (1978) *English Social History* New illustrated edition with introduction by Asa Briggs, Longman, London, p.491. 'From 1875 the catastrophe set in. A series of bad seasons aggravated its initial stages, but the cause was the development of the American prairies as grain lands within reach of the English market ... in 1846 Disraeli had prophesied the ruin of agriculture as an inevitable result of free trade in corn. For thirty years he had been wrong. Now he was suddenly right ... yet he did nothing about it, and allowed the "curse of Cobden" to blight the English cornfields ... statesmen regarded the fate of agriculture with all the more indifference because it involved no acute problem of unemployment.'

[12] *Crockford's Clerical Directory, 1885* under R Tacon entry: when the next Incumbent, Grundy took over in 1935 the population had decreased to 456 - *Crockford's 1935* under R Grundy entry.

[13] 1875 August 25th. The first swimmer from Dover to Calais in 21 hours 45 minutes.

effort than the fact that rural labourers were at the point of starvation. Having said this I must confess that the labourers themselves were excited by this particular event as they were when there was talk of greyhound racing being introduced in Yarmouth.[14] The divisions in society are more apparent in city and town society. I travelled to London and observed Cleopatra's needle[15] being berthed, and while there I observed the stark differences between the slums of the East End, the growth of a well-off middle-class in the suburbs and the wealth to be found in the city. In Rollesby there are the few gentry left, one or two farmers, and the rest are labourers. In the city and towns are found the 'new money' people, especially in the banking systems. They do not always have it their way. Not longer after I arrived Sir Robert Harvey the banker shot himself.[16] Rumours spread about his Crown Bank and they proved founded. The crash came the very next day after his death. The baronet had shot himself because of some poor speculation on the stock exchange. The treasurers of City, Council and Church had considerable deposits in Crown Bank. The City, for example, had £5000 lodged in that bank and the Norwich Board of Guardians lost some £6000. The Messrs. Kerrison, father and son partners in the bank, were ruined. Their property was valued at £88,000 and was given up to customers of the bank. Much money had been transferred to the Crown Bank because of the collapse of the Overend and Gurney Company in 1866.[17]

Yarmouth also had a branch of the Crown Bank but there was not so much investment there. When His Royal Highness, The Prince of Wales, had recovered from his fever at Sandringham he paid a three-day visit to Yarmouth,[18] and I was amongst those who greeted him at Southtown railway station. I did not stay in the crowd too long because there had been rumours of smallpox. This illness is devastating and during the winter months of 1871-2 this wretched illness killed 600 souls in Norwich alone.[19] Smallpox hits the poorer classes on the whole but it is no respecter of social

[14] 1876 October 7th. Greyhound racing with an artificial hare staged experimentally at Hendon. 1926 July 24th. First Greyhound track opens, Belle Vue, Manchester.

[15] 1878 January. Cleopatra's Needle reaches London from Alexandria after 4 month voyage.

[16] 1870 June 15th.

[17] Bayne, A D (circa 1880) *History of Eastern England* James MacDonald, Yarmouth. Vol.II, p.492.

[18] 1872 June 26-29th.

[19] Bayne, A D (circa 1880) *History of Eastern England* James MacDonald, Yarmouth. Vol.II, p.515.

classes.

It is true that at the end of the last century the lower classes were starving, but the class divisions were not so apparent. That was the same year that a European war nearly broke out but the Russians and others saw sense[20] and it was a pleasure to hear of Beaconsfield arriving in Dover to declare that he had 'brought peace with honour'. With what has happened since it was a tragedy that more treaties were not signed before wars broke out.

It was in 1878 I married my wife, Caroline Ballard (7th May) and together we were to have five sons and three daughters. These were excellent days and a good marriage. My wife died several years ago (May 5th 1921) two days before our next wedding anniversary. Caroline helped with all kinds of entertainment arrangements, which ranged from luncheons at the Savoy in London for family friends to entertaining the local constabulary of the East and West Flegg Hundreds.[21] We often entertained all the householders of Rollesby to an evening meal; this was some one hundred and forty people, and although old Mr Tooke did the catering, Caroline did the organising.

Before the onset of the 20th century I travelled everywhere on one of my horses and can recall the amusement of seeing the first cycles being used. First the penny-farthing and then later the development of bikes with pneumatic tyres.[22] I have to confess to being tempted myself when I was younger, more so as cars developed, but the rural roads around Rollesby meant my horse was still the safest and most comfortable way to travel. The horse also enabled me to be able to stop and speak to parishioners with ease.

I recall young Goodwin had purchased a cycle and fell off into the ditch by Heath Farm: he was hardly hurt, but since he had survived the Zulu wars[23] it would have been truly ironical if he were damaged by a mere accident in Rollesby. The horse managed the back lanes in those days better than any wheels. Young Goodwin's accident was not helped by the darkness of the evening, and to think that was about the same time that they had

---

[20] 1878 July 13th. Treaty of Berlin signed.

[21] 1887 December 24th. R Tacon's private papers.

[22] 1878. Cyclists' Touring Club established - 1888 John Boyd Dunlop patents a pneumatic tyre.

[23] 1879 January 22nd. Zulus defeat British at Battle of Isandhlwana, massacring 826 whites and about 800 black soldiers. January 22nd-23rd. Battle of Rorke's Drift.

introduced electric street lighting on Waterloo Bridge to light up the night, an extraordinary luxury.[24] It was not long after this event that young Goodwin signed on again and went to what we call the first Boer War.[25] I could hardly blame a young man for seeking his fortune in the army given the lack of work in the fields of Rollesby.

I always made a point of remembering young Goodwin in our prayers. In the church I found that Morning Prayer was considerably more popular than Evening Prayer: I have never quite understood why. The service became a little more acceptable to some when we took to reading the Revised Version[26] of the New Testament: the words were more accessible to country people who rarely read much other than newspapers. There seemed much to pray about in those days: the Boer War, the activities of the extreme Fenians in Ireland and wars in Egypt and all round the globe. When I look back from 1929 I realise that they were comfortable days. I can recall my considerable enjoyment of international cricket when Australia lost the first match to England at Kennington Oval.[27] When in 1882 Australia beat us at home, some wag in the *Sporting Times* referred to 'the ashes' as a mock obituary for English Cricket's loss, and now the wretched title seems to have caught on. No doubt by the time this is read, the pundits will no longer refer to the 'ashes'.

The 1880s were, with the benefit of hindsight, strange days. On the one hand we were preoccupied with news of the Empire and on the other, petty matters. I remember the death of Gordon when the Mahdi's troops stormed Khartoum[28] and we all thought this the most frightful business. Gladstone even considered his resignation when Queen Victoria sent a telegram critical of the government's handling of the business. The public was in outrage: 'foreigners' having the nerve to kill a high ranking British soldier. We did not know then what lay ahead in the Great War of this century. No sooner had the country overcome the shock of Gordon's death than they were up in

[24] 1879 October. Electric lighting in London, on north side of embankment and Waterloo Bridge.

[25] 1880 October 16th. First Boer War between Britain and restored Transvaal begins.

[26] 1881. Revised Version of the New Testament, encouraged by Convocation of Canterbury, is published.

[27] 1880 September 6-8th.

[28] 1885 January 26th.

arms simply because the budget put more tax on spirits and beers,[29] and the next moment they were discussing which was the best dog at a dog show of all things.[30] The world has changed a good deal since then, but when one is caught up in the events of the day it is perhaps a good thing that we do not know what the future holds.

Church attendance is waning[31] yet we are increasing the number of clergy in the towns.[32] Not only did it strike me that the Church was changing but so was all social and political life at a rapid pace.

It is a good thing that God does not let us know what is ahead of us. In January 1887 I was at the Hall having a celebratory meal with my old friend, Major-General Sarel C.B. and the next day he was dead. Dr Mayo from Yarmouth was called in the night but it was too late. General Sarel had served with distinction in the Punjab and India generally, and was popular in the village. On the day of his funeral everyone shut down and all the curtains were drawn:[33] his memorial will stay in the church as long as the church stands. We have placed his memorial on the tower wall. He was, after all, also the one time Governor of Guernsey. When his soldier son, Clement, died we placed the brass lectern in its place in memory of him and his father, two fine soldiers.

The 1880s were the beginning of our technological advance. They built a tunnel under the River Severn for railways, and it took fourteen years, a remarkable achievement.[34] Some wags claim that they will one day build one under the English Channel to France: I am sure that not only will this be physically impossible but hardly expedient, politically. I recall at the time reading in the paper that there were 35 warships at the first Spithead Naval

---

[29] 1885 June 7th. Hostile demonstrations in Hyde Park at budget's proposed increases on spirits and beer duties.

[30] 1885 March 10th. Cruft's Dog Show first held, in London.

[31] Chadwick, H (Editor) (2000) *Not Angels but Anglicans* Canterbury Press, Norwich, p.228. 'By the 1880s, church attendance was failing to keep pace with population growth. Outright decline was not to occur until the 20th century.'

[32] Chadwick, H (Editor) (2000) *Not Angels but Anglicans* Canterbury Press, Norwich, p.229. 'The Victorians vastly increased the physical presence of Anglicanism in the new towns, cities and suburbs of Britain. They increased the number of clergy and improved their training...'. p.257. '...communicant figures touched a new low point in 1917 ... in 1931 the adult strength of the Church of England amounted to nearly ten per cent of the total population.'

[33] *Eastern Daily Press* January 8th 1887.

[34] 1886. Severn Tunnel, at 4 miles 628 yards the longest railway tunnel in Britain, is opened after 14 years of engineering, supervised by Sir John Hawkshaw.

Review[35] and feeling very proud of our achievements as a country. Then I read of this infamous Jack the Ripper[36] and realised that although we were making technological and scientific progress, there were still considerable elements of barbarity in our society. I doubled my efforts with the local school and took my role as a governor of the endowed Paston School, North Walsham very seriously. I had to play my part in trying to civilise the next generation. I have now been a governor of that school for fifty-five years.[37] As regards the National School in Rollesby I organised its enlargement in 1892[38] in order that it could increase its roll up to 100 children. It had originally been built in 1824 and was somewhat small and out of date. Later in 1924 we closed this old edifice and built the modern school on the Main Road. I also helped some of the girls by making them monitors at 2d a week. For this they had to clean the school and scrub the lavatories. While you are digging the ground the devil cannot catch you and it also brought some welcome money into their homes.[39] I know that today's generation looks back to the second half of the Victorian era as one of strict, ethical, indeed puritanical, behaviour,[40] but there was as always distinct human weakness, and unless we educate the young people appropriately we lay up serious misfortune for the future. I encouraged boys in the choir[41] and to pump the organ if only to keep a fatherly eye on them. I always paid them a few pennies for attendance and took them to Yarmouth[42] as an outing from time to time.[43] The seaside resort is becoming a popular pastime for everyone, especially from those places that are within easy reach of the cities by rail. Yarmouth is reasonably popular, but not as much as Scarborough and

---

[35] 1887 July.

[36] 1888 August 8th-November 9th. Six prostitutes murdered in Whitechapel.

[37] Forder, C (1975) *A History of the Paston School* UEA Printing Unit, Norwich, p.134.

[38] Women's Institute Federation (1990) *The Norfolk Village Book* Countryside Books, Norwich, p.174.

[39] Evans, George Ewart (1977) *Ask the Fellows who Cut the Hay* Faber & Faber, Boston, p.161.

[40] Trevelyan, G M. (1978) *English Social History* New illustrated edition with introduction by Asa Briggs, Longman, London, p.501.

[41] Flegg Parish Magazines 1907-10. The March 1907 magazine indicates a strong choir with the top annual attendances recorded as: Willie Shrive at 103 attendances, P Harrison 102, James Parker 102, John Piggin 102, Charles Parker 101, Percy Took 101, and John Durrant 96.

[42] Flegg Parish Magazines 1907-10. In April 1908 the magazine refers to another choir treat when the boys were treated to a supper in the schoolroom during which plum puddings with silver coins and a gold ring were eaten!

[43] Interview with Frederick Youngs, one of the choirboys still alive. 27th July 2000.

Ramsgate, in Kent.[44] Of course the boys come and go, but I have always managed a choir of least ten with a few adults. One of the problems with young people is that they see adults misbehave and feel that they may imitate. I was deeply distressed to hear that the then future king, the Prince of Wales, was rumoured to have various affairs, and indeed was obliged to give evidence as a witness in a libel action brought by a Guards Officer accused of cheating at baccarat.[45] I recall shuddering at the thought that this man would be the head of the Church of England soon. Equally distressing was the public news about Oscar Wilde.[46]

The young are like sensitive plants and I was pleased when the government abolished all fees for elementary education.[47] We have to be careful what political thoughts the young adopt: the new Independent Labour Party[48] is a new and dangerous element. I admire the intellectual ability of Mr James Keir Hardie, MP for West Ham, who founded it, but he has no understanding of the way that ordinary labourers expect him to change the world for their benefit. I used to think it a passing nonsense, and although I watched the party grow in strength, I could never see it being strong enough to form a government: how wrong I was![49]

Socially things change slowly, but change they will without revolution and radical socialism. I can still recall the Local Government Act in the mid 1890s[50] when the government established Parish Councils and actually gave women equality with men as voters and candidates for council election. My old Parish Clerk, Richard Annison,[51] who had been clerk for some thirty-six years, had always talked of the need for a Parish Council, but he would not have understood the need for women to vote. He would also have had palpitations had he heard the same rumour prevalent in those days that there had

---

[44] Day trips to the seaside increased in popularity from now and through to the Edwardian period. This was the period when Southend Pier was constructed in Essex and Blackpool Tower was built.

[45] 1891 June 2nd.

[46] 1895 May 25th. Oscar Wilde sentenced to 2 years' hard labour for homosexuality.

[47] 1891. Education Act.

[48] 1893 January 13th. Independent Labour Party founded in Bradford.

[49] 1924 January 23rd. Ramsay MacDonald forms minority Labour government while Rev R Tacon is in his 70s.

[50] 1894 March 1st. Local Government Act.

[51] Gravestone in Rollesby South Graveyard by wall: 'Richard Steward Annison died April 5th 1887 aged 78. Clerk of Parish for 36 years, tomb erected by RJ Tacon. Also his wife Mary, died 1902 aged 94.'

been informal talks between the Papacy and the Church of England.[52] Dear old Richard and his wife Mary even distrusted the Methodists down Main Road. With the Prince of Wales and authors such as Oscar Wilde behaving the way they do it is not surprising that the ordinary people misbehave.

I became a Justice of the Peace in 1874,[53] mainly working at the Court House on a Tuesday afternoon. I might add that at the time of writing I am the oldest magistrate in the county! It was not an onerous task but I was always surprised with the different types of parishioners who came before me. Many of them can hardly read, and if they do it is only the *Daily Mail.*[54] I had high hopes that when the Workers' Education Association was set up this would help with their general education.[55] Many of these malcontents soon joined the army because the end of the century saw the start of the serious Boer War. When I look back, the Boer War was compared to the Great War singularly unimportant, but at the time news of it filled our papers and it was always in our intercessory prayers. I can still remember the shock of hearing of British defeats at the battle of Magersfontein and Stormberg:[56] we had always expected that British forces must and would win. It was indeed a black week. As we turned into the twentieth century we hoped for better news with the appointment of Lord Roberts as Commander in Chief in South Africa with Kitchener as his chief of staff. Sir John French relieved Kimberley;[57] Buller relieved Ladysmith after a 118-day siege,[58] and Baden-Powell, Mafeking.[59] The public was joyful, but in my more contemplative moods, while wandering the parish on my horse, I could not but feel that we would not always be invincible. To say so in public would have been damning. I still, as I do to this day, believe our cause to be just, and when a cause is just then it must be triumphant, but modern warfare has proved a great equaliser and of the most painful sort. Despite what the papers were claiming, I detected that the South African War was

[52] 1894. Informal talks in Rome by Viscount Halifax on possible reconciliation between Papacy and the Anglicans: it continued intermittently for two years.

[53] *Crockford's Clerical List 1899* under R Tacon entry.

[54] 1896 May. *Daily Mail* goes on sale at 1/2d.

[55] 1904 October.

[56] 1899 December 11th and 10th.

[57] 1900 February 15th.

[58] 1900 February 28th.

[59] 1900 May 16th.

not a success, and then Queen Victoria died[60] leaving King Edward VII and his gambling ways upon the throne and as head of the Church. Though I gathered later this King had winning ways and even managed to impress the French that we are a reasonable people;[61] I suppose even the worst types have some good in them.

At the turn of the century I was pleased to see my uncle, Thomas Tacon, mentioned in the New Year's Honours list as a new Knight.[62] He was a JP for Suffolk and Norfolk. He enjoyed congenial company, but was not ostentatious and never mixed with the wrong company. I wish some of our national leaders had the behaviour of our local gentry.

It was about this time I invested some money in a motor car, not that I can call it an investment in hindsight,[63] as it cost me more money than a horse and would never start unless my stableman was there to crank it into life. I remember purchasing it in the week that we nearly declared war on Russia: the Russian fleet had mistaken some Hull trawlers as Japanese torpedo-boats and sank one causing two deaths.[64] Fortunately the French mediated and we avoided what could have been a catastrophic war. I cannot but muse on the way I manage to recall world events with what I was doing in a rural area like Rollesby.

In the same vein I recall 1906 well. It was not an important year in many ways but some silly fool invented the term 'suffragette'[65] for militant women campaigners at the same time as several of my clerical colleagues were deviating from the proper Anglican services. Quite why these two concepts should merge in my mind is a mystery, a kind of nightmare that one day the Church will ordain women as priests. I think at a more rational level it was because the suffragettes disrupted the state opening of Parliament,[66] the very Parliament that authorised a Royal Commission on Ecclesiastical Discipline to examine the encroachment of practices contrary to Anglican

---

[60] 1901 January 22nd. Queen Victoria dies at Osborne House; Prince of Wales accedes as King Edward VII.

[61] 1903 May 1st-4th. Edward VII's state visit to Paris breaks down traditional French suspicion of Britain.

[62] *Eastern Daily Press*, January 1st 1900.

[63] 1904 January 1st. Licensing of motor cars, and fitting of number plates, introduced; 23,000 registered cars with a speed limit of 20 mph.

[64] 1904 October 21-28th. The Dogger Bank incident.

[65] 1906 January 10th. *Daily Mail* invents this term.

[66] 1906 October 23rd.

teaching. They recommended a Prayer Book revision and new Dioceses. As I write these notes in 1929 I cannot but smile that it took until 1927 to bring the revised Prayer Book before Parliament and then they threw it out.[67] I was bitterly opposed to women having the vote at the time, but confess with an open heart that I have since changed my mind. The Great War might not have happened if women had had a say in governance. The women marched in peace but at the same time, in the Falls Road of Belfast, our troops opened fire and killed four Roman Catholics.[68] The Irish problem is very serious but I am sure it will soon be resolved. The Sinn Fein League is a passing phase, and I think that although it will take a few years the Irish will come to their senses.[69] Once more it is back to my earlier point that we must educate our young people: I was pleased when Baden-Powell formed the Boy Scouts, and we now have our own troop in Rollesby.[70] It is better to put money and effort into the young than into the elderly:[71] the young are our future. It is a sad state of affairs when the cities have to have special Juvenile Courts[72] for some youngsters when at the same time a young Frenchman can fly the Channel like a bird.[73] The world seemed upside down even then. On the one hand a suffragette at Bristol Railway station attacked Winston Churchill,[74] and on the other King Edward VII spent his time at horse racing and winning the Derby.[75] Minor politicians of no consequence, like Churchill, take the headlines, the next a royal horse and in the meantime our youngsters line up at Juvenile Courts!

Perhaps I ought not to be too scathing about Edward VII; I felt quite sad when he died,[76] but given the circumstances of the years to follow, it was perhaps better that we had King George V on the throne. I still find it mildly ironical that at the King's funeral cortège amongst the eight kings and

---

[67] 1927. House of Commons rejects Revised Prayer Book, 238 votes to 205.

[68] 1907 August 12th. 62 years later to the day, in 1969 August 12th saw the start of three days of street fighting in Londonderry.

[69] 1907. Sinn Fein League formally constituted in Ireland.

[70] 1907 July 25th. Baden-Powell forms first Boy Scouts; camp at Brownsea Island.

[71] 1909 January 1st. First payment of old-age pension: 5/- a week for those over 70 years of age.

[72] 1910 January 10th. A Juvenile Court opens in London.

[73] 1909 July 25th. Louis Blériot first man to fly the Channel to Dover in 43 minutes.

[74] 1909 November 14th.

[75] 1909 May 26th. King Edward VII sees his horse Minoru win the Derby.

[76] 1910 May 6th. King Edward VII dies at Buckingham Palace; Prince of Wales accedes as King George V.

five heirs there was the German Kaiser, a royal relative who was to bring so much suffering to this world.

From 1929 and at my desk in the Rectory study, I find it almost difficult to recall the years before the Great War; it seems almost a haze. I remember the excitement in the parish over Dr Crippen, the murderer, being arrested aboard *SS Montrose* by a radio signal,[77] and when in London the excitement of being carried upwards by an electric escalator.[78] They were almost balmy days; nothing seemed as if life would change, just a world of inventions and a growing confidence that life would improve for the masses. We had become accustomed to the news of war around the globe in faraway lands, we had also become used to the idea that war was around the corner but would always be avoided, as with the Russians I mentioned earlier. When the Great War started I was startled that it had actually happened. I must confess that, like many others, I believed it would be over in a few months. Indeed even in Rollesby there was a certain war fever, and many of our young men joined up for what everyone thought would be an adventure. Looking back from my old age, I realise now how wrong we all were, but it is impossible to have any sensible perspective when you live through the events of the day. I still put the blame squarely on the Kaiser, but do agree with some modern historians that Europe's build-up of industrial weaponry gave war a certain inevitability. Whatever the reason the tragedy of modern warfare certainly came home to roost in every city, town, village and home.

In this area of Rollesby it came sooner than to other parts of the country because German naval airships bombed Yarmouth and King's Lynn.[79] Most of us knew someone or other who was affected by this outrageous attack on civilians. I really do not want to dwell too long on this war; it still has unbearably painful and deeply personal memories, even now over a decade later. I can recall vividly the horror reading about one of the early battles at a place called Neuve Chapelle,[80] where we suffered 12,000 casualties for 1,200 yards, a thousand men for a hundred yards. We heard about poison gas and names like Ypres and Somme became part of our daily vocabulary. At the start of the war there was almost a feeling of exultation because we as

---

[77] 1910 July 31st. And he was hanged November 23rd.

[78] 1911 October 4th. First electric escalators at Earl's Court underground, London.

[79] 1915 January 19th.

[80] 1915 March 10th-12th.

a country were destined to put the Kaiser in his place; the British Empire was to be supreme. As the casualty lists were published there was almost a national gasp of horror. As the telegrams arrived it became a sickening revulsion and a deep sadness at what had been unleashed. When the first troops left for Flanders the crowds came out and the drums were sounded, but as the war entrenched itself the soldiers left at night, as if we were all ashamed.

My parish of Rollesby was small, just over five hundred souls and mainly old because younger people had sought their fortune whether in the cities or overseas. Even here we sent sixteen young men to fight, and thirteen were killed, and three returned maimed but were never themselves again. Neighbour was embarrassed to speak with neighbours who lost their children; it was as if we were all involved in a conspiracy. When I wrote earlier that I find recollecting the Edwardian era vague it was because the Great War has left a scar across my memory. I can recall it detail by bitter detail, but I care little for noting it down here. I remember in September 1916, the start of the new term at school, going to see Mr and Mrs Beck, their son George Daniel,[81] a Private in the 1st Battalion of the Norfolk Regiment had been killed at some remote village called Bapaume. He had died with thousands of others in the Somme battle, and across the country thousands of families would have received identical telegrams, but I remember Mrs Beck's face, wet with tears, and Mr Beck standing speechless for hours. I sat with them for two hours, but what could I say? Looking back I can see that for Rollesby 1917 seemed the very worst of those terrible years. The Walpoles[82] were so sickened by the loss of their son they packed up and left without saying anything to anyone at the beginning of May 1917. Then there was Donald Chapman, William Platter, Fred Dyball, John Olley, Leslie Ransome, George and Charles Wright and Billy Palmer their friend. The telegrams came and did not stop coming. In September of 1917 Bob Piggin, a Gunner from the Royal Garrison Artillery died in Belgium. I went to see Robert his father and we just sat in silence for the morning. I thought Bob Piggin[83] was a survivor, he was thirty-six and had gone through the war mainly unscathed. I could recall when I sat there how some silly girl in 1914

---

[81] Commonwealth War Graves Commission, Thiepval Memorial, Somme, Private 3/7992.

[82] F Walpole Private 40562 died Saturday 28th April 1917 at Arras. CWGC.

[83] CWGC Vlamertinghe New Military cemetery, Ieper, West-Vlaanderen, Gunner 20213.

had given him a white feather: she was now married to an entertainer in Yarmouth who had somehow managed to avoid conscription.

All my five sons served in the Great War. Richard, my eldest who had been educated at Harrow and Trinity College, Cambridge and served in Salonika, was mentioned in despatches.[84] My second son, Waveney, in the Norfolks, fought in France and Mesopotamia. Dudley, whom I had educated at the finest school in the world, Eton, was a Captain and also mentioned in despatches. Then Thomas, was a Major with the Military Cross and is now a solicitor. He would have done better had he gone to Eton and not Harrow. Then my youngest, Ernest, dear Ernest, I shall never recover from the pain.

The telegram came to the Rectory; my youngest son Ernest, a Second Lieutenant in the Lancashire Hussars had been killed on the Ypres Salient at a place called Tyne Cot. Ernest was only twenty-one, a boy who may well have entered Holy Orders and taken over from me. Caroline and I were shattered. Like my parishioners we just sat together trying to understand what had happened. The servants moved about quietly, understanding the grief, because they too had suffered in their families. In the afternoon I took my horse and rode down to the quietness of Rollesby Broad. I read a letter he had written home. In this he spoke of having to censor 300 letters, and wrote of the terrible flies and thirst.[85] I sat by the Broad and wept until I could cry no more.

Despite all my efforts in the parish over the previous forty years I had never felt as much a part of the place as I did after this tragedy. I had given comfort to others as far as I was ever able, but now they comforted me: we had suffered together. This war killed all, the sons of gentry and farm labourers alike, the gifted and the dull, the educated and the illiterate: death in the trenches bound them and us at home together. That Christmas of 1917 my wife and I spent quietly, and on Boxing Day went for supper with the Brownswords at Rollesby Hall. I knew that as soon as Harry walked in from answering the door he too had faced the same tragedy that very day: he held the familiar telegram in his hand. His son Douglas had been killed on Christmas Day. While we were celebrating Midnight Mass Douglas had

[84] Richard Charles Tacon was to become the next patron of the Parish and his son, Richard is the current patron (31 July 2000).

[85] Letter 13th August 1917 amongst private papers of R Tacon.

been killed in a support trench called Oxford Road. He had been a Captain in the Army Service Corps[86] and had died in the same area as my own son, Ernest, and the lad Bob Piggin. Normally they would have all been at Midnight Mass in Rollesby: instead 1917 claimed their lives within a few weeks of one another in the same godless area. Mabel Brownsword needed smelling salts and my wife thought we ought to go. Harry asked us to stay; he knew we too had suffered such a shock and took some comfort that where he was we had been. My faith took me for a time into a spiritual wilderness, how could a God allow this to happen? It was irrational, and I knew that as humans we are responsible for our own free will, and that God cannot interfere in our daily lives to deprive us of free will. It took months for me to gain any understanding in my prayers again. Parishioners who lost their children in the trenches did not reproach me on such theological issues but I knew they felt it. What was the point of prayer if all that happened was death and desolation? On Easter Sunday 1918 I preached on God giving his only son, the suffering Christ, and I could feel within myself and others that our faith was binding us together.

At the end of the war there was considerable rejoicing, but for those of us who had lost members of our family it was muted. Of course we were relieved that the war had stopped, but the victory felt hollow. We put the memorial up in the entrance to the graveyard, and although I took the service I had to brace myself as I read the names: not just because Ernest was among them, but I knew the pain all my fellow parishioners felt. That cross in the graveyard is opposite my family vault,[87] and I never pass by that memorial without acknowledging it and the suffering that flowed from those years.

I look back with horror to the time I supported the war: I was never quite as outspoken as Arthur Winnington-Ingram, Bishop of London,[88] who tried to make the war a holy war and always ensured he was photographed in military uniform. Prime Minister Asquith described him as an 'intensely silly bishop' and I am grateful that most of us realised before too long the folly of modern war. Christianity may have lost its way because of

---

[86] CWGC Captain Douglas Anderson Brownsword, Army Service Corps, died Tuesday, 25th December 1917, aged 25. Oxford Road Cemetery, Ieper, West-Vlaanderen.

[87] The memorial stone stands above the vault.

[88] Chadwick, H (Editor) (2000) *Not Angels but Anglicans* Canterbury Press, Norwich, p.256-7.

the Church's attitudes, but we changed just in time. It was significant that the grave of the Unknown Warrior was still placed in the Abbey and not the Cenotaph: this contrasted with the French who placed theirs in the entirely secular place of the Arc de Triomphe.[89]

As a parish clergyman I had a duty to give strength to others, and I pursued my duties and life with a new vigour. I hid my pain and bitter memories and forced myself to smile and work as if the world were a new place. I became busy in my personal affairs and increased my field holdings, rented out the Grange to the Silcots and even built a shop down in the village.[90] During the war the army had taken over the old Workhouse and Court Rooms, and they left it in a thorough mess. We demolished parts of the old building and the Board of Guardians continued to meet on Tuesday mornings[91] with little to discuss. The Court continued as usual after 1918 and I busied myself as a JP. They wanted to move even the Court to Ormesby but I blocked this silliness.[92]

I let out Hall Farm to Tooke: he lived opposite the Horse and Groom, which was now being run by Arthur Tooke. It was not long before the village was back to normal, but with the obvious lack of young men. I busied myself as a governor of Paston School as I mentioned earlier, and was pleased when the government raised the school leaving age to fourteen.[93] Boys could stay even longer so long as they could be supported. We rebuilt the local school down Main Road[94] and the old school we used for Parish affairs, calling it the 'Rector's Rooms'. The war changed my mind on many things, not least women's right to vote. I trust that women will not push themselves too forward though, as it does not seem right for the fairer sex to do this. I thought my nightmare of women clergy was becoming real when I heard that an Anglican woman had become Britain's first woman minister at the Congregationalist City Temple.[95] The article caught my attention

---

[89] Chadwick, H (Editor) (2000) *Not Angels but Anglicans* Canterbury Press, Norwich, p.259.

[90] Now by Beck's Garage.

[91] Information from Frederick Youngs - 29 February 2000.

[92] During World War II the Court function ceased, it moved to Ormesby Village Hall and then to Yarmouth. The army took the Court House and old Workhouse over between 1939-45 and after the war it was sold for £1000. In the mid-1990s it changed hands at over £100,000.

[93] 1918 August. Education Act introduced by H A L Fisher.

[94] 1924. Still stands with modern extensions.

[95] 1917. Maude Royden.

only because I had read somewhere that a Rollesby man called Goodwin had been the first minister there. I actually own the cottage in which he was born. It was with a sigh of relief that I found that she was a Congregationalist minister, which is not the same as a clerk in Holy Orders.

I have to say that women's dress is conspicuously anti-feminine these days: almost tubular with breasts flattened and a mock waist around their hips. At Oxford women can become full members of the University and are actually able to receive degrees.[96] Ernest told me, when once on leave, the brave and sterling work they had done in the field hospitals, so I do not grudge them that, but I do wish they would dress more like women. Women have equal rights in divorce suits; wives can actually divorce their husbands for adultery.[97]

The Russian Revolution has now embedded itself and we are faced with Communism. I recall after the Great War the relief when we withdrew our own troops from Russia:[98] we had been supporting the Tsar's troops, the White Russians, but we have all had enough of war. I suspect that Communism is here to stay and I can only pray it does not lead to another war, because the way weapons have developed I dread to think what would be the outcome.[99] There is even now a Communist Party in this country![100] So long as they only talk I care little. I attended the dedication by King George V of the Cenotaph and the burial of the Unknown Soldier at Westminster Abbey. I could not help but wonder whether it was my old choirboy, John Olley,[101] whose body was never identified. They say it was the war to end wars, I only hope the pundits are right: I have my doubts. Even in Ireland there is war, the Black and Tans killed twelve people by shooting into a football crowd and the IRA shot eleven officers in Dublin:[102] when will it stop? The Irish even killed their own man, Michael Collins,[103] but now the Irish Free State Constitution Act has come into

---

[96] 1920.

[97] 1923 July 18th. Matrimonial Causes Act.

[98] 1919 September 27th. British troops withdrawn from Archangel; withdrawn from Murmansk, 12th October.

[99] 1927 May 27th. Britain breaks off diplomatic relations with Soviet Russia.

[100] 1920 July 31st. Communist Party of Great Britain founded.

[101] John Olley on Rollesby Memorial but no sign of him in Commonwealth Graves Commission.

[102] 1920 November 21st.

[103] 1922 August 22nd.

force I hope this ends the Irish problem.[104]

I became too old for my trusted horse during the last ten years, and I purchased a Morris-Cowley,[105] a fine car and it gives me much pleasure in the local area. On long journeys my chauffeur drives me in the Rolls Royce. We went to London in this vehicle; it took all day but it was a pleasurable drive. I watched the wedding of the Duke of York to Lady Elizabeth Bowes-Lyon: she was a beautiful bride and I only hope she keeps her beauty even if she lives to be a hundred.[106] While there I met an old Italian friend who told me about their new Prime Minister, Benito Mussolini:[107] I listened with respect to his eulogies on the man, but from what I have read I do not trust this new approach to government. It smacks too much of the Dark Ages when the strong survive and the weak and elderly go the wall.

I hope that we as a nation always steer clear of such politics and simply enjoy our democratic way of life and sport. I was thrilled when Eric Liddell and Harold Abrahams won gold medals in the Olympics.[108] The Wembley Stadium has been opened and Bolton Wanderers beat West Ham 2-1;[109] it is a wonderful stadium and should last for hundreds of years. In Rollesby we have a very active soccer and cricket team; I am still President of the Rollesby Football Club! George Wallis, the Vicar of Ormesby St Margaret, the next door parish, had a curate called George Raymond Grundy[110] who was keen on sports and won all the local competitions. He is a good man and I have my eye on him to take over from me when I have gone, and that is not too far off. Rollesby will have better teams under a man like that. At the moment Grundy is Rector of Thrigby, as well as my curate in Rollesby. It's the quality that is important, not the size of the village. I thought this when reading about the New Zealand All Blacks who won all their thirty matches in their second Rugby Union Tour:[111] they are only a nation of some one to two million. I am sure they cannot keep this standard of rugby going.

---

[104] 1922 December 6th.

[105] Cost in 1922 £425.

[106] 1923 April 26th. The future King George VI and Queen Elizabeth.

[107] 1922 October 30th. Benito Mussolini becomes Italian Prime Minister.

[108] 1924. VI Olympiad in Paris.

[109] 1923 April 28th.

[110] Curate at Ormesby 1919-20 who assisted at the Reverend Tacon's funeral and then took over as Rector.

[111] 1924.

I am not sure how long I can keep going. Life is still busy in the parish, only last year I was elected President of the East Norfolk Agricultural Society and I had three years as President of the Acle Agricultural Show.[112] I put a good deal of effort and personal finance into St George's church.[113] In 1884 I restored the church at a cost of nearly £2,000 with new oak roofs to the nave aisles and porch. I rebuilt the brick buttresses, restored the window frames from the rotting wood, took out the ridiculous box pews replacing them with pitch pine and had built a splendid organ.[114] More recently I have replaced three windows, one in memory of my youngest son Ernest killed in the Great War; one for my beloved wife, Caroline, and to my daughter, Ethel, who was a brilliant organist; and one, a little conceited, for my fifty years service to the church. It has been money consumptive and tiring work.

Nor am I sure I can keep this letter going too long: I tire easily these days. I have just opened a letter from the Bishop pointing out that we may use the new Revised 1928 Prayer Book if authorised by a diocesan bishop. When I started this letter a few days ago I noted that this Prayer Book had been thrown out:[115] all is change and it exhausts me. When I came to this parish in 1872 we were truly rural: it was idyllic apart from the farming problems. In my brief time here I have watched engines develop into cars and man fly. With the cars we have made tanks and with the planes bombers. There is still vast unemployment and suffering, and I am not convinced that the Great War was the war to end wars. I apologise for ending on a sad note, but I am not convinced that mankind has made the necessary spiritual and moral progress alongside the scientific advances, and I shall not be unhappy for my Lord to call me home.

---

[112] R Tacon's private papers.

[113] Richard Tacon virtually rebuilt the church. He restored the chancel (1875) and the nave (1884), put new roofing on, fixed the tracery to windows, installed new seating and a new font of Purbeck marble (1885), restored the tower (1897), organised the new organ via the good offices of Major C P S Ensor (1897), placed the great West window in memory of his 50 years as Rector (1922), and put in windows for his wife, Caroline and son, Ernest.

[114] *Evening Press* 1884 June 14th.

[115] 1928. Modified version again defeated in House of Commons by 266 votes to 220: the 1928 book can be used if authorised by a diocesan bishop. Chadwick, H (Editor) (2000) *Not Angels but Anglicans* Canterbury Press, Norwich, p.257. 'The new structures were, though, to be severely tested in 1927 and 1928, when the revised Book of Common Prayer, overwhelmingly approved by all three Houses of the Church Assembly, was twice rejected by the Commons. The affair revealed the continuing force of Protestant sentiment, in opposition to the more Catholic tendency of the new book.'

CHAPTER 34

ooooo

George Raymond Grundy (1930-1950)

World War II

Dear Future Readers,

I am writing this letter propped up in a hospital bed in Yarmouth as the nurses are putting up Christmas decorations. I am not sure whether I will live to see the New Year, 1950,[1] or how far into the future this letter will be read; indeed if there is much of a future the way mankind is developing atomic weapons. As for myself I was born on September 11th 1889, at 16 Effingham Road, Lee, London. My father was the Reverend George William Grundy and he came from Cork, in Ireland, making me half Irish. My father married one of the Worthington brewery daughters and my mother was a formidable person. I studied at the London College of Divinity and was deaconed and priested in Chelmsford Cathedral in 1915 and 1916 respectively. I served my first curacy at Little Ilford, under the Reverend Hugh Guy. It was while there I met my wife, the Rector's daughter, Muriel Emily. Her father officiated at our wedding on April 18th 1918, held in my next curacy at St Thomas Heigham. It was a joint wedding because my wife's sister was married at the same time.[2] After this I moved to Ormesby St Margaret as curate with oversight of Ormesby St Michael for two years in 1919-20.[3] The incumbent of that parish was the Reverend

---

[1] Raymond Grundy died in Great Yarmouth Hospital on January 2nd 1950 from throat cancer.

[2] Family details from son, George Grundy. 6 August 2000.

[3] *Crockford's Clerical Directory, 1935* under G R Grundy entry.

George Charles Wallis, BD, a man whom I liked and who recommended me to the Bishop to be Rector of Thrigby. This is a small village with little to do so I was also curate to the Reverend Richard Tacon in Rollesby. He died in 1929 and with the Archdeacon I helped bury a man I greatly loved. My admiration of Richard Tacon does not mean I did not have my ups and downs with him. I am partly Irish as already mentioned, and people do say I am a law unto myself.[4] I was headstrong as a young man, and Richard Tacon was more like the Lord of the Manor. He used to visit people of the parish on a horse, was a well-known JP and drove to his school meetings in a chauffeured Rolls Royce. I doubt whether the Church of England will ever see such old-style parsons again. He and his family virtually owned the parish and its farmlands and it was this that brought me into a slight clash with them once I was inducted as Rector. Richard Tacon had allowed me to live in the Grange once the Silcots had gone, but I had anticipated living in the Rectory as became my position as Rector. The Tacons stubbornly refused to leave what they regarded as their natural home. The Bishop and Diocese, ever conscious that they were the patrons of the living, did little about the matter. Rollesby had a population of some 456 souls and my tithe rent charges came to £648 per annum, but I had some money and purchased White Farm and a few acres to farm from old man Christmas. The Tacons did eventually move over to the Grange but not without some difficult moments between us. I got along well enough with the new patron, Dudley Tacon (the previous Rector's son), and he never interfered in the running of the church.

The Reverend Richard Tacon had been very keen on his presidency of the Rollesby Football Club and had encouraged me to run it well. He would have been proud of my 1931-2 team who won the Wiltshire Cup and Shield: the photograph of my team sits proudly on my desk.[5] Then, during the Spanish Civil War, we opened the old Rectory to Spanish refugees: some of them were top football players, so after that we won everything!

I also took over another mantle from the Reverend Tacon and became a JP working from the Old Court House. I was actively involved in local politics during the 1930s; I was a Councillor for the Fleggs, and also a Norfolk

[4] Comment by his son, George Grundy aged 81 in interview of 6 August 2000.

[5] Photograph now in the possession of Miss A Bates.

County Councillor. I enjoyed the electioneering: I used to borrow old Arthur Lanham's car and had 'Vote for Grundy' all over its bodywork.[6] I was also Masonic Chaplain at St Mary's Lodge, Great Yarmouth. I confess to thoroughly enjoying the social side of being a Mason. I would dine well, and on more than one occasion drive my old Ford into a muddy field on the way home. I would then have to contact my sons, George and John, who would fetch Black Beauty, our trusted horse, to drag my car out of the mire.[7]

It was about this time that a close friend of my wife's died in India and we virtually adopted his two children: Miles, whom we always knew as Smiler, and his sister Margaret. Smiler went to Forest Gate School, London, and Margaret to Ealing, but they spent their holidays with us. I would always take them to the Regal cinema in Yarmouth for a Saturday afternoon outing: while they watched the film I would wander the docks area. Annie our maid particularly enjoyed these afternoons: I gathered later that the young organist at the cinema would often ask my wife to play so he could slip away and meet his girlfriend. My wife was an accomplished organist, but I do wish that she would avoid her favourite jazz pieces in church.

Apart from my wife's occasional outburst with jazz during Evensong the music in the church was good. Old Kelly Hodds[8] was my main organ blower, and he was assisted by Freddy Baldry. Fred was my general handyman, grave digger and organ pump man: he was a simple soul and had I allowed him he would have followed me everywhere.[9] The choir was strong; we had Freddy Moore, Tommy Piggin, Ken Ransome, Tom Evans, Edgar Mace, and Fred, William and John Symonds. They were not sophisticated musicians but they could sing even the dullest psalms with a good heart.

The parish was developing with a few new houses when I arrived, down by the Old Court House with some more houses down Main Road. Nevertheless, it was not an easy time for employment. After the Wall Street crash[10] there were serious reverberations in this country, and unemployment

[6] From Granville Lanham, Arthur Lanham's son (8 August 2000).

[7] George Grundy (6 August 2000).

[8] See Appendix 3 for some details of local people in the 1930s.

[9] When this rector died Freddy slept by his grave for the first night: information given by Mr Symonds who was a choir member in those days.

[10] 1929 October 28th. Sharp fall in share values on Stock Exchange following start of Wall Street crash on 24th October.

reached dismal levels. The government seemed more concerned with matters abroad than at home. We heard a great deal about Gandhi, in India,[11] naval treaties[12] that proved to be useless, and an Airship R101[13] that proved as disastrous as the silly attempts to keep the Germans in check. The R101 and other airships were mere puffs: compared to the Supermarine S6 seaplane winning the Schneider Trophy in 1929 the airship was nothing. This plane was to develop into the Spitfire, now much beloved and so essential a few years ago. I do not think that in the 1930s any of us realised how important aircraft development was going to be. We took it for granted when Amy Johnson flew solo to Australia in a Gipsy Moth biplane[14] and James Mollison flew from Australia to London in eight days nineteen hours.[15]

I recall my anger when I read that Oswald Mosley[16] had founded the British Union of Fascists, and how agreeable it was when he was greeted by hostile crowds in London and was eventually incarcerated during the war. In Rollesby people kept their heads; being country people we were pleasantly isolated from the extremism of the cities. We had, to my knowledge, no Fascists or Communists in our parish; we had a few socialists but our main concern was our daily work and trying to improve living conditions.

Conditions in the church were not good: we had little money and little hope of reliable money coming in to support the work of the gospel. A huge amount of money was spent by Lieutenant-Colonel Hubert Yates on a stained glass window in our north aisle. It was placed there in memory of his wife, Gertrude Loetitia Molyneux. She had been the fourth daughter of General Sarel buried by Richard Tacon. Gertrude was actually buried in Cornwall but the window was placed here because of family connections. It is a beautiful window but we would have been better off with a donation. There is no religious zeal in the Church at large, no enthusiasm amongst

---

[11] 1930 March 12th. Gandhi begins a peaceful civil disobedience campaign.

[12] 1930 April 22nd. Treaty of London on naval disarmament: limitations on submarines and aircraft carriers.

[13] 1930 October 7th. Airship R101 crashes near Beauvais on maiden flight to India, killing 44, including the Air Minister, Lord Thomson.

[14] 1930 May 5th. She took off from Croydon airport and reached Darwin on May 24th.

[15] 1931 August 6th.

[16] 1932 October.

the people.[17] Indeed, it strikes me that more churches close than open![18]

Living in the country is always the dream of town and urban people but in reality it can be quite a tough life. We are, as rural people, a great deal more passive than urban dwellers. When we suffer unemployment we look for work and tend our gardens, and we do not look for a fight either with society as a whole or the police.[19] On the other hand we can let the rest of the world pass by with too little comment if we are not careful. I recall very early on in my ministry a discussion in the Horse and Groom that became very strong, so much so that the landlord, Curtis, was worried about his glasses. It started over the subject of Jews. It was not that there was any hostility about Jews, which tends to operate more in golf clubs and middle-class circles, but about the situation in Germany. There had been protests in Hyde Park about the treatment of Jews in Germany[20] and there were those who thought it just to be old anti-Hun propaganda, and those who suspected the Germans of vile doings. There were those who wanted to believe that the Germans had returned to the fold and those who believed Germans could never be trusted again. I calmed it all down when Curtis asked me to step in; the local parson can still wield some authority. My point is that in the country we did not actually stop to ask what was happening in Germany: it was too far away from the reality of what we understood, the village. We were more concerned with how much the bus service to Yarmouth was costing than the plight of people in another country. Even the wireless[21] failed to draw our attention to other people in other countries. I remember reading about Winston Churchill warning against the Germans re-arming,[22] but he was almost laughed out of the House. I have to confess I thought him a war-monger at that time, but because I read a good deal by 1935 I was listening to his warnings with greater apprehension.

---

[17] Hastings, A (1991) *A History of English Christianity* SCM, London, p.679. '...within English history there have been waves of religious enthusiasm, of attempts to convert and truly Christianize a rather nominally Christian England. We see such waves in the 13th, the 17th and the 19th centuries. Hitherto, at least, ours has not been such an age.'

[18] Hastings, A (1991) *A History of English Christianity* SCM, London, p.602. 'The closure of doors is unquestionable. Between 1969-1984 the Church of England declared 1,086 churches redundant ... one church was demolished every nine days.'

[19] 1931 October 30th. Series of violent clashes between police and unemployed marchers in London.

[20] 1933 July 20th.

[21] 1932 March 15th. First transmission from Broadcasting House: Henry Hall conducts his BBC Dance Orchestra.

[22] 1933 August 12th. Churchill's first speech warning of German rearmament.

The 1930s were a strange mix between relaxation at home and disturbing news from abroad. I had taken a brief holiday to watch tennis at Wimbledon. Fred Perry and Dorothy Round had won both the singles finals for Britain:[23] I am sure we will always dominate Wimbledon. Between matches I read my *Times* and I was transfixed by what was happening in Germany. The 'Night of the Long Knives'[24] in which at least a hundred of Hitler's enemies were murdered, and Hitler had been the German Chancellor since the previous year. Now, in 1949, we know he was more than capable of this, but in 1934 it seemed inconceivable, sitting in strawberry-laden Wimbledon that a head of a modern European state could have his opponents murdered.

The British public would not have put up with such felony. I remember in 1935 that when the Cabinet approved a partition plan for Ethiopia arranged by our own man, Hoare, and the French Foreign Minister, Laval,[25] the public rage was such that both men had to resign. Simply to appease Mussolini they had decided to divide another country up as if it were a game of chess. The French and British public would not put up with such an outrage. In the same way the public resented the extremist stupidity of Oswald Mosley: Jew and Gentile turned out in riotous mood to attack him and his followers. It needed the Public Order Bill in order to ban political private armies and control marches, though I suspect every normal Englishman was behind the barrow boys of Whitechapel when Mosley's march was stopped.[26] When I look back at the events of history I wish that the public had a means of expressing their feelings more than just through the right to vote every four or five years.

The turmoil abroad and on our London streets was overshadowed by the death of King George V[27] and then by the abdication of Edward VIII over the issue of Mrs Simpson. Baldwin, our Prime Minister then, was caught between various factions. Edward VIII had made himself popular in some

[23] 1934 July 7th.

[24] 1934 June 30th.

[25] 1935 December 9th.

[26] 1936 November 10th. Public Order Bill introduced into House of Commons following the 'Battle of Cable Street' when a provocative march into Whitechapel by Mosley's BUF was halted by anti-Fascists. The Bill became effective from January 1st 1937.

[27] George V dies at Sandringham: Prince of Wales accedes as Edward VIII.

quarters, especially after his tour of the slums in South Wales[28] and with some politicians like Winston Churchill. At the end of the day the truth will be allowed to seep out, but it is my considered opinion that the Archbishop of Canterbury, Cosmo Gordon Lang, refused to crown the man. The King's brother took his place as George VI[29] and, given the troubled years to follow, thank goodness he did. During all this upheaval Crystal Palace burned to the ground;[30] it felt like a prophetic warning of things to come. It all left a very bad taste in one's mouth, especially the news that German troops had occupied the demilitarised Rhineland.[31]

The world was clearly heating up again. Amongst the trivia such as the Duke of Windsor marrying Mrs Simpson[32] and the happy couple visiting Hitler[33] there was at the same time the bombing of Guernica[34] in the Spanish Civil War by German planes and the invasion of China by Japan.[35] I remember discussing this with the Patron, Dudley Tacon: we both agreed that the use of aircraft was going to be significant in the next war, and both of us suddenly realised we had assumed 'another' war. I had a similar conversation with some friends at the opening of Norwich City Hall,[36] with the same assumption that war was inevitable. The majority of acquaintances were of the opinion that war had become too dreadful in its sophistication to allow it to happen. I used to argue that they were right, but only in theory. As a priest I have some understanding of human nature, and the silly behaviour of some neighbours in Rollesby was only a reflection of what could and did happen at international level. Even when Chamberlain returned with 'peace in our time' I was still convinced it was only a matter of time before all hell would break lose.

As soon as war started I tried to join the army as a chaplain but was informed that I was too old. I found this faintly ridiculous and I was determined to be involved, if only in my pastoral priestly care. The Bishop of

[28] 1936 November 18-19th.

[29] 1936 December 10th.

[30] 1936 November 30th.

[31] 1936 March 7th.

[32] 1937 June 3rd.

[33] 1937 October 11-23rd. Duke and Duchess of Windsor visit Nazi Germany and meet Hitler.

[34] 1937 April 27th.

[35] 1937 July 7th.

[36] 1938. The Hall was completed; designed by C James and R Pierce.

Norwich was not helpful. He suggested that since I had trained for the priesthood during the First War and so missed it I was desirous to be early for the next. On February 3rd 1940 I buried my last parishioner, one Esther Daniels, and as I committed the dear old seventy-six-year-old I decided then and there to do something constructive. I joined the Church Army and bought a van with Church Army emblazoned on the side. On one side of the van I had a tea urn to sustain the troops and on the other an altar for spiritual sustenance. Bracecamp, my old friend the Vicar of Ormesby, promised to look after Rollesby for three months while I was away: neither he nor I expected it to be three years. Bracecamp and I were good enough friends to do this. Rumour had it that Bracecamp's nickname was 'coal-ticket' because if parishioners attended church ten times in a row he gave them five tons of coal as chairman of the Fuel Allotment Committee. With a friend I set sail for the continent. I chose to head towards what I deemed to be the front line at Dammes Carnier just as the German army pushed into France. I found myself the only person responsible for looking after 4,000 refugees and some wounded soldiers in Lille, when the Germans turned up. Sadly I think I must have been one of the earliest to fall victim to becoming a prisoner of war. How important all this is to the Parish of Rollesby I am uncertain.

Perhaps Bracecamp, the Vicar of Ormesby, or my wife should take over because they looked after Rollesby in my absence. My wife was an accomplished organist and would also take the prayers for Matins and Evensong. I remember arguing with a large German officer that I was Church Army and not Army, but to no avail. I had a large selection of Bibles with me and they allowed me to keep these and my altar equipment, but they confiscated my van. I was able to give these Bibles to various soldiers imprisoned with me.[37] As a Church Army chaplain they allowed me to attend the hospital where the wounded troops were lodged. I was moved from camp to camp[38] after this, suffering all the usual indignities of any prisoner of war. Eventually I was placed in Oflag 9 and was known as the 'Gaffer' because I was the old-

[37] 1999 November. One such Bible emerged from an old soldier's effects: inside was written 'Thomas Stanley Houstord, November 1st 1940 Presented as a token of friendship at Enghien Hospital German Prison, Belgium by The Rev G Raymond Grundy Rollesby Rectory Gt Yarmouth Church Army Chaplain captured near Dammes Carnier.'

[38] He ended up in Oflag IX AH at Lille: there he was known as the 'Gaffer' because he was the oldest in the camp. Note from George Grundy, his son.

est prisoner there.[39] The main problem in the camp was the complete lack of tobacco; the German guards simply confiscated any that came into the camp. In the early stages of my imprisonment I convinced the German Commandant to allow me to conduct the occasional service in Lille. I was allowed to do this under guard and during the Communion service many of the locals slipped 'fags' into an empty chalice to enable me to smuggle them back into camp.[40]

In 1942 I was still suffering from piles: they used to drive me mad. I also developed a serious pain in my throat, it was not just a sore throat, and I eventually went to see a Naval doctor who to my horror looked worried. He told me that it did not look good but he needed better facilities to check the nature of my illness before he would pronounce what he suspected. I pestered him of course but he was insistent. He went to the camp commandant and the next thing I knew I was being taken under guard to a Nuremberg hospital, of all places. I have to confess I was well looked after. The nurse and the doctor, despite being German, were extremely kind. I was not wearing my dog collar, and as far as they were concerned I was simply an enemy prisoner of war. After a day's examination they diagnosed throat cancer and I sat there stunned as the doctor explained to me that it was really a matter of time. He explained to me that they could prescribe some drugs, which would help with the pain, but there was no cure.

Back in the camp I saw the senior officer and explained my predicament. He was a decent sort of chap and saw the German military authority about my repatriation. As English we were not popular; in the air raids on Hamburg[41] we had killed thousands. Nevertheless, I was packed up and returned to England via Sweden. For many it was seen as good luck, for me I had mixed feelings; I was being returned because I was dying. The one thing that did strike me was that amidst all the killing, the mayhem and murder, the individual Germans I met at the hospital and through the repatriation effort showed a degree of compassion I had not expected. There was a special Red Cross boat travelling via Sweden to Leith in Scotland.[42] It was a long, tiring journey, and an anxious one.

---

[39] George Grundy (6 August 2000).

[40] George Grundy (6 August 2000).

[41] 1943 July 26th - August 3rd.

[42] 1943 Monday October 25th.

On my return to Rollesby it was a world I had difficulty in recognising. Bracecamp, the Vicar of Ormesby, met and collected me from Yarmouth station, but we hardly knew one another. I had seen men killed in the most terrifying of situations, guns and hand grenades blowing my ear drums to pieces, men dying from indescribable wounds. I had seen men starving in the prison camps, losing their minds through boredom. As I travelled through Germany on the way home I had seen the bloodletting of revenge. Here in Rollesby nothing had changed. The fields were growing corn, the pub still sold beer, and people came to Evensong. There seemed to be two worlds in existence at the same time. I returned to White House Farm and there for a few months just rested and tried to regain some lost energy. I was interviewed at length by various War Office officials and some backroom boys who needed to know what was happening in the POW Camps - what sort of things the prisoners needed to facilitate their escaping. When I said how dangerous it was they did not seem to mind. It was not so much that they needed men back, except for pilots, but for every man who escaped, even if it were a canteen supervisor, it tied up German resources. I was also interviewed by W A Nicholson of the *Daily Mail* and was something of a nine-hour celebrity in the national press. It was a brief piece of unwanted fame, war was raging around the world, men and women dying, my two sons, George and John were both away serving, and I was not keen on the publicity.

By 1944 I resumed my duties back in St George's, though I was so tired from my illness that Bracecamp lent me a curate and I would sit in my stall and let him take the service. I heard the appalling news that one of my young football team players, Fred Dublack, had died in a Japanese prisoner of war camp. After the war I gather he was buried in Chungkai War Cemetery.[43] He was a good athlete and was only twenty-seven years old when he died. Also Percy Shreeve, who had joined the South Staffordshire Regiment, died at only twenty-four in Burma.[44] I went to see Charles and Elisabeth Shreeve; they were of course inconsolable. By the end of the war Teddy Alexander, Cyril Brown, Cecil Moore and Stan Wymer were also

[43] CWGC under F J Dublack, Private 5777163, 5th Bn; Royal Norfolk Regiment: Chungkai War Cemetery is approximately 5 kilometres west of Kanchanaburi War Cemetery. It does not appear on any map but was a hamlet on the River Kwai Noi about 117 kilometres west of Bangkok.

[44] CWGC under Percy James Shreeve, Private 5781860; Taukkyan War Cemetery, Myanmar; the cemetery is outside Yangon (formerly Rangoon) near the airport adjoining the village of Taukkyan.

dead. Teddy died of wounds on the 1st of May in Tunisia, he had joined the 9th Battalion of the Royal Fusiliers, a City of London Regiment; he was only twenty years of age.[45] They died in faraway places with strange names, places very distant in every meaning of the word from rural Rollesby.

When D-Day came in 1944 our hearts were in our mouths; we all had the distinct impression it was now or never. Norfolk had been flooded with American troops and Air Force officers; the soldiers had disappeared and we had all guessed that an invasion had been imminent. The soldiers had taken over the great Jacobean Hall and the Court House as well as the old school. They had managed to ruin all three. The Jacobean Hall had also been home to some evacuees, but they had not taken kindly to rural life. They came, I was informed, into the village looking for the cinema and fish and chip shop, and were dismayed to find only a post office and a store. It was not as if the locals were unkind, but the young city children could not cope with country life.

The last year of the war, 1945, brought mixed messages to the home front. We heard of places like Auschwitz and Dachau and found such cruelty inconceivable.[46] I had received nothing but fair dealing from the Wehrmacht and I could only speculate that the Nazis had perpetrated such wickedness. There was the joy of German surrender along with news of yet more casualty lists, the fear of a menacing Russia,[47] but above all the news of the atomic bomb on August 6th. I shall never forget that August 6th is the day of our Lord's Transfiguration on the Holy Mountain. We celebrated that day in St George's; God's bright light while Hiroshima felt the death and destruction of man's bright light. I found it awesome, almost terrifying that August 6th carried both these events. To this day I am not sure what I feel about that event. I remember being angry that Bishop Bell of Chichester had denounced the bombing of Germany as 'terror bombing',[48] but Hiroshima was too awful to contemplate. I suppose that if I had been a soldier preparing to invade Japan with its fanatical fighting and no-surren-

---

[45] CWGC Fusilier 5783234 Enfidaville War Cemetery, Tunisia, Grave reference VIII.C.31.

[46] Chadwick, H (Editor) (2000) *Not Angels but Anglicans* Canterbury Press, Norwich, p.258. 'Although there was now more space for Christian pacifism, acceptance of overt criticism of the war was still limited. When Bishop Bell condemned in the House of Lords the saturation bombing of German cities, he found himself an isolated figure. His courageous stance antagonised Churchill and the King ...'

[47] 1946 March 5th. Churchill's Iron Curtain speech at Fulton.

[48] 1944 February 9th. In the House of Lords.

der policy I may have agreed. It is a difficult problem, but I am certain the second bomb was not necessary: either way we have a very dangerous world. Our only hope is the new United Nations,[49] but my fear is that it will go the same way as the old League of Nations: in short it will have no real teeth.

There are some reforms under the new Labour Government, not least the National Health Service Bill,[50] though it is probably too late for me. I was surprised when Churchill was thrown out of power. Having met many of the troops in the Prisoner of War Camp I knew that although they admired him as a war leader they wanted to return to a better more socially equitable world, and they were convinced that only the Labour party would achieve such a thing. The Royal Commission on granting women equal pay[51] would not have happened under a Conservative government. There are new changes in the air, even in the Church. Attendance has dropped, and Archbishop Fisher of Canterbury preached a sermon at Cambridge where he urged full communion with other churches.[52] I think that will always be a pious hope in the sky.

At the end of 1946 my wife's parents fell seriously ill and her youngest sister died unexpectedly. I agreed that my wife should nurse them while I looked after myself with the help of a housekeeper, a Miss Jackson. She is still with me. 1947 started as one of the coldest years in Rollesby I have ever known. Even the news that eleven leading Nazis had been hanged at Nuremberg for war crimes could not cheer up that winter.[53] The Broads froze and because rationing was still in force the times felt just as hard as they had in the middle of the war. Coal was particularly difficult to get hold of[54] but mercifully rural life at least gave us plenty of wood to burn. The snow blizzards were unbearable and even the size of newspapers had to be cut.[55] In the meantime there was a degree of anti-Jewish feeling because of

---

[49] 1946 January 10th. First session of UN General Assembly opens in London.

[50] 1946 November 6th.

[51] 1946 November 6th.

[52] 1946 November 3rd.

[53] 1946 October 16th.

[54] 1947 January 13th. The coldest winter since 1883 necessitated coal rationing to homes and industry.

[55] 1947 March 6th. Blizzards cut off 15 towns and closed 300 roads; newspapers and magazines cut down in size.

the disturbances in Palestine:[56] despite what had happened in the recent war I found it difficult to calm down people's feelings. It did not last long, and soon everyone had an opinion on the mass nationalisation that was proceeding: especially when British Railways came into effect.[57] Four hundred souls in Rollesby had between them three hundred opinions: I explained to my friends that British Railways was here to stay whatever they thought. Mercifully the political clutter of opinion died down a little when bread rationing came to a halt;[58] quite why it had lasted that long I shall never understand. There was even greater rejoicing amongst the village children when sweet rationing stopped.[59] I managed to purchase a new type of modern car, a Morris Minor,[60] but to be quite honest I have not had much energy to enjoy it since my throat cancer is wearing me down more and more. In fact I am writing this only because I am currently bedridden.

I know my life is ebbing away, and as I sit and ponder this letter-writing task I cannot but reflect on the suffering mankind has imposed on itself in this century. The First War was so unnecessary and bloodletting, and made the Second World War so necessary, with so much more bloodletting. The Second War with its nuclear weapons and planned genocide has made me wonder whether as a human race we have made any progress since Atilla the Hun. We talk about the barbaric past but we have made the slaughter of fellow human beings so much easier with our sophisticated weapons. Morally we have taken hardly a step forward and I wonder how effective the Church will ever be in the new climate I detect coming into being. Even in Rollesby the state has taken over many functions of the Church; education and even the charities we run are of little consequence in the welfare state. I suspect that the next priest will find a different world in which he has to be God's servant to this parish.

---

[56] 1947 July 31st. Bodies of two British sergeants, kidnapped by Irgun terrorists, found hanging near Haifa, Palestine. August 1st. Anti-Jewish demonstrations in Lancashire when news of these deaths were made public.

[57] 1948 January 1st.

[58] 1948 July 25th.

[59] 1949 April 24th.

[60] 1948. The new compact version goes on show at the Motor Show with Rover's Landrover.

CHAPTER 35

ooooo

Henry Gascoigne (1950-1958)

The 1950s and Teddy Boys

Dear Future,

This strange request arrived in the vestry unannounced, and I am not certain whether it is a joke or not, but either way I feel it to be quite a good idea to try and summarise my time here in this part of Norfolk. I was ordained late in life having been an organist at Gloucester Cathedral. I trained at King's College, London and was priested in Gloucester in 1941 during the war years. I served my first curacy at Holy Trinity in Cheltenham and then became Rector of Stokesby with Herringby between 1942 and 1950. I came to this neck of the woods in 1950 as Curate in charge of Rollesby and was eventually made Rector in 1953. I was also Curate in charge of Burgh St Mary with Billockby from 1953. I always had a special affection for Rollesby and was thrilled to help choose the stained glass window[1] in memory of Dudley Tacon's sister, Ethel Safford. She had been a brilliant organist in her time; Dudley and I chose a picture of St Michael, and now I feel as if I have added something to the St George's history. The day of a cleric for each small village and hamlet have gone: I have a geographically large area and a small population. I did not live in Rollesby but Clippesby Rectory.[2] I found the situation a difficult one as did the vari-

---

[1] Chancel, north wall.

[2] Personal information from *Crockford's 1961/62*.

ous congregations. They had been accustomed to having their own priest and suddenly they were sharing one between several parishes. Logistically it had to happen. I had the custom of standing outside the church to greet people as they entered and they always commented on the fact it was good to see me there, but in the same breath ask whether I could spend more time in their particular parish. After the war there was a shortage of both money and clergy, and small country parishes had no choice but to be joined together in loose federations: the word benefice became a popular word for this, rather than parishes. Each parish considered they had ownership of the cleric and became parochial in their attitudes. If I were seen too much in one parish it was claimed I was not doing my job in another. Some churches had to change their service times because if they all had services at ten or eleven in the morning I could not be in three places at the same time. Changing hymn books or the nature of any service always causes an uproar, but changing the times of a service was a political quagmire. At times there was a distinct resentment and even the best of the churchwardens could at times be caustic about the situation. In the traditional single parishes the cleric would have three services a day: in the country I could have five or six and it was exhausting. It was not easy travelling between the churches, cars are not always reliable and are always expensive.

'We are the larger parish, Rector, we don't expect more than one service on Sundays but we do expect to see you in the parish at least half the week.'

'But,' I would reply, 'that leaves me a day in each other parish, then there's Sunday and I have no day off.'

'But with your job do you need a day off?'

I could barely bring myself to answer this but explained every labourer needs some time to relax.

'I work five days a week, I come to church on Sundays and on Saturdays I help at the church, tell me Rector, when's my day off?'

'You only attend one service on a Sunday, I am at it all day.'

'But my one attendance stops me going out for the rest of the day.'

I do not want to mention the warden in question, but he really expected me to be on call, wandering the parishes, visiting the sick, burying the dead and preparing sermons and services seven days a week. Eventually I published the fact I would like Fridays free of parish activity. On the first day off up comes this warden and tells me that 'I knew I would catch you in, because it's your day off.' It meant that I could not relax at home, but if I wanted time out I had to go away to Norwich or somewhere else.

It was particularly difficult for the Rollesby people; they were the larger parish and had been used to their own rector living either in the rectory or at a private farm as with my predecessor. The Diocese had sold the rectory; thus I lived outside the main parish: it really was very taxing, for me as well as the parishioners. I knew that something had to be done and the wardens, the Patron, Dudley Tacon, and Parochial Church Council pestered the Diocese until they gave in. My successor will now move into a custom-built modern rectory next door to the church. The Diocese could hardly argue because the Patron, Dudley Tacon, gave them the land on which to build the new house. Sadly I doubt if I will ever live in it: time is against me. I recall standing in the shop in Martham Road listening to parishioners discussing the fact I never gave enough time to the parish. Ironically the ones who were bleating the most never came to church anyway. This shop had been built by the old Rector, Richard Tacon, and Clowes of Yarmouth had purchased it: now they have sold or leased it to Hacon and then the Tookes. I was visiting old Mrs Tooke in her backroom when I overheard this conversation. In the end I could not resist it and popped my head around the corner and asked them why they were chattering about me when I was doing my job in the next room. They were astonished and silenced: unfortunately because of my lisp I could not be as sharp and authoritative as I would like to have been. I used to speak to Miss King the headmistress of the local school, and even Curtis in the Horse and Groom, and they would both tell me not to worry, but it was easier said than done. Even down at Allards general store on Main Road, currently run by the Smiths, I knew that I could be the topic of discussion. As I mentioned earlier I have a slight lisp and this always makes clear discussion uneasy.

In my last eight years here I have never managed to cope with the fact that whatever I do I am always the subject of so much idle talk, and believe me I am not paranoid. I also found this doubly irritating because there were so many other things going on in the world that should have concerned us.

The Korean War meant involvement by our soldiers yet again,[3] and there was a real danger it could have escalated into an atomic confrontation.[4] We had already taken part in the work of developing atomic weaponry, and then Churchill announces that we have our own atomic bomb as if it's a prize,[5] and explodes it in the Monte Bello islands[6] to advertise its devastation. The recent Campaign for Nuclear Disarmament has my total support, but my parishioners do not share my views.[7] Every time there is any conflict I wonder whether it is going to be the end of the world. Although the war ended in 1945 we have too many crises of a military nature. We killed harmless Egyptians because they were nationalists,[8] the IRA have been building up arms again,[9] there was a state of emergency in Cyprus,[10] we invaded Egypt and were told to get out by the Americans,[11] and we have even had trouble in Aden[12] and Kenya.[13] All this with the nuclear world becoming more dangerous, and all the parishioners can do is talk about where I am and how much time I spend in their village. I know why the Church has had to unite so many parishes but it does not make life on the ground that easy for the parish priests.

Rural parish life is an exhausting experience and I have found it necessary to take extensive holidays when I could afford them. I went to the Coronation of Queen Elizabeth II[14] and thoroughly enjoyed the occasion. At least there was no smog,[15] which always concerned me when in that part of the world: it kills so many people and causes so many accidents. London always strikes me as a place of despair, and I was not surprised to hear that Chad Varah at St Stephen's, Wallbrook started the Samaritans to help peo-

[3] 1950 August 29th. First two battalions of British troops reach Korea.

[4] 1950 December 4th. Attlee flies to Washington to urge Americans not to use nuclear weapons.

[5] 1952 February 26th.

[6] 1952 October 3rd.

[7] 1958 February 17th. CND led by Bertrand Russell and Canon Collins launched at Westminster.

[8] 1952 January 24th. British troops kill 41 Egyptians rioting at Ismailia in the Suez Canal zone.

[9] 1955 IRA (inactive since 1939) raids army camp at Arborsfield, Berks in search of weapons.

[10] 1955 November 26th. State of emergency declared.

[11] 1956 November 15th. British transfer captured positions to UN Emergency Force.

[12] 1958 May 2nd. Anti-British unrest in Aden leading to state of emergency.

[13] 1959 June 16th. House of Commons debates killing at Hola Camp, Kenya, of eleven Mau Mau detainees.

[14] 1952. George VI dies at Sandringham, Queen Elizabeth crowned June 2nd 1953.

[15] 1952 December. Smog in London held responsible for over 2,000 deaths.

ple desperate in their lonely lives in that great city.[16] Nevertheless, I enjoyed my trips to London; I was there when I heard that Stalin had died;[17] I went to listen to Dr Billy Graham,[18] and also happened by when they hanged Ruth Ellis in Holloway prison.[19] I was pleased with Stalin's death, not impressed by Dr Graham and felt the hanging of a female a dreadful crime in a so-called civilised society. London was an escape from Rollesby and its environs, but I stopped going after I had a dangerous encounter with a group of hooligans calling themselves 'Teddy Boys'.[20] At least in rural Norfolk the only danger is a driver who has had too much to drink. The authorities will have to do something about drunken drivers; it simply should not be allowed. They have opened a super fast motorway[21] and if people drink on such roads we could face many deaths. The only problem is that I cannot see any government taking away our liberty to drink. Roger Bannister may have run a four-minute mile[22] but some cars and motorcycles can reach a hundred miles an hour. The roads around Rollesby are not motorways but they are dangerous enough when some of our farmers are unwinding after a day in the fields. I have no doubt it will not be long before there are major motorways leading all the way to Norwich.

My trips to London ceased after the near collision with the Teddy Boys, but I now note that some of the boys down Coronation Avenue are dressing in the same silly manner and throw their weight around in Yarmouth. Fortunately Rollesby is too quiet a place for them to spend much time in. Rollesby does have its problems. Even in the church there has been considerable debate over the nature of the services. Some of the congregation feel that we should have more Communions, some feel we should use more modern hymns, others want Evensong in the afternoon, and some say we should experiment beyond the Book of Common Prayer. It is becoming a veritable minefield; every lay person has an opinion on matters of liturgy. I am sure it was not like this in the days of Grundy and Tacon: they laid down

---

[16] Revd E Chad Varah founds Samaritans in 1953.

[17] 1953 March 5th. Stalin dies: Khrushchev succeeds him as Communist Party Secretary.

[18] 1954 May 6th. The first evangelistic crusade at Harringay: it lasted three months.

[19] 1955 July 13th. Last woman to be executed in Britain.

[20] In fashion by 1955.

[21] 1959 November 2nd. Southern section of M1 opened.

[22] 1954 May 6th. At Oxford.

the law and that was that! Times are changing, and although there is a part of me that resents interference another more prayerful insight tells me that I should be happy that lay people are interested. This is especially true as congregation numbers appear to decline. The number of times this is mentioned to me as if it is somehow my fault. Yet when I check the registers from the past the numbers are always around the twenty to thirty mark. It does not help that the church is somewhat removed from where the main bulk of people live. But I stray from my main point: the silly arguments that sometimes develop over the most trivial of matters. We purchased a new set of prayer books and they had red covers instead of the usual black. I heard nothing for months but one lady stopped coming to church.

'But, my dear,' I explained, 'it was not my choice, they only had red covered books and it did not seem important, in fact I thought they made a colourful change.'

'This church,' she replied sternly, 'has always had black covered prayer books. What would you think if you were told to wear a red cassock?'

'In some churches choirs and altar boys do wear red cassocks.'

'Don't bandy words with me, we don't have altar boys here, we are a Protestant church, and you are not a choir boy, though I sometimes wonder.'

I ignored her barb and tried a touch of humour. 'I could wear a purple cassock one day like a bishop.'

'Now you are being frivolous.'

I was being frivolous but it did hurt a trifle that the thought of me being a bishop was so ludicrous. She never returned to church, and later that year she died. At her funeral I dug out the old black prayer books and used them: the congregation said nothing, for once. I put some flowers on her grave only this morning, but I will not mention names because I am not sure how far distant this will be read.

Another problem was the flowers. I dislike flowers on the altar; in the sanctuary it is fine, but not on the altar. Nor do I hold strictly to the tradition of no flowers in Advent, but prefer none in Lent. Some of the ladies felt the flowers should reflect the colours of the liturgical seasons, others thought one vase was quite sufficient, another group wanted the church like a perpetual flower festival, and one group thought we should never purchase flowers but use only plants from the hedgerows. The flowers in church became a major issue and soon we wasted three Parochial Church Meetings on the subject. Finally, we managed to draw up some guidelines and a rota of who did flowers and when. It was nearly a civil war in the pews, two groups of elderly ladies virtually stopped talking to one another, and two never came back to church. One made a public point of joining the Methodists and the other went down to Ormesby, where she fell out on another issue before attending Martham, the village to the north. Somehow I got the blame: I lacked spirited leadership and so forth. I tried to explain that I did not view myself as a Chief Executive or Managing Director, nor did I have God's omnicompetence, and that Christ had died for all of us and not for us to squabble over flowers. I even preached on the matter in a roundabout way, but the people who needed to hear this were not in the pews by this stage.

Naturally, when news spread to the other churches in my benefice that there was virtually an all out flower civil war, I was sad to see their rejoicing.

'Never mind, Rector,' I too frequently heard, 'it's not like that here, you know we all admire the way you do things here.'

Several parishes within a single benefice led to its own civil-type war without it coming to actual blows. Each considered itself the prime parish, each considered itself the most thoughtful and caring place, and each thought the rest behind the times and unfair to the Rector. I gather from the *Church Times* that there are rumblings about changing from the Book of Common Prayer to more modern services. I suspect that it is only a rumble, the Book of Common Prayer is here to stay, but I hope I am dead or retired before these modern services happen, I would not be able to cope with the conflict that would be bound to ensue. If they fight over the colour of book covers and flowers, heaven knows how they will cope with new services. I have one nagging doubt in my mind, no two. The first is that if my leadership had been more determined then perhaps such problems might not have arisen. On the other hand I see myself as a servant to the community and not their boss. I lose either way. The second problem is the lack of definition in the nature of my work. Because everyone expects me to be in their parish, I work and visit and hardly stop. The job is like a piece of endless string, I do not know where it stops or where I do. I work all day and then feel I have still not done enough. I become exhausted and take a day off or a brief holiday and then feel guilty. I sometimes hanker after a Monday to Friday job with hours from eight to five with a one-hour lunch break. In my better moments I realise I do not have a job, I have a life, but I hope I retire before I die.

CHAPTER 36

ooooo

Roger MacKenzie Boys (1959-1961)

CND, apartheid, etc

Dear Friends,

I feel quite pleased to add my bit for the future. It will be only a small piece because I was not the rector, but simply a temporary Priest in Charge while they looked for a suitable man to take over the benefice. I was far too old still to be going, especially when you recall I was at Oxford in 1899, gained my MA in 1903, and am still operational in 1960! When the Bishop and Archdeacon asked me to stand in I said I would but had little desire to drop dead while in harness: the Bishop seemed to think it better to die in harness than in retired dotage. I wanted to be an academic, and was Canon Scholar, in Lincolnshire in 1900, but moved on after priesting in 1902 and became Curate of St Mark's, Lakenham, and followed a parish ministry up to retirement and now at Rollesby well beyond retirement. I actually retired in 1956 but have been given permission to officiate. I do not live in Rollesby but between Catfield and Stalham. I actually married a local Thurne girl, and many people looked down their noses on the extraordinary grounds that clergy did not marry local girls. It is a strange world when clergy are often accused of being snobbish but when we do something ordinary like everyone else we are criticised. People accuse us of being on some sort of social platform and enjoy watching us fall off it, but if we climb down they resent it just as much.

It is also a good thing that there is this long interregnum in the parish because it is enabling the Diocese to complete the new custom-built rectory for the new incumbent. It was silly my predecessor having to live out of the major parish because the poor devil was always being criticised for being elsewhere. At least with the new rectory it will always ensure that Rollesby has its own rector living on the doorstep. They are hardly going to recycle a 1960 purpose-built rectory as the 'Old Rectory': that would mean two 'Old Rectories' in the same tiny village.

Because of my age and the need to travel between several parishes lay people are becoming much more involved in the arrangements of services. In the old days I would travel to my church, have to open it up, switch lights on, ignite the boilers, set books out, light candles and prepare the altar. Now the lay people do it in preparation: it is a sheer luxury and I hope the younger clergy who will follow me appreciate this development. The lay people in the Rollesby congregation have been particularly good. I have been here two years now and have thoroughly enjoyed my time.

I was part and parcel of the opening of the new Parish Hall. It was built on the site of the old school that burned down during the last war thanks to the carelessness of the army. It was actually the East Suffolks who were responsible. The village awoke at eight in the morning to find the old school ablaze. The bit that was left was then used by the Home Guard. Frederick Youngs had wanted the hall built on the playing fields near the school; this was a sensible idea but the insurance people would not co-operate. As far as they were concerned they were replacing a building not in the business of providing cash for another. It was bureaucratic stupidity but we had no choice. The hall was designed by Mr Seabert, a local architect, and very sensibly designed if I may be permitted to say so. The opening day was warm; although only July it felt like the middle of August, and young Glenda Youngs, Frederick's four-year-old daughter presented flowers to Mrs Lincoln Ralphs after she had opened the doors. Mrs Lincoln Ralphs was the wife of the Chief Education Officer. There followed the usual bun fight, and I had the distinct impression that this facility would serve the future Rollesby well. I sat with Mr Miller and we thoroughly enjoyed the occasion.

This particular gentleman had seen all the highs and lows of the village because he had run the Post Office since 1947. He was a man who understood the community and had started the 'Over 60s' club called the 'Happy Rollers' with over fifty members: he was the chairman.[1]

I enjoyed the turn of the decade, and hoped that 1960 would bring more peace to our world. There were anti-apartheid protests outside South Africa House,[2] CND demonstrations in Trafalgar Square,[3] and in June the House of Commons rejected Sir John Wolfenden's report on homosexuality.[4] The sixties could be the silly years; never in a hundred years will South Africa reject apartheid, the Soviet Union is here to stay and so is the nuclear threat, and homosexuality will never be acceptable in our type of society.

Nevertheless, the few years I spent in Rollesby were peaceful, and I enjoyed the Beetle Drives and Whist Club in the new parish hall: before the hall was built they used to have whist drives in the rectory's old stable. I was pleased to give way to the next man so I did not have to die in harness. I have left these notes in the drawer, and I do hope they are picked up eventually. I think the 1960s are going to be an interesting decade; it is not so much the technical development but the social changes taking place. Young people are tending to be much more dominant, and there seems to be greater freedom of thought and expression. Had I married my Thurne wife today nobody would have batted an eyelid!

---

[1] *Norfolk Fair - County Magazine,* Sept 1977, article by Clare Howes, p.27.

[2] 1960 March 21st. Fifty demonstrators arrested protesting at the death of sixty-seven Africans shot dead at Sharpeville.

[3] 1960 April 18th. Some 100,000 CND supporters demonstrate in Trafalgar Square after Aldermaston march.

[4] 1960 June 29th. Recommendations rejected in House of Commons by 213 to 99 votes.

CHAPTER 37

ooooo

Peter Ernest Jefford (1961-1970)

The 'Swinging Sixties'

Dear Andrew Sangster,[1]

I was pleased to receive your letter and to learn that you are now the incumbent of Rollesby.[2] What happened to Fleggburgh and Billockby? Who are they with now? Your letter has forced me to unlock a whole Pandora's box of memories that come flooding out. I have never been back to Rollesby since the early 1980s, before we went to Devon, but one day I would like to come and see the church. Have you any news of Mrs Clayton the widow of John, or Ann Bates who did a wonderful job as treasurer?

To my letter: I was born in 1929 the year the Reverend Raymond Grundy was installed as rector. I trained at King's College, London, and my further training was at Warminster, the same place as you went, I gather. I was priested in 1955 and after a couple of curacies my first incumbency was Rollesby, Burgh St Mary and St Margaret with Billockby, first as Priest in Charge, then as rector. I served first in the Diocese of Gloucester in a large rural parish so this served as a good introduction to Rollesby. I was inducted on August 21st 1961, St Bartholomew's Day,[3] by the Diocesan Bishop; the Archdeacon was Meiklejohn and he belonged to the old school, gaiters,

---

[1] This letter, for which I am very grateful, was supplied in note form by Peter Jefford.

[2] The parish grew in population during this decade: in October 1962 the population was 388; in October 1968 590 and in October 1969 604.

[3] Amongst the little coincidences of life was that the notes for this letter, from Peter Jefford, arrived on August 24th - St Bartholomew's Day.

severity, the lot. It was the last induction he did before he retired. Dudley Tacon at the Grange and Dr Tom Royden of Fleggburgh interviewed my wife, Celia, and me, amongst others. The offer was the incumbency with a new group of parishes as I outlined above. We were to move into a brand new rectory in Heath Lane on land given by the Patron, Dudley Tacon.

During my time we worked hard to restore the church because it had decayed somewhat during the previous fifty years. We launched an appeal in the February of 1962 and by 1969 we had redecorated the church and had a special service led by the Archdeacon of Norwich, the Venerable Aubrey Aitken.[4] Everyone was happy with the renovation except a few who did not want to see the removal of the tin scrolls from the chancel walls. They read, 'He shall feed his flock like a shepherd,' and although the sentiment was first class, the tin work and paint had become tatty.

It was all change for us and for the parishes. If we are to understand the Church we must first understand 'nature', and the primary lesson of nature that is always 'the lesson of change': to ignore this is to fly in the face of reason. Even small changes can frighten people; the introduction of the New English Bible[5] unsettled many. Some change brings hope: Michael Ramsey, Archbishop of Canterbury,[6] allowed three Anglican representatives to take part in the second Vatican Council;[7] these seemed like exciting changes. This was especially true when Pope Paul VI and our archbishop held a joint service in St Paul's Basilica, Rome.[8] There was talk of union between Methodists and Anglicans:[9] George Nunnerley our local Methodist colleague was quite excited by this prospective change. In 1969 the Methodist Conference voted in favour but the Anglican convocation gave insufficient backing. Colin Riches the new Methodist minister in Rollesby had a few pointed comments on this lack of change. Then John Robinson wrote his book *Honest to God*[10] and this sent the pigeons fluttering to the roof. I recall that this was about the time that Norwich developed its own university: a

[4] Report in *Yarmouth Mercury*, April 18th 1969.

[5] 1961 March 14th. New Testament version.

[6] Enthroned as 100th Archbishop on June 27th 1961.

[7] 1962 October 11th - December 1965.

[8] 1966 March 24th.

[9] 1963. Anglican-Methodist Commission Report, *Conversations between the Church of England and the Methodist Church,* outlines programme for gradual union.

[10] 1963 March.

fine development but it still provoked criticism for such a change.[11]

Some change is exciting and I can recall the pleasure of living in a new house and having a car to use for the first time after four years without one. Fields and the graveyard surrounded the rectory; there were no pavements, no streetlights, no zebra crossings and just three shops in the village. All I could see was barley ready for the harvest and sugar beet. The headmaster of the school, John Clayton, proved to be a good friend and was also an excellent parish reader. He had been a prisoner of war to the Japanese; a subject best steered clear of. The greatest change was the formation of the new benefice and the different parishes having to learn to share the one incumbent, and this was not always easy for them or me. I would attend all three churches every Sunday, sharing the services between 8.00am Holy Communion, to the Main Service at 10.00am or 11.00am and then Evensong at 6.30pm. It made for a hectic day. I should not complain, because when I visited people in the council houses I discovered they had no gas and their only real amenity was a water tap for cold water. There was no indoor sanitation but a bucket in the shed that was emptied on the basis of night soil collection! They had no bathroom and no bath.

I was also lucky to be surrounded by some good people. In Rollesby I had an excellent organist in Willie Allard, a retired market gardener; there was little he could not play. Not only was Willie a man who played only by ear, but he did it all for free. Bob who was totally deaf pumped the organ, so Willie Allard had to switch on a light to let him know when to stop and start. My churchwardens were Dudley Tacon and Walter Miller, but in those days the PCC did not even have a bank account or a cheque book until Ann Bates came along and did a marvellous job bringing us into the modern world. Walter Miller used to keep the Post Office and had done the accounts in the old fashioned way that took Ann Bates months to unravel. There was a sense of change all around. The new bishop[12] had set his sights on raising the expectations of the Diocese and all clergy were expected to attend chapter meetings and deanery meetings as a 'duty'. In November 1961 I was appointed as the first Flegg Deanery Chapter Clerk. The Bishop also wanted to raise clergy stipends and give a children's allowance so we

---

[11] 1963.

[12] 1971-85. Maurice Arthur Ponsonby Wood.

were assessed for a parish quota to help pay these bills. I am pleased to note that Rollesby always paid up on time. I can tell you something about inflation because in those days the quota was only £30 per annum, and we struggled to pay that! Our eldest child was going to school at this time, and we always cycled everywhere: it was safer in those days than today. We all found the Norfolk dialect a little difficult to understand at first, but we soon became accustomed to it. One thing we did discover about Norfolk people was that once they came to trust you, you had a friend for life. The people who came to church were always extremely loyal and worked hard; in addition to this they were generous in so many ways.

Our first summer was hot and then came our first autumn. I recall the sugar beet campaign, with the old ladies working in the fields day and night wearing oil skins: it was hard labour indeed. They also wore sacks around their waists and worked with their hooks in a fast and competent way. Even if it poured with rain and wind beat down they never stopped. We may see life in the rural world as idyllic, but the hard work of these ladies told another story. The shooting season was noisy; the pheasants seemed to take refuge in our back garden and it was an important rural industry in Norfolk. I suppose that is why the King purchased the Sandringham estate in the first place. It was ducks in September (flighting) and pheasants from November: I quite enjoyed the season and was a beater on Rollesby Hall estate and on another at Filby. Though I suppose in the old days the incumbent would have been shooting with his own set of guns!

The Estate and Hall were owned by Captain Benn, promoted to Major just before we arrived, and recently married to his Norwegian bride. He had also been promoted to Sir Patrick Benn, Bart., and had rebuilt the Hall to a Norwegian design. There were of course different opinions about this design, but I always found him very kind. Sir Patrick had inherited the Hall from Sir Ion Benn, his grandfather.

The question of money was never far from my mind, and we had a great campaign to raise money for new choir robes both for the adults and the children. I set this effort going as early as 1961. The graveyard was in a terrible state, everything was overgrown and there were thick brambles everywhere. The church gutters were not working, and the water had penetrated the walls and damaged the timber in the north and south aisles. The walls were badly stained and the fact was that the building was not waterproof. We had to redecorate the walls after damp proofing, and then rewire because all the old wires had perished with the rain. The architect[13] who had designed the Rectory also carried out the church's first ever quinquennial inspection and the report came through marked 'urgent'. From memory I think the original costs amounted to the astronomical figure of £65,000. Given that Clippesby Rectory had just been sold for £4,000 this will give some idea of the enormity of the problem. I enlisted the help of the Bishop, the Archdeacon, Aubrey Aitken, and the two wardens, Dudley Tacon and Sir Patrick Benn and set about a major appeal.

We raised money in every way we could. We had the traditional summer fetes, whist drives, dances, bingo, jumble sales, bowls, collecting waste paper, carol singing and lunches at the Hall. Saturday afternoons were set aside for clearing the graveyard. My wife took a serious hand in this, as did many others, including Bernard Parker, and Michael and Keith Hodds and bit by bit the old church could once again be seen in all its glory.

It seemed a hectic time, and on one occasion Freddy Baldry accidentally locked me in the church. Only ringing the bell at the wrong time saved me from being lost all night. On another occasion I had climbed on the south aisle roof to clean the gutters and the ladder fell away: I shouted for help and was eventually rescued by David Edmonds. Meanwhile, I was just as busy in the two schools of Rollesby and Fleggburgh, I was especially pleased to be able to take assemblies in John Clayton's[14] school. It was a busy time and I tried to knock on all parish doors, visiting from Monday to Friday.

Communication was one major problem and my next task was to try and produce a parish magazine each month. The first step was the purchase of a second-hand duplicator, stencils, tubes of ink, staples and paper. I was lucky in so far that in the Old Rectory lived Bridget Hayton, a member of the choir who was also a secretary to a firm of solicitors in Yarmouth. She nobly cut all the stencils and continued to do so until she married. We sold 270 copies a month and made a small profit, but it was really hard work. It took five days a month just to distribute them to the shops and the distributors.

---

[13] Architect was Peter Codling of Feilden and Mawson.

[14] John Clayton was later to be ordained and worked as a curate at Ormesby St Michael before he died.

Very early on I became a chaplain to the local British Legion and I recall those services well. Dudley Tacon and Sir Patrick Benn wore their bowler hats and medals, and those Sunday mornings of Remembrance Day were always wet, cold, windy or frosty. I can recall the names of many people who attended these and other services: Lawn, Hayton, Curtis, Shreeve, Wymer, Ransome, Baldry, Tooke and Miller. I can even recall some of their nick-names, Tiddler Wymer, Jack or Rabbit Ransome, and Shiner Shreeve.

We did start to make progress. The choir robes arrived, and we fitted an electric discus blower to the organ thus obviating the need for the organ blower. The Benns gave us a lovely new carpet. They were good days with parties up at the Hall and I continued to enjoy my days in the local school. I remember a new teacher being appointed of whom we had high hopes, but he left after a year to become a professional bingo caller! These were the days when we had our own local 'Bobby', Arthur Youngs, who would call by on his bike and gently tease me, hoping that I was keeping an eye on things.

In 1963 we had the great freeze. It was cold, bitter cold. Even the flowers froze in their jars in the church. The Broads froze over and I learned to ice skate and watched ice hockey. I went out on my bike and got frostbite in my finger. It was during this great freeze that our third son, Stephen, was born. It was potentially dangerous but no more so than the time I was acting as a beater beside the Broad and I fell into quicksand that had been created by the great freeze. I was terrified and I shall never forget Les Goodwin, the old gamekeeper, who very quietly said, 'Crawl on your stomach, Rector.' This I did and came out safely. The gamekeeper was a good friend of old Mr Brunson who laid my lawns. Les Goodwin came to my rescue on another occasion when he found me trapped in my car and caught in a snowdrift, and fortunately dug me out.

There had been a quarry up on Heath Lane and the council filled it in with rubbish. Throughout the summer, dustcarts plagued us, and then we had a plague of insects, next ladybirds, then flies and finally a house full of crickets. I have some idea how Pharaoh felt in the story of Moses.

It was not all fun. Like the rest of the world we were concerned that the end of the world was in sight. The Cuban missile crisis[15] illustrated how close to the nuclear brink we were. I really did anticipate a nuclear war and

---

[15] 1962 October 22nd - 28th.

wondered what a post-nuclear-war world would be like. There was the devastating news of Kennedy's assassination,[16] problems with Rhodesia,[17] mass demonstrations in London against the Vietnam War,[18] and in Ireland British troops took responsibility for the streets.[19] Yet the War Office fortunately renamed itself the Ministry of Defence:[20] a civilised nomenclature in a world teetering on the edge of nuclear war and minor wars of a serious nature.

Sometimes the numbers in church were disappointing. In 1962 I had especially prepared the Good Friday service, and only six people turned up. On another occasion I nearly died of shock when unlocking the church I then opened the piscina[21] and a huge black cat jumped out at me. I shall never know how it came to be in there. That day there were only three parishioners and the black cat.

People did turn out for special occasions (Good Friday did improve) especially the carol singing. When we sang at the Hall the refreshments were always welcome and they were liberal in their generosity, which meant we sometimes forgot the lines. Then we would sing around the village, landing up outside the old Court House at one in the morning, totally exhausted. After harvest festivals I would take the produce down to the Fisherman's Hospital in Great Yarmouth for the residents.

On the edges of Rollesby things were changing. Gas exploration was taking place in the North Sea and Yarmouth was full of supply ships and helicopters. We even had an American gas engineer move into the village: it was like taking an alien on board our rural world. It was no more alien than the shock that a cabinet minister had been caught lying[22] and yet another spy, Kim Philby, emerged from the woodwork.[23] The Labour Party won a major election with Harold Wilson as Prime Minister[24] and 'Mods and

---

[16] 1963 November 22nd.

[17] 1966 January 31st. Britain bans trade with Rhodesia.

[18] 1968 March 17th.

[19] 1969 August 12th - 15th. Three days of street fighting in Londonderry and on August 19th troops moved in.

[20] 1964 April 1st.

[21] A cupboard where the elements were kept.

[22] 1963 March 22nd. John Profumo scandal with Christine Keeler weakens government's standing.

[23] 1963 July 1st.

[24] 1964 October 15th.

Rockers' were swarming all over Great Yarmouth and using the main road as a race-track. Some civilised things did happen, not least the abolition of the death penalty[25] and the passing of the Race Relations Act.[26] I recall the Queen visiting Germany, the first royal visit to that country since 1913[27] and it seemed that Europe was being healed until De Gaulle vetoed our entry into the European Market time and time again.[28] We were quite pleased when he resigned![29]

The world was up and down but life in Rollesby always seemed very steady and pleasant. I would like to wish everyone well and say we are very happy in our retirement in Oxford. We have four grandchildren and we have travelled much. Even in my retirement I help out in thirty-nine different parishes. I am not sure whether the figure thirty-nine reminds me of the thirty-nine steps or the Thirty-Nine Articles of religion! My wife Celia is well and I am chaplain to a small Oxford College and this is our forty-sixth wedding anniversary. With my prayers and all our good wishes to you all in Rollesby.

---

[25] 1965 November 8th.

[26] 1965 November 8th. Race Relations Act: prohibits public racial discrimination.

[27] 1965 May 13th.

[28] 1967 November 27th. And again on December 19th and on September 27th 1968.

[29] 1969 April 29th.

CHAPTER 38

ooooo

Robin Howard Elphick (1971-1984)

Decimalization, the ECC and ecumenism

Dear Ex-parishioners,

Andrew Sangster, your current rector, approached me; I gather he is acting as editor for this unusual account of the history of Rollesby and its church life. My wife Jane and I met him on August 16th 2000 and gave him a brief account of our time in Rollesby. Many of you will remember us and indeed we are still in touch with a few of you.

I trained at the London College of Divinity and was deaconed in 1965 and priested in 1965 in the Southwark Diocese. My first curacy was at St Barnabas, Clapham Common and my next was at Woking St Peter in Guildford Diocese. I had always wanted to be a parish priest in a rural area; my wife Jane had been brought up on a farm. Strangely, Maurice Wood took one of my ordination retreats and I told him this: later in 1971 he was consecrated as Bishop of Norwich and I came to the Diocese at virtually the same time. I was made Rector of Rollesby with Burgh with Billockby. Later the benefice changed and after a brief time as Priest in Charge I was also made Rector of Ashby with Oby, Thurne, and Clippesby, in which position I stayed until we left for Frinton in 1984.

I shall never forget my visit to Rollesby. A friend of mine had given my name to the then Bishop of Norwich, William Launcelot Scott Fleming.

His reply was not encouraging as he already had a number of men in his Diocese looking for livings, but he promised to put my name on the list. Then, during the postal strike in early 1971, the phone rang one evening and I heard for the first time the throaty whisper of Aubrey Aitken, the Archdeacon of Norwich. He was an avid supporter of Norwich City Football Club and rarely preached a sermon without some reference to the team! He told me about the vacancy at Rollesby and invited Jane and me to come up and look at the three parishes. He met us at Thorpe Station and took us back for lunch at his house in The Close. After lunch we helped with the washing-up and he later jokingly told me that this had helped me get the job!

We met my predecessor, Peter Jefford, and were shown around the churches on a day when it poured with rain. Later I stayed at the Hall and was interviewed by the six wardens. Dudley Tacon, the Patron and also the warden of Rollesby, thought me far too young for the post. I was thirty-five but looked younger. Dudley Tacon and Sir Patrick belonged to another generation. I recall that Dudley thought my expenses of £50 a year were excessive. But unlike previous clergy of the parish I had a stipend of only £1400 per annum on which to live. I think if I had asked for fifty guineas they may have understood me better. When we went to decimal currency it was a living nightmare for many of the older generation.[1]

We arrived at the purpose-built rectory next to the church with our three children. It was Simon's fifth birthday, Vicky was three and Jeremy was three weeks old. I had to oversee the removal as Jane was busy with the children and recovering from giving birth to Jeremy. After the two-up, two-down curate's house in Woking, the rectory seemed very spacious. We all enjoyed the large garden where many games of football and cricket were played with our children and their friends from the village. The village at least had a sense of identity, and it was pleasing. I can recall the pride that the locals felt when Pauline Tacon, the old Patron's wife, unveiled the new village sign on the playing field in 1977, to mark the Queen's jubilee.

When I first arrived in Rollesby, the churchwardens were Sir Patrick Benn and Dudley Tacon, who was by then an old man. Sir Patrick lived in the Hall and rarely attended church, except when he was on duty as a sides-

[1] 1971 February 15th. Decimal coinage replaces shillings and pence.

man and on Remembrance Sunday. On that day he would gather all the men at the Horse and Groom and, equipped with bowler hat and rolled umbrella, would march them up to the church for the service. Soon however, most of them became too old and this custom lapsed.

Dudley Tacon died in 1972[2] and Sir Patrick was eventually voted out of office when three others were nominated for the post. For that Annual General Meeting, held at the Village Hall, I asked Robert Chase,[3] who at that time lived at 'Peddars Croft' on the main road, to act as teller.

There was a small degree of animosity towards the old wardens because they represented a landed interest and reflected the days of the Manor. Indeed, Jane, my wife, never forgot the time she crossed the graveyard in jeans and a lady curtsied to her - she was careful how she dressed after that!

For several years my chuchwardens were Cyril Burton and Peter Trueman, who later trained to be a Reader and was a great help when I took on Thurne and Clippesby. The PCC was active and we were blessed in having an excellent treasurer in Ann Bates who worked as a cashier at Barclays.

I had several immediate tasks on hand as soon as I arrived. One was building up a nucleus of faithful worshippers and getting them accustomed to a quarterly benefice service. To be quite honest I found it easier working with people who had either moved into Norfolk or Norfolk people who had been away and returned. It was very difficult with residents who had lived all their lives there and expected nothing to change. We had to spend some money repairing the top of the tower, which was crumbling away, and we built a screen[4] across the base of the tower, thus giving the church its first vestry. Outside the front of the church was an allotment that we converted into a useful car park. I remember the day we were thinking of this plan it suddenly seemed trivialised by the news that British soldiers had killed thirteen demonstrators in Northern Ireland; this soon came to be known as Bloody Sunday.[5] It was the same year that we prayed for the developing tragedy in Uganda when President Amin, a tyrant, expelled 40,000 British Asians from that country. We didn't foresee the bloodshed that was to fol-

---

[2] Dudley Tacon was buried in the family vault on November 6th 1972. The vault is below the path, just in front of the Tacon memorial.

[3] Later to be a Chairman of Norwich City Football Club.

[4] In memory of John Clayton: see later.

[5] 1972 January 30th.

low, but that unhappy country was constantly in our intercessions.[6] Not only did thousands suffer but the Anglican Archbishop of Uganda, Dr Janani Luwum, was killed by this man when under detention.[7] I had the privilege of knowing Janani Luwum as he spent a year at the London College of Divinity during my time and lived in the next room to me. He was a gracious, Christ-like man.

When I look back I am astounded at the number of tragic deaths I had to deal with during my time in Rollesby. Rollesby had a population of some eight hundred, and yet the sad deaths were disproportionate. There were two cot deaths - one in the Thain family; Diane Nudd, a young sixteen-year-old was killed crossing the road after she got off a bus in the village; young Harrison, whose father ran a motorcycle shop called Jay Bee in Yarmouth, was killed on a motorbike; Arthur Tooke's daughter had flu symptoms then died at the age of twenty-five, as did Janet Gedge at the same age; young Debby Manson was killed in another motorbike accident; a man called Brown was found drowned in the village pond, and he was only in his forties; and Joe Beckett was knocked down on the Martham Road and killed. The place seemed fraught with accidents. It seemed to me that much of my ministry was with bereavement.

The congregation grew to between thirty and forty and we built up a smaller nucleus of committed Christians, drawn from all the parishes, who met regularly for fellowship. Towards the end of my ministry a man called Robin Baker moved into the Runham area. He claimed to have had a vision of revival in Norfolk and set up a house church, which sadly attracted away a number of our members. Several people were 're-baptised' in their bath, but in the end the group wrecked the faith of one or two people.

A similar breakaway group operated in the Hemsby area and at one stage were all set to go to America. In the end they brought about the divorce of a couple who often came to our services at Rollesby.

I specially enjoyed my summers in Rollesby because of my love for cricket and for many years I played for the village team. They were happy days and we travelled all over Norfolk. In 1978 we won the Norfolk Junior Cup. It is the only sporting trophy I have ever won and it still stands proudly in

---

[6] 1972 August 4th.

[7] 1977 February 17th.

my study. For many years I helped Cecil Miller, the life and soul of Rollesby Cricket Club, to cut the pitch on Friday evenings. The team contained some talented players - not least George Catchpole, the three Harrison brothers and the two Wymer brothers. Mr Grundy may have had a good soccer team, but our cricket was good and came from local people, not the Spanish refugees!

Towards the end of my time, it was a great pleasure that my son Simon also played in the team and on one occasion Jeremy was included as well!

After home matches we always adjourned to the Horse and Groom, presided over in those days by Buster Curtis. He was a blunt man. Once when I ordered a shandy I remember him suggesting that I should have a 'man's drink'!

In the summer of 1972 Dudley Tacon, who was a member of the MCC, gave me two tickets for the Lord's Test against the Australians. Barney Wymer came with me and the highlight of the day was watching Greg Chappell score a magnificent century for Australia.

During my time in Rollesby the services started to change, and we took on board the new Series 3:[8] I was pleasantly surprised how adaptable everyone was and it soon felt as if it had been our service for generations. I know in some other parishes that the updating and modernising of services caused serious divisions: not in Rollesby. The local headmaster, John Clayton,[9] was a lay reader and helped in this transition. He was an interesting man. He had been a Japanese prisoner of war and had an undying hatred for anything Japanese. As a result of war wounds he had a wooden arm and he was said to hit the children with it! As I mentioned earlier, the Rollesby congregation took to change easily, but not so easily when it came to politics: there were few public gatherings that did not discuss our joining the EEC[10] and when VAT[11] was introduced a few months later this increased the debate. It did not help the matter that VAT started on April 1st, Fool's Day! Politics was a tussle between Labour's Harold Wilson and the Conservative's Ted

[8] PCC Minutes 27 February 1973. It was also agreed at this time that Evensong be tried on the second Sunday of every month. It was moved from 6.30pm to 3.30 in the afternoon, and this ceased from May 1974 and there was a return to the main morning service.

[9] John Clayton was eventually ordained and assisted in the Parish of Ormesby St Michael. He died on October 11th 1979 and a screen was placed at the base of the bell tower in memory of his work and life in the church.

[10] 1973 January 1st. Britain with Denmark and Ireland join EEC.

[11] 1973 April 1st.

Heath and always at the core was the threat of strikes, especially with the coal miners. When Margaret Thatcher[12] came to power in the Conservative Party, there was a plebiscite[13] for and against the EEC. We all know the consequences but it never healed the different opinions. Meanwhile the IRA was being active and life looked fairly dismal on the political front. Throughout my ministry we were always praying for peace in Ireland. It seemed particularly bad in 1979 when Earl Mountbatten was murdered[14] as well as eighteen of our soldiers.[15] Margaret Thatcher had just been elected Prime Minister following the debacle of potential devolution in Scotland and Wales and the loss of confidence in Callaghan.[16] To add to the scandals of the end of that decade, Sir Anthony Blunt, a distinguished art historian, was denounced by Mrs Thatcher as a Soviet spy and had his knighthood annulled. In the following year of 1980 we boycotted the Olympics in Russia because of their invasion of Afghanistan. There was much material for our prayers.

In 1975 Bishop Maurice came up with a scheme to equip all his clergy with mopeds. If a clergyman wanted one, then the Bishop had a fund that made a grant of £50,000 for the Diocese, and the parishes had to find the balance - they were about £75.00 each. Delivery took place in front of the Bishop's house with the press and TV in attendance. Pictures appeared in all the major daily papers and Giles drew a cartoon of the scene. Because I had a motorcycle licence I was able to get the next model up from the moped and in 1979 changed it to a Honda '90'. I found the machines very useful for getting around, though I soon discovered that you had to have the right clothes or you got very cold! Jane needed the car for her work as a care assistant at the John Grant School in Caister. She did a lot of good work here, and set up the Rollesby Group Riding Centre for disabled people, in Richard Tacon's farmyard. Before we left it moved to a custom-built centre out of the village. It was a pleasing initiative. My wife also started the Rollesby Play Group down in the village hall and I gather that it is still

---

[12] 1975 February 10th.

[13] 1975 May 8th. Britain's first ever referendum, carried out on June 5th. 64% of electorate voted in favour.

[14] 1979 August 27th. Along with three companions.

[15] 1979 August 27th. IRA kills eighteen British soldiers at Warrenpoint, South Armagh.

[16] 1979 March 28th. Callaghan loses a no confidence motion by a single vote and agrees to dissolve Parliament.

going to this day. Jane was also a governor of the local school that our children attended, under the good offices of the new headmistress, Anna Devitt.

At the end of the 1970s Molly Wolsey[17] and her husband arrived and set up the organisation called FORC, 'Friends of Rollesby Church'. This group set about raising money for the essential repairs the building needed. Their first task was the reconstruction of the graveyard boundary wall along the Fleggburgh Road. It suddenly happened, indeed it happened overnight and without a faculty: I worried about that for a time but the DAC[18] never turned up and the graveyard looked much better as a result of this effort. We did not have an appropriate Communion table and after much discussion and investigation we found one in a redundant church at Coslaney:[19] it took nearly a year to go through the formalities but we managed and I am pleased to see it is still used. We were then very conscious of our antiquity as a church and proud of our heritage and Ann Bates wrote a brief history and guide for the church.

We had a little crisis over parish boundaries. In 1977 it was discovered that Martham was expanding, with a large housing estate that encroached on our parish. It was agreed that Mr Trueman and Mr Wolsey would attempt to change the parish boundaries so we did not have this encroachment. They eventually succeeded in this effort.[20]

When our friends heard that we were going to live in Norfolk, they shivered and muttered about the east wind 'straight from Siberia'. We did have some cold winters but we certainly enjoyed some baking hot summers. However, we never found the climate as cold as outsiders seemed to think it was! In the February of 1979[21] the snow was so deep that Main Road was blocked for a week. We had to walk to Martham for food supplies, and the drifts of snow against the church were so high we had to hold the Sunday service in the village hall. It was strange how people reacted in such adversity. Everyone was prepared to help everyone else; indeed people went out of

---

[17] PCC Minutes 1980 January 21st.

[18] Diocesan Advisory Committee, which has to pass any work on churches through a procedure called a Faculty Application.

[19] PCC Minutes 13th May 1975.

[20] PCC Minutes 17th October 1977.

[21] 1978 and 1979. Severe snow in January and February brought many parts of the UK to a standstill.

their way to ensure all was well with their neighbours. When the snow had gone they all retreated behind their own front doors. Not long after this winter the Diocese sold the old rectory at Oby and they gave some of the proceeds to enlarge our drawing room so that we could hold larger gatherings there. This was welcome both as a public facility and to ease life for us.

Our main undertakers were the Jary brothers and Mr Brundish, the latter insisting that his men wore overcoats even on the hottest of summer days. On one occasion a funeral nearly cost me great embarrassment. I had been into Yarmouth early one morning and was driving back for a funeral at Rollesby at 11.30. On the Caister by-pass I found myself passing the Jarys' hearse and thought they must be going somewhere else. To my increasing consternation they continued to follow me all the way back to Rollesby. Eventually I stopped them at the Horse and Groom and discovered that the service was at 11.00am! By now it was 10.50! I asked them to go very slowly round to pick up the family and sped off to get ready. I managed to pick up Willie Allard, our organist, and be at the church gates as the hearse came up the road - but it was a close shave.

Money was not always easy, especially with inflation. During my time I was ex-officio chairman of the Poor Trustees - an archaic charity that rented out land and used the income to buy coal for the 'poor'. It was never easy deciding who was poor, and many individuals expected to receive a distribution as of right once they reached sixty-five!

On one occasion I had to prepare a young couple for marriage and shortly before the big day, heard that the lad was letting it be known in the Horse and Groom that his wedding gift to his wife was going to be a packet of nappies; the implication being that she was pregnant. I was anxious to know the truth about this rumour for the girl's sake and was concerned about his apparent lack of love towards her. I duly approached him, but he hotly denied it. I was further hauled over the coals in my study by his father for daring to suspect such a thing of his son. I should have read him Archbishop Donald Coggan's personal call to the nation on moral direction, that he gave on the occasion of his enthronement.[22] I recall that about this time we were asked to discuss a Church publication called 'Marriage and the Church's Task', a document about whether we should marry divorced

---

[22] 1975 January 24th.

people or not. This was not dissimilar to what is being discussed today[23] and seven out of eleven of our PCC favoured some relaxation in the rules.[24]

At the beginning of the 1980s Dr Robert Runcie was enthroned as Archbishop of Canterbury and Cardinal Hume read the epistle. This struck me as a hopeful sign for the future: a closer working relationship between the Churches. The visit by Pope John Paul II to England[25] and the joint service with our Archbishop at Canterbury Cathedral further encouraged us all that the various denominations were moving closer together.

The Falklands War[26] caused mix feelings within Rollesby and the nation as a whole, and when Archbishop Runcie, at the thanksgiving service, prayed for the dead and wounded on both sides he upset Margaret Thatcher, but expressed an opinion felt by most Christians. Generally speaking we rarely discussed politics in Rollesby with the possible exception of the cut and thrust in the Horse and Groom. We picked up on the suffering of the world and prayed.

Looking back to our time in Rollesby we made many friends and it was a happy time. After nearly thirteen years we felt that there was not much more we could do and so we moved. No doubt the people of Rollesby roll on, if you will forgive me my pun, despite the changes that are part and parcel of life in a village encompassed in the wider scene of the ups and downs of the world in which we all live.

---

[23] 2000 The Church of England discusses the Winchester Report.

[24] PCC Minutes 19th November 1979. (NB. The voting this time (May 2000) was 100% in favour of some relaxation of rules.)

[25] First Papal visit to England (UK) May 1982.

[26] 1982 April 2nd. Argentina attempted to annexe Falkland Islands.

CHAPTER 39

ooooo

Kenneth Newton (1984-1989)

The Margaret Thatcher era

Dear Whoever you are,

I intend to keep this short. I am not well and tomorrow, the eighth day of the new year, I intend to resign;[1] I have enjoyed myself in Rollesby but my health is letting me down badly. In your notes you have asked me to say something about myself. I was born in 1924 and trained at St Aiden's, Birkenhead, eventually being priested in 1953.[2] My first curacy was in Felling, Durham then I was appointed Priest in Charge at St George's, Gateshead. Before I came to St George's, Rollesby, I held five other incumbencies and served two periods overseas in Bermuda, a place I loved. My wife, Mona, also particularly enjoyed our time in Belize. I was sixty when appointed to Rollesby with Burgh with Billockby and Ashby with Oby, and it was meant to be my last post: I had intended to stay longer but I have not been a well man since I arrived. I was not everything the joint representatives had wanted, but who would be? They wanted somebody with the experience of an archbishop yet young enough to stay for at least twenty years. They wanted somebody from low to centre in churchmanship[3] when they really meant someone really low. I was a late academic, starting with an early Open University BA in 1974 but since then acquired a doctorate that

[1] 1989 8th January. The PCC Minutes.

[2] *Crockford's Clerical Directories* 1880-2000.

[3] 1984 21st May. The PCC Minutes.

impressed them at the interview. I should have guessed the Norfolk climate would not be good for my health on the day of the interview;[4] it was a damp, cold and miserable October day and I do not think I saw any sun in Rollesby for any length of time for the next five years. The rumour gained ground that I had come to Rollesby 'to take things easy' and one churchwarden resigned because she did not like the way I did things. It was all because I asked her to meet the architect for a quinquennial inspection and then forget to tell her he was not coming. She complained that I never kept wardens in the picture and I confess I may have been somewhat remiss on this point. I was certainly not intending to flog myself to death, and gained great comfort out of my hobby of playing jazz on the piano. I especially enjoyed going to the Lloyds for Sunday lunch where I would play piano to my heart's content. My music was useful in Thurne where, more often than not, there was no organist. When we arrived we had no furniture and the parishioners found all we needed: then our furniture eventually arrived and I had the problem of getting rid of the gifts. I do not think everyone appreciated this or me for that matter. I found some of the Rollesby people to be a mixture of the sophisticated to the very rough and ready. I was bemused to read in a local history of East Flegg that 'all these places ending with a "by" are of Danish origin, this district having been peopled by the Danes, and their descendants are a very rough race to this day'.[5] I could not help but smile and see the truth of this in some of the people I met.

Financially it was a struggle for them and me. In 1986 the parish quota rose by a massive 25%, based on £82 for each person in the congregation.[6] This meant we owed the Diocese £2,884 and we knew we could not meet such a demand. I protested at once, and by December had managed to reduce the figure to £2,395 because of the habitually low attendance at all services.[7] After this problem we tried to keep the parochial electoral roll to a sensible level, at least a level that reflected our ability to pay. It was even a struggle to pay our magazine bills and I lost the treasurer on account of this. The congregation was small, some fresh blood appeared from time to time, a Dr A Lloyd had purchased White Farm, where the Reverend Raymond

---

[4] 1984 3rd October.

[5] Bayne, A D (circa 1880) *History of Eastern England*: James MacDonald, Yarmouth. Vol.II, p.193.

[6] 1986 8th January. The PCC Minutes.

[7] 1986 3rd December. The PCC Minutes.

Grundy had lived, and Dr Lloyd's wife, Lisa, joined the PCC.[8] Despite the comings and goings of congregation members our numbers always fluctuated around the eighteen mark as an average, and in 1988 Mrs Catchpole did a parish attendance survey for the Diocese and our numbers were still only an average seventeen.

One of the main problems was heating what must be one of the coldest and dampest churches in Norfolk. We tried everything, from gas to paraffin to garage heaters given by Don Beck, the garage owner on Martham Road. The organ was horrendous until Dr Lloyd gave nearly £200 to have it repaired in memory of an uncle and aunt. We did have extra lighting installed in the nave in memory of Colwyn Wolsey, the founder of FORC:[9] he died on August 15th 1983. We had a brass plaque installed to commemorate this gift and it certainly made the old Norman church seem brighter and lighter.

The main problem was trying to run so many churches and trying to be in too many places at the same time. I became 'schizophrenic', waking up in the night sweating with worry that I had missed a service at Rollesby or Oby. In terms of the population the benefice was not large. A city priest I knew in Southampton laughed when I told him that Rollesby had nearly a thousand souls and with the other parishes another thousand. In his parish he had nine thousand people, but he had only the one church and two curates to help. I agree that his baptisms, weddings and funerals, his hatchings, matchings and dispatchings would be heavy, but Sunday would have been a doddle for him. I could have up to six services on a Sunday and it became very confusing. This led to mistakes and naturally I was the one who always got the blame. The PCC asked me to make sure there were proper rotas for sidesmen and organists[10] because the service always started with too much confusion. I did my best but such rotas should be organised by the lay people. The last straw was last month when they complained about a lack of organisation on Remembrance Sunday:[11] next year they will have an interregnum and it will be interesting to see how they manage. Even if I am not there, I shall get the blame! Whilst I was on holiday a

---

[8] 1986 28th April.

[9] Friends of Rollesby Church.

[10] 1987 29th April. The PCC Minutes.

[11] 1988 7th December. The PCC Minutes.

funeral occurred and when the undertaker arrived with the imported priest the church was locked. I was away and someone had not had the common sense to contact the verger, yet when I returned from my all too brief break, I was the one who had to do all the apologising and explain to the PCC again.[12] My organisational skills were not the best. We had been considering a faculty for the tower, and I am sure I sent it in and assured everyone that I had. In fact I forgot, but this will not be discovered until I have gone. I hope that the next chap will have the energy to pursue the endless red tape involved in the faculty procedure. The world events of the day made faculty procedures seem so silly. The IRA blew up the Grand Hotel at Brighton during the Conservative Party Conference[13] and all the PCC wanted to discuss was magazine distribution. Margaret Thatcher ruled the country with an iron fist without the velvet glove, and the Bishop of Durham was convincing everyone that it was easier to be an atheist. The IRA were active all over the country, the *Herald of Free Enterprise*, a cross-Channel ferry, turned over killing hundreds[14] and I am expected to fuss over a faculty procedure! Life in the parish all seemed so trivial.

I had good friends here and I enjoyed the social side of life: visiting the Lloyds, and Don Beck's company, but I have to confess that spiritually I would have been better off in a larger parish or back in Bermuda. Perhaps after a lifetime in a varied and interesting ministry it was a mistake to finish in a rural parish, and I cannot be the first incumbent to think like this. Rollesby is a pleasant enough area but when some of the congregation said I preached above their heads, I knew instinctively I was in the wrong place for them and me.

---

[12] 1986 7th July. The PCC Minutes.

[13] 1984 October 12th.

[14] 1987 March 7th.

CHAPTER 40

ooooo

Christopher Cousins (1990-1998)

Women priests in the last decade of the old millennium

Dear Andrew,[1]

I came to Rollesby in the May of 1990, having served my title at St Hilary, Wallasey in the Diocese of Chester. The living had, at that time, reverted to the Archbishop of Canterbury, Robert Runcie, because the vacancy had lasted for eighteen months.

I was inducted into the united benefice of Rollesby and Burgh with Billockby, and Thurne with Oby and Ashby and Clippesby on the 18th May 1990, by the then Bishop of Thetford, Timothy Dudley-Smith. It was interesting that I was ordained by Michael Baughen, Bishop of Chester, another hymn writer!

You asked me to comment on the times through which we lived in Rollesby. I actually find this quite difficult. From the wider Church perspective it was the time of the great debate regarding women priests. I personally had no problem with this apart from the fear that it would divide the church on yet another issue. I can recall the murder of the children in Dunblane, but quite honestly I was too wrapped up in parish work to recall many of the issues outside the parish boundaries.

When I first came, Rollesby was the major parish within the benefice although there was a high degree of competition from Fleggburgh parish.

---

[1] This letter was written by Chris Cousins.

Fleggburgh was much the same size as Rollesby and there was a good deal of inter-village rivalry between the two villages. There was some alleged hearsay that the origins of this rivalry was something to do with someone throwing stones at someone else many years previously, or someone or another stealing another's girlfriend! All very suspicious but likely.

One of the first things I had to deal with was the major tower repairs in Rollesby church. A faculty was obtained and the work put in hand through Bannesters of Stalham. The work took some time to complete because the condition of the tower was substantially worse than originally believed. The cross-beams had rotted and stonework had become unstable in many places. The final repair bill was over double the original estimate: the difference being paid mainly by English Heritage, nearly £24,000!

At another level it was important to try and get the five churches of the benefice pulling together as a group. To this end a Group Council was formed which from memory, consisted mostly of the churchwardens. It was also necessary to arrange a manageable schedule of services. It was my aim to try and be in each church each and every Sunday for a service. I did this for about eighteen months, at the end of which I found it necessary to back down a bit.

In Rollesby itself we had Stephen Cobb and later Richard Tacon with Lisa Lloyd as churchwardens and so we began a very positive period of church life. There were a large number of baptisms in the initial period due to my predecessor not having been long in the parish and his predecessor having operated a restricted baptism policy. The result of this was that we built up a regular family-orientated congregation of about forty. We also made the south-west corner of the nave into a children's corner. Richard Tacon managed to get some carpet free from Bruce Sturrock and together Richard and I purchased some cheap office partitions. In this corner we began a Sunday School, which my wife Jenny led with the help of Lisa Lloyd's daughters.

Mr Hawes the organist retired. He had played at Rollesby for a good while and was quite ancient. His music had deteriorated to the extent that the wedding march was unrecognisable! Geoff Hewitt joined as organist and Tania Lloyd, the daughter of my churchwarden, also ably assisted us at times.

My first three years was a very good time. Living in Rollesby, I was able to mix with everyone; it was a friendly village, though somewhat spread out geographically. The Friends of Rollesby Church (FORC) played a large part in providing funds for repairs and so forth, and since the congregation was small, income was also, but we just about made ends meet.

We held some united harvest suppers in the group. These were very happy events held at Jean Lindsey's holiday camp in Clippesby. I remember my first suggestion of a united harvest supper was met with horror but I persevered. The next year, not wanting to force my will upon the people I asked what they wanted to do about harvest supper and whether they would like separate ones. 'Good Lord! No.' came back the reply. 'We want our traditional united harvest supper.'

During my time at Rollesby, I began my M.Th. studies at Westminster College, Oxford. After two years I gained my Dip.Th.. Then the course changed and Oxford University allowed Westminster students to do an Oxford degree. Because Oxford had its own peculiar M.A. it was decided that a M.Th. should be introduced. I gained my degree and this course greatly helped me in my ministry. I shall always be grateful to the Rollesby group for getting me started with both encouragement and some financial support.

In 1992, as a result of the losses sustained by the Church Commissioners, there was considerable pressure being exerted by the Norwich Diocese, to reduce clergy posts. As a result, and following discussions between John Wilson,[2] then Rural Dean, and the clergy, a pastoral scheme was suggested. This entailed Rollesby being split from its original grouping and being joined with Ormesby St Michael and Ormesby St Margaret with Scratby. Clippesby and Thurne went into the Martham group and Fleggburgh with the Filby group. This scheme was put before the PCCs of the Rollesby group and it was almost unanimously, though reluctantly, agreed. Life now started to change.

Faced with having to look after Ormesby St Margaret, a village substantially larger than Rollesby, Jenny and I took the decision that we would have to move out of the Rollesby rectory and down to Ormesby. Ormesby had

---

[2] Vicar of Ormesby 1982-1992, affectionately known as 'Jumbo'.

the designated rectory according to the pastoral scheme.

This decision was reluctantly taken on my part, and was not popular in Rollesby. I think it was felt that I was deserting Rollesby in favour of Ormesby. The loss of a resident rector after all this time and with such a history as Rollesby's was a hard blow. I understood the feelings, though I was hurt by the inference of desertion.

I tried very hard to continue to treat Rollesby in the same way as I had when resident. I continued to take assemblies in Rollesby School, to visit the Windmill Nursing Home and to 'be around' as much as was possible. Inevitably, I could not be around as much as I had been, and this was regarded as confirming expectations. However, whilst I was down in Ormesby, Rollesby church received a substantial bequest from Barbara Rudd that should help them in the future. This made finances much easier and we were able to have the bells repaired and re-hung. However, for safety's sake, it was felt that the bells should swing rather than rotate so as not to risk damaging the tower. We were also able to purchase a new set of altar frontals. This had become an ambition of mine since arriving in the parish and learning that a predecessor had put the frontals away in a box following his arrival. They had duly got damp and rotted.

I think we also brought some semblance of order to the graveyard. Here, various headstones had been allowed contrary to regulations. I tried hard to stick as closely to the regulations as possible and we developed a really nice section in the north-west corner. The PCC commissioned a survey and record of the graveyard and this was undertaken by Virginia Lloyd.

In the early days we had some truly lovely services. We had a Midnight Eucharist, Christingles, carol services and family services. These were all well attended and things were going really well. There was little choice at the time but to agree to the proposed pastoral scheme in order to save clergy posts and money. Looking back on it I think it was particularly difficult for Jenny and me. We had grown very attached to Rollesby and to the group. There was a sense in which the move satisfied no one, only the financial needs. I think Rollesby felt I was deserting them and Ormesby felt that they did not really choose me as they would have done in the usual way. It was necessary for me to leave when I did to allow for a new beginning for the new benefice in which Rollesby now finds itself, under a new rector who could not be blamed!

One of the joys of the new arrangement was the strong link that developed between Rollesby and Ormesby St Michael. Looking to the future, I feel this will greatly help the new benefice to thrive and I believe this co-operation continues.

Latterly at Rollesby, numbers began to diminish for various reasons. Some families moved, others grew up and their children began doing other things on a Sunday. It is easy to look back and see the early part of my time in Rollesby as good and the latter part as less so. To do so, though, would be negative. I firmly believe that the pastoral re-organisation was God's will for the area. The decision was agreed by all PCCs involved, readily but reluctantly. The development of the Flegg Group of churches under Peter Paine's[3] splendid chairmanship was another way in which the area's churches were very definitely brought together.

As a family we retain very happy memories of Rollesby and my first incumbency. It was a lovely experience for which we are very thankful.

---

[3] Rector of Martham.

CHAPTER 41

ooooo

Andrew Sangster (1999-)

Dear Reader,

I was trained at King's College, University of London and then at the theological college of St Boniface in Warminster, after which I was ordained in Rochester Cathedral on Trinity Sunday, 1969; a similar background to some of my predecessors in this book. This particular reflection occurred to me while I was standing in St George's church looking at the list of rectors; it caused me think about their past. Who were they? What did they see and do? What were their hopes and fears for themselves and the parish: if only I could wake them up and have a chat!

As a young priest I served the usual curacy in Kent and was later an incumbent in Southampton. In those days I did not feel very comfortable with parish life so I spent most of my ministry in school chaplaincy work and teaching. Eventually I climbed the greasy pension pole and after nine years as a headmaster in the independent system felt compelled to return to the Church. Carol and I were intending to take up the offer of a parish in Stoke on Trent when we heard from one of the warden-representatives from this Norfolk benefice. As I had not heard anything from Norfolk for two months, I had assumed that this particular application had been rejected. And so it was that the very morning I was writing a letter of acceptance for the Stoke on Trent post, a request to interview me arrived. My first inclination was to refuse, but Geoff Freeman, a churchwarden of Ormesby St Margaret, was very persuasive in pointing out that we had applied to be considered for this vacancy and ought to attend. I had intended to jump through the various hoops and say 'no' as graciously as possible, but having met the interviewing representatives[1] Carol and I enjoyed the experience so much we were pleased to accept the offer, and have never regretted the deci-

[1] For Rollesby the representatives were Dorothy Bracey and Ann Bates; for Ormesby St Michael, Granville Lanham and Elizabeth Hirst, for Ormesby St Margaret, Geoff Freeman and Chris Ellis. The churchwardens of Rollesby were, and still are at the date of writing, Mrs Lisa Lloyd and Mrs Dorothy Bracey.

sion. We also enjoyed meeting the Rollesby Patron in the Bishop's interview. He was Richard Tacon, grandson of the Reverend Richard Tacon, who had virtually rebuilt St George's at the turn of the last century, and was probably the most significant incumbent St George's ever had in its long history.

All our friends and acquaintances warned us that the Norfolk people were insular and parochial in attitude. Carol and I found this to be totally unfounded. In my visits around the parish there has always been a welcome and St George's church people are totally supportive of the benefice as a whole. The six wardens from the three parishes[2] meet formally four times a year and to date there has never been the slightest tension.

As I have been in post for only two years there is little point in my writing about this period, but I will make a brief comment on the plans for the future and potential problems as I see them.

St George's on a winter's day can very cold and damp. When I open the doors on a Thursday or Friday morning (when it is St George's turn for Daily Offices) it is similar to opening a fridge door; the cold air comes out. Books left overnight feel damp and my breath is more visible inside the church than out. A small group of people faithfully turn out for the Daily Offices and it occurred to me that we needed a small warm room somewhere within the church. I spoke to Lisa Lloyd and Dorothy Bracey, the two committed wardens, and I discovered that there had been plans for similar ventures, not least FORC saving money for a water supply to be laid to the church. We soon appointed an architect[3] and requested the DAC[4] to give us preliminary permission for a room at the west end of the south nave, with toilet facilities and kitchen in the base of the tower, and a platform above for the bell ringers. The patron, wardens and PCC moved with remarkable alacrity and I felt we would achieve everything within a few months. We were all to be disappointed. My predecessor has already noted that English Heritage had put £24,000 into saving the tower and this virtually gave the rights of the building over to this national body. They are still dithering (at the time of writing) with mild formalities and the length of

[2] Rollesby was attached to Ormesby St Margaret and St Michael as described in the letter from Christopher Cousins.

[3] Bryan, George.

[4] Diocesan Advisory Committee.

time they take to respond is a cause of deep irritation. They treat us as if we are vandals 'having a go' at one of their museums or tourist attractions while we see ourselves as an active rural Christian community. English Heritage is a formidable organisation that has wrapped itself into a fortress of impregnable red tape while the congregation freezes and the lack of toilet facilities continues to be an embarrassment. St George's is a beautiful church and we are looking forward to completing these plans one day with a view to redecorating the inside and changing the heating system.

Congregational life is very reasonable for a rural parish, especially when one recalls that the church is nearly a mile away from the three focal points of Rollesby village. When I visit parishioners who rarely come to church, or those who come only for the occasional offices, I always find that the church is held in high esteem and affection. This observation leads me on to what I perceive to be the major problem.

Rollesby had several old rectories but no longer a resident rector; even the new rectory has been sold and I live four miles away in Ormesby St Margaret. I try to compensate by ensuring that Rollesby has a service every Sunday, and that I am around the village at least two days a week, and hold Daily Offices in the church on those days. In addition to this I insist that the Rollesby PCC meets in Ormesby rectory because it is Rollesby's rectory as well as Ormesby's. Nevertheless, the parish could, as it has in time past, benefit from its own resident priest. The parish faithfully pays its quota and maintains itself with a small but loyal group of worshippers. Rollesby has a population of only just over a thousand souls but even on a good Sunday can produce only just over thirty in the congregation; yet many non-going parishioners do benefit from the presence of the church and its priest. I know it is not practicable with today's logistics for Rollesby to have its own priest but there is always the fear that more pastoral schemes will be introduced and the benefice be made wider than it is at the moment. Currently I can cycle everywhere and so get to know people: enlarge it further and the individual approach will be lost. Team ministries are not the answer. Before I came back into parish life I read Roger Lloyd's book on the Church of England and in particular his passage where he thought the team or group ministry was the future for rural communities.[5] Before coming to Norfolk I

[5] Lloyd, R (1966) *The Church of England 1900-1965* SCM, London, p.535.

looked at other possibilities, and every time I encountered a group or team ministry there was always an underlying tension of one sort or another. In one group in which I was offered a post the antagonistic feelings within the group were almost palpable. I was not surprised to read in the *Church Times* and the daily press that this particular team had become headline news involving the courts. I also discovered that many lay people intensely disliked not having their own priest and objected to not knowing which member of the team was to be with them. The clue to a successful ministry is I believe in the business of visiting; some may see this as a small talk with coffee and biscuits but visiting acts as an amalgam to a parish and is best done by a priest who knows his particular area. At this moment Rollesby is just about comfortable with a priest who comes in from a larger parish, but any further watering down because of financial pressures and the church in this area will be lost. This would be a tragedy because over the last two years I have come to realise that the strength of the Church of England is to be found in such rural areas as Rollesby. A village like Rollesby and many others of a similar socio-economic structure have a loyalty to the parish church and the wider Church that is seldom found in suburbia and cities.

I appear to be looking to a gloomy future and I hope I am wrong. The reason I fear the watering down of the rural parish ministry is because at a recent Chapter meeting a diocesan financial adviser prophesied that within ten years there would be very few full-time incumbents left, and that parishes would be run by non-stipendiary ministers. All around the Diocese there appear to be many parishes that cannot pay their quotas and eventually this will lead to further cutting back of front line troops, namely the parish priests. I have no magic answers. I frequently make myself unpopular in clerical circles by pointing out that the administrative system of the Church of England is far too top heavy and that all clergy (residential canons, archdeacons and bishops) should all be paid the same minimum stipend (only the expenses of office should differ). But I may as well try and stop smoking my pipe. Nor am I convinced that this will solve the problem. If this benefice declared unilateral independence (God forbid) it could survive and even contribute towards supporting others. In moments of prayerful solitude I often find myself wondering whether the Church of England needs a total restructuring. I allow this type of heresy to creep into my mind only because I feel that with the possible demise of the parish priest the future will indeed be bleak. I often wondered how my predecessors coped in their days, thus I wrote to them and hence this book.

In the meantime, like all my predecessors in Rollesby, I lead the congregational worship, coach people to come and worship, and do my best to act as a servant both to the faithful and also to the rest of the parish. Having read so much about the parish I feel as if I have been here a thousand years; I hope St George's is still active under God's hand for another thousand years.

INDEX TO APPENDICES

Translation from French article on John Mapes Ensor – Vice-Consul 319
Notes from *White's 1845 Directory* 322
Residents from *Kelly's Directory 1933* 324
Methodist ministers associated with Rollesby 325
Rollesby deaths as recorded in Graveyard and Register 326

APPENDIX I

Translation from *Quest-France* 31 October – 1st November 1998: 'Thoughts on All Saints' Day'

Modest Tomb for the Consul

Cemeteries of the past were more a reflection of society than they are today: imposing vaults and notable chapels set within high railings bordered the main pathways, a lesson to all who saw them. The more humble graves would be found in a maze of closely packed rows. However, time can sometimes obliterate these sharp distinctions and, just two steps away from the important graves, can be found a grave of the nobility long since abandoned, such is the case with that of John Mapes Ensor. Not far from the main gate of the town cemetery, bordering the main path, is a grave so small one could believe it is that of a child. A broken slate slab on some lopsided piers. Once a year at All Saints' Day an unknown person places a modest floral tribute, to honour him like the other notables. A warmhearted gesture in an unfeeling age! Here lies, nevertheless, a gentleman of the best society, whom one would have addressed as M'sieur le Consul. With a little patience, the dark slab reveals a Latin inscription: 'Since February 1852 this has been the resting place of John Mapes Ensor, vice-consul of Her Gracious Majesty Queen Victoria' thus uncovering part of the mystery. Why then did this Englishman stationed at Lorient come to die at Concarneau at only fifty-five years of age? All that could be said, is that some days previously, a ship from London carrying grain had been seriously damaged near the Glénans and had to put into port at Concarneau to make an assessment of the cargo. As the ship in difficulty was English, this would justify the presence of the nearest British consul.

Aristocratic Family

Of the English gentry, the family can pride themselves on their name, which was already established in the eleventh century. John, for his part, was descended from Thomas Ensor known from 1530. Born in 1797, the eighth child, he grew up at Rollesby Hall in Norfolk. Inherited from his grandmother Mapes, the manor house, built in 1618, had fine style with its high chimneys, spacious entrance hall and oak panelling. The estate comprised more than twenty hectares of hunting land, a large lake and several farms. Is it this John who shot the great sea eagle with its wingspan of 2.20 metres? This is known only to family memory. Although he inherited the estate he preferred to travel. Some years later he married Marie-Ann Webb, with whom he had three children. He left England.

In April 1850, John Mapes Ensor received his commission of vice-consul of Great Britain at Lorient. He came to be installed, with his wife and daughter, at Port-Louis. In his new residence in La Place du Tertre, not far from the citadel, he had a housekeeper and a coachman and made no secret of his wealth and position. He was quickly adopted by the shipowners and grand merchants. The Administrator noted elsewhere that he was 'surrounded by the greatest attention' and was 'totally commendable'.

The old rivalry of the Indies Companies is long forgotten, but at the time, good relations particularly with the English, over the importing of coal, were essential. The presence of a British representative thus would only make things easier, and those in power wished him to stay a long time in post.

Last Stroke of Fate

However, in less than three years after his arrival, John Mapes Ensor died at Concarneau.

Unfortunately the Act of civil-state does not mention the cause of his death. It was Gustave Le Guillou de Penanros, one of the richest of the town's inhabitants, and Justice of the Peace, Louis de Malherbe, who would come to make the declaration. Curiously, he was not to be returned either to Port-Louis, or to his native Norfolk, but would be interred at Concarneau. His widow returned to England where she died thirty-four years later. Rollesby Hall passed into the hands of Revd. Edmund Ensor, to be sold in 1906, thus changing the continuity forever.

For a long time, the Parks Department of the town were commissioned to put flowers on the grave of the Englishman in the old cemetery on All Saints' Day. Scrupulously, the gravedigger placed a chrysanthemum on an impressive, ivy-covered tomb, presuming it to be the right one. Until one day the stone was cleaned, revealing that it carried only the names of 'dyed in the wool' Concarneau inhabitants. Not an English name in sight, yet only a short distance away lay the deserving John Mapes Ensor. At the same time the concession had been made to honour the vice-consul perpetually, without doubt the Mayor of that time never failed to do this. So for many years, without a word spoken, the poor gentleman was honoured at a burial place which was not his own. Goodness!

MICHEL GUEGUEN

APPENDIX 2

Notes from *White's 1845 Directory: Norfolk* (pp.304-5)

includes prominent locals in 1845

Rollesby is a large scattered village and parish, 8 miles N.W. by N. of Yarmouth, containing 589 inhabitants, 1407 acres of enclosed land, and about 200 acres of the waters, called the Broads. J. M. Ensor, Esq., now in France, owns most of the soil, and is lord of the manor. He formerly resided at the Hall, a handsome building, which was in the Elizabethan style, but was new fronted with white brick, and otherwise improved, about 18 years ago. It is now unoccupied, and delightfully situated east of the village, in the vale of the Broads, eight of which unite, and covering a long strip of 400 acres, form the largest fresh water lake in the county. The Church (St. George) stands on an eminence, at the west end of the village, and has monuments of the Claxton, Gleane, and Mapes families. The Living is a discharged rectory, valued in K.B. at £17, and now having a clear yearly rent of £648 in lieu of tithes, by commutation in 1839. J. M. Ensor, Esq., is patron, and the Rev. E. S. Ensor, B.A., incumbent. The Workhouse for the incorporated Hundreds of East and West Flegg, stands in this parish, on a declivity near the Broads, and is already noticed at page 293. In 1836, it was partly destroyed by fire, (supposed to be the work of an incendiary,) and its restoration cost about £2000. A fire-engine is now kept on the premises. The Poor's Allotment, awarded at the enclosure of Rollesby in 1816, comprises 23A. 1a. 32p., now let for about £15 a year, which is distributed in coals. In 1620 and 1669, cphr. .Amys and Leonard Mapes left to the poor parishioners 1A. of land, now let for £4.10s., which is applied towards the support of a Sunday School, which was opened as a daily National School, in 1844.

Annison Rd. *steward, wheelwright*
Annison Rt. *thatcher and beerhouse*
Baldry Win. *shoemaker*
Boyce Mr John
Brown Benj. vict. *Horse and Groom*
Day Mr John
Derry Rt. *thatcher*
Ensor Jno. M. Esq. *Hall. (in France)*
Ensor Rev Edmund S., B.A. *Rectory*
Frosdick Danl. *beerhs. & shopkr*
Frosdick Dl. sen. *carrier to Yarmouth*
Gaze Richd. sen. & jun. *joiners*
Gorble Wm. *gardener*
Harris George, *farrier*
Laws Jas. *parish clerk and schoolr.*
Mason Win, *shopkeeper*
Mountseer John, *master of the Workhouse and Superintdt. Registrar*
Norman Rd. Briton, *canvass, tarpauling, sacking, net, &c.*
Ransome Edw. *overseer & surveyor*

Blacksmiths
Appleton John
Nicholls Win.
Skoyles 'Nm.

*Farmers (*are owners)*
Baldry George
*Chapman Jas.
*Christmas John
Clarke Win.
Curtis Richard
*Denham John
Durrant Robert
*Fabb Richard
Hartnan Henry
Kemp Robert
Lincoln James *(farm bailiff)*
Ransome John
Vellum Win.
Wright Ann

APPENDIX 3

Residents from *Kelly's Directory 1933* (pp.439-440)

*(*farm 150 acres or over)*

Alexander Robert. *Boot repairer*

Allard Jn. *Shopkeeper*

Benn Lt-Col. Ion Brides Hamilton JP. Rollesby Hall.

Benn & Power **Farmers.* Broad Farm.

Bloom Albert. *Blacksmith*

Clowe's *Grocers*

Curtis Wm. Horse & Groom Inn (Rollesby Bowling Club).

Daniels & Howes *Farmers*

Evans Cyril H Shenton., Broad House.

Frosdick Sidney. *Farmer*

Gaze Sidney. *Farmer*

Green Joseph. *Market gardener*

Grundy Rev George Raymond (Rector). The Rectory.

Hewitt Herbert. *Farmer*

Howes William. *Farmer*

Laxon Walter. *Miller*

Mace Edgar Jn. *Farmer*

Miller Walter. James. Clerk to Parish Council, Post Office. *Carpenter*

Nichols Charles George. Woodbine Villa. *Market gardener*

Powells Percy Edgar. Sowells Farm. *Farmer*

Rudd Arthur, Taconville.

Sharman Edith. *Shopkeeper*

Shreeve Charles. Low Farm. *Farmer*

Shreeve Jn. *Farmer*

Smith Louisa. *Shopkeeper*

Spall Mrs. Broadlands.

Tacon Richard Charles MA, JP., The Grange.

Tooke *Arthur Harry. *Farmer*

Tooke Emma. *Smallholder*

Townend William Edward. *Market gar-dener*

Wyatt Jn. *Farmer*

Wymer Edward. *Smallholder*

Youngs Hy. *Market gardener*

APPENDIX 4

Methodist ministers associated with Rollesby

1883-1886	George C Normandale
1886-1891	George Rudram
1891-1895	William Moore
1895-1899	James Cooper
1899-1902	Matthew S Cushing
1902-1912	Francis C France
1912-1916	William H Lawson
1916-1918	Henry R Didcock
1918-1920	John Norton
1920-1924	Ernest C Hudson
1924-1930	Ernest S France
1930-1935	Abraham Hill
1935-1938	A Barrett Gowers
1938-1942	Harry W Hart
1942-1946	Harold W Pope
1946-1950	John E Ogden
1950-1952	Reginald T Wagstaffe
1952-1955	Leonard G Jones
1955-1961	William H Nicholas
1961-1967	George R Nunnerley
1967-1976	Colin E Riches
1976-1985	N Roy Coppack
1985-1993	Stephen G Yelland
1993-2001	Ralph Shepherd Webb

Rollesby Deaths as recorded in Graveyard and Register

Name	*Date*	*Age*
Abbot Charles	Sept 26 1702	67
Alexander Alice	Nov 27 1956	94
Alexander Edward Ernest	Feb 12 1907	9 mths
Alexander George Henry	Jun 10 1964	68
Alexander Hilda Louise	Jul 30 1966	71
Alexander Robert	Jan 8 1931	69
Alexander Robert Edward Charles	Mar 15 1962	68
Alexander Victoria Maud	Jul 4 1927	26
Allard Eva	May 21 1999	90
Allard Harriet	Apr 19 1949	73
Allard John William	Mar 14 1967	92
Allard John William George	Nov 10 1993	93
Allen George	Mar 9 1912	74
Almagioni Elizabeth	May 31 1956	92
Annison Edward	Mar 9 1812	62
Annison George William	Oct 25 1911	1 mth
Annison James Frederick	Feb 24 1949	77
Annison Maria	Nov 3 1849	45
Annison Mary	Oct 5 1902	92
Annison Mary Ann	Oct 10 1902	94
Annison Richard Steward	Apr 5 1887	78
Annison Rose Belinda	Feb 2 1912	4 mths
Annison Rose Belinda	Dec 10 1948	76
Annison Susan	Nov 7 1852	90
Annison William	Jul 20 1995	81
Appleton Elizabeth	Mar 4 1820	48
Appleton May	July 1810	65
Ashford Patricia Evelyn	Sep 20 1923	6
Atkins Amy	Jan 10 1968	86
Bailey Mary Annie	Nov 3 1921	41
Baldrey Frederick Henry	Mar 1 1974	74
Baldry Charles John	Jun 15 1920	69
Baldry John	Dec 1 1884	60
Baldry Martha Elizabrth	Feb 16 1915	66
Baldry Mary	Oct 2 1890	72
Baldry Olive Elizabeth	Mar 25 1930	74
Baldry Sydney Burton	Jun 27 1920	41
Barber Alice May	Feb 23 1956	73
Barber Constance Gladys	Oct 15 1914	14 days
Barber Ernest	Oct 28 1941	60
Barber Mildred	Apr 4 1934	46
Barber Sarah Ann	Feb 25 1930	77
Barlow Harold Edmund	Jul 25 1990	76
Bartlett Flora Lydia	Jul 5 1948	65
Bates Benjamin	Jan 28 1949	57
Bates Charles	May 26 1967	96
Bates Florence Charlotte	Oct 12 1960	69
Bates Florence Letitia	Dec 6 1948	77
Bates Jame	Jun 23 1988	82
Bates Robert Charles	Dec 9 1946	48
Bawdry Peter Ernest	Feb 18 1993	58
Beare Richard Stanley	May 14 1987	78
Beck Augusta	Jun 19 1907	65
Beck Benjamin	Apr 27 1898	91

Name	*Date*	*Age*
Beck Benjamin	Feb 20 1890	50
Beck Harriet Augusta	Jun 24 1907	65
Beck Mary Ann	May 25 1871	58
Beckett Alan James	Sep 24 1980	44
Beckett Alice Bertha	Jan 12 1963	64
Beckett Russell George	Oct 4 1968	70
Bell Maria	Feb 7 1882	89
Bell Maria	Dec 27 1833	15
Bell William	Oct 19 1865	82
Benn Sir Patrick Ion Hamilton	Apr 10 1992	70
Benn the Hon Lady Edel Jorgine	Apr 27 1994	72
Benns Arthur	Aug 8 1951	85
Bensley Mabel Janet	May 9 1997	79
Bensly Maurice	Feb 16 1940	1
Berrett Ethel Francis	Jun 10 1949	64
Blogg Elsie May	Mar 26 1976	72
Blogg Stanley James	Apr 2 1982	75
Bloom Daisy Alice	Jul 13 1972	87
Bloom Edward	Mar 3 1977	95
Boardley Bessie Edith	Jun 28 1990	97
Boardley Reginald Thomas	May 25 1961	68
Boult Hannah	Jan 19 1885	83
Boult Louisa	Apr 12 1916	85
Boult Thomas Cubit	Dec 12 1901	66
Boyce Emily	Mar 13 1937	91
Brett Esreller	Oct 5 1860	65
Brett John	Mar 2 1853	55
Brighton Agnes Augusta	Nov 5 1928	67
Brighton Charles	Feb 7 1935	71
Brighton Stanley Edward	Dec 2 1908	5 mths
Bronson Cyril Robert	Nov 24 1980	77
Brooks David Arthur	Apr 11 1973	41
Brooks Emily Louisa	Feb 25 1932	22
Brown Emily	Jun 12 1962	86
Brown Florence Selina	Nov 5 1907	2
Brown Gertrude Sarah	Nov 22 1955	48
Brown Henry Horace	Jun 11 1976	78
Brown Horace Henry	Sep 13 1942	66
Brown Mary-Ann	Dec 14 1885	39
Brown Percy Charles	Mar 9 1949	38
Brown Samuel	Feb 19 1915	88
Brown Sidney Oliver	Jul 13 1973	69
Brunson Edith Freda	Apr 26 1993	88
Bull John Frederick	Feb 5 1971	10 hrs
Burgess Charles	Sep 29 1906	64
Burgess Charles William	Jan 10 1906	7 wks

Name	*Date*	*Age*
Burgess Dorothea Mary	Feb 17 1905	2 mths
Burgess Evangeline	Aug 8 1933	77
Burgress William -fishing accident	July 18 1895	22
Bush Charles William	Apr 24 1957	83
Bush Harriet Anne	Mar 3 1957	86
Bush Rosannah Sarah	Nov 30 1906	36
Butt Inez Agnes	May 25 1957	91
Byles Mary Ann Ellen	Aug 31 1962	87
Cainton Ellen (?) poor hwriting	Jun 19 1927	52
Calver Alfred James Frederick	Aug 25 1992	78
Calver Iris Margaret Emma	Nov 8 1991	72
Cantelo Henry William	Mar 10 1931	73
Cantelo Maria Hilda	Aug 27 1913	51
Carr Frederick	Apr 11 1983	73
Carter Ben	Jul 17 1787	32
Catchpole Emily Mary	Feb 12 1972	72
Catchpole Lewis Henry	Jan 20 1968	67
Chapman Thomas	Jun 31 1917	84
Chilvers George	Feb 25 1924	74
Christmas Charles	Aug 5 1892	74
Christmas Jane	Apr 2 1889	82
Church Ann	Feb 15 1911	73
Church Benjamin	Apr 17 1919	75
Cobb Alfred Henry	May 2 1909	4
Cobb Ann	Mar 30 1801	89
Cobb Francis	Jul 10 1809	
Cobb-Green Elizabeth	Jan 6 1836	35
Codman Elizabeth	Apr 11 1936	89
Codman Robert	Jan 5 1933	78
Coe Robert	Apr 4 1932	84
Coe Susan	Jul 5 1924	71
Connop Ernest Mosely	Sep 15 1911	
Connop Ernest Mosley	Sep 19 1911	63
Connop Merry	Mar 15 1907	58
Coppin Anna-Maria	Mar 21 1883	15
Coppin Sarah-Ann	Jan 7 1881	22
Cornish Gerald Clement	Apr 30 1976	61
Cornish Herbert	Nov 20 1942	61
Cornish Lilly	Nov 30 1958	79
Crane Ernest William	Jul 10 1984	65
Crane Issac	Sep 4 1822	21
Crane Joan Gladys	Jan 4 1974	52
Crowe Malcolm John	Aug 1 1990	37
Curtis Ethel Edith Tryphera	Jan 7 1964	29
Curtis Eve Joyce	Jul 11 1979	63
Curtis George William	Jan 2 1932	3

Name	Date	Age
Curtis Noel Frederick Lawrence	Jul 4 1989	78
Curtis William George	Jun 17 1982	77
Daniels Elizabeth	Dec 1 1889	
Daniels Emma Elizabeth	Jun 13 1969	82
Daniels Frederick Charles	Apr 23 1899	37
Daniels George	Mar 1897	82
Daniels George	Jul 12 1807	82
Daniels Herbert Edward	May 27 1891	33
Daniels John Christmas	Dec 18 1951	91
Davey Hannah	May 25 1907	89
Davey Kenneth John	Aug 8 1990	66
Davey Luke Alan	Oct 13 1992	9 mths
Day Ann		
Day Eleanor	Sep 27 1850	
Day John	Oct 30 1849	
Day Mary	Jan 6 1825	79
Deacon Harold	May 8 1981	82
Deacon Winifred Dorothy	Mar 11 1991	90
Deary William	Mar 4 1800	86
Dickerson Alice Harriett	May 31 1944	76
Dickerson William	Nov 30 1938	81
Docking Abraham	Jul 27 1807	77
Docking George	Jan 7 1790	61
Docking Margaret	Oct 28 1775	37
Docking Sarah	Jan 10 1807	69
Docking William	Jan 14 1790	1
Dorking Elizabeth	Mar 26 1908	73
Dorking George William	Nov 17 1958	83
Dorking Louisa Charlotte	Au 14 1906	29
Dorking Rachael	Dec 28 1943	66
Dorman Harman	May 17 1836	35
Duck Mary	Jan 7 1802	81
Dunham Elizabeth	Dec 21 1899	86
Dunham George		
Dunham John	Jul 4 1850	18
Dunham John	May 26 1879	75
Durrant Anna	Nov 17 1936	93
Durrant Samuel	May 29 1908	65
Durrant Samuel	Feb 1 1911	73
Dybal Reginald	Dec 4 1979	78
Dyball Edith May	Oct 11 1923	1
Dyball Frederick John	Jul 23 1907	4 mths
Dyball Mabel May	Aug 21 1961	58
Eaton Benjamin	Oct 1 1795	91
Eaton Sarah	Aug 11 1787	78
Edmonds Benjamin	Dec 5 1934	79

Name	Date	Age
Edmonds Brian Albert	Mar 16 1979	48
Edmonds Mildred Harriet	Mar 18 1964	79
Elizabeth	Dec 20 1798	83
Ensor Capt Leonard Smith	Dec 16 1915	69
Ensor Edmund Alfred le-Fleming	Dec 22 1903	41
Ensor Ellen Eliza	Jun 26 1917	78
Ensor May Amelia	Nov 19 1928	83
Etheridge Percy Charle	Jul 23 1986	66
Evans Jennifer	Sep 10 1943	3 days
Farrow Bejamin	Dec 6 1948	85
Farrow Charlotte Easter	Dec 12 1928	60
Farrow Edna May	Mar 30 1994	85
Fenn James	Dec 15 1913	80
Fisher Anne	Aug 2 1822	82
Frances Catherine	Jul 5 1862	87
Frances Harriet	Sep 5 1890	76
Frances John	Apr 12 1887	76
Frances Robert John	Nov 2 1869	44
Frosdick Albert	Feb 9 1899	19
Frosdick Ann Hannah	Feb 16 1973	94
Frosdick Avis Betty	Jan 10 1983	59
Frosdick Benjamin	Nov 3 1926	87
Frosdick Daniel	Apr 6 1864	86
Frosdick David	Jan 31 1911	78
Frosdick Elizabeth	Jan 5 1867	41
Frosdick Elizabeth	Dec 2 1859	73
Frosdick Emily Eveline	Apr 25 1986	86
Frosdick Ethel Florence	Apr 5 1972	86
Frosdick Gladys Daisy	Dec 5 1975	79
Frosdick Horace Henry	Jun 3 1871	10
Frosdick James	May 27 1896	78
Frosdick James	Jan 13 1925	84
Frosdick James William	Apr 4 1894	19
Frosdick Jonathan John	Mar 21 1956	80
Frosdick Margaret	Oct 25 1809	81
Frosdick Mary Ann	Jul 11 1903	77
Frosdick Mary Ann	May 24 1922	83
Frosdick Mary Ann	Mar 5 1930	84
Frosdick Robert Sidney	Sep 14 1956	74
Frosdick Sidney James	Mar 13 1981	70
Frosdick Thomas	Feb 17 1855	39
Frost Charles	Nov 6 1887	
Frost Sarah	Aug 28 1872	71
Gadge-Danials Sarah	Nov 22 18?3	70
Gadge-Danials William		
Gamble Dorcos	Oct 12 1822	23

Name	Date	Age
Gane Ellen	Aug 21 1961	91
Garman Barbara Dorothy	Jul 15 1983	46
Gaze Adelaide May	Oct 8 1981	92
Gaze Anna Janet	May 7 1885	11
Gaze Daphne Adelaide	Jun 25 1924	10 mths
Gaze Elizabeth	Jan 13 1860	68
Gaze George	Aug 21 1906	49
Gaze George	May 8 1850	29
Gaze James	Jun 16 1882	62
Gaze James & Rebecca	1851	
Gaze Mary	Jan 3 1818	76
Gaze Mary-Ann	Jul 4 1851	6
Gaze Rebecca	Oct 28 1881	73
Gaze Richard	Apr 2 1864	69
Gaze Richard	Apr 30 1840	76
Gaze Richard	Jul 23 1851	7
Gaze Robert	Nov 24 1858	51
Gaze Robert & Mary-Ann		
Gaze Sidney Isaac	Aug 1 1972	82
Gaze Susannah	Dec 30 1934	80
Gaze William	Nov 16 1841	17
Gedge Janet Anne	Apr 3 1975	25
Gedge Jerima	1837	
Gedge John	Feb 14 1821	60
Gedge Sarah	Jan 29 1860	65
George Emily Ann	Dec 15 1871	57
George James	Dec 18 1913	72
George Ronald Charles	Aug 13 1992	72
Gibbs Samuel Arthur	Apr 19 1926	77
Gibbs Thirza Ann	Jun 6 1924	72
Gilbert Rose	May 25 1835	35
Goodmon Kathleen Lucy	Sep 17 1975	62
Goodrum Robert	Sep 7 1967	3 hrs
Goodrum Steven	Sep 7 1967	11 hrs
Gornhw? John	17--	
Gotts Winifred Amy	Jun 25 1994	75
Grapes Florence Lilian	Jan 13 1988	84
Green Alice	Feb 6 1953	72
Green Bertha	Apr 29 1902	1 mth
Green Edward	Aug 20 1913	79
Green Elizabeth	Jan 6 1864	2
Green Frederick	Sept 28 1866	
Green George Frederick	Mar 7 1903	2 days
Green George William	Jul 15 1921	46
Green Issac	Jul 10 1816	50
Green John	Aug 4 1903	60
Green John Harry	May 12 1871	8
Green Joseph William	Nov 15 1961	101
Green Rebecca	Feb 2 1834	74
Green Robert Henry	Jul 13 1904	29
Green Sarah	Oct 9 1875	51
Green Thomas	Jun 30 1807	82
Green William	Oct 1 1821	60
Grimble Prudence	Nov 23 1906	67
Grimble William	May 16 1901	64
Grimmer Amelia May	Dec 2 1972	76
Grimmer Frederick Lewis	Dec 24 1968	70
Grimmer Hilda	Jan 16 1998	99
Grimmer Mary Elizabeth	Jan 4 1944	81
Grimmer Walter William	Jul 29 1923	5 mths
Grimmer William Henry	May 6 1965	79
Grundy George Raymond	Jan 4 1950	60
Gummer John Samuel	May 9 1942	85
Gummer William	May 30 1942	1 wk
Hall Ann Elizabeth	Jun 12 1919	86
Hall Eliza	Mar 20 1907	56
Hall Elsie Edith	Dec 5 1988	66
Hall Forence John	Jul 21 1965	67
Hall Harry Basil	Feb 3 1981	59
Hall James	Sep 18 1912	73
Hall Thomas James George	Jul 8 1940	39
Hammond-Green Martha	Dec 24 1852	20
Hammonds Reginald Bertie	Feb 11 1975	62
Handly Susan	Dec 22 1822	59
Harman Susanna	Aug-29	6
Harris George	Dec 16 1861	48
Harris Mary Anne	Oct 26 1859	35
Harris Stella Mary	Jul 11 1950	26
Harrison	Feb 29 1894	92
Harrison Agnes Louisa	Sep 9 1901	28
Harrison Daniel	May 31 1886	92
Harrison Daniel - fishing accident	July 18 1895	20
Harrison Ellen Rose	Jan 1 1952	69
Harrison Harriet	Nov 3 1929	80
Harrison James	Jan 18 1933	92
Harrison John Charles	Jan 1 1935	89
Harrison John Henry	Sep 1 1992	84
Harrison John Robert	Jun 3 1902	7 mths
Harrison Mary Ann	Oct 12 1901	57
Harrison Minnie	Jun 6 1961	80
Harrison Robert Daniel	May 20 1950	73
Harrison Sarah	Jan 18 1898	54

Name	Date	Age
Harvey Elizabeth	Nov 16 1872	102
Harvey James	Jan 6 1862	81
Hawkins Harriet Jane	Nov 14 1960	75
Hayne Hilton John William	Jun 16 1986	90
Hayton Doris	Mar 22 1925	22
Hayton Edward	Jan 7 1980	73
Hayton James	Aug 6 1911	70
Hayton James Albert	Jul 24 1954	82
Hayton Julia	Mar 20 1946	75
Head May	May 29 1962	59
Hedges William Reverend	Jul 15 1850	61
Hewitt Arthur Robert William	Dec 20 1952	78
Hewitt Beryl Kathleen	Feb 17 1923	6 mths
Hewitt Emma Emmeline	Dec 31 1965	91
Hewitt Hannah	Sep 5 1904	29
Hewitt Hannah May	Jan 8 1969	77
Hewitt Leslie Barry	Sep 29 1997	51
Hewitt Matilda Kathleen	Sep 28 1949	50
Hewitt Ralph (Manny)	May 4 2000	60
Hewitt Sidney Elijah	Jul 19 1963	76
High Kenneth George	Sep 26 1985	53
Hill Arthur Walter Henry	Sep 5 1990	79
Hill Violet Rose	Sep 11 1987	83
Hinton Peter John Lee	Nov 17 1994	71
Hinton Valda Agnus	Nov 18 1991	70
Hodds Ellen Elizabeth	Aug 18 1961	77
Hodds Gordon Raymond	Feb 6 1981	64
Hodds Henry	Feb 8 1923	80
Hodds Henry George	Jun 23 1976	64
Hodds Philip Henry	Aug 18 1969	93
Hodds Sally Gwen	Jan 12 1972	21 hrs
Hodds Sarah Ann	Aug 31 1923	53
Hodds Winifred Ada	Aug 25 1976	68
Holt Donald	Nov 4 1983	70
Howes Elder May	Nov 4 1966	82
Howes Lorna Ethel	Mar 8 1919	2
Howes May Emma	Jan 24 1997	?
Howes William	Jun 2 1958	82
Hoyne Mary Ann	Nov 23 1962	66
Hunt Catherine	Jan 18 1937	67
Hunt Frederick James	Sep 24 1937	74
Hunt Sarah Ann	Oct 29 1909	75
Hunt William	Dec 27 1905	71
Ingram Laura Avice (Tommie)	Aug 4 1925	34
Izat Keith Walter	Dec 3 1990	44
Jeary Doris May	Mar 22 1991	74
Jeary Harrison John	Jan 21 1941	63
Johnson David	Jul 1 1949	3 days
Johnson Eliza Jane	Mar 10 1944	91
Jones George James	Feb 12 1900	68
Jones Maria	Jul 11 1921	84
Kemp Maria	Jun 22 1888	70
Kemp Mary	Dec 14 1859	70
Kemp Rebecca	Jun 23 1831	21
Kittle Milicent Louisa	Feb 14 1974	84
Kittle Raymond Walter	Oct 13 1982	61
Kittle Sidney Charles	May 9 1968	80
Lambert Arthur Ray	Jul 23 1984	51
Lambert Emma Louisa	Jul 16 1963	74
Lambert Joseph William	May 7 1952	63
Lambert Leslie Frank	Oct 13 1992	70
Lambert Roy Harold	Aug 4 1951	27
Lambert Stanley Oliver	Mar 12 1983	56
Lawson Ann Elizabeth	Jun 30 1851	10
Laxon Alfred	Feb 13 1963	79
Laxon Annie Jane	Sep 30 1954	71
Laxon Dora May	Oct 9 1956	65
Laxon Hilda Jessie	Mar 26 1986	82
Laxon Walter	Jan 28 1972	80
Legett John	Sep 6 1798	60
Legett Sarah	Nov 1790	60
Lewell James	Feb 24 1890	50
Lewis Gerald Arthur	Sep 25 1991	64
Lock George	May 13 1922	77
Lock James	Jan 19 1915	41
Lowne David	Nov 12 1917	91
Lowne Emily Frances	Feb 11 1936	52
Lowne Ernest George	Mar 3 1933	61
Lowne Sarah Ann	Oct 13 1902	73
Mace Ethel May	Jan 21 1976	84
Mace Eva Eliza	Nov 20 1987	79
Mace Henry Clarence	Jul 12 1991	81
Mace Paul Edward	Jun 21 1995	58
Machell Lucy Harriet	Dec 21 1890	47
Manson David Albert	May 1 1984	16
Mason James Robert	Dec 5 1942	82
Massingham George Maynard	Jul 1 1953	62
Matteu Sarah	Feb 1 1906	77
Mayhew Frank John	Sep 1 1907	10
Mayhew Gerchaiu William	May 15 1907	19
Mayhew Moses William	Aug 17 1907	41
Mayhew Thomas Gordon	May 15 1907	2

ame	Date	Age
cColville Walter	Aug 9 1933	45
cCulloch Brian David John	Feb 3 1989	58
een-Brown Charles Edward		4 mths
een-Brown James	June 15 1869	17
ickel-Burgh John Henry	Apr 6 1861	1
ile Elizabeth	Jan 18 1869	22
iles Edmund	Apr 7th 1795	34
iles Frances	Aug 6 1791	68
iles Mary	Mar 7 1799	75
iles Mary Ann	Aug 28 1912	82
mp Robert	May 14 1862	87
mp Robert	Sept 2 1825	80
mp William	Mar 23 1866	52
rrison Cecil John Richard	Jun 1 1987	86
rrison Ethel May	Mar 14 1986	85
rrison Janet Ann	Aug 29 1936	11 days
rrison Maud Eliza	Mar 18 1958	79
rrison Robert	Mar 7 1955	86
rrison Robert John	Oct 15 1915	4
rrison Rosanna	May 10 1941	69
rrison William	Jun 12 1923	12
ttle Joseph	Aug 25 1926	56
ng Jane	June 23 1851	5
ng Mary	Mar 4 1859	75
iller Ann Elizabeth	Nov 10 1938	76
iller Doris Catherine	Sep 25 1986	72
iller Hannah Ann	Dec 3 1941	89
iller John	May 2 1820	20
iller John	May 1 1842	72
iller John	Jan 9 1875	55
iller Kenneth Hugh	Feb 26 1924	7 days
iller Nora Beatrice	May 31 1957	70
iller Sarah	May 24 1828	55
iller Thomas	Sep 1 1852	14
iller Walter George	Aug 24 1924	69
iller Walter James	Dec 11 1964	79
olyneux-Sarel Clement Vincent	Jul 20 1895	27
olyneux-Sarel Henry Walter	Jun 16 1941	68
olyneux-Sarel Leut RN	Aug 2 1875	
onesy Lily Elizabeth	Mar 2 1953	41
onsey Alice Eliza	Oct 14 1936	62
onsey Bertie William	Jan 24 1989	77
onsey Edward Thomas	Apr 25 1975	71
onsey Gertrude	Jan 9 1961	59
onsey Henry William	Jan 27 1937	65
oody Katherine Marie	Nov 18 1970	5 wks

Name	Date	Age
Moore John	Dec 14 1963	80
Moore Rose Ann	Jul 26 1939	77
Moore Sarah	May 18 1961	81
Morris Emma	Dec 3 1922	71
Morris Mary Ann	Nov 18 1903	62
Mortimer George	Aug 14 1910	82
Mortimer Harriett Elizabeth	Jan 3 1918	76
Mortimer William George	Mar 15 1935	73
Motts Rebecca	Jan 9 1908	79
Myhill Albert Arthur	Feb 11 1915	38
Myhill Benjamin	Mar 2 1860	2
Myhill George	Jul 20 1866	21
Myhill Hannnah	Mar 19 1908	78
Myhill Mary Ann Elizabeth	Jan 14 1954	77
Myhill William	Jan 28 1909	77
Narborough Nora	Aug 5 1997	80
Newark Mary Ann	Feb 15 1906	75
Nicherpon Phoebe Priscilla	Dec 27 1933	64
Nicholls John Green Gedge	Aug 13 1929	69
Nichols Alfred	Sep 24 1958	59
Nichols Audrey Francis	Sep 2 1988	78
Nichols Celia	Apr 2 1976	91
Nichols Charles George	Mar 21 1975	82
Nichols Dorothy	Feb 26 1915	13
Nichols Edith mary	Nov 21 1972	87
Nichols Edmund	Mar 21 1862	82
Nichols Elizabeth Ann	July 8 1902	39
Nichols Ellen Sarah	Jun 14 1974	80
Nichols Geoffrey James	Oct 5 1981	87
Nichols George	Jun 19 1922	61
Nichols Harry	Oct 25 1990	81
Nichols James William	Jun 18 1937	60
Nichols Jane	Feb 24 1942	55
Nichols Joan	Oct 21 1975	57
Nichols Joseph	Apr 10 1937	84
Nichols Joseph William	Jan 19 1955	80
Nichols Lilian	Jan 25 1973	73
Nichols Mary	Nov 21 1928	74
Nichols Mary	Sep 4 1879	76
Nichols Rebecca	Jun 21 1889	
Nichols Rosanna	Aug 1 1950	76
Nichols Sarah	Feb 26 1958	88
Nichols Sarah Elizabeth	Aug 9 1922	52
Nichols Thomas George	Oct 26 1893	65
Nichols William	Dec 12 1838	30
Nichols William Wiseman	Aug 14 1887	65

Name	Date	Age
Nichols Winifred Louise	Mar 5 1953	56
Notley Agnes	Nov 22 1951	84
Notley Doris Hilda	Feb 13 1980	67
Notley Penelope	Apr 19 1952	83
Notley Robert	Oct 22 1945	80
Notley Roland Alfred	May 3 1991	87
Notley Ronald Frank	Mar 28 1996	89
Notley Ruth	Mar 4 1985	82
Nunn George William	Feb 13 1935	48
Nunn Hannah	Mar 10 1923	78
Nunn James	Apr 22 1909	74
Pacey David Lionel	Feb 9 1995	52
Page Ann	Apr 6 1802	24
Page Helen Maud	Apr 12 1967	77
Page James George	Jun 10 1950	59
Palgrave Alfred Joseph	Apr 4 1918	51
Palgrave George	Jan 31 1901	64
Palgrave Lucy	Feb 3 1933	83
Palgrave Selina Louise	Nov 5 1965	67
Palgrove Albert Sidney	Nov 15 1883	5
Palgrove Edith Ann	Feb 22 1894	22
Palgrove Rebecca	Jun 5 1851	
Palgrove Richard	Apr 28 1878	56
Palgrove Sussana	Jun 25 1851	
Palmer Ethel May	Jun 15 1965	77
Parker Ann Eliza	May 6 1848	21
Parker Bernard Arthur	Feb 2 1996	77
Parker Bessie Alice	Oct 29 1951	76
Parker Charles	Feb 1 1919	90
Parker Charles Edward	Jan 29 1931	72
Parker Edith Ellen	Jun 14 1937	72
Parker Emily	Dec 15 1910	84
Parker Emily Ann	Feb 22 1943	70
Parker Hannah Elizxabeth	Jul 12 1935	68
Parker Harriet	Dec 2 1905	71
Parker Harriet Maud	Jan 13 1979	67
Parker James	Jun 22 1835	53
Parker James Alfred	Dec 17 1918	55
Parker John	May 10 1939	68
Parker Laura Juliana	May 16 1933	66
Parker Louisa	Sep 30 1942	90
Parker Richard	Nov 4 1917	43
Parker Robert Edward	May 8 1940	81
Parker Sarah	Nov 30 1860	76
Parker William	May 15 1930	76
Parmenter Ivy Kathleen	Dec 16 1981	79

Name	Date	Age
Parmenter Robin Arthur	Jan 17 1984	44
Pattison Ernest	Dec 3 1955	30 mi
Pearce Arthur	Aug 28 1952	72
Pearce Edith Alice	Jan 9 1982	76
Pearsons Arthur Stanley	Oct 6 1978	74
Pearsons Ruth Mary	Mar 23 1984	75
Piggin Alice Louisa	Jun 27 1956	71
Piggin George Jebez	May 20 1952	71
Piggin Leonard Ralph	Jan 8 1940	67
Piggin Nora Maria	Feb 19 1912	9 mth
Pilgran (?) Elizabeth	Feb 14 1876	
Pitchford William George	Mar 22 1980	70
Platten Elizabeth	Mar 5 1945	85
Platten Elsie emily	Aug 19 1910	5 mth
Platten Freda Anna Majorie	Mar 7 1906	1
Platten Louisa Amelia	Mar 7 1932	70
Platten Walter Robert	Dec 26 1930	79
Pooke William James	Feb 28 1916	47
Porter Benjamin	Oct 2 1917	83
Powley Ann Eliza	Nov 3 1936	75
Powley Herbert	Jun 13 1938	81
Powley Herbert Walter Chapman	Dec 21 1959	60
Powley Maria	Oct 19 1899	73
Powley Robert	Mar 6 1900	74
Preston Elizabeth	Aug 28 1763	48
Preston John	Dec 27 1778	66
Price Vernon Haydn	Sep 25 1991	65
Procter Anne Elizabeth	Apr 11 1934	72
Procter George	Dec 5 1921	57
Proctor Lydia	Mar 17 1905	76
Ransome Ann	Jun 6 1845	
Ransome Ann	Nov 22 1847	
Ransome Anne Sarah	Jul 25 1974	63
Ransome Austin George	Sep 5 1918	12
Ransome Charlotte	Jan 12 1922	86
Ransome Daisy Elizabeth	Jan 20 1902	4 mths
Ransome Edith Alice	Sep 27 1957	74
Ransome Ellen Rose	Jun 30 1998	91
Ransome Ernest Ezekiel	Jan 4 1971	61
Ransome Ethel Maud & stillborn ch	Feb 19 1957	42
Ransome Frances Lois	Feb 21 1848	
Ransome George	Nov 25 1847	59
Ransome Harriet	Apr 24 1844	14
Ransome Herbert Charles William	Jan 9 1979	83
Ransome John	Aug 20 1855	57
Ransome John George	May 7 1905	75

Name	Date	Age
ansome John Samuel	Mar 10 1978	88
ansome John William	May 2 1949	85
ansome Mary Ann	Apr 28 1925	55
ansome Mary Jane	Feb 23 1978	86
ansome Olive May	Nov 18 1907	4 mths
ansome Patricia Linda	Mar 3 1951	2 mths
ansome Richard	May 7 1828	17
ansome Robert	Mar 9 1853	24
ansome Robert Joseph George	Sep 25 1912	4
ansome Robert Leslie	Mar 25 1918	20
ansome Susannah	Jan 13 1916	47
ansome Thirza		
eynolds Ann	Aug 9 1919	90
eynolds Stanley Charles	Sept 19 1901	2
eynolds William	Dec 12 1903	81
ice Helen May	Mar 20 1914	16 mths
iddle-Smith Robert	Oct 11 1819	60
itchie Catherine Mary	Mar 10 1957	73
itchie Ewing Thompson	May 14 1926	69
itchie Mary Ellen	Sep 24 1943	88
ivett Amelia	May 9 1933	64
obinson Arthur Charles	Apr 23 1956	72
obinson Edith	Mar 1 1956	68
opes Henry William	Aug 19 1941	68
ose Geoffrey Herbert	Sep 10 1975	82
ose Hilda May	Oct 9 1958	52
ales Ann Maria	Feb 23 1951	86
ales Jack Honaine	Aug 25 1988	73
ales John	May 19 1913	59
ales Violet	Sep 29 1970	58
arel Henry Andrew Leut Gen	Jan 2 1887	
arel Margaret Jane Phyllis	Dec 12 1919	74
chofield Sarah	Aug 19 1841	78
hingles Benjamin	May 12 1903	71
hingles James William	Jan 7 1888	28
hingles Mary Ann	Mar 9 1909	73
hreeve Alice	Jun 19 1875	6
hreeve Ambrose Bertie	Sep 27 1962	73
hreeve Bejamin Henry	Jun 2 1912	67
hreeve Frederick	Jan 10 1924	1 day
hreeve James	Jan 26 1875	27
hreeve Louisa Ann	Jul 23 1938	92
hreeve Mary Ann	Jun 23 1901	75
hreeve Rosa Maxa	Dec 27 1945	58
hreeve Walter Robert	Feb 22 1909	18
immonds Cissie Edith	Dec 13 1952	45

Name	Date	Age
Simnett Mary Ann	Apr 14 1890	61
Skipper Ann	Jun 2 1850	62
Skipper John	Jan 11 1876	92
Skoyles George John	Apr 20 1927	73
Skoyles Mary Ann	Mar 3 1929	73
Slaughter Elizabeth	Jun 14 1918	91
Smith Archie Ronald	Oct 29 1970	60
Smith Desmond John	Jan 14 1992	68
Smith Edward	Oct 13 1953	70
Smith Elsie Madeline	Jul 1 1949	3 days
Smith Emi Gertrude	Sep 8 1987	69
Smith Ethel Elizabeth	May 26 1977	91
Smith Frederick John	Feb 23 1951	68
Smith Getrude Maria	Sep 6 1972	62
Smith Harriot	Mar 6 1919	80
Smith Harry Charles	Mar 19 1914	6
Smith John	Mar 5 1857	58
Smith Louisa Edith	Jan 29 1958	68
Smith Mary	Sep 13 1920	79
Smith Raymond John	Dec 7 1928	3 days
Smithurst Dennis	Aug 26 1994	74
Spall Edward Charles	Oct 25 1928	58
Spall Emily Grace	May 26 1952	79
Spall Gerald Rupert	Dec 4 1974	62
Spall Margaret McHarg	Oct 7 1987	77
Spink Maurice Bert Thomas	Nov 3 1969	48
Staines Doris Ellen	Jun 11 1992	72
Starkings Friday Samuel August	Oct 5 1979	71
Starkings Nora Dorothy	Feb 6 1992	82
Steadman Emily Rachel	Dec 4 1975	4 mths
Steaggle Ann Mary	Oct 15 1895	49
Steaggles Amelia	Nov 13 1901	40
Stevenson Roland Cecil	Jun 15 1930	28
Stones William the fishing accident	July 18 1895	27
Swift Edith Emily	Aug 2 1965	90
Swift James	Jun 26 1959	82
Symonds Ellen Eliza	Nov 12 1965	72
Tacon Betty	Jul 12 1956	27
Tacon Caroline Ballard	May 5 1921	70
Tacon Dudly George Tomline	Nov 11 1972	86
Tacon Ernest JB	Oct 9 1917	21
Tacon Ethel (Safford Andrew)	Jul 17 1952	73
Tacon Pauline Violet Pearl	Oct 4 1979	68
Tacon Richard Charles	May 3 1934	52
Tacon Richard John	Mar 11 1929	82
Tacon Thomas Henry Warcup MC	Oct 22 1973	83

Name	Date	Age
Tacon Waveney Pitt	Apr 2 1954	71
Thain Jeanette Louise	Jan 17 1980	14 mths
Thain Robert Joseph	Aug 8 2000	84
Thompson Sarah Ann	Oct 16 1931	90
Thompson William	Apr 9 1915	89
Toll Jack	Jan23 1934	8 days
Tooke Amelia (Rivett)	May 5 1933	65
Tooke Arthur Harry	Oct 11 1965	93
Tooke Arthur Sidney	Aug 8 1966	69
Tooke Edith	Aug 23 1990	91
Tooke Edith Emma	Feb 26 1953	79
Tooke Edna May	Mar 15 1927	1
Tooke Elsie Patience	Jan 9 1968	73
Tooke Emma	Apr 24 1935	78
Tooke Gladys May	Mar 30 1920	4 mths
Tooke Jennifer Marguerite	Jun11 1975	24
Tooke Muriel Charlotte	May 16 1994	79
Tooke Percy Horace	Aug 11 1977	86
Tooke Queenie Hilda May	Nov 29 1991	94
Tooke Sidney	Jan 25 1977	81
Tooke William	Jul 28 1913	68
Tooke William James	Mar 3 1916	47
Torr Joyce Ethel	Apr 23 1953	34
Torr Oswald Addison	Jul 28 1997	86
Townsend Eliza	Mar 4 1959	93
Townsend William Edward	Jun 1 1943	76
Trueman Elsie	Sep 17 1982	91
Turner Benjamin	Sep 21 1905	77
Turner Martha	Jul 24 1885	57
Turner Robert Samuel	Sep 7 1964	82
Turner Ruth Louisa	Mar 28 1967	76
Utting Mary	Jan 11 1781	79
Varle Baby stillborn	Jul 22 1988	0
Varle Nicole	Dec 21 1985	11
Veale James Scott	Jan 25 1941	72
Walpole Albert Ernest	Oct 13 1981	86
Walpole Ann Elizabeth	Dec 12 1930	68
Walpole Bertie	Feb 19 1941	36
Walpole Charles Thomas	Jun 14 1904	18
Walpole Frederick	Apr 27 1909	53
Walpole Gladys Emily	Dec 21 1964	69
Walpole Henry William	Jun 6 1933	73
Walpole Rachel	May 29 1905	42
Walpole Rosena	Jan 7 1929	42
Walpole Samuel John	Oct 6 1944	69
Walpole Walter Thomas	Dec 23 1904	52
Ward Anna Elizabeth	Sep 9 1918	47

Name	Date	Age
Warnes George Thomas Valentine	Jan 26 1962	75
Warnes Helen Maud	Mar 26 1964	77
Watson Sarah	Feb 28 1907	83
Watson Susan Jillian	Dec 13 1988	24
Webb Charles	Jan 31 1967	74
Webb Elizabeth Catherine	Sep 1 1981	89
Webster Ann	Jan 26 1920	73
Webster Thomas	Feb 14 1909	59
Wells Barnard Doughty	Apr 4 1907	58
Wensley John Scott	Oct 26 1971	6 wks
Westgate Anna Eliza	Feb 26 1903	12
Westgate Elizabeth	Aug 16 1916	61
Wilkinson Elizabeth	Jul 5 1926	76
Wilkinson Walter Reuben	May 12 1942	80
Wilson Clifford	Dec 1 1994	79
Woodhouse Ethel May	May 15 1986	78
Woodman Ellen Marie	Dec 31 1980	81
Woodman William Horace	Oct 30 1980	49
Woolston Betty Eleanor	Nov 27 1918	10 wks
Woolston Frederick Henry	Jan 23 1917	57
Woolston Harriet	Dec 27 1937	81
Woolston Henry John	Jun 20 1912	28
Wooltorton Edith Ellen	May 15 1918	47
Wrench George Henry	Apr 4 1986	83
Wrench Vena Lilian	Jan 11 1990	?
Wright Arthur William	Jul 9 1933	63
Wright Georgina	Apr 12 1946	83
Wright James William	Mar 10 1933	70
Wright Percyy Williams	Jan 1 1905	5 mths
Wright Rebecca	Mar 3 1947	76
Wyatt Mabel Lucy	Oct 18 1933	30
Wymer Arthur Edward	Jun 4 1975	70
Wymer Edith Maud	Jun 6 1997	90
Wymer Edward	Oct 28 1958	84
Wymer Gertrude Eliza	Apr 24 1957	58
Wymer Rosanna	Oct 19 1957	75
Wymer Thelma Maud	Jan 26 1929	2
Wymer Wilham	Aug 11 1959	81
Young Mable Maud Victoria	Aug 12 1984	87
Youngs Charles	Apr 24 1899	70
Youngs Eleanor May	Sep 12 1957	77
Youngs Elizabeth	Dec 30 1913	70
Youngs Fred	Sep 13 1917	83
Youngs Gladys	Jun 26 2000	83
Youngs Henry	Dec 14 1960	75
Youngs Mary Ann	Aug 24 1902	66

Bibliography

Bayne, A D (circa 1880) *History of Eastern England: Volumes I-II,* James MacDonald, Yarmouth.

Burke's Landed Gentry (1937) Centenary Edition.

Barber, R (Editor) (1981) *The Pastons* Folio Society, London.

Chadwick, H (Editor) (2000) *Not Angels but Anglicans* Canterbury Press, Norwich.

Champion, M & Sotherton, N (1999) *Kett's Rebellion 1549* Timescape Publishing, Norfolk.

Churchill, Winston S (1956) *A History of the English Speaking Peoples Vols 1-4* Cassell, London.

Ecclestone (1971) *A W Henry Manship's Great Yarmouth* Buckle, Gt Yarmouth.

Ellis, Ted (1982) *Countryside Reflections* Wilson-Polle, Norwich.

Elton, G R (1997) *England Under the Tudors* Folio Society, London.

Evans, George Ewart (1977) *Ask the Fellows who Cut the Hay* Faber & Faber, Boston.

Fletcher, R (1980) *The East Anglians* Patrick Stephens, Cambridge.

Forder, C (1975) *A History of the Paston School* UEA Printing Unit, Norwich.

Hastings, A (1991) *A History of English Christianity* SCM, London.

Land, S K (1977) *Kett's Rebellion: The Norfolk Rising of 1549* Boydell Press, Ipswich.

Lloyd, R (1966) *The Church of England 1900-1965* SCM, London.

Morrill, J (Editor) (1996) *The Oxford Illustrated History of Tudor and Stuart Britain* Oxford UP.

Norfolk and Norwich Archaeological Society Vols 1-49 (1959) N&NAS, Norwich.

Outhwaite, R B (1997) *Scandal in the Church: Dr Edward Drax Free 1764-1843* CUP.

Palmer, A & V (1996) *The Pimlico Chronology of British History* Pimlico Press, London.

Palmer, C H (Editor) (1847) *Foundation of Great Yarmouth (Henry Manship's MS)* Charles Sloman, Yarmouth.

Patterson, Arthur (circa 1900) *From Hayloft to Temple (1865).*

Pevsner, N (1976) *The Buildings of England: North-East Norfolk and Norwich* Penguin Books, Middlesex.

Porter, R (1998) *England in the Eighteenth Century* Folio Society, London.

Powicke, M (1962) 'The Thirteenth Century' in *The Oxford History of England.*

Trevelyan, G M (1945) *English Social History* Longmans, London.

Trevelyan, G M (1978) *English Social History* New illustrated edition with introduction by Asa Briggs, Longman, London.

Wallace, D & Bagnall-Oakeley, R P (1951) *Norfolk* Robert Hale, London.

White, W (1969) *White's 1845 Norfolk* David & Charles reprints, Redwood Press, Trowbridge.

Women's Institute Federation (1990) *The Norfolk Village Book* Countryside Books, Norwich.

Woodforde, James (Editor) Beresford, John (1978) *The Diary of a Country Parson 1758-1802* OUP.

Ziegler, P (1997) *The Black Death* Folio Society, London.

Magazines, Newspapers and Periodicals

Crockford's Clerical Directories 1880-2000.

Eastern Daily Press 1886-1900.

Flegg Parish Magazines 1907-10.

Kelly's Directory of Norfolk 1933, published by London Kelly's Directories.

Norfolk Fair – County Magazine, May 1971, article by D A Palgrave.

Norfolk Fair – County Magazine, Sept 1977, article by Clare Howes.

White's Norfolk, 1836, 1845, 1846, 1875.

Primary Sources

Bates, Ann. Private Research from the *Norfolk Archaeological Society*.

Commonwealth War Graves Commission
http://yard.ccta.gov.uk/cwgc/register.nst/ = CWGC

List of Rectors in Rollesby Church.

Lloyd, Virginia *Landscape Analysis: A Study of the Parish of Rollesby, Norfolk* unpublished private research.

MacAllan, Dr Barbara: private research.

Palgrave, Derek A *The Palgraves of Rollesby, 1773-1973* Private publication, undated.

Rollesby Parochial Church Council Minutes 1950-2000. (PCC)

Tacon, Richard: private papers. The Tacon family were the Patrons of the parish throughout the 20th century.

University of East Anglia web site:
http://www.uea.ac.uk/his/virtualnorfolk/migration/ormesby.htm

Interviews

Granville Lanham, long time farmer in the area.

George Grundy, son of Raymond Grundy.

Mr F Symonds, member of choir before World War II.

Frederick Youngs, a smallholder and stallholder through most of the 20th century.

Index

A

Abbey of St Benets of Holm 16
Abrahams, Harold 257
Acle Agricultural Show 258
Act of Uniformity 1552 120
Act of Uniformity 1662 156
Act of Union 1707 170
Adams, William Junior 185-98
Adams, William Senior 173-8, 199
Aden 276
Agincourt 75
Agricultural strike 1874 240
Airship R101 262
Aitken, Aubrey - Archdeacon 286, 289, 294
Alexander, Teddy 268
All Black Tour 1924 257
Allard, Willie 287, 300
Allards general stores 275
Altars 120, 127, 299
American Civil War 228
American War of Independence 192
Amin, President 295
Andeley, James 79-83
Anmere, William de 21-25, 27
Annison, Edward 211
Annison, Richard 247
Ansbach, Caroline of 183
Anti-Catholcism 161
Anti-clerical feeling in 14th cent 62
Anti-ritual demonstrations 1859 220
Apartheid 283
Aragon, Catherine of 108
Archbishop Chichele 80
Archbishop Cosmo Gordon Lang 265
Archbishop Donald Coggan 300
Archbishop Dr Robert Runcie 301
Archbishop Fisher on Christian unity 270
Archbishop Michael Ramsey 286
Archbishop Sancroft 167
Archbishop Scrope 74
Archery 48
Arne, Thomas 184
Arnold, Thomas 86
Articles of Religion 120, 123, 128, 135
Ascot 202
Ascripti glebae 24
Ashley's Mines Act 1842 216
Asquith 254
Atlantic telegraph 1858 220
Atlee 276
Atomic weapons 276
Auschwitz and Dachau 269
Austen, Jane 204
Austrian War of Succession 186
Avignon Popes 62

B

Babingley, Simon de 61-4, 65
Babington, Sir Anthony 134
Back'us boys 234

Baden-Powell 248, 250
Baker, Robin 296
Baker, Thomas 199-211, 213
Baldry, Freddy 261, 289
Ball, John 67-8
Balliol, Edward 47
Bank Holidays start 1871 235
Bank of England established 169
Bannister, Roger 277
Baptists 200
Bare-fist boxing 226
Barnado, Dr Thomas 229
Bateman, Sir Bartholomew 57
Bateman, William Bishop of Norwich 57
Bates, Ann 285, 287, 295, 313
Battle of Austerlitz 1805 203
Battle of Cable Street 264
Battle of Corunna 203
Battle of Crecy 51
Battle of Dettingen 1743 187
Battle of Empingham 1470 100
Battle of Flodden 1513 108
Battle of Guinegate 1513 108
Battle of Inkerman 219
Battle of La Rochelle 1372 62
Battle of Leipzig 1813 203
Battle of Magersfontein 1899 248
Battle of Malplaquet 174
Battle of Mons 174
Battle of Mortimer's Cross 1461 99
Battle of Neuve Chapelle 251
Battle of Oxford 1646 149
Battle of Plassey 1757 189
Battle of Poiters 1356 59
Battle of Sedgemoor 1685 166
Battle of Sluys 1340 51
Battle of Somme 251, 252
Battle of Stoke 1487 107
Battle of Stormberg 1899 248
Battle of the Spurs 1513 108
Battle of Trafalgar 203
Battle of Vitoria 1813 203
Battle of Wakefield 1460 99
Battle of Waterloo 1815 204
Battle of Ypres 251, 253
Battles of Sheriffmiur and Preston 175
Baynard, Robert 92
Beck, Don 305, 306
Beck, George Daniel 252
Becket, Thomas 18
Beckett, Joe 296
Benn family 288, 289, 290, 294, 295
Bennington, Charles H 233-7
Berking, John 81
Berking Manor 22, 91, 118
Berking, Richard de and wife Joan 50, 59
Berlin Decree 1806 203
Biblical criticism 237
Bigot, Roger 16
Bill of Pains and Penalties 1722 182
Bilney, Thomas 119
Bishop Bell of Chichester 269
Bishop Chaderton 125
Bishop John Fisher 120
Bishop of Elmham 16
Bishop of London, Winnington-Ingram 254
Bishop of Norwich - Edmund Freke 128
Bishop of Norwich - Henry Despenser 69
Bishop of Norwich - John Hopton 128
Bishop of Norwich - John Parkhurst 128
Bishop of Norwich - John Salmon 28
Bishop of Norwich - John Wakeryng 80
Bishop of Norwich - Launcelot Fleming 293
Bishop of Norwich - Maurice Wood 287, 293, 298
Bishop of Norwich - Richard Nykke (Nix) 112
Bishop of Norwich - Rugge 118
Bishop of Norwich - William Middleton 21
Bishop of Norwich - William Rugge 122
Bishop of Norwich - Alexander de Tottington 77
Bishop of Rochester - Francis Atterbury 182
Bishop of Thetford 16
Bishop of Winchester - Cardinal Beaufort 86

Bishop Stapledon 40
Black Death 55-9, 61
Black Death rumours 52
Black Friday in the City - 1866 228
Black Hole of Calcutta 189
Black Prince 66
Bleriot, Louis 250
Blomevyle, John 125-32, 133
Blucher 204
Blunt, Sir Anthony 298
Boer War 244, 248
Bois, John de 73, 86
Bois, Richard 106, 118
Bois, Roger 81
Bois, Thomas 81
Boleyn, Anne 117, 119
Bolingbroke 1715 174
Bollinge, William 139, 141
Bonnie Prince Charlie 187
Booth, William 228
Bow Street Runners 193
Bowes-Lyon, Lady Elizabeth 257
Bowler hats introduced 218
Boxing 229
Boy Scouts 250
Boys, Roger MacKenzie 281-3
Bracecamp 266, 268
Bracey, Dorothy 314
Bradmore, Thomas 73-8, 79
British Union of Facists 262
Britten, Norman 201
Brooke, Thomas 121, 133
Brookes, Matthew 146
Brown, Cyril 268
Brown family 296
Brownsword, Harry 253
Brownsword, Mabel 254
Brownsword, Douglas 253
Brownswords of Rollesby Hall 253
Bruce, Robert 30
Brundish Funeral Directors 300
Brunson 290
Bryan, George 314
Brygge, John 97-104, 105
Buckingham, execution in 1483 102
Bullyvaunt, William 140
Bulman, John 105, 106
Bunyan, John 161
Burt, Robert 206
Burton, Cyril 295
Butt, Mrs 241
Byng, Admiral 189

Cabot, John 102
Cade, Jack 92, 94
Caesarean clergy 70
Calendar, change of 1752 189
Calendar, Gregorian 189
Calendar, Julian 189
California - origin of name 218
Callaghan 298
Cambrensis Giraldus 17
Cambridge Higher Local Examination 230
Camlet weavers in Norwich 207
Canal construction 1772 194
Capgrave, John Friar 76
Cappes, William and Ethelreda 118, 130
Captain Cook 192
Captain Swing agrarian riots of 1830 207
Cardinal Pole 129
Carmen, Mary 186
Carr, Nicholas 111-5
Carter, John 150
Carteret 184
Carver family 148
Catchpole family 297, 305
Cathedral cloisters 29
Cathedral tower clock 1321 39
Cato Street Conspiracy 205
Caylly, John de 27-32, 35

Cecil, William 128
Cenotaph 255, 256
Census 1801 201
Census 1861 227
Chapman, Donald 252
Chapman, John 201
Chappell, Greg 297
Charles I 143, 147, 157
Charles II 150, 153, 160, 165, 175
Chartists 216
Chase, Robert 295
Cholera in early Victorian period 209, 216
Chungkai War Cemetery 268
Church Army 266
Church attendance in England and Wales 245
Churche, Edmund 104
Churchill, John 168
Churchill, Winston 250, 263, 265, 270, 276
Circumspecte Agatis 1286 Writ 21
Cistercians 17
Civil War 147, 149, 150, 153, 156
Clapham Sect 205
Clarendon Constitutions 18
Clarke, Christopher 140
Claxton, Hamo(n) 145-154, 155
Claxton family 143, 146
Claxton, Laurance 146
Clayton, John 285, 287, 289, 295, 297
Cleopatra's Needle -1878 242
Clere, Edward 92
Clere, John Sir 122
Clere, Richard 113
Clergy Disqualification Act 1801 202
Clerical celibacy 70
Clericis Laicos 1296 Papal Bull 22
Cleves, Anne of 118
Closh and kayles 101
Cloth trade 46, 121
Clothing in 14th century 57, 58
CND 281, 283
Cobb, Stephen 308
Cobham, Eleanor mistress of Gloucester 86
Codling, Peter 289
Coinage 1344 51
Coinage 1489 108
Coinage 1549 121
Colenso, J W 237
Collins, Mr 175
Columbus, Christopher 102
Communist Party 256
Compurgation 19
Coney (rabbit) 37
Congregationalists appoint woman minister 256
Conventicle Act 1664 156
Corn Laws of 1840s 217
Corpus Christi 1318 40
Corrody 41
Countess of Yarmouth 1730s 183
Cousins, Christopher 307-11
Crabb, Henry 203
Cranmer 117, 125, 129
Cricket 244, 297
Cricket and the MCC 229
Cricket, first documented match 188, 221
Crimean War 219
Crippen, Dr 251
Cromwell, Oliver 147, 149, 150, 151, 152, 153
Cromwell, Thomas 118, 119
Crowmer, William - Sheriff of Kent 93
Crufts Dog Show 1885 245
Crystal Palace 219, 265
Cuban crisis 290
Cubitt, William 140
Curtis family 263, 275, 290, 297
Cycles first used 243
Cyclists' Touring Club 243
Cyprus - state of emergency 276

D

DAC 299, 314
Daily Mail 249

Daily Mail — Nicholson, W A 268
Daily Telegraph 220
Daily Universal Register 195
Damme, John 86
Daniels, Esther 266
Darwin, Charles 221, 237
Davis, Emily 230
D-Day 1944 269
De Gaulle and European Market 292
Deave, Renden 290
Decimal coinage 294
Declaration of Indulgence 1687 167
Declaration of Rights 1689 168
Defoe, Daniel 176, 181
Despensers 30
Devitt, Anna 299
Dickens, Charles 217
Directory of Public Worship 149
Dispossessed clergy 124
Dissenters 160
Dog collar 214
Dogger Bank Incident 249
Domesday Book 16
Dowe family 148
Downing Street Number 10 183
Drake, Francis 135
Drax, Dr Edward 200
Dredge, J 241
Drewry (Drury) family 139, 146, 151
Drummond, Edward 217
Dublack, Fred 268
Duke of Norfolk 1546 122
Duke of Buckingham 1521 114
Duke of Cumberland 1740s 187
Duke of Gloucester 86
Duke of Marlborough 1705 170, 174
Duke of Monmouth 1685 166
Duke of Norfolk 30
Duke of Norfolk - 1569 130
Duke of Norfolk 1530 118
Duke of Somerset 1449 86, 92
Duke of Suffolk 1450 92
Duke of Windsor 265
Duke of York 1681 160, 161
Dunblane murder 307
Dunkirk 174
Dutch War 1665 157
Dybal, Fred 252

E

Earl of Bute 191
Earl of Oxford 1714 174
Earl of Suffolk 1523 108
Earl of Surrey 1513 108
Earl of Wilmington 1742 184
Earthquake 1756 189
Easdell, Baldwin 133-7
East Anglia Rising of 1477 101
Eastern Association 149
Eastow family 148
Ebenezer Chapel Rollesby 225
Edmonds, David 289
Education Act 1870 234
Education Act 1891 247
Education Act 1918 255
Edward I 21
Edward II 30, 40
Edward III 39, 45, 49, 55
Edward IV 97, 99, 101
Edward V 97, 101
Edward VI 117, 124, 127
Edward VII 213, 214, 249, 250
Edward VIII 264
EEC 297, 298
Electric lighting in London 244
Eleven articles of 1553 124
Elgin Marbles 204
Elizabeth I 139, 141, 142
Ellis, Christopher 313
Ellis, Ruth 277
Elphick, Robin Howard 293-301

Ely, Alan de 27
Emigration to America 1637 148
English Bible 69, 120
English Heritage 308, 314, 315
English, Symond 122
English translation of Bible 113
Ensor family 155, 202, 211, 213, 215, 258
Ensor, Edmund Smith 213-23, 225
Escalators on the underground 251
Essex Earl of 1599 142
Established Church Act 1836 208
Estreford, Roger de 59
Eton College foundation 85
Evangelical Alliance 218
Evans, Tom 261
Evelyn, John 152
Expulsion of Jewish money lenders 22

F

Factory Act 1833 207
Factory Act 1844 218
Factory Act 1874 240
Falklands 195
Falklands War 301
Fastolf, Sir John 102
Fawkes, Guy 142
Fenians 244
Feudal system collapsing - early 1400s 83
Fferyer, Robert 118
Field of Gold 113
Fielding, Henry and John 193
Fifth Monarch Sect 151
Filby, Robert de 28
Fire at Whitehall 1698 169
Fire of Southwark 1676 162
First Trade Unions Congress 1868 229
Fitzherbert, Anthony 113
Fitzherbert, Mrs Maria 206
Five Mile Act 1665 156
Fleet Mutiny in Yarmouth 1797 202
Flegg 16
Flegg, Richard 16
Flete, John de 50
Flowerdew 123
Folstaff, Laurence 39-43
Football - first international 1872 235
Football Association 1872 235
Football first called - 1486 102
FORC 299, 305, 309, 314
Forrest, Friar 119
Forster, William Edward 234
Foundry 196
Fox, Edward 112
Francis, Robert John 225-31
Fransham, Agatha 86
Freeman, Geoffrey 313
Freemasons 205
Freethinkers 230
French raid ports 1338 50
French raid Rye and Hastings 1377 67
French, Sir John 248
Friars & Monks in 14th cent 45, 46
Frosdick, Robert 211
Frost, Henry 68

G

Gaddesden, John of 31
Gambling in 18th century 194
Gardiner, Stephen 112
Garrick of Drury Lane 193
Gascoigne, Henry 273-80
Gaveston, Piers 30
Gawdays, Thomas 130
Gedge, Janet 296
General Enclosure Act 1801 202
George I 173, 179, 181
George II 183, 185, 186, 188, 191
George III 185, 191, 204, 206
George IV 206
George V 250, 256, 264

George VI 265
Ghandi 262
Gibraltar 174, 181
Gibson, John 165-72
Giles - cartoonist 298
Gin Act 1751 187, 189
Gin shops 188
Gladstone 244
Glendower, Owen 74
Godwin, Thomas and Margaret 135
Golf - 1754 188
Goodwin, Les 290
Goodwin, Thomas 145, 147, 149, 151, 152
Gordon, General 244
Gordon Riots 194
Gorleston, Kett's Rebellion 123
Grace W G 229
Graham, Billy 277
Great Exhibition -1851 219
Great Fire of London 1666 157
Great frost of 1739 184
Great War 1914-18 251, 252, 253
Green-side shift 56
Grubbers and dock-chisels 136
Grundy, George 261
Grundy, George Raymond 257, 259-71, 297, 304, 305
Grundy, John 261
Guernica 265
Gunton Manor 16, 22
Gunton, Roger de 16, 46

H

Hackett, John 152
Hales, John MP 121
Halifax talks 1894 248
Hampden 148
Handel's Messiah 188
Happisburgh 193
Happy Rollers 283
Hardie, James Keir MP 247
Hardy, Thomas 240
Harrison family 297
Harvest failure 1692 169
Harvests of 1842 215
Harvey, Sir Robert 242
Hawes 308
Hayton 290
Hayton, Bridget 289
Heachaam, Gilbert de 29
Heath Lane 24
Heath, Ted 297, 298
Heath, William 179-84, 185
Henley 209
Henry II 17
Henry IV 73, 74, 77,
Henry, Prince of Wales 1612 142
Henry V 73, 75, 77, 79
Henry VI 73, 79, 80, 85, 88, 91, 92, 97, 98, 100
Henry VI - judicial tour of Norfolk 94
Henry VII 97, 102, 105, 106, 108
Henry VIII 105, 108, 111, 117, 118, 127
Herald of Free Enterprise 306
Herald, Roger 56
Hereward the Wake 16
Heriot 32
Herling, John de 31
Hewitt, Geoffrey 308
Heydon, John 94
Heydon, Sir Christopher 130
Highwaymen 169, 182
Hiroshima 269
Hirst, Elizabeth 313
Hitler 264, 265
HMS Albert 226
HMS Warrior 226
Hoare Laval Treaty 1935 264
Hockering, William 46, 56
Hodds, Kelly 261
Hodds, Michael and Keith 289
Hogarth and gin 180

Hogshead of ale 63
Holt fire 1708 190
Holy relics 82
Hoper, William 97
Hopkins, Matthew 150
Horse racing 173, 202
Houstord, Thomas Stanley 266
Howard, Catherine 118
Hungerford, Robert - Lord Moleyns 94, 103
Hurnard, William 185
Hurry, Walter 49-53, 55
Huskisson, William 209
Hymns Ancient and Modern 226
Hymns early 18th century 170

I

Income tax 1842 215
Indian Mutiny 220
Interdenominational Sunday Schools 202
Irish famine 217
Irish Problems 244, 250, 256, 276, 291, 295, 298, 306
Iron Curtain Speech 269

J

Jack the Ripper 246
Jacobites 175
James I 139, 142, 174
James II 161, 165, 166, 167
Jary Funeral Directors 300
Jefford, Peter Ernest 285-92, 294
Jenkins, Captain Robert 156
Jermouth (Yarmouth nomenclature) 36
Jesuits 133, 135
Jewish Naturalisation Act 1753 193
Joan of Arc 79
John Grant School 298
John of Gaunt 62, 65, 66, 68, 70, 86
Johnson, Amy 262
Judge Jeffreys 166
Julian of Norwich 70, 71
Julyan, Henry 155-8
Justices of Eyre 19
Juvenile Courts 250

K

Kaiser Wilhelm II 221
Keble 208
Keeler - brewing tub 236
Keeler, Christine 291
Kempe, Margery 89
Kempe, William 142
Kennedy's assassination 291
Kenya 276
Kerrisons 242
Kett, Robert 121, 122, 123
Kett's Rebellion 121, 122, 123
Khrushchev 277
Kimberley 248
King, Miss 275
King's College, London 209
King's Lynn bombed 251
Kirk, Colonel 166
Knolls, John 91-5
Korean War 276

L

Labour Party 247
Ladysmith 248
Lakenham 196
Lambeth Conference 1867 229
Lancaster, Joseph 201
Langele, Robert de, Prior 23
Langland 61
Lanham, Arthur 261
Lanham, Granville 313
Latimer, Hugh 121, 122
Laud, William 147, 148, 149, 152

Laud, William's tortoise 186
Lavenham, Firminus de 35-8
Law against sport 1314 31
Law against sport 1340s 51
Lawn 290
Leopold I of Belguim 227
Licensing of motor cars 249
Liddell, Eric 257
Lillywhite, Fred 221
Lincoln, Simon de 22
Lloyd family 304, 305, 306, 308, 310, 313
Local Government Act 1894 247
Lollards 75, 79, 80, 126
London Rising 1326 40
London smog 276
Longbow usage in 14th cent 36
Lopez, Roderigo 141
Lord Cardigan 219
Lord North 130
Lord North 1770 194
Lord Roberts 248
Lord Say 93
Lord Somerset 1549 121
Losinga, Herbert 16
Lottery of 1768 190
Louis XIV 168
Lowestoft 183
Lowestoft - Civil War 149
Lowestoft - Kett's Rebellion 122
Luddites 207
Ludham 80
Luther, Martin 112
Luwum, Dr Janani 296
Lyons, Arnold de 65
Lyons, Nicholas de 65-72

M

Macaulays 205
Mace, Edgar 261
MacDonald, Ramsay 247
McNaghten Rules 217
Mafeking 248
Magdalen College 167
Mahdi in Kartoum 244
Mail coaches 209
Mail service established 195
Manson, Debby 296
Mapes Ensor family 140, 143, 148, 155, 190, 215
Marquis of Queensberry 229
Marriage Act 1753 193
Marriage Act 1836 208
Marriage of clergy 124
Married Women's Property Act 1870 234
Marston family 148
Martham 16
Martham Mill fire 240
Mary of Modena 160
Mary Queen of Scots 134
Matrimonal Causes Act 1923 256
Maud (Matilda) and Stephen Civil War 17
Mayo, Dr 245
Measles outbreak 1723 180
Meiklejohn, Archdeacon 285
Merchet 32
Merciless Parliament 71
Methodism 182, 195, 196, 200, 205, 225, 226
Methodist – Anglican talks 286
Methwold, Thomas de 57
Miles, Francis 192
Miles the Gunner 123
Miller - post office 282
Miller, Cecil 297
Miller, Walter 287
Milton, John 158
Minorca 174, 189
Mollison, James 262
Molyneux, Gertrude Loetitia 262
Monastries 1530-40 120
Moody, Dwight 240

Moon eclipse in 1345 57
Moore, Cecil 268
Moore, Freddy 261
Morality play 58
More, Sir Thomas 112, 120
Mort d'Ancestor 19
Mortimer 1323 36
Mortimer, Robert 86
Mortimer, Sibilla 86
Mortimers 74
Mosley, Oswald 262, 264
Motorcars first arrive 228
Moulton family 148
Muggletonians 146
Mussolini, Benito 257, 264

N

Napoleon 196, 202
National Health Service Bill 1950 270
National School in Rollesby 210, 215, 246
National Society 202
Nationalisation of railways 271
Nave building and tower 23, 24
Nelson 196, 203
Neville, Alexander 121
Neville family - Earl of Warwick 93
New English Bible 286
Newman, John Henry 208, 217
Newton, Kenneth 303-6
Night of the Long Knives 264
Nightingale, Florence 219
Nonconformist ministers 156
North Briton 191
Northern, Bartholomew 105-110, 111
Norwich - Cathedral burned 1272 23
Norwich - Cathedral fire 1413 77
Norwich - City Hall opened 265
Norwich - cloth makers 41
Norwich - Church Congress 1865 230
Norwich - collpase of Crown Bank 242
Norwich - fire of 1751 190
Norwich - infamous murder of 1851 236
Norwich - smallpox outbreak 1870s 242
Norwich visited by Wesley brothers 195
Norwich 1810 German mercenaries 201
Norwich Crusade 1383 to Flanders 69
Norwich Guilds 78
Norwich Postman 175
Norwich Weekly Mercury 175
Nudd, Diane 296
Nuremberg trials 270

O

Oates, Titus 161
Oflag IX AH 266
Old age pensioners first paid 250
Old Sarum 187
Old World Cottage 135
Oldecastle 75
Olivers, Thomas 196
Olley, John 252, 256
Olympics 1924 257
Olympics 1980 298
Ormesby, origin of name 16
Ormesby, Sir William de 27
Overend and Gurney Company 242
Owen, Robert 201
Oxford debates 228
Oxford Holy Club 182
Oxford Movement 205, 214

P

Page family 148
Paine, Peter 311
Palestine problems post-WW II 271
Palgrave family 186, 211, 234
Palmer, Billy 252
Palmer family 148
Palmer, William 106

Papal schism 74
Pardoners 40
Parish boundaries 299
Parish chest 134
Parish Clerk's rights 241
Parish Councils established 247
Parish quotas 288, 304
Parish reorganisation 309
Parker, Bernard 289
Parliamentary Reform Act 1867 229
Parr, Catherine 118
Paston, John 103
Paston School 246, 255
Paston, William 87
Peat digging 16
Peche, Juliana de 22, 28
Peche, Simon de 22, 28
Peche, William 28
Pecke, William 122
Peel 217
Penn, William 156, 169
Penny post 209
Penry, John 141
Percy family 93
Percys of Northumbria 74
Perry, Fred 264
Peterloo Massacre 205
Peter's boat 127
Peter's Pence - papal tax 106
Philby, Kim 291
Piggin, Bob 252, 254
Piggin, Robert 252
Piggin, Tommy 261
Pilgimages 88, 89
Pillar boxes introduced 1855 220
Pitt, William 183, 186, 190, 192, 194
Plague 1592 139, 140
Platter, William 252
Pluralities Act 1838 217
Pneumatic tyres 243
Pocket boroughs 207
Pole, Michael de la impeaches Bishop of Norwich 69
Poll tax 67
Ponder, Dr John 139-44
Poor Law Amendment Act 207
Pope Adrian VI 112
Pope Clement VII 112
Pope Leo X 111
Pope Martin 75
Pope Paul John II 301
Pope Paul VI 286
Porch of St George's built 104
Praemunire II Statute 1365 62
Praemunire III Statute 1393 71
Prayer Book 134, 152
Prayer Book 1549 120
Prayer Book 1559 127
Prayer Book 1662 156
Prayer Book 1928 250, 258
President Buchanan 220
Prime Minister office 175
Primogeniture 21
Prince Albert of Saxe-Coburg 209, 227
Prince Arthur 108
Prince of Wales 1890s 248
Prince Rupert 149
Prince William of Orange 167
Princess Caroline of Brunswick 206
Princess Henrietta Maria 143
Profumo, John 291
Protestant Packet 175
Protestants 126
Prynne, William 148
Public executions 1868 229
Public Order Bill 1936 264
Public Worship Regulation Act 1874 240
Purcell, Henry 162
Purgatory and all souls 120
Puritans 148, 152
Pym 148

Q

Quakers 156, 167, 205
Queen Anne 170, 173, 175
Queen Anne's Bounty 170
Queen Elizabeth I 127, 133, 139
Queen Elizabeth II 276
Queen Mary 117, 118, 124, 125, 129
Queen Victoria 209, 219, 220, 239, 244, 249
Queen's Jubilee village sign 294
Quinns, William 140

R

Rabbits - hollow meat 199
Race Relations Act 1965 292
Rainham, William 140
Ralphs, Mrs Lincoln 282
Ransome, Jack (Rabbit) 290
Ransome, Ken 261
Ransome, Leslie 252
Rectory moves to St Margaret's 309
Rectory new in Rollesby 282
Redman, George 130
Reform Bill 1832 207
Relics 89
Reppes, William and Thomas de 28
Restoration, The 153
Revised Code of Education 1862 228
Revised Standard Version of Bible 244
Rhodesia UDI 291
Richard II, his death 71
Richard III 97, 101, 102
Riches, Colin 286
Rigmarden, John 125
Rites, Sarum, Norwich, Hereford 32
River Thames freezes 227
Road Locomotion Act 1865 228
Robberds 207
Robin Hood 61
Robin of Redesdale revolt 100
Robinson, John 286
Rollesby - Parish Hall opened 282
Rollesby - tower in 1990s 308
Rollesby chuch restoration 1884 258
Rollesby church choir in 1907-10 246
Rollesby, Ernald of 22
Rollesby fire appliance 1898 240
Rollesby Hall 140, 147, 193, 209, 269, 288
Rollesby Poor House 192, 197, 200, 207, 209, 215
Rollesby, Richard de 16
Rollesby, Robert of 29
Rollesby war memorial 254
Rollesby, William of 22
Rollesby, origins of name 16
Rollesby, Simon de 28
Rollesby, the ale-house 236
Rood screens 129
Round, Dorothy 264
Royal Commission on Ecclesiastical Discipline 249
Royal Commission on Town Health 1844 216
Royal Lancastrian Institution 201
Royden, Dr Tom 286
Royden, Maude 255
Rugby Football Union started 1871 235
Rugg, Walter 15-20
Rule Britannia 184
Runhale, Warine de 56
Russell, Bertrand 276
Russian Revolution 256
Ruyter 157
Rykenhale Simon de 55-60

S

Saint George - possible date of dedication 74
Salvaton Army 228
Samaritans 276
Sangster, Andrew 313-7
Sankey and Moody Hymn Book 240

Sankey, Ira David 240
Sarel, Clement 245
Sarel, Major General 245, 262
Sawtrey, William Lollard martyr 75
Scormfet, Nicholas 77
Scottish Wars 14th cent 47
Scratby 218, 226
Seabert, Mr 282
Seaside resorts developed 246
Seditious Meeting Acts 1816 204
Seed drill 180
Seige of Sebastopol 219
Selot, John 91
Series III 297
Severn Tunnel 1886 245
Seymour, Jane 118
Shakespeare 141, 142
Shancke, Robert 133
Sharp, Jack - Lollard rebellion 80
Sheep breeding 14th century 41
Sheppard, Jack 182
Shipwreckers 1860s 226
Shreeve family 268, 290
Shreeve, Percy 268
Shreeve, Shiner 290
Silcok, Mr 241
Silcots 255
Simnel, Lambert 107
Sinn Fein 250
Slave ships 183
Slavery 207
Sleaze 1720 175
Smith, John 159-64
Smith, John Chancellor of Norwich 97
Smith, John le 56
Smyth, John 140
Snuff 1700s 170
Sophia of Hanover 174
Sotterby, Thomas and Elizabeth 91
Soup kitchens 201
South Sea Bubble 179, 185
South Sea Company 175
Southwark fire 226
Southwell, Robert 141
Spanish Armada 135
Spanish Civil War 260, 265
Spenser (see Despenser) 69
Spitfire & Schneider Trophy 262
Spithead Naval Review 1887 245, 246
Sporting Times 244
St Andrew's, Norwich 22
St Margaret of Antioch 126
St Paul's consecrated 169
St Paul's struck by lightning - 1561 129
Stagecoaches 209
Stalin 277
Stapleton, Sir Miles 92
Star Chamber 109, 134
Statute against Vagabonds 1531 120
Statute of Labourers 1351 59
Stephenson's Rocket 209
Storm of 1771 193
Street lighting 1685 169
Strip farming 24
Strumpshaw 193
Stuart Mill, John 229
Sturrock, Bruce 308
Succession Act 1534 119
Suckling House 22
Suez Canal 227
Suez Canal problem 276
Suffragette 249
Sunday Schools 222
Swannington 123
Sweating sickness 1528 127
Symonds - Fred, William and John 261

T

Tacon, Charles 239
Tacon, Caroline 243, 258
Tacon, Dudley 260, 273, 275, 286, 287, 289,

290, 294, 295, 297
Tacon, Ernest 253, 254, 258
Tacon, Ethel 241, 258
Tacon, Pauline 294
Tacon, Richard 239-58, 260
Tacon, Richard (current patron) 253, 308, 314
Tacon (Safford), Ethel 273
Tacon, Thomas 253
Tacon, Waveney 253
Teddy Boys 277
Test Act 1673 160
Thain family 296
Thames unhealthy - 1858 221
Thatcher, Margaret 298, 301, 306
The English Hymnal **226**
The Times 203, 222
Thedlef, Henry 30
Thedlef, Semeine 30
Thelnetham 139
Thelwell 196
Thirty-Nine Articles 217
Thistlewood, Arthur 205
Thomas Cook's Holidays 226
Thor 15
Thorntons 205
Thrulby, William 85-9, 91
Tithes 136
Toleration Act 1689 168
Tolpuddle 207
Tomblands 23, 29
Tooke family 243, 255, 275, 296
Tooke, Rev John Horne 202
Townshend 175, 183
Tractarianism 218
Transportation of convicts 229
Transubstantiation 126
Treaty of Berlin 1878 243
Treaty of London 1930 262
Treaty of Paris 1763 191
Treaty of Utrecht 174
Treaty of Westminster 1674 160
Trollope, Anthony 220
Trinity College, Cambridge 57
Trowse 117
Trueman, Peter 295
Tuddenham, Sir Thomas 94
Tull, Jethro 180, 183
Turnpikes and tolls 181
Twyford, Hugh 125
Tyburn 141
Tyeburn Hospital 49
Tyler, Wat 68, 69
Tyndale, William 113
Tyrone 142

U

Underground Railway - London 1863 228
United Nations 270
University Boat Race 209
University College 209
USA war of 1812 203
Utopia 112

Valence, Aymer de 28
Varah, Chad 276
VAT 297
Vatican Council II 286
Venns 205
Vere, Robert de 71
Victoria Cross 220
Victorian fashion in 1870s 240
Vietnam War 291
Villeins 66

Wall Street crash 261
Wallis, George 260

Walpole 175, 181, 183, 184
Walpole family in Rollesby 252
Walton, William 77
War of Roses 97
Warbeck, Perkin 107
Warwick - the King maker 100
Watt, James 194
Watts, Isaac 170
Webb, Matthew 241
Webster, Thomas 241
Weekly Courant 175
Weekly Packet 175
Wellerton, Gilbert de 49
Welsh revolt 22
Wembley Stadium 257
Wentworth, Peter MP 134, 141
Wesley, Charles 182, 195, 196
Wesley, John 182, 195, 196
Westacre, William 77
Whigs and Tories late 17th century 161
White (Whight), William 117-24
White House Farm 16, 179, 260, 268, 304
White, William, Norfolk Lollard 80
Whitefield, George 182
Whitehead, Robert 226
Wilberforce, William 205
Wild, Jonathan 182
Wilde, Oscar 247, 248
Wilkes 191, 195
William and Mary 165, 169
William III 168
Williams, George 218
Wilson, Harold 291
Wilson, John (Jumbo) 309
Wimbledon 264
Windmill Nursing Home 310
Window Tax 192
Winter of 1665 157
Winter of 1709 173
Winter of 1947 270
Wireless 1932 263
Witch hunts 150
Witchcraft in 15th century 86, 87, 88
Wittenberg 112
Wolfe of Quebec 190
Wolfenden Report 283
Wolsey, Colwyn 305
Wolsey, Molly (Wilson) 299
Wolsey, Thomas 108, 109, 110, 112
Wool 51
Workhouse, Rollesby see Rollesby Poor House
Workers Education Association 248
Wren, Sir Christopher 162
Wright, George and Charles 252
Wyclif 70, 71
Wymer family 268, 290, 297
Wymondham 123

Yarmouth - 1720s 175
Yarmouth - Admiralty Court 131
Yarmouth - body snatching 236
Yarmouth - Dutch royalty 1795 196
Yarmouth - flooding in 1825 206
Yarmouth - greyhound racing 242
Yarmouth - Kett's Rebellion 122
Yarmouth - Masonic Lodge, St Mary's 261
Yarmouth - muringers 47
Yarmouth - Nelson's visit 196
Yarmouth - politcial fighting 1795 196
Yarmouth - royal visit 1515 110
Yarmouth - royal visit 1578 131
Yarmouth - royal vist 1872 242
Yarmouth - tragic accident of 1846 218
Yarmouth and the Cinque Ports 63
Yarmouth bombed 251
Yarmouth in 16th century 131
Yarmouth in Civil War 149
Yarmouth Methodism 196
Yarmouth smuggling 1760s 193

Yarmouth visited by Wesley brothers 196
Yates, Lieutenant-Colonel Hubert 262
Yeates, John 118
YMCA 218
York and Lancaster - first dissension 93
Young MP, 1450 98
Youngs, Arthur 290
Youngs, Frederick 282
Youngs, Glenda 282

Z

Zulu Wars 1879 243